The Annals of Imperial Rome

By Cornelius Tacitus

Translated by Alfred John Church and William Jackson Brodribb

2

A Digireads.com Book
Digireads.com Publishing
16212 Riggs Rd
Stilwell, KS, 66085

The Annals of Imperial Rome
By Cornelius Tacitus
Translated by Alfred John Church and William Jackson Brodribb
ISBN: 1-4209-2668-3

Please visit *www.digireads.com*

TABLE OF CONTENTS

BOOK I—A.D. 14, 15, p. 5

BOOK II—A.D. 16-19, p. 33

BOOK III—A.D. 20-22, p. 60

BOOK IV—A.D. 23-28, p. 84

BOOK V—A.D. 29-31, p. 109

BOOK VI—A.D. 32-37, p. 112

BOOK VII-X—A.D. 37, 47, p. 130

BOOK XI—A.D. 47, 48, p. 131

BOOK XII—A.D. 48-54, p. 143

BOOK XIII—A.D. 54-58, p. 163

BOOK XIV—A.D. 59-62, p. 182

BOOK XV—A.D. 62-65, p. 203

BOOK XVI—A.D. 65, 66, p. 227

BOOK I, A.D. 14, 15

Rome at the beginning was ruled by kings. Freedom and the consulship were established by Lucius Brutus. Dictatorships were held for a temporary crisis. The power of the decemvirs did not last beyond two years, nor was the consular jurisdiction of the military tribunes of long duration. The despotisms of Cinna and Sulla were brief; the rule of Pompeius and of Crassus soon yielded before Caesar; the arms of Lepidus and Antonius before Augustus; who, when the world was wearied by civil strife, subjected it to empire under the title of "Prince." But the successes and reverses of the old Roman people have been recorded by famous historians; and fine intellects were not wanting to describe the times of Augustus, till growing sycophancy scared them away. The histories of Tiberius, Caius, Claudius, and Nero, while they were in power, were falsified through terror, and after their death were written under the irritation of a recent hatred. Hence my purpose is to relate a few facts about Augustus—more particularly his last acts, then the reign of Tiberius, and all which follows, without either bitterness or partiality, from any motives to which I am far removed.

When after the destruction of Brutus and Cassius there was no longer any army of the Commonwealth, when Pompeius was crushed in Sicily, and when, with Lepidus pushed aside and Antonius slain, even the Julian faction had only Caesar left to lead it, then, dropping the title of triumvir, and giving out that he was a Consul, and was satisfied with a tribune's authority for the protection of the people, Augustus won over the soldiers with gifts, the populace with cheap corn, and all men with the sweets of repose, and so grew greater by degrees, while he concentrated in himself the functions of the Senate, the magistrates, and the laws. He was wholly unopposed, for the boldest spirits had fallen in battle, or in the proscription, while the remaining nobles, the readier they were to be slaves, were raised the higher by wealth and promotion, so that, aggrandised by revolution, they preferred the safety of the present to the dangerous past. Nor did the provinces dislike that condition of affairs, for they distrusted the government of the Senate and the people, because of the rivalries between the leading men and the rapacity of the officials, while the protection of the laws was unavailing, as they were continually deranged by violence, intrigue, and finally by corruption.

Augustus meanwhile, as supports to his despotism, raised to the pontificate and curule aedileship Claudius Marcellus, his sister's son, while a mere stripling, and Marcus Agrippa, of humble birth, a good soldier, and one who had shared his victory, to two consecutive consulships, and as Marcellus soon afterwards died, he also accepted him as his son-in-law. Tiberius Nero and Claudius Drusus, his stepsons, he honoured with imperial tides, although his own family was as yet undiminished. For he had admitted the children of Agrippa, Caius and Lucius, into the house of the Caesars; and before they had yet laid aside the dress of boyhood he had most fervently desired, with an outward show of reluctance, that they should be entitled "princes of the youth," and be consuls-elect. When Agrippa died, and Lucius Caesar as he was on his way to our armies in Spain, and Caius while returning from Armenia, still suffering from a wound, were prematurely cut off by destiny, or by their step-mother Livia's treachery, Drusus too having long been dead, Nero remained alone of the stepsons, and in him everything tended to centre. He was adopted as a son, as a colleague in empire and a partner in the tribunitian power, and paraded through all the armies, no longer through his mother's secret intrigues, but at her open suggestion. For she had gained such a hold on the aged Augustus that he drove out as an exile into the island of Planasia, his only grandson, Agrippa Postumus, who, though devoid of worthy qualities, and having only the brute courage of physical strength, had not been convicted of any gross offence. And yet Augustus had appointed Germanicus, Drusus's offspring, to the command of eight legions on the Rhine, and required Tiberius to adopt him, although Tiberius had a son, now a young man, in his house; but he did it that he might have several safeguards to rest on. He had no war at the time on his hands except against the Germans, which was rather to wipe out the disgrace of the loss of Quintilius Varus and his army than out of an ambition to extend the empire, or for any adequate recompense. At home all was tranquil, and there were magistrates with the same titles; there was a younger generation, sprung up since the victory of Actium, and even many of the older men had been born during the civil wars. How few were left who had seen the republic!

Thus the State had been revolutionised, and there was not a vestige left of the old sound morality. Stript of equality, all looked up to the commands of a sovereign without the least apprehension for the present, while Augustus in the vigour of life, could maintain his own position, that of his house, and the general tranquillity. When in advanced old age, he was worn out by a sickly frame, and the end was near and new prospects opened, a few spoke in vain of the blessings of freedom, but most people dreaded and some longed for war. The popular gossip of the large majority fastened itself variously on their future masters. "Agrippa was savage, and had been exasperated by insult, and neither from age nor experience in affairs was equal to so great a burden. Tiberius Nero was of mature years, and had established his fame in war, but he had the old arrogance inbred in the Claudian family, and many symptoms of a cruel temper, though they were repressed, now and then broke out. He had also from earliest infancy been reared in an imperial house; consulships and triumphs had been heaped on him in his younger days; even in the years which, on the pretext of seclusion he spent in exile at Rhodes, he had had no thoughts but of wrath, hypocrisy, and secret sensuality. There was his mother too with a woman caprice. They must, it seemed, be subject to a female and to two striplings besides, who for a while would burden, and some day rend asunder the State."

While these and like topics were discussed, the infirmities of Augustus increased, and some suspected guilt on his wife's part. For a rumour had gone abroad that a few months before he had sailed to Planasia on a visit to Agrippa, with the knowledge of some chosen friends, and with one companion, Fabius Maximus; that many tears were shed on both sides, with expressions of affection, and that thus there was a hope of the young man being restored to the home of his grandfather. This, it was said, Maximus had divulged to his wife Marcia, she again to Livia. All was known to Caesar, and when Maximus soon afterwards died, by a death some thought to be self-inflicted, there were heard at his funeral wailings from Marcia, in which she reproached herself for having been the cause of her husband's destruction. Whatever the fact was, Tiberius as he was just entering Illyria was summoned home by an urgent letter from his mother, and it has not been thoroughly ascertained whether at the city of Nola he found Augustus still breathing or quite lifeless. For Livia had surrounded the house and its approaches with a strict watch, and favourable bulletins were published from time to time, till, provision having been made for the demands of the crisis, one and the same report told men that Augustus was dead and that Tiberius Nero was master of the State.

The first crime of the new reign was the murder of Postumus Agrippa. Though he was surprised and unarmed, a centurion of the firmest resolution despatched him with difficulty. Tiberius gave no explanation of the matter to the Senate; he pretended that there were directions from his father ordering the tribune in charge of the prisoner not to delay the slaughter of Agrippa, whenever he should himself have breathed his last. Beyond a doubt, Augustus had often complained of the young man's character, and had thus succeeded in obtaining the sanction of a decree of the Senate for his banishment. But he never was hard-hearted enough to destroy any of his kinsfolk, nor was it credible that death was to be the sentence of the grandson in order that the stepson might feel secure. It was more probable that Tiberius and Livia, the one from fear, the other from a stepmother's enmity, hurried on the destruction of a youth whom they suspected and hated. When the centurion reported, according to military custom, that he had executed the command, Tiberius replied that he had not given the command, and that the act must be justified to the Senate.

As soon as Sallustius Crispus who shared the secret (he had, in fact, sent the written order to the tribune) knew this, fearing that the charge would be shifted on himself, and that his peril would be the same whether he uttered fiction or truth, he advised Livia not to divulge the secrets of her house or the counsels of friends, or any services performed by the soldiers, nor to let Tiberius weaken the strength of imperial power by referring everything to the Senate, for "the condition," he said, "of holding empire is that an account cannot be balanced unless it be rendered to one person."

Meanwhile at Rome people plunged into slavery—consuls, senators, knights. The higher a man's rank, the more eager his hypocrisy, and his looks the more carefully studied, so as neither to betray joy at the decease of one emperor nor sorrow at the rise of another, while he mingled delight and lamentations with his flattery. Sextus Pompeius and Sextus Apuleius, the consuls, were the first to swear allegiance to Tiberius Caesar, and in their presence the oath was taken by Seius Strabo and Caius Turranius, respectively the commander of the praetorian cohorts and the superintendent of the corn supplies. Then the Senate, the soldiers and the people did the same. For Tiberius would inaugurate everything with the consuls, as though the ancient constitution remained, and he hesitated about being emperor. Even the proclamation by which he summoned the senators to their chamber, he issued merely with the title of Tribune, which he had received under Augustus. The wording of the proclamation was brief, and in a very modest tone. "He would," it said, "provide for the honours due to his father, and not leave the lifeless body, and this was the only public duty he now claimed."

As soon, however, as Augustus was dead, he had given the watchword to the praetorian cohorts, as commander-in-chief. He had the guard under arms, with all the other adjuncts of a court; soldiers attended him to the forum; soldiers went with him to the Senate House. He sent letters to the different armies, as though supreme power was now his, and showed hesitation only when he spoke in the Senate. His chief motive was fear that Germanicus, who had at his disposal so many legions, such vast auxiliary forces of the allies, and such wonderful popularity, might prefer the possession to the expectation of empire. He looked also at public opinion, wishing to have the credit of having been called and elected by the State rather than of having crept into power through the intrigues of a wife and a dotard's adoption. It was subsequently understood that he assumed a wavering attitude, to test likewise the temper of the nobles. For he would twist a word or a look into a crime and treasure it up in his memory.

On the first day of the Senate he allowed nothing to be discussed but the funeral of Augustus, whose will, which was brought in by the Vestal Virgins, named as his heirs Tiberius and Livia. The latter was to be admitted into the Julian family with the name of

Augusta; next in expectation were the grand and great-grandchildren. In the third place, he had named the chief men of the State, most of whom he hated, simply out of ostentation and to win credit with posterity. His legacies were not beyond the scale of a private citizen, except a bequest of forty-three million five hundred thousand sesterces "to the people and populace of Rome," of one thousand to every praetorian soldier, and of three hundred to every man in the legionary cohorts composed of Roman citizens.

Next followed a deliberation about funeral honours. Of these the most imposing were thought fitting. The procession was to be conducted through "the gate of triumph," on the motion of Gallus Asinius; the titles of the laws passed, the names of the nations conquered by Augustus were to be borne in front, on that of Lucius Arruntius. Messala Valerius further proposed that the oath of allegiance to Tiberius should be yearly renewed, and when Tiberius asked him whether it was at his bidding that he had brought forward this motion, he replied that he had proposed it spontaneously, and that in whatever concerned the State he would use only his own discretion, even at the risk of offending. This was the only style of adulation which yet remained. The Senators unanimously exclaimed that the body ought to be borne on their shoulders to the funeral pile. The emperor left the point to them with disdainful moderation, he then admonished the people by a proclamation not to indulge in that tumultuous enthusiasm which had distracted the funeral of the Divine Julius, or express a wish that Augustus should be burnt in the Forum instead of in his appointed resting-place in the Campus Martius.

On the day of the funeral soldiers stood round as a guard, amid much ridicule from those who had either themselves witnessed or who had heard from their parents of the famous day when slavery was still something fresh, and freedom had been resought in vain, when the slaying of Caesar, the Dictator, seemed to some the vilest, to others, the most glorious of deeds. "Now," they said, "an aged sovereign, whose power had lasted long, who had provided his heirs with abundant means to coerce the State, requires forsooth the defence of soldiers that his burial may be undisturbed."

Then followed much talk about Augustus himself, and many expressed an idle wonder that the same day marked the beginning of his assumption of empire and the close of his life, and, again, that he had ended his days at Nola in the same house and room as his father Octavius. People extolled too the number of his consulships, in which he had equalled Valerius Corvus and Caius Marius combined, the continuance for thirty-seven years of the tribunitian power, the title of Imperator twenty-one times earned, and his other honours which had either frequently repeated or were wholly new. Sensible men, however, spoke variously of his life with praise and censure. Some said "that dutiful feeling towards a father, and the necessities of the State in which laws had then no place, drove him into civil war, which can neither be planned nor conducted on any right principles. He had often yielded to Antonius, while he was taking vengeance on his father's murderers, often also to Lepidus. When the latter sank into feeble dotage and the former had been ruined by his profligacy, the only remedy for his distracted country was the rule of a single man. Yet the State had been organized under the name neither of a kingdom nor a dictatorship, but under that of a prince. The ocean and remote rivers were the boundaries of the empire; the legions, provinces, fleets, all things were linked together; there was law for the citizens; there was respect shown to the allies. The capital had been embellished on a grand scale; only in a few instances had he resorted to force, simply to secure general tranquillity."

It was said, on the other hand, "that filial duty and State necessity were merely assumed as a mask. It was really from a lust of sovereignty that he had excited the veterans by bribery, had, when a young man and a subject, raised an army, tampered with the Consul's legions, and feigned an attachment to the faction of Pompeius. Then, when by a decree of the Senate he had usurped the high functions and authority of Praetor when Hirtius and Pansa were slain—whether they were destroyed by the enemy, or Pansa by poison infused into a wound, Hirtius by his own soldiers and Caesar's treacherous machinations—he at once possessed himself of both their armies, wrested the consulate from a reluctant Senate, and turned against the State the arms with which he had been intrusted against Antonius. Citizens were proscribed, lands divided, without so much as the approval of those who executed these deeds. Even granting that the deaths of Cassius and of the Bruti were sacrifices to a hereditary enmity (though duty requires us to waive private feuds for the sake of the public welfare), still Pompeius had been deluded by the phantom of peace, and Lepidus by the mask of friendship. Subsequently, Antonius had been lured on by the treaties of Tarentum and Brundisium, and by his marriage with the sister, and paid by his death the penalty of a treacherous alliance. No doubt, there was peace after all this, but it was a peace stained with blood; there were the disasters of Lollius and Varus, the murders at Rome of the Varros, Egnatii, and Juli."

The domestic life too of Augustus was not spared. "Nero's wife had been taken from him, and there had been the farce of consulting the pontiffs, whether, with a child conceived and not yet born, she could properly marry. There were the excesses of Quintus Tedius and Vedius Pollio; last of all, there was Livia, terrible to the State as a mother, terrible to the house of the Caesars as a stepmother. No honour was left for the gods, when Augustus chose to be himself worshipped with temples and statues, like those of the deities, and with flamens and priests. He had not even adopted Tiberius as his successor out of affection or any regard to the State, but, having thoroughly seen his arrogant and savage temper, he had sought glory for himself by a contrast of extreme wickedness." For, in fact, Augustus, a few years before, when he was a second time asking from the Senate the tribunitian power for Tiberius, though his speech was complimentary, had thrown out certain hints as to his manners, style, and habits of life, which he meant as reproaches, while he seemed to excuse. However, when his obsequies had been duly performed, a temple with a religious ritual was decreed him.

After this all prayers were addressed to Tiberius. He, on his part, urged various considerations, the greatness of the empire, his distrust of himself. "Only," he said, "the intellect of the Divine Augustus was equal to such a burden. Called as he had been by him to share his anxieties, he had learnt by experience how exposed to fortune's caprices was the task of universal rule. Consequently, in a state which had the support of so many great men, they should not put everything on one man, as many, by uniting their efforts would more easily discharge public functions." There was more grand sentiment than good faith in such words. Tiberius's language even in matters which he did not care to conceal, either from nature or habit, was always hesitating and obscure, and now that he was struggling to hide his feelings completely, it was all the more involved in uncertainty and doubt. The Senators, however, whose only fear was lest they might seem to understand him, burst into complaints, tears, and prayers. They raised their hands to the gods, to the statue of Augustus, and to the knees of Tiberius, when he ordered a document to be produced and read. This contained a description of the resources of the State, of the number of citizens and allies under arms, of the fleets, subject kingdoms, provinces, taxes, direct and indirect, necessary expenses and customary bounties. All these details Augustus had written with his own hand, and had added a counsel, that the empire should be confined to its present limits, either from fear or out of jealousy.

Meantime, while the Senate stooped to the most abject supplication, Tiberius happened to say that although he was not equal to the whole burden of the State, yet he would undertake the charge of whatever part of it might be intrusted to him. Thereupon Asinius Gallus said, "I ask you, Caesar, what part of the State you wish to have intrusted to you?" Confounded by the sudden inquiry he was silent for a few moments; then, recovering his presence of mind, he replied that it would by no means become his modesty to choose or to avoid in a case where he would prefer to be wholly excused. Then Gallus again, who had inferred anger from his looks, said that the question had not been asked with the intention of dividing what could not be separated, but to convince him by his own admission that the body of the State was one, and must be directed by a single mind. He further spoke in praise of Augustus, and reminded Tiberius himself of his victories, and of his admirable deeds for many years as a civilian. Still, he did not thereby soften the emperor's resentment, for he had long been detested from an impression that, as he had married Vipsania, daughter of Marcus Agrippa, who had once been the wife of Tiberius, he aspired to be more than a citizen, and kept up the arrogant tone of his father, Asinius Pollio.

Next, Lucius Arruntius, who differed but little from the speech of Gallus, gave like offence, though Tiberius had no old grudge against him, but simply mistrusted him, because he was rich and daring, had brilliant accomplishments, and corresponding popularity. For Augustus, when in his last conversations he was discussing who would refuse the highest place, though sufficiently capable, who would aspire to it without being equal to it, and who would unite both the ability and ambition, had described Marcus Lepidus as able but contemptuously indifferent, Gallus Asinius as ambitious and incapable, Lucius Arruntius as not unworthy of it, and, should the chance be given him, sure to make the venture. About the two first there is a general agreement, but instead of Arruntius some have mentioned Cneius Piso, and all these men, except Lepidus, were soon afterwards destroyed by various charges through the contrivance of Tiberius. Quintus Haterius too and Mamercus Scaurus ruffled his suspicious temper, Haterius by having said—"How long, Caesar, will you suffer the State to be without a head?" Scaurus by the remark that there was a hope that the Senate's prayers would not be fruitless, seeing that he had not used his right as Tribune to negative the motion of the Consuls. Tiberius instantly broke out into invective against Haterius; Scaurus, with whom he was far more deeply displeased, he passed over in silence. Wearied at last by the assembly's clamorous importunity and the urgent demands of individual Senators, he gave way by degrees, not admitting that he undertook empire, but yet ceasing to refuse it and to be entreated. It is known that Haterius having entered the palace to ask pardon, and thrown himself at the knees of Tiberius as he was walking, was almost killed by the soldiers, because Tiberius fell forward, accidentally or from being entangled by the suppliant's hands. Yet the peril of so great a man did not make him relent, till Haterius went with entreaties to Augusta, and was saved by her very earnest intercessions.

Great too was the Senate's sycophancy to Augusta. Some would have her styled "parent"; others "mother of the country," and a majority proposed that to the name of Caesar should be added "son of Julia." The emperor repeatedly asserted that there must be a limit to the honours paid to women, and that he would observe similar moderation in those bestowed on himself, but annoyed at the invidious proposal, and indeed regarding a woman's elevation as a slight to himself, he would not allow so much as a lictor to be assigned her, and forbade the erection of an altar in memory of her adoption, and any like distinction. But for Germanicus Caesar he asked pro-consular powers, and envoys were despatched to confer them on him, and also to express sympathy with his grief at the death of Augustus. The same request was not made for Drusus, because he was consul elect and present at Rome. Twelve candidates were named for the praetorship, the number which Augustus had handed down, and when the Senate urged Tiberius to increase it, he bound himself by an oath not to exceed it.

It was then for the first time that the elections were transferred from the Campus Martius to the Senate. For up to that day, though the most important rested with the emperor's choice, some were settled by the partialities of the tribes. Nor did the people complain of having the right taken from them, except in mere idle talk, and the Senate, being now released from the necessity of bribery and of degrading solicitations, gladly upheld the change, Tiberius confining himself to the recommendation of only four candidates who were to be nominated without rejection or canvass. Meanwhile the tribunes of the people asked leave to exhibit at their own expense games to be named after Augustus and added to the Calendar as the Augustales. Money was, however, voted from the exchequer, and though the use of the triumphal robe in the circus was prescribed, it was not allowed them to ride in a chariot. Soon the annual celebration was transferred to the praetor, to whose lot fell the administration of justice between citizens and foreigners.

This was the state of affairs at Rome when a mutiny broke out in the legions of Pannonia, which could be traced to no fresh cause except the change of emperors and the prospect it held out of license in tumult and of profit from a civil war. In the summer camp three legions were quartered, under the command of Junius Blaesus, who on hearing of the death of Augustus and the accession of Tiberius, had allowed his men a rest from military duties, either for mourning or rejoicing. This was the beginning of demoralization among the troops, of quarreling, of listening to the talk of every pestilent fellow, in short, of craving for luxury and idleness and loathing discipline and toil. In the camp was one Percennius, who had once been a leader of one of the theatrical factions, then became a common soldier, had a saucy tongue, and had learnt from his applause of actors how to stir up a crowd. By working on ignorant minds, which doubted as to what would be the terms of military service after Augustus, this man gradually influenced them in conversations at night or at nightfall, and when the better men had dispersed, he gathered round him all the worst spirits.

At last, when there were others ready to be abettors of a mutiny, he asked, in the tone of a demagogue, why, like slaves, they submitted to a few centurions and still fewer tribunes. "When," he said, "will you dare to demand relief, if you do not go with your prayers or arms to a new and yet tottering throne? We have blundered enough by our tameness for so many years, in having to endure thirty or forty campaigns till we grow old, most of us with bodies maimed by wounds. Even dismissal is not the end of our service, but, quartered under a legion's standard we toil through the same hardships under another title. If a soldier survives so many risks, he is still dragged into remote regions where, under the name of lands, he receives soaking swamps or mountainous wastes. Assuredly, military service itself is burdensome and unprofitable; ten as a day is the value set on life and limb; out of this, clothing, arms, tents, as well as the mercy of centurions and exemptions from duty have to be purchased. But indeed of floggings and wounds, of hard winters, wearisome summers, of terrible war, or barren peace, there is no end. Our only relief can come from military life being entered on under fixed conditions, from receiving each the pay of a denarius, and from the sixteenth year terminating our service. We must be retained no longer under a standard, but in the same camp a compensation in money must be paid us. Do the praetorian cohorts, which have just got their two denarii per man, and which after sixteen years are restored to their homes, encounter more perils? We do not disparage the guards of the capital; still, here amid barbarous tribes we have to face the enemy from our tents."

The throng applauded from various motives, some pointing with indignation to the marks of the lash, others to their grey locks, and most of them to their threadbare garments and naked limbs. At, last, in their fury they went so far as to propose to combine the three legions into one. Driven from their purpose by the jealousy with which every one sought the chief honour for his own legion, they turned to other thoughts, and set up in one spot the three eagles, with the ensigns of the cohorts. At the same time they piled up turf and raised a mound, that they might have a more conspicuous meeting-place. Amid the bustle Blaesus came up. He upbraided them and held back man after man with the exclamation, "Better imbrue your hands in my blood: it will be less guilt to slay your commander than it is to be in revolt from the emperor. Either living I will uphold the loyalty of the legions, or Pierced to the heart I will hasten on your repentance."

None the less however was the mound piled up, and it was quite breast high when, at last overcome by his persistency, they gave up their purpose. Blaesus, with the consummate tact of an orator, said, "It is not through mutiny and tumult that the desires of the army ought to be communicated to Caesar, nor did our soldiers of old ever ask so novel a boon of ancient commanders, nor have you yourselves asked it of the Divine Augustus. It is far from opportune that the emperor's cares, now in their first beginning, should be aggravated. If, however, you are bent upon attempting in peace what even after your victory in the civil wars you did not demand, why, contrary to the habit of obedience, contrary to the law of discipline, do you meditate violence? Decide on sending envoys, and give them instructions in your presence."

It was carried by acclamation that the son of Blaesus, one of the tribunes, should undertake the mission, and demand for the soldiers release from service after sixteen years. He was to have the rest of their message when the first part had been successful. After the young man departure there was comparative quiet, but there was an arrogant tone among the soldiers, to whom the fact that their commander's son was pleading their common cause clearly showed that they had wrested by compulsion what they had failed to obtain by good behaviour.

Meanwhile the companies which previous to the mutiny had been sent to Nauportus to make roads and bridges and for other purposes, when they heard of the tumult in the camp, tore up the standards, and having plundered the neighbouring villages and Nauportus itself, which was like a town, assailed the centurions who restrained them with jeers and insults, last of all, with blows. Their chief rage was against Aufidienus Rufus, the camp-prefect, whom they dragged from a waggon, loaded with baggage, and drove on at the head of the column, asking him in ridicule whether he liked to bear such huge burdens and such long marches. Rufus, who had long been a common soldier, then a centurion, and subsequently camp-prefect, tried to revive the old severe discipline, inured as he was to work and toil, and all the sterner because he had endured.

On the arrival of these troops the mutiny broke out afresh, and straggling from the camp they plundered the neighbourhood. Blaesus ordered a few who had conspicuously loaded themselves with spoil to be scourged and imprisoned as a terror to the rest; for, even as it then was, the commander was still obeyed by the centurions and by all the best men among the soldiers. As the men were dragged off, they struggled violently, clasped the knees of the bystanders, called to their comrades by name, or to the company, cohort, or legion to which they respectively belonged, exclaiming that all were threatened with the same fate. At the same time they heaped abuse on the commander; they appealed to heaven and to the gods, and left nothing undone by which they might excite resentment and pity, alarm and rage. They all rushed to the spot, broke open the guardhouse, unbound the prisoners, and were in a moment fraternising with deserters and men convicted on capital charges.

Thence arose a more furious outbreak, with more leaders of the mutiny. Vibulenus, a common soldier, was hoisted in front of the general's tribunal on the shoulders of the bystanders and addressed the excited throng, who eagerly awaited his intentions. "You have indeed," he said, "restored light and air to these innocent and most unhappy men, but who restores to my brother his life, or my brother to myself? Sent to you by the German army in our common cause, he was last night butchered by the gladiators whom the general keeps and arms for the destruction of his soldiers. Answer, Blaesus, where you have flung aside the corpse? Even an enemy grudges not burial. When, with embraces and tears, I have sated my grief, order me also to be slain, provided only that when we have been destroyed for no crime, but only because we consulted the good of the legions, we may be buried by these men around me."

He inflamed their excitement by weeping and smiting his breast and face with his hands. Then, hurling aside those who bore him on their shoulders, and impetuously flinging himself at the feet of one man after another, he roused such dismay and indignation that some of the soldiers put fetters on the gladiators who were among the number of Blaesus's slaves, others did the like to the rest of his household, while a third party hurried out to look for the corpse. And had it not quickly been known that no corpse was found, that the slaves, when tortures were applied, denied the murder, and that the man never had a brother, they would have been on the point of destroying the general. As it was, they thrust out the tribunes and the camp-prefect; they plundered the baggage of the fugitives, and they killed a centurion, Lucilius, to whom, with soldiers' humour, they had given the name "Bring another," because when he had broken one vine-stick on a man's back, he would call in a loud voice for another and another. The rest sheltered themselves in concealment, and one only was detained, Clemens Julius, whom the soldiers considered a fit person to carry messages, from his ready wit. Two legions, the eighth and the fifteenth, were actually drawing swords against each other, the former demanding the death of a centurion, whom they nicknamed Sirpicus, while the men of the fifteenth defended him, but the soldiers of the ninth interposed their entreaties, and when these were disregarded, their menaces.

This intelligence had such an effect on Tiberius, close as he was, and most careful to hush up every very serious disaster, that he despatched his son Drusus with the leading men of the State and with two praetorian cohorts, without any definite instructions, to take suitable measures. The cohorts were strengthened beyond their usual force with some picked troops. There was in addition a considerable part of the Praetorian cavalry, and the flower of the German soldiery, which was then the emperor's guard. With them too was the commander of the praetorians, Aelius Sejanus, who had been associated with his own father, Strabo, had great influence with Tiberius, and was to advise and direct the young prince, and to hold out punishment or reward to the soldiers. When Drusus approached, the legions, as a mark of respect, met him, not as usual, with glad looks or the glitter of military decorations, but in unsightly squalor, and faces which, though they simulated grief, rather expressed defiance.

As soon as he entered the entrenchments, they secured the gates with sentries, and ordered bodies of armed men to be in readiness at certain points of the camp. The rest crowded round the general's tribunal in a dense mass. Drusus stood there, and with a gesture of his hand demanded silence. As often as they turned their eyes back on the throng, they broke into savage exclamations, then looking up to Drusus they trembled. There was a confused hum, a fierce shouting, and a sudden lull. Urged by conflicting emotions, they felt panic and they caused the like. At last, in an interval of the uproar, Drusus read his father's letter, in which it was fully stated that he had a special care for the brave legions with which he had endured a number of campaigns; that, as soon as his mind had recovered from its grief, he would lay their demands before the Senators; that meanwhile he had sent his son to concede unhesitatingly what could be immediately granted, and that the rest must be reserved for the Senate, which ought to have a voice in showing either favour or severity.

The crowd replied that they had delivered their instructions to Clemens, one of the centurions, which he was to convey to Rome. He began to speak of the soldiers' discharge after sixteen years, of the rewards of completed service, of the daily pay being a denarius, and of the veterans not being detained under a standard. When Drusus pleaded in answer reference to the Senate and to his father, he was interrupted by a tumultuous shout. "Why had he come, neither to increase the soldiers' pay, nor to alleviate their hardships, in a word, with no power to better their lot? Yet heaven knew that all were allowed to scourge and to execute. Tiberius used formerly in the name of Augustus to frustrate the wishes of the legions, and the same tricks were now revived by Drusus. Was it only sons who were to visit them? Certainly, it was a new thing for the emperor to refer to the Senate merely what concerned the soldier's interests. Was then the same Senate to be consulted whenever notice was given of an execution or of a battle? Were their rewards to be at the discretion of absolute rulers, their punishments to be without appeal?"

At last they deserted the general's tribunal, and to any praetorian soldier or friend of Caesar's who met them, they used those threatening gestures which are the cause of strife and the beginning of a conflict, with special rage against Cneius Lentulus, because they thought that he above all others, by his age and warlike renown, encouraged Drusus, and was the first to scorn such blots on military discipline. Soon after, as he was leaving with Drusus to betake himself in foresight of his danger to the winter can they surrounded him, and asked him again and again whither he was going; was it to the emperor or to the Senate, there also to oppose the interests of the legions. At the same moment they menaced him savagely and flung stones. And now, bleeding from a blow, and feeling destruction certain, he was rescued by the hurried arrival of the throng which had accompanied Drusus.

That terrible night which threatened an explosion of crime was tranquillised by a mere accident. Suddenly in a clear sky the moon's radiance seemed to die away. This the soldiers in their ignorance of the cause regarded as an omen of their condition, comparing the failure of her light to their own efforts, and imagining that their attempts would end prosperously should her brightness and splendour be restored to the goddess. And so they raised a din with brazen instruments and the combined notes of trumpets and horns, with joy or sorrow, as she brightened or grew dark. When clouds arose and obstructed their sight, and it was thought she was buried in the gloom, with that proneness to superstition which steals over minds once thoroughly cowed, they lamented that this was a portent of never-ending hardship, and that heaven frowned on their deeds.

Drusus, thinking that he ought to avail himself of this change in their temper and turn what chance had offered to a wise account, ordered the tents to be visited. Clemens, the centurion was summoned with all others who for their good qualities were liked by the common soldiers. These men made their way among the patrols, sentries and guards of the camp-gates, suggesting hope or holding out threats. "How long will you besiege the emperor's son? What is to be the end of our strifes? Will Percennius and Vibulenus give pay to the soldiers and land to those who have earned their discharge? In a word, are they, instead of the Neros and the Drusi, to control the empire of the Roman people? Why are we not rather first in our repentance as we were last in the offence? Demands made in common are granted slowly; a separate favour you may deserve and receive at the same moment."

With minds affected by these words and growing mutually suspicious, they divided off the new troops from the old, and one legion from another. Then by degrees the instinct of obedience returned. They quitted the gates and restored to their places the standards which at the beginning of the mutiny they had grouped into one spot.

At daybreak Drusus called them to an assembly, and, though not a practised speaker, yet with natural dignity upbraided them for their past and commended their present behaviour. He was not, he said, to be conquered by terror or by threats. Were he to see them inclining to submission and hear the language of entreaty, he would write to his father, that he might be merciful and receive the legions' petition. At their prayer, Blaesus and Lucius Apronius, a Roman knight on Drusus's staff, with Justus Catonius, a first-rank centurion, were again sent to Tiberius. Then ensued a conflict of opinion among them, some maintaining that it was best to wait the envoys' return and meanwhile humour the soldiers, others, that stronger measures ought to be used, inasmuch as the rabble knows no mean, and inspires fear, unless they are afraid, though when they have once been overawed, they can be safely despised. "While superstition still swayed them, the general should apply terror by removing the leaders of the mutiny."

Drusus's temper was inclined to harsh measures. He summoned Vibulenus and Percennius and ordered them to be put to death. The common account is that they were buried in the general's tent, though according to some their bodies were flung outside the entrenchments for all to see.

Search was then made for all the chief mutineers. Some as they roamed outside the camp were cut down by the centurions or by soldiers of the praetorian cohorts. Some even the companies gave up in proof of their loyalty. The men's troubles were increased by an early winter with continuous storms so violent that they could not go beyond their tents or meet together or keep the standards in their places, from which they were perpetually torn by hurricane and rain. And there still lingered the dread of the divine wrath; nor was it without meaning, they thought, that, hostile to an impious host, the stars grew dim and storms burst over them. Their only relief from misery was to quit an ill-omened and polluted camp, and, having purged themselves of their guilt, to betake themselves again every one to his winter-quarters. First the eighth, then the fifteenth legion returned; the ninth cried again and again that they ought to wait for the letter from Tiberius, but soon finding themselves isolated by the departure of the rest, they voluntarily forestalled their inevitable fate. Drusus, without awaiting the envoys' return, as for the present all was quiet, went back to Rome.

About the same time, from the same causes, the legions of Germany rose in mutiny, with a fury proportioned to their greater numbers, in the confident hope that Germanicus Caesar would not be able to endure another's supremacy and offer himself to the legions, whose strength would carry everything before it. There were two armies on the bank of the Rhine; that named the upper army had Caius Silius for general; the lower was under the charge of Aulus Caecina. The supreme direction rested with Germanicus, then busily employed in conducting the assessment of Gaul. The troops under the control of Silius, with minds yet in suspense, watched the issue of mutiny elsewhere; but the soldiers of the lower army fell into a frenzy, which had its beginning in the men of the twenty-first and fifth legions, and into which the first and twentieth were also drawn. For they were all quartered in the same summer-camp, in the territory of the Ubii, enjoying ease or having only light on hearing of the death of Augustus, a rabble of city slaves, who had been enlisted under a recent levy at Rome, habituated to laxity and impatient of hardship, filled the ignorant minds of the other soldiers with notions that the time had come when the veteran might demand a timely discharge, the young, more liberal pay, all, an end of their miseries, and vengeance on the cruelty of centurions.

It was not one alone who spoke thus, as did Percennius among the legions of Pannonia, nor was it in the ears of trembling soldiers, who looked with apprehension to other and mightier armies, but there was sedition in many a face and voice. "The Roman world," they said, was in their hand; their victories aggrandised the State; it was from them that emperors received their titles."

Nor did their commander check them. Indeed, the blind rage of so many had robbed him of his resolution., In a sudden frenzy they rushed with drawn swords on the centurions, the immemorial object of the soldiers' resentment and the first cause of savage fury. They threw them to the earth and beat them sorely, sixty to one, so as to correspond with the number of centurions. Then tearing them from the ground, mangled, and some lifeless, they flung them outside the entrenchments or into the river Rhine. One Septimius, who fled to the tribunal and was grovelling at Caecina's feet, was persistently demanded till he was given up to destruction. Cassius Chaerea, who won for himself a memory with posterity by the murder of Caius Caesar, being then a youth of high spirit, cleared a passage with his sword through the armed and opposing throng. Neither tribune nor camp-prefect maintained authority any longer. Patrols, sentries, and whatever else the needs of the time required, were distributed by the men themselves. To those who could guess the temper of soldiers with some penetration, the strongest symptom of a wide-spread and intractable commotion, was the fact that, instead of being divided or instigated by a few persons, they were unanimous in their fury and equally unanimous in their composure, with so uniform a consistency that one would have thought them to be under command.

Meantime Germanicus, while, as I have related, he was collecting the taxes of Gaul, received news of the death of Augustus. He was married to the granddaughter of Augustus, Agrippina, by whom he had several children, and though he was himself the son of Drusus, brother of Tiberius, and grandson of Augusta, he was troubled by the secret hatred of his uncle and grandmother, the motives for which were the more venomous because unjust. For the memory of Drusus was held in honour by the Roman people, and they believed that had he obtained empire, he would have restored freedom. Hence they regarded Germanicus with favour and with the same hope. He was indeed a young man of unaspiring temper, and of wonderful kindliness, contrasting strongly with the proud and mysterious reserve that marked the conversation and the features of Tiberius. Then, there were feminine jealousies, Livia feeling a stepmother's bitterness towards Agrippina, and Agrippina herself too being rather excitable, only her purity and love of her husband gave a right direction to her otherwise imperious disposition.

But the nearer Germanicus was to the highest hope, the more laboriously did he exert himself for Tiberius, and he made the neighbouring Sequani and all the Belgic states swear obedience to him. On hearing of the mutiny in the legions, he instantly went to the spot, and met them outside the camp, eyes fixed on the ground, and seemingly repentant. As soon as he entered the entrenchments, confused murmurs became audible. Some men, seizing his hand under pretence of kissing it, thrust his fingers into their mouths, that he might touch their toothless gums; others showed him their limbs bowed with age. He ordered the throng which stood near him, as it seemed a promiscuous gathering, to separate itself into its military companies. They replied that they would hear better as they were. The standards were then to be advanced, so that thus at least the cohorts might be distinguished. The soldiers obeyed reluctantly. Then beginning with a reverent mention of Augustus, he passed on to the victories and triumphs of Tiberius, dwelling with especial praise on his glorious achievements with those legions in Germany. Next, he extolled the unity of Italy, the loyalty of Gaul, the entire absence of turbulence or strife. He was heard in silence or with but a slight murmur.

As soon as he touched on the mutiny and asked what had become of soldierly obedience, of the glory of ancient discipline, whither they had driven their tribunes and centurions, they all bared their bodies and taunted him with the scars of their wounds and the marks of the lash. And then with confused exclamations they spoke bitterly of the prices of exemptions, of their scanty pay, of the severity of their tasks, with special mention of the entrenchment, the fosse, the conveyance of fodder, building-timber, firewood, and whatever else had to be procured from necessity, or as a check on idleness in the camp. The fiercest clamour arose from the veteran soldiers, who, as they counted their thirty campaigns or more, implored him to relieve worn-out men, and not let them die under the same hardships, but have an end of such harassing service, and repose without beggary. Some even claimed the legacy of the Divine Augustus, with words of good omen for Germanicus, and, should he wish for empire, they showed themselves abundantly willing. Thereupon, as though he were contracting the pollution of guilt, he leapt impetuously from the tribunal. The men opposed his departure with their weapons, threatening him repeatedly if he would not go back. But Germanicus protesting that he would die rather than cast off his loyalty, plucked his sword from his side, raised it aloft and was plunging it into his breast, when those nearest him seized his hand and held it by force. The remotest and most densely crowded part of the throng, and, what almost passes belief, some, who came close up to him, urged him to strike the blow, and a soldier, by name Calusidius, offered him a drawn sword, saying that it was sharper than his own. Even in their fury, this seemed to them a savage act and one of evil precedent, and there was a pause during which Caesar's friends hurried him into his tent.

There they took counsel how to heal matters. For news was also brought that the soldiers were preparing the despatch of envoys who were to draw the upper army into their cause; that the capital of the Ubii was marked out for destruction, and that hands with the stain of plunder on them would soon be daring enough for the pillage of Gaul. The alarm was heightened by the knowledge that the enemy was aware of the Roman mutiny, and would certainly attack if the Rhine bank were undefended. Yet if the auxiliary troops and allies were to be armed against the retiring legions, civil war was in fact begun. Severity would be dangerous; profuse liberality would be scandalous. Whether all or nothing were conceded to the soldiery, the State was equally in jeopardy.

Accordingly, having weighed their plans one against each other, they decided that a letter should be written in the prince's name, to the effect that full discharge was granted to those who had served in twenty campaigns; that there was a conditional release for those who had served sixteen, and that they were to be retained under a standard with immunity from everything except actually keeping off the enemy; that the legacies which they had asked, were to be paid and doubled.

The soldiers perceived that all this was invented for the occasion, and instantly pressed their demands. The discharge from service was quickly arranged by the tribunes. Payment was put off till they reached their respective winter-quarters. The men of the fifth and twenty-first legions refused to go till in the summer-camp where they stood the money was made up out of the purses of Germanicus himself and his friends, and paid in full. The first and twentieth legions were led back by their officer Caecina to the canton of the Ubii, marching in disgrace, since sums of money which had been extorted from the general were carried among the eagles and standards. Germanicus went to the Upper Army, and the second, thirteenth, and sixteenth legions, without any delay, accepted from him the oath of allegiance. The fourteenth hesitated a little, but their money and the discharge were offered even without their demanding it.

Meanwhile there was an outbreak among the Chauci, begun by some veterans of the mutinous legions on garrison duty. They were quelled for a time by the instant execution of two soldiers. Such was the order of Mennius, the camp-prefect, more as a salutary warning than as a legal act. Then, when the commotion increased, he fled and having been discovered, as his hiding place was now unsafe, he borrowed a resource from audacity. "It was not," he told them, "the camp-prefect, it was Germanicus, their general, it was Tiberius, their emperor, whom they were insulting." At the same moment, overawing all resistance, he seized the standard, faced round towards the river-bank, and exclaiming that whoever left the ranks, he would hold as a deserter, he led them back into their winter-quarters, disaffected indeed, but cowed.

Meanwhile envoys from the Senate had an interview with Germanicus, who had now returned, at the Altar of the Ubii. Two legions, the first and twentieth, with veterans discharged and serving under a standard, were there in winter-quarters. In the bewilderment of terror and conscious guilt they were penetrated by an apprehension that persons had come at the Senate's orders to cancel the concessions they had extorted by mutiny. And as it is the way with a mob to fix any charge, however groundless, on some particular person, they reproached Manatius Plancus, an ex-consul and the chief envoy, with being the author of the Senate's decree. At midnight they began to demand the imperial standard kept in Germanicus's quarters, and having rushed together to the entrance, burst the door, dragged Caesar from his bed, and forced him by menaces of death to give up the standard. Then roaming through the camp-streets, they met the envoys, who on hearing of the tumult were hastening to Germanicus. They loaded them with insults, and were on the point of murdering them, Plancus especially, whose high rank had deterred him from flight. In his peril he found safety only in the camp of the first legion. There clasping the standards and the eagle, he sought to protect himself under their sanctity. And had not the eagle-bearer, Calpurnius, saved him from the worst violence, the blood of an envoy of the Roman people, an occurrence rare even among our foes, would in a Roman camp have stained the altars of the gods.

At last, with the light of day, when the general and the soldiers and the whole affair were clearly recognised, Germanicus entered the camp, ordered Plancus to be conducted to him, and received him on the tribunal. He then upbraided them with their fatal infatuation, revived not so much by the anger of the soldiers as by that of heaven, and explained the reasons of the envoys' arrival. On the rights of ambassadors, on the dreadful and undeserved peril of Plancus, and also on the disgrace into which the legion had brought itself, he dwelt with the eloquence of pity, and while the throng was confounded rather than appeased, he dismissed the envoys with an escort of auxiliary cavalry.

Amid the alarm all condemned Germanicus for not going to the Upper Army, where he might find obedience and help against the rebels. "Enough and more than enough blunders," they said, "had been made by granting discharges and money, indeed, by conciliatory measures. Even if Germanicus held his own life cheap, why should he keep a little son and a pregnant wife among madmen who outraged every human right? Let these, at least, be restored safely to their grandsire and to the State."

When his wife spurned the notion, protesting that she was a descendant of the Divine Augustus and could face peril with no degenerate spirit, he at last embraced her and the son of their love with many tears, and after long delay compelled her to depart. Slowly moved along a pitiable procession of women, a general's fugitive wife with a little son in her bosom, her friends' wives weeping round her, as with her they were dragging themselves from the camp. Not less sorrowful were those who remained.

There was no appearance of the triumphant general about Germanicus, and he seemed to be in a conquered city rather than in his own camp, while groans and wailings attracted the ears and looks even of the soldiers. They came out of their tents, asking "what was that mournful sound? What meant the sad sight? Here were ladies of rank, not a centurion to escort them, not a soldier, no sign of a prince's wife, none of the usual retinue. Could they be going to the Treveri, to be subjects of the foreigner?" Then they felt shame and pity, and remembered his father Agrippa, her grandfather Augustus, her father-in-law Drusus, her own glory as a mother of children, her noble purity. And there was her little child too, born in the camp, brought up amid the tents of the legions, whom they used to call in soldiers' fashion, Caligula, because he often wore the shoe so called, to win the men's goodwill. But nothing moved them so much as jealousy towards the Treveri. They entreated, stopped the way, that Agrippina might return and remain, some running to meet her, while most of them went back to Germanicus. He, with a grief and anger that were yet fresh, thus began to address the throng around him—

"Neither wife nor son are dearer to me than my father and the State. But he will surely have the protection of his own majesty, the empire of Rome that of our other armies. My wife and children whom, were it a question of your glory, I would willingly expose to destruction, I now remove to a distance from your fury, so that whatever wickedness is thereby threatened, may be expiated by my blood only, and that you may not be made more guilty by the slaughter of a great-grandson of Augustus, and the murder of a daughter-in-law of Tiberius. For what have you not dared, what have you not profaned during these days? What name shall I give to this gathering? Am I to call you soldiers, you who have beset with entrenchments and arms your general's son, or citizens, when you have trampled under foot the authority of the Senate? Even the rights of public enemies, the sacred character of the ambassador, and the law of nations have been violated by you. The Divine Julius once quelled an army's mutiny with a single word by calling those who were renouncing their military obedience 'citizens.' The Divine Augustus cowed the legions who had fought at Actium with one look of his face. Though I am not yet what they were, still, descended as I am from them, it would be a strange and unworthy thing should I be spurned by the soldiery of Spain or Syria. First and twentieth legions, you who received your standards from Tiberius, you, men of the twentieth who have shared with me so many battles and have been enriched with so many rewards, is not this a fine gratitude with which you are repaying your general? Are these the tidings which I shall have to carry to my father when he hears only joyful intelligence from our other provinces, that his own recruits, his own veterans are not satisfied with discharge or pay; that here only centurions are murdered, tribunes driven away, envoys imprisoned, camps and rivers stained with blood, while I am myself dragging on a precarious existence amid those who hate me?

"Why, on the first day of our meeting, why did you, my friends, wrest from me, in your blindness, the steel which I was preparing to plunge into my breast? Better and more loving was the act of the man who offered me the sword. At any rate I should have perished before I was as yet conscious of all the disgraces of my army, while you would have chosen a general who though he might allow my death to pass unpunished would avenge the death of Varus and his three legions. Never indeed may heaven suffer the Belgae, though they proffer their aid, to have the glory and honour of having rescued the name of Rome and quelled the tribes of Germany. It is thy spirit, Divine Augustus, now received into heaven, thine image, father Drusus, and the remembrance of thee, which, with these same soldiers who are now stimulated by shame and ambition, should wipe out this blot and turn the wrath of civil strife to the destruction of the foe. You too, in whose faces and in whose hearts I perceive a change, if only you restore to the Senate their envoys, to the emperor his due allegiance, to myself my wife and son, do you stand aloof from pollution and separate the mutinous from among you. This will be a pledge of your repentance, a guarantee of your loyalty."

Thereupon, as suppliants confessing that his reproaches were true, they implored him to punish the guilty, pardon those who had erred, and lead them against the enemy. And he was to recall his wife, to let the nursling of the legions return and not be handed over as a hostage to the Gauls. As to Agrippina's return, he made the excuse of her approaching confinement and of winter. His son, he said, would come, and the rest they might settle themselves. Away they hurried hither and thither, altered men, and dragged the chief mutineers in chains to Caius Caetronius commander of the first legion, who tried and punished them one by one in the following fashion. In front of the throng stood the legions with drawn swords. Each accused man was on a raised platform and was pointed out by a tribune. If they shouted out that he was guilty, he was thrown headlong and cut to pieces. The soldiers gloated over the bloodshed as though it gave them absolution. Nor did Caesar check them, seeing that without any order from himself the same men were responsible for all the cruelty and all the odium of the deed.

The example was followed by the veterans, who were soon afterwards sent into Raetia, nominally to defend the province against a threatened invasion of the Suevi but really that they might tear themselves from a camp stamped with the horror of a dreadful remedy no less than with the memory of guilt. Then the general revised the list of centurions. Each, at his summons, stated his name, his rank, his birthplace, the number of his campaigns, what brave deeds he had done in battle, his military rewards, if any. If the tribunes and the legion commended his energy and good behaviour, he retained his rank; where they unanimously charged him with rapacity or cruelty, he was dismissed the service.

Quiet being thus restored for the present, a no less formidable difficulty remained through the turbulence of the fifth and twenty-first legions, who were in winter quarters sixty miles away at Old Camp, as the place was called. These, in fact, had been the first to begin the mutiny, and the most atrocious deeds had been committed by their hands. Unawed by the punishment of their comrades, and unmoved by their contrition, they still retained their resentment. Caesar accordingly proposed to send an armed fleet with some of our allies down the Rhine, resolved to make war on them should they reject his authority.

At Rome, meanwhile, when the result of affairs in Illyrium was not yet known, and men had heard of the commotion among the German legions, the citizens in alarm reproached Tiberius for the hypocritical irresolution with which he was befooling the senate and the people, feeble and disarmed as they were, while the soldiery were all the time in revolt, and could not be quelled by the yet imperfectly-matured authority of two striplings. "He ought to have gone himself and confronted with his imperial majesty those who would have soon yielded, when they once saw a sovereign of long experience, who was the supreme dispenser of rigour or of bounty. Could Augustus, with the feebleness of age on him, so often visit Germany, and is Tiberius, in the vigour of life, to sit in the Senate and criticise its members' words? He had taken good care that there should be slavery at Rome; he should now apply some soothing medicine to the spirit of soldiers, that they might be willing to endure peace."

Notwithstanding these remonstrances, it was the inflexible purpose of Tiberius not to quit the head-quarters of empire or to imperil himself and the State. Indeed, many conflicting thoughts troubled him. The army in Germany was the stronger; that in Pannonia the nearer; the first was supported by all the strength of Gaul; the latter menaced Italy. Which was he to prefer, without the fear that those whom he slighted would be infuriated by the affront? But his sons might alike visit both, and not compromise the imperial dignity, which inspired the greatest awe at a distance. There was also an excuse for mere youths referring some matters to their father, with the possibility that he could conciliate or crush those who resisted Germanicus or Drusus. What resource remained, if they despised the emperor? However, as if on the eve of departure, he selected his attendants, provided his camp-equipage, and prepared a fleet; then winter and matters of business were the various pretexts with which he amused, first, sensible men, then the populace, last, and longest of all, the provinces.

Germanicus meantime, though he had concentrated his army and prepared vengeance against the mutineers, thought that he ought still to allow them an interval, in case they might, with the late warning before them, regard their safety. He sent a despatch to Caecina, which said that he was on the way with a strong force, and that, unless they forestalled his arrival by the execution of the guilty, he would resort to an indiscriminate massacre. Caecina read the letter confidentially to the eagle and standard-bearers, and to all in the camp who were least tainted by disloyalty, and urged them to save the whole army from disgrace, and themselves from destruction. "In peace," he said, "the merits of a man's case are carefully weighed; when war bursts on us, innocent and guilty alike perish."

Upon this, they sounded those whom they thought best for their purpose, and when they saw that a majority of their legions remained loyal, at the commander's suggestion they fixed a time for falling with the sword on all the vilest and foremost of the mutineers. Then, at a mutually given signal, they rushed into the tents, and butchered the unsuspecting men, none but those in the secret knowing what was the beginning or what was to be the end of the slaughter.

The scene was a contrast to all civil wars which have ever occurred. It was not in battle, it was not from opposing camps, it was from those same dwellings where day saw them at their common meals, night resting from labour, that they divided themselves into two factions, and showered on each other their missiles. Uproar, wounds, bloodshed, were everywhere visible; the cause was a mystery. All else was at the disposal of chance. Even some loyal men were slain, for, on its being once understood who were the objects of fury, some of the worst mutineers too had seized on weapons. Neither commander nor tribune was present to control them; the men were allowed license and vengeance to their heart's content. Soon afterwards Germanicus entered the camp, and exclaiming with a flood of tears, that this was destruction rather than remedy, ordered the bodies to be burnt.

Even then their savage spirit was seized with desire to march against the enemy, as an atonement for their frenzy, and it was felt that the shades of their fellow-soldiers could be appeased only by exposing such impious breasts to honourable scars. Caesar followed up the enthusiasm of the men, and having bridged over the Rhine, he sent across it 12,000 from the legions, with six-and-twenty allied cohorts, and eight squadrons of cavalry, whose discipline had been without a stain during the mutiny.

There was exultation among the Germans, not far off, as long as we were detained by the public mourning for the loss of Augustus, and then by our dissensions. But the Roman general in a forced march, cut through the Caesian forest and the barrier which had been begun by Tiberius, and pitched his camp on this barrier, his front and rear being defended by intrenchments, his flanks by timber barricades. He then penetrated some forest passes but little known, and, as there were two routes, he deliberated whether he should pursue the short and ordinary route, or that which was more difficult unexplored, and consequently unguarded by the enemy. He chose the longer way, and hurried on every remaining preparation, for his scouts had brought word that among the Germans it was a night of festivity, with games, and one of their grand banquets. Caecina had orders to advance with some light cohorts, and to clear away any obstructions from the woods. The legions followed at a moderate interval. They were helped by a night of bright starlight, reached the villages of the Marsi, and threw their pickets round the enemy, who even then were stretched on beds or at their tables, without the least fear, or any sentries before their camp, so complete was their carelessness and disorder; and of war indeed there was no apprehension. Peace it certainly was not—merely the languid and heedless ease of half-intoxicated people.

Caesar, to spread devastation widely, divided his eager legions into four columns, and ravaged a space of fifty miles with fire and sword. Neither sex nor age moved his compassion. Everything, sacred or profane, the temple too of Tamfana, as they called it, the special resort of all those tribes, was levelled to the ground. There was not a wound among our soldiers, who cut down a half-asleep, an unarmed, or a straggling foe. The Bructeri, Tubantes, and Usipetes, were roused by this slaughter, and they beset the forest passes through which the army had to return. The general knew this, and he marched, prepared both to advance and to fight. Part of the cavalry, and some of the auxiliary cohorts led the van; then came the first legion, and, with the baggage in the centre, the men of the twenty-first closed up the left, those of the fifth, the right flank. The twentieth legion secured the rear, and, next, were the rest of the allies.

Meanwhile the enemy moved not till the army began to defile in column through the woods, then made slight skirmishing attacks on its flanks and van, and with his whole force charged the rear. The light cohorts were thrown into confusion by the dense masses of the Germans, when Caesar rode up to the men of the twentieth legion, and in a loud voice exclaimed that this was the time for wiping out the mutiny. "Advance," he said, "and hasten to turn your guilt into glory." This fired their courage, and at a single dash they broke through the enemy, and drove him back with great slaughter into the open country. At the same moment the troops of the van emerged from the woods and intrenched a camp. After this their march was uninterrupted, and the soldiery, with the confidence of recent success, and forgetful of the past, were placed in winter-quarters.

The news was a source of joy and also of anxiety to Tiberius. He rejoiced that the mutiny was crushed, but the fact that Germanicus had won the soldiers' favour by lavishing money, and promptly granting the discharge, as well as his fame as a soldier, annoyed him. Still, he brought his achievements under the notice of the Senate, and spoke much of his greatness in language elaborated for effect, more so than could be believed to come from his inmost heart. He bestowed a briefer praise on Drusus, and on the termination of the disturbance in Illyricum, but he was more earnest, and his speech more hearty. And he confirmed, too, in the armies of Pannonia all the concessions of Germanicus.

That same year Julia ended her days. For her profligacy she had formerly been confined by her father Augustus in the island of Pandateria, and then in the town of the Regini on the shores of the straits of Sicily. She had been the wife of Tiberius while Caius and Lucius Caesar were in their glory, and had disdained him as an unequal match. This was Tiberius's special reason for retiring to Rhodes. When he obtained the empire, he left her in banishment and disgrace, deprived of all hope after the murder of Postumus Agrippa, and let her perish by a lingering death of destitution, with the idea that an obscurity would hang over her end from the length of her exile. He had a like motive for cruel vengeance on Sempronius Gracchus, a man of noble family, of shrewd understanding, and a perverse eloquence, who had seduced this same Julia when she was the wife of Marcus Agrippa. And this was not the end of the intrigue. When she had been handed over to Tiberius, her persistent paramour inflamed her with disobedience and hatred towards her husband; and a letter which Julia wrote to her father, Augustus, inveighing against Tiberius, was supposed to be the composition of Gracchus. He was accordingly banished to Cercina, where he endured an exile of fourteen years. Then the soldiers who were sent to slay him, found him on a promontory, expecting no good. On their arrival, he begged a brief interval in which to give by letter his last instructions to his wife Alliaria, and then offered his neck to the executioners, dying with a courage not unworthy of the Sempronian name, which his degenerate life had dishonoured. Some have related that these soldiers were not sent from Rome, but by Lucius Asprenas, proconsul of Africa, on the authority of Tiberius, who had vainly hoped that the infamy of the murder might be shifted on Asprenas.

The same year witnessed the establishment of religious ceremonies in a new priesthood of the brotherhood of the Augustales, just as in former days Titus Tatius, to retain the rites of the Sabines, had instituted the Titian brotherhood. Twenty-one were chosen by lot from the chief men of the State; Tiberius, Drusus, Claudius, and Germanicus, were added to the number. The Augustal game's which were then inaugurated, were disturbed by quarrels arising out of rivalry between the actors. Augustus had shown indulgence to the entertainment by way of humouring Maecenas's extravagant passion for Bathyllus, nor did he himself dislike such amusements, and he thought it citizenlike to mingle in the pleasures of the populace. Very different was the tendency of Tiberius's character. But a people so many years indulgently treated, he did not yet venture to put under harsher control.

In the consulship of Drusus Caesar and Caius Norbanus, Germanicus had a triumph decreed him, though war still lasted. And though it was for the summer campaign that he was most vigorously preparing, he anticipated it by a sudden inroad on the Chatti in the beginning of spring. There had, in fact, sprung up a hope of the enemy being divided between Arminius and Segestes, famous, respectively, for treachery and loyalty towards us. Arminius was the disturber of Germany. Segestes often revealed the fact that a rebellion was being organized, more especially at that last banquet after which they rushed to arms, and he urged Varus to arrest himself and Arminius and all the other chiefs, assuring him that the people would attempt nothing if the leading men were removed, and that he would then have an opportunity of sifting accusations and distinguishing the innocent. But Varus fell by fate and by the sword of Arminius, with whom Segestes, though dragged into war by the unanimous voice of the nation, continued to be at feud, his resentment being heightened by personal motives, as Arminius had married his daughter who was betrothed to another. With a son-in-law detested, and fathers-in-law also at enmity, what are bonds of love between united hearts became with bitter foes incentives to fury.

Germanicus accordingly gave Caecina four legions, five thousand auxiliaries, with some hastily raised levies from the Germans dwelling on the left bank of the Rhine. He was himself at the head of an equal number of legions and twice as many allies. Having established a fort on the site of his father's entrenchments on Mount Taunus he hurried his troops in quick marching order against the Chatti, leaving Lucius Apronius to direct works connected with roads and bridges. With a dry season and comparatively shallow streams, a rare circumstance in that climate, he had accomplished, without obstruction, rapid march, and he feared for his return heavy rains and swollen rivers. But so suddenly did he come on the Chatti that all the helpless from age or sex were at once captured or slaughtered. Their able-bodied men had swum across the river Adrana, and were trying to keep back the Romans as they were commencing a bridge. Subsequently they were driven back by missiles and arrows, and having in vain attempted for peace, some took refuge with Germanicus, while the rest leaving their cantons and villages dispersed themselves in their forests.

After burning Mattium, the capital of the tribe, and ravaging the open country, Germanicus marched back towards the Rhine, the enemy not daring to harass the rear of the retiring army, which was his usual practice whenever he fell back by way of stratagem rather than from panic. It had been the intention of the Cherusci to help the Chatti; but Caecina thoroughly cowed them, carrying his arms everywhere, and the Marsi who ventured to engage him, he repulsed in a successful battle.

Not long after envoys came from Segestes, imploring aid against the violence of his fellow-countrymen, by whom he was hemmed in, and with whom Arminius had greater influence, because he counselled war. For with barbarians, the more eager a man's daring, the more does he inspire confidence, and the more highly is he esteemed in times of revolution. With the envoys Segestes had associated his son, by name Segimundus, but the youth hung back from a consciousness of guilt. For in the year of the revolt of Germany he had been appointed a priest at the altar of the Ubii, and had rent the sacred garlands, and fled to the rebels. Induced, however, to hope for mercy from Rome, he brought his father's message; he was graciously received and sent with an escort to the Gallic bank of the Rhine.

It was now worth while for Germanicus to march back his army. A battle was fought against the besiegers and Segestes was rescued with a numerous band of kinsfolk and dependents. In the number were some women of rank; among them, the wife of Arminius, who was also the daughter of Segestes, but who exhibited the spirit of her husband rather than of her father, subdued neither to tears nor to the tones of a suppliant, her hands tightly clasped within her bosom, and eyes which dwelt on her hope of offspring. The spoils also taken in the defeat of Varus were brought in, having been given as plunder to many of those who were then being surrendered.

Segestes too was there in person, a stately figure, fearless in the remembrance of having been a faithful ally. His speech was to this effect. "This is not my first day of steadfast loyalty towards the Roman people. From the time that the Divine Augustus gave me the citizenship, I have chosen my friends and foes with an eye to your advantage, not from hatred of my fatherland (for traitors are detested even by those whom they prefer) but because I held that Romans and Germans have the same interests, and that peace is better than war. And therefore I denounced to Varus, who then commanded your army, Arminius, the ravisher of my daughter, the violater of your treaty. I was put off by that dilatory general, and, as I found but little protection in the laws, I urged him to arrest myself, Arminius, and his accomplices. That night is my witness; would that it had been my last. What followed, may be deplored rather than defended. However, I threw Arminius into chains and I endured to have them put on myself by his partisans. And as soon as give opportunity, I show my preference for the old over the new, for peace over commotion, not to get a reward, but that I may clear myself from treachery and be at the same time a fit mediator for a German people, should they choose repentance rather than ruin, For the youth and error of my son I entreat forgiveness. As for my daughter, I admit that it is by compulsion she has been brought here. It will be for you to consider which fact weighs most with you, that she is with child by Arminius or that she owes her being to me."

Caesar in a gracious reply promised safety to his children and kinsfolk and a home for himself in the old province. He then led back the army and received on the proposal of Tiberius the title of Imperator. The wife of Arminius gave birth to a male child; the boy, who was brought up at Ravenna, soon afterwards suffered an insult, which at the proper time I shall relate.

The report of the surrender and kind reception of Segestes, when generally known, was heard with hope or grief according as men shrank from war or desired it. Arminius, with his naturally furious temper, was driven to frenzy by the seizure of his wife and the foredooming to slavery of his wife's unborn child. He flew hither and thither among the Cherusci, demanding "war against Segestes, war against Caesar." And he refrained not from taunts. "Noble the father," he would say, "mighty the general, brave the army which, with such strength, has carried off one weak woman. Before me, three legions, three commanders have fallen. Not by treachery, not against pregnant women, but openly against armed men do I wage war. There are still to be seen in the groves of Germany the Roman standards which I hung up to our country's gods. Let Segestes dwell on the conquered bank; let him restore to his son his priestly office; one thing there is which Germans will never thoroughly excuse, their having seen between the Elbe and the Rhine the Roman rods, axes, and toga. Other nations in their ignorance of Roman rule, have no experience of punishments, know nothing of tributes, and, as we have shaken them off, as the great Augustus, ranked among deities, and his chosen heir Tiberius, departed from us, baffled, let us not quail before an inexperienced stripling, before a mutinous army. If you prefer your fatherland, your ancestors, your ancient life to tyrants and to new colonies, follow as your leader Arminius to glory and to freedom rather than Segestes to ignominious servitude."

This language roused not only the Cherusci but the neighbouring tribes and drew to their side Inguiomerus, the uncle of Arminius, who had long been respected by the

Romans. This increased Caesar's alarm. That the war might not burst in all its fury on one point, he sent Caecina through the Bructeri to the river Amisia with forty Roman cohorts to distract the enemy, while the cavalry was led by its commander Pedo by the territories of the Frisii. Germanicus himself put four legions on shipboard and conveyed them through the lakes, and the infantry, cavalry, and fleet met simultaneously at the river already mentioned. The Chauci, on promising aid, were associated with us in military fellowship. Lucius Stertinius was despatched by Germanicus with a flying column and routed the Bructeri as they were burning their possessions, and amid the carnage and plunder, found the eagle of the nineteenth legion which had been lost with Varus. The troops were then marched to the furthest frontier of the Bructeri, and all the country between the rivers Amisia and Luppia was ravaged, not far from the forest of Teutoburgium where the remains of Varus and his legions were said to lie unburied.

Germanicus upon this was seized with an eager longing to pay the last honour to those soldiers and their general, while the whole army present was moved to compassion by the thought of their kinsfolk and friends, and, indeed, of the calamities of wars and the lot of mankind. Having sent on Caecina in advance to reconnoitre the obscure forest-passes, and to raise bridges and causeways over watery swamps and treacherous plains, they visited the mournful scenes, with their horrible sights and associations. Varus's first camp with its wide circumference and the measurements of its central space clearly indicated the handiwork of three legions. Further on, the partially fallen rampart and the shallow fosse suggested the inference that it was a shattered remnant of the army which had there taken up a position. In the centre of the field were the whitening bones of men, as they had fled, or stood their ground, strewn everywhere or piled in heaps. Near, lay fragments of weapons and limbs of horses, and also human heads, prominently nailed to trunks of trees. In the adjacent groves were the barbarous altars, on which they had immolated tribunes and first-rank centurions. Some survivors of the disaster who had escaped from the battle or from captivity, described how this was the spot where the officers fell, how yonder the eagles were captured, where Varus was pierced by his first wound, where too by the stroke of his own ill-starred hand he found for himself death. They pointed out too the raised ground from which Arminius had harangued his army, the number of gibbets for the captives, the pits for the living, and how in his exultation he insulted the standards and eagles.

And so the Roman army now on the spot, six years after the disaster, in grief and anger, began to bury the bones of the three legions, not a soldier knowing whether he was interring the relics of a relative or a stranger, but looking on all as kinsfolk and of their own blood, while their wrath rose higher than ever against the foe. In raising the barrow Caesar laid the first sod, rendering thus a most welcome honour to the dead, and sharing also in the sorrow of those present. This Tiberius did not approve, either interpreting unfavourably every act of Germanicus, or because he thought that the spectacle of the slain and unburied made the army slow to fight and more afraid of the enemy, and that a general invested with the augurate and its very ancient ceremonies ought not to have polluted himself with funeral rites.

Germanicus, however, pursued Arminius as he fell back into trackless wilds, and as soon as he had the opportunity, ordered his cavalry to sally forth and scour the plains occupied by the enemy. Arminius having bidden his men to concentrate themselves and keep close to the woods, suddenly wheeled round, and soon gave those whom he had concealed in the forest passes the signal to rush to the attack. Thereupon our cavalry was thrown into disorder by this new force, and some cohorts in reserve were sent, which, broken by the shock of flying troops, increased the panic. They were being pushed into a swamp, well known to the victorious assailants, perilous to men unacquainted with it, when Caesar led forth his legions in battle array. This struck terror into the enemy and gave confidence to our men, and they separated without advantage to either.

Soon afterwards Germanicus led back his army to the Amisia, taking his legions by the fleet, as he had brought them up. Part of the cavalry was ordered to make for the Rhine along the sea-coast. Caecina, who commanded a division of his own, was advised, though he was returning by a route which he knew, to pass Long Bridges with all possible speed. This was a narrow road amid vast swamps, which had formerly been constructed by Lucius Domitius; on every side were quagmires of thick clinging mud, or perilous with streams. Around were woods on a gradual slope, which Arminius now completely occupied, as soon as by a short route and quick march he had outstripped troops heavily laden with baggage and arms. As Caecina was in doubt how he could possibly replace bridges which were ruinous from age, and at the same time hold back the enemy, he resolved to encamp on the spot, that some might begin the repair and others the attack.

The barbarians attempted to break through the outposts and to throw themselves on the engineering parties, which they harassed, pacing round them and continually charging them. There was a confused din from the men at work and the combatants. Everything alike was unfavourable to the Romans, the place with its deep swamps, insecure to the foot and slippery as one advanced, limbs burdened with coats of mail, and the impossibility of aiming their javelins amid the water. The Cherusci, on the other hand, were familiar with fighting in fens; they had huge frames, and lances long enough to inflict wounds even at a distance. Night at last released the legions, which were now wavering, from a disastrous engagement. The Germans whom success rendered unwearied, without even then taking any rest, turned all the streams which rose from the slopes of the surrounding hills into the lands beneath. The ground being thus flooded and the completed portion of our works submerged, the soldiers' labour was doubled.

This was Caecina's fortieth campaign as a subordinate or a commander, and, with such experience of success and peril, he was perfectly fearless. As he thought over future possibilities, he could devise no plan but to keep the enemy within the woods, till the wounded and the more encumbered troops were in advance. For between the hills and the swamps there stretched a plain which would admit of an extended line. The legions had their assigned places, the fifth on the right wing, the twenty-first on the left, the men of the first to lead the van, the twentieth to repel pursuers.

It was a restless night for different reasons, the barbarians in their festivity filling the valleys under the hills and the echoing glens with merry song or savage shouts, while in the Roman camp were flickering fires, broken exclamations, and the men lay scattered along the intrenchments or wandered from tent to tent, wakeful rather than watchful. A ghastly dream appalled the general. He seemed to see Quintilius Varus, covered with blood, rising out of the swamps, and to hear him, as it were, calling to him, but he did not, as he imagined, obey the call; he even repelled his hand, as he stretched it over him. At daybreak the legions, posted on the wings, from panic or perversity, deserted their position and hastily occupied a plain beyond the morass. Yet Arminius, though free to attack, did not at the moment rush out on them. But when the baggage was clogged in the mud and in the fosses, the soldiers around it in disorder, the array of the standards in confusion, every one in selfish haste and all ears deaf to the word of command he ordered the Germans to charge, exclaiming again and again, "Behold a Varus and legions once more entangled in Varus's fate." As he spoke, he cut through the column with some picked men, inflicting wounds chiefly on the horses. Staggering in their blood on the slippery marsh, they shook off their riders, driving hither and thither all in their way, and trampling on the fallen. The struggle was hottest round the eagles, which could neither be carried in the face of the storm of missiles, nor planted in the miry soil. Caecina, while he was keeping up the battle, fell from his horse, which was pierced under him, and was being hemmed in, when the first legion threw itself in the way. The greed of the foe helped him, for they left the slaughter to secure the spoil, and the legions, towards evening, struggled on to open and firm ground.

Nor did this end their miseries. Entrenchments had to be thrown up, materials sought for earthworks, while the army had lost to a great extent their implements for digging earth and cutting turf. There were no tents for the rank and file, no comforts for the wounded. As they shared their food, soiled by mire or blood, they bewailed the darkness with its awful omen, and the one day which yet remained to so many thousand men.

It chanced that a horse, which had broken its halter and wandered wildly in fright at the uproar, overthrew some men against whom it dashed. Thence arose such a panic, from the belief that the Germans had burst into the camp, that all rushed to the gates. Of these the decuman gate was the point chiefly sought, as it was furthest from the enemy and safer for flight. Caecina, having ascertained that the alarm was groundless, yet being unable to stop or stay the soldiers by authority or entreaties or even by force, threw himself to the earth in the gateway, and at last by an appeal to their pity, as they would have had to pass over the body of their commander, closed the way. At the same moment the tribunes and the centurions convinced them that it was a false alarm.

Having then assembled them at his headquarters, and ordered them to hear his words in silence, he reminded them of the urgency of the crisis. "Their safety," he said, "lay in their arms, which they must, however, use with discretion, and they must remain within the entrenchments, till the enemy approached closer, in the hope of storming them; then, there must be a general sortie; by that sortie the Rhine might be reached. Whereas if they fled, more forests, deeper swamps, and a savage foe awaited them; but if they were victorious, glory and renown would be theirs." He dwelt on all that was dear to them at home, all that testified to their honour in the camp, without any allusion to disaster. Next he handed over the horses, beginning with his own, of the officers and tribunes, to the bravest fighters in the army, quite impartially, that these first, and then the infantry, might charge the enemy.

There was as much restlessness in the German host with its hopes, its eager longings, and the conflicting opinions of its chiefs. Arminius advised that they should allow the Romans to quit their position, and, when they had quitted it, again surprise them in swampy and intricate ground. Inguiomerus, with fiercer counsels, heartily welcome to barbarians, was for beleaguering the entrenchment in armed array, as to storm them would, he said, be easy, and there would be more prisoners and the booty unspoilt. So at daybreak they trampled in the fosses, flung hurdles into them, seized the upper part of the breastwork, where the troops were thinly distributed and seemingly paralysed by fear. When they were fairly within the fortifications, the signal was given to the cohorts, and the horns and trumpets sounded. Instantly, with a shout and sudden rush, our men threw themselves on the German rear, with taunts, that here were no woods or swamps, but that they were on equal ground, with equal chances. The sound of trumpets, the gleam of arms, which were so unexpected, burst with all the greater effect on the enemy, thinking only, as they were, of the easy destruction of a few half-armed men, and they were struck down, as unprepared for a reverse as they had been elated by success. Arminius and Inguiomerus fled from the battle, the first unhurt, the other severely wounded. Their followers were slaughtered, as long as our fury and the light of day lasted. It was not till night that the legions returned, and though more wounds and the same want of provisions distressed them, yet they found strength, healing, sustenance, everything indeed, in their victory.

Meanwhile a rumour had spread that our army was cut off, and that a furious German host was marching on Gaul. And had not Agrippina prevented the bridge over the Rhine from being destroyed, some in their cowardice would have dared that base act. A woman of heroic spirit, she assumed during those days the duties of a general, and distributed clothes or medicine among the soldiers, as they were destitute or wounded. According to Caius Plinius, the historian of the German wars, she stood at the extremity of the bridge, and bestowed praise and thanks on the returning legions. This made a deep impression on the mind of Tiberius. "Such zeal," he thought, "could not be guileless; it was not against a foreign foe that she was thus courting the soldiers. Generals had nothing left them when a woman went among the companies, attended the standards, ventured on bribery, as though it showed but slight ambition to parade her son in a common soldier's uniform, and wish him to be called Caesar Caligula. Agrippina had now more power with the armies than officers, than generals. A woman had quelled a mutiny which the sovereign's name could not check." All this was inflamed and aggravated by Sejanus, who, with his thorough comprehension of the character of Tiberius, sowed for a distant future hatreds which the emperor might treasure up and might exhibit when fully matured.

Of the legions which he had conveyed by ship, Germanicus gave the second and fourteenth to Publius Vitellius, to be marched by land, so that the fleet might sail more easily over a sea full of shoals, or take the ground more lightly at the ebb-tide. Vitellius at first pursued his route without interruption, having a dry shore, or the waves coming in gently. After a while, through the force of the north wind and the equinoctial season, when the sea swells to its highest, his army was driven and tossed hither and thither. The country too was flooded; sea, shore, fields presented one aspect, nor could the treacherous quicksands be distinguished from solid ground or shallows from deep water. Men were swept away by the waves or sucked under by eddies; beasts of burden, baggage, lifeless bodies floated about and blocked their way. The companies were mingled in confusion, now with the breast, now with the head only above water, sometimes losing their footing and parted from their comrades or drowned. The voice of mutual encouragement availed not against the adverse force of the waves. There was nothing to distinguish the brave from the coward, the prudent from the careless, forethought from chance; the same strong power swept everything before it. At last Vitellius struggled out to higher ground and led his men up to it. There they passed the night, without necessary food, without fire, many of them with bare or bruised limbs, in a plight as pitiable as that of men besieged by an enemy. For such, at least, have the opportunity of a glorious death, while here was destruction without honour. Daylight restored land to their sight, and they pushed their way to the river Visurgis, where Caesar had arrived with the fleet. The legions then embarked, while a rumour was flying about that they were drowned. Nor was there a belief in their safety till they saw Caesar and the army returned.

By this time Stertinius, who had been despatched to receive the surrender of Segimerus, brother of Segestes, had conducted the chief, together with his son, to the canton of the Ubii. Both were pardoned, Segimerus readily, the son with some hesitation, because it was said that he had insulted the corpse of Quintilius Varus. Meanwhile Gaul, Spain, and Italy vied in repairing the losses of the army, offering whatever they had at hand, arms, horses, gold. Germanicus having praised their zeal, took only for the war their arms and horses, and relieved the soldiers out of his own purse. And that he might also soften the remembrance of the disaster by kindness, he went round to the wounded, applauded the feats of soldier after soldier, examined their wounds, raised the hopes of one, the ambition of another, and the spirits of all by his encouragement and interest, thus strengthening their ardour for himself and for battle.

That year triumphal honours were decreed to Aulus Caecina, Lucius Apronius, Caius Silius for their achievements under Germanicus. The title of "father of his country," which the people had so often thrust on him, Tiberius refused, nor would he allow obedience to be sworn to his enactments, though the Senate voted it, for he said repeatedly that all human things were uncertain, and that the more he had obtained, the more precarious was his position. But he did not thereby create a belief in his patriotism, for he had revived the law of treason, the name of which indeed was known in ancient times, though other matters came under its jurisdiction, such as the betrayal of an army, or seditious stirring up of the people, or, in short, any corrupt act by which a man had impaired "the majesty of the people of Rome." Deeds only were liable to accusation; words went unpunished. It was Augustus who first, under colour of this law, applied legal inquiry to libellous writings provoked, as he had been, by the licentious freedom with which Cassius Severus had defamed men and women of distinction in his insulting satires. Soon afterwards, Tiberius, when consulted by Pompeius Macer, the praetor, as to whether prosecutions for treason should be revived, replied that the laws must be enforced. He too had been exasperated by the publication of verses of uncertain authorship, pointed at his cruelty, his arrogance, and his dissensions with his mother.

It will not be uninteresting if I relate in the cases of Falanius and Rubrius, Roman knights of moderate fortune, the first experiments at such accusations, in order to explain the origin of a most terrible scourge, how by Tiberius's cunning it crept in among us, how subsequently it was checked, finally, how it burst into flame and consumed everything. Against Falanius it was alleged by his accuser that he had admitted among the votaries of Augustus, who in every great house were associated into a kind of brotherhood, one Cassius, a buffoon of infamous life, and that he had also in selling his gardens included in the sale a statue of Augustus. Against Rubrius the charge was that he had violated by perjury the divinity of Augustus. When this was known to Tiberius, he wrote to the consuls "that his father had not had a place in heaven decreed to him, that the honour might be turned to the destruction of the citizens. Cassius, the actor, with men of the same profession, used to take part in the games which had been consecrated by his mother to the memory of Augustus. Nor was it contrary to the religion of the State for the emperor's image, like those of other deities, to be added to a sale of gardens and houses. As to the oath, the thing ought to be considered as if the man had deceived Jupiter. Wrongs done to the gods were the gods' concern."

Not long afterwards, Granius Marcellus, proconsul of Bithynia, was accused of treason by his quaestor, Caepio Crispinus, and the charge was supported by Romanus Hispo. Crispinus then entered on a line of life afterwards rendered notorious by the miseries of the age and men's shamelessness. Needy, obscure, and restless, he wormed himself by stealthy informations into the confidence of a vindictive prince, and soon imperilled all the most distinguished citizens; and having thus gained influence with one, hatred from all besides, he left an example in following which beggars became wealthy, the insignificant, formidable, and brought ruin first on others, finally on themselves. He alleged against Marcellus that he had made some disrespectful remarks about Tiberius, a charge not to be evaded, inasmuch as the accuser selected the worst features of the emperor's character and grounded his case on them. The things were true, and so were believed to have been said.

Hispo added that Marcellus had placed his own statue above those of the Caesars, and had set the bust of Tiberius on another statue from which he had struck off the head of Augustus. At this the emperor's wrath blazed forth, and, breaking through his habitual silence, he exclaimed that in such a case he would himself too give his vote openly on oath, that the rest might be under the same obligation. There lingered even then a few signs of expiring freedom. And so Cneius Piso asked, "In what order will you vote, Caesar? If first, I shall know what to follow; if last, I fear that I may differ from you unwillingly." Tiberius was deeply moved, and repenting of the outburst, all the more because of its thoughtlessness, he quietly allowed the accused to be acquitted of the charges of treason. As for the question of extortion, it was referred to a special commission.

Not satisfied with judicial proceedings in the Senate, the emperor would sit at one end of the Praetor's tribunal, but so as not to displace him from the official seat. Many decisions were given in his presence, in opposition to improper influence and the solicitations of great men. This, though it promoted justice, ruined freedom. Pius Aurelius, for example, a senator, complained that the foundations of his house had been weakened by the pressure of a public road and aqueduct, and he appealed to the Senate for assistance. He was opposed by the praetors of the treasury, but the emperor helped him, and paid him the value of his house, for he liked to spend money on a good purpose, a virtue which he long retained, when he cast off all others. To Propertius Celer, an ex-praetor, who sought because of his indigence to be excused from his rank as a senator, he gave a million sesterces, having ascertained that he had inherited poverty. He bade others, who attempted the same, prove their case to the Senate, as from his love of strictness he was harsh even where he acted on right grounds. Consequently every one else preferred silence and poverty to confession and relief.

In the same year the Tiber, swollen by continuous rains, flooded the level portions of the city. Its subsidence was followed by a destruction of buildings and of life. Thereupon Asinius Gallus proposed to consult the Sibylline books. Tiberius refused, veiling in obscurity the divine as well as the human. However, the devising of means to confine the river was intrusted to Ateius Capito and Lucius Arruntius.

Achaia and Macedonia, on complaining of their burdens, were, it was decided, to be relieved for a time from proconsular government and to be transferred to the emperor. Drusus presided over a show of gladiators which he gave in his own name and in that of his brother Germanicus, for he gloated intensely over bloodshed, however cheap its victims. This was alarming to the populace, and his father had, it was said, rebuked him. Why Tiberius kept away from the spectacle was variously explained. According to some, it was his loathing of a crowd, according to others, his gloomy temper, and a fear of contrast with the gracious presence of Augustus. I cannot believe that he deliberately gave his son the opportunity of displaying his ferocity and provoking the people's disgust, though even this was said.

Meanwhile the unruly tone of the theatre which first showed itself in the preceding year, broke out with worse violence, and some soldiers and a centurion, besides several of the populace, were killed, and the tribune of a praetorian cohort was wounded, while they were trying to stop insults to the magistrates and the strife of the mob. This disturbance was the subject of a debate in the Senate, and opinions were expressed in favour of the praetors having authority to scourge actors. Haterius Agrippa, tribune of the people, interposed his veto, and was sharply censured in a speech from Asinius Gallus, without a word from Tiberius, who liked to allow the Senate such shows of freedom. Still the interposition was successful, because Augustus had once pronounced that actors were exempt from the scourge, and it was not lawful for Tiberius to infringe his decisions. Many enactments were passed to fix the amount of their pay and to check the disorderly behaviour of their partisans. Of these the chief were that no Senator should enter the house of a pantomime player, that Roman knights should not crowd round them in the public streets, that they should exhibit themselves only in the theatre, and that the praetors should be empowered to punish with banishment any riotous conduct in the spectators.

A request from the Spaniards that they might erect a temple to Augustus in the colony of Tarraco was granted, and a precedent thus given for all the provinces. When the people of Rome asked for a remission of the one per cent. tax on all saleable commodities, Tiberius declared by edict "that the military exchequer depended on that branch of revenue, and, further, that the State was unequal to the burden, unless the twentieth year of service were to be that of the veteran's discharge." Thus the ill-advised results of the late mutiny, by which a limit of sixteen campaigns had been extorted, were cancelled for the future.

A question was then raised in the Senate by Arruntius and Ateius whether, in order to restrain the inundations of the Tiber, the rivers and lakes which swell its waters should be diverted from their courses. A hearing was given to embassies from the municipal towns and colonies, and the people of Florentia begged that the Clanis might not be turned out of its channel and made to flow into the Arnus, as that would bring ruin on themselves. Similar arguments were used by the inhabitants of Interamna. The most fruitful plains of Italy, they said, would be destroyed if the river Nar (for this was the plan proposed) were to be divided into several streams and overflow the country. Nor did the people of Reate remain silent. They remonstrated against the closing up of the Veline lake, where it empties itself into the Nar, "as it would burst in a flood on the entire neighbourhood. Nature had admirably provided for human interests in having assigned to rivers their mouths, their channels, and their limits, as well as their sources. Regard, too, must be paid to the different religions of the allies, who had dedicated sacred rites, groves, and altars to the rivers of their country. Tiber himself would be altogether unwilling to be deprived of his neighbour streams and to flow with less glory." Either the entreaties of the colonies, or the difficulty of the work or superstitious motives prevailed, and they yielded to Piso's opinion, who declared himself against any change.

Poppaeus Sabinus was continued in his government of the province of Moesia with the addition of Achaia and Macedonia. It was part of Tiberius' character to prolong indefinitely military commands and to keep many men to the end of their life with the same armies and in the same administrations. Various motives have been assigned for this. Some say that, out of aversion to any fresh anxiety, he retained what he had once approved as a permanent arrangement; others, that he grudged to see many enjoying promotion. Some, again, think that though he had an acute intellect, his judgment was irresolute, for he did not seek out eminent merit, and yet he detested vice. From the best men he apprehended danger to himself, from the worst, disgrace to the State. He went so far at last in this irresolution, that he appointed to provinces men whom he did not mean to allow to leave Rome.

I can hardly venture on any positive statement about the consular elections, now held for the first time under this emperor, or, indeed, subsequently, so conflicting are the accounts we find not only in historians but in Tiberius' own speeches. Sometimes he kept back the names of the candidates, describing their origin, their life and military career, so that it might be understood who they were. Occasionally even these hints were withheld, and, after urging them not to disturb the elections by canvassing, he would promise his own help towards the result. Generally he declared that only those had offered themselves to him as candidates whose names he had given to the consuls, and that others might offer themselves if they had confidence in their influence or merit. A plausible profession this in words, but really unmeaning and delusive, and the greater the disguise of freedom which marked it, the more cruel the enslavement into which it was soon to plunge us.

BOOK II, A.D. 16-19

In the consulship of Sisenna Statilius Taurus and Lucius Libo there was a commotion in the kingdoms and Roman provinces of the East. It had its origin among the Parthians, who disdained as a foreigner a king whom they had sought and received from Rome, though he was of the family of the Arsacids. This was Vonones, who had been given as an hostage to Augustus by Phraates. For although he had driven before him armies and generals from Rome, Phraates had shown to Augustus every token of reverence and had sent him some of his children, to cement the friendship, not so much from dread of us as from distrust of the loyalty of his countrymen.

After the death of Phraates and the succeeding kings in the bloodshed of civil wars, there came to Rome envoys from the chief men of Parthia, in quest of Vonones, his eldest son. Caesar thought this a great honour to himself, and loaded Vonones with wealth. The barbarians, too, welcomed him with rejoicing, as is usual with new rulers. Soon they felt shame at Parthians having become degenerate, at their having sought a king from another world, one too infected with the training of the enemy, at the throne of the Arsacids now being possessed and given away among the provinces of Rome. "Where," they asked, "was the glory of the men who slew Crassus, who drove out Antonius, if Caesar's drudge, after an endurance of so many years' slavery, were to rule over Parthians."

Vonones himself too further provoked their disdain, by his contrast with their ancestral manners, by his rare indulgence in the chase, by his feeble interest in horses, by the litter in which he was carried whenever he made a progress through their cities, and by his contemptuous dislike of their national festivities. They also ridiculed his Greek attendants and his keeping under seal the commonest household articles. But he was easy of approach; his courtesy was open to all, and he had thus virtues with which the Parthians were unfamiliar, and vices new to them. And as his ways were quite alien from theirs they hated alike what was bad and what was good in him.

Accordingly they summoned Artabanus, an Arsacid by blood, who had grown to manhood among the Dahae, and who, though routed in the first encounter, rallied his forces and possessed himself of the kingdom. The conquered Vonones found a refuge in Armenia, then a free country, and exposed to the power of Parthia and Rome, without being trusted by either, in consequence of the crime of Antonius, who, under the guise of friendship, had inveigled Artavasdes, king of the Armenians, then loaded him with chains, and finally murdered him. His son, Artaxias, our bitter foe because of his father's memory, found defence for himself and his kingdom in the might of the Arsacids. When he was slain by the treachery of kinsmen, Caesar gave Tigranes to the Armenians, and he was put in possession of the kingdom under the escort of Tiberius Nero. But neither Tigranes nor his children reigned long, though, in foreign fashion, they were united in marriage and in royal power.

Next, at the bidding of Augustus, Artavasdes was set on the throne, nor was he deposed without disaster to ourselves. Caius Caesar was then appointed to restore order in Armenia. He put over the Armenians Ariobarzanes, a Mede by birth, whom they willingly accepted, because of his singularly handsome person and noble spirit. On the death of Ariobarzanes through a fatal accident, they would not endure his son. Having tried the government of a woman named Erato and having soon afterwards driven her from them, bewildered and disorganised, rather indeed without a ruler than enjoying freedom, they received for their king the fugitive Vonones. When, however, Artabanus began to threaten, and but feeble support could be given by the Armenians, or war with Parthia would have to be undertaken, if Vonones was to be upheld by our arms, the governor of Syria, Creticus Silanus, sent for him and kept him under surveillance, letting him retain his royal pomp and title. How Vonones meditated an escape from this mockery, I will relate in the proper place.

Meanwhile the commotion in the East was rather pleasing to Tiberius, as it was a pretext for withdrawing Germanicus from the legions which knew him well, and placing him over new provinces where he would be exposed both to treachery and to disasters. Germanicus, however, in proportion to the strength of the soldiers' attachment and to his uncle's dislike, was eager to hasten his victory, and he pondered on plans of battle, and on the reverses or successes which during more than three years of war had fallen to his lot. The Germans, he knew, were beaten in the field and on fair ground; they were helped by woods, swamps, short summers, and early winters. His own troops were affected not so much by wounds as by long marches and damage to their arms. Gaul had been exhausted by supplying horses; a long baggage-train presented facilities for ambuscades, and was embarrassing to its defenders. But by embarking on the sea, invasion would be easy for them, and a surprise to the enemy, while a campaign too would be more quickly begun, the legions and supplies would be brought up simultaneously, and the cavalry with their horses would arrive, in good condition, by the river-mouths and channels, at the heart of Germany.

To this accordingly he gave his mind, and sent Publius Vitellius and Caius Antius to collect the taxes of Gaul. Silius, Anteius, and Caecina had the charge of building a fleet. It seemed that a thousand vessels were required, and they were speedily constructed, some of small draught with a narrow stem and stern and a broad centre, that they might bear the waves more easily; some flat-bottomed, that they might ground without being injured; several, furnished with a rudder at each end, so that by a sudden shifting of the oars they might be run into shore either way. Many were covered in with decks, on which engines for missiles might be conveyed, and were also fit for the carrying of horses or supplies, and being equipped with sails as well as rapidly moved by oars, they assumed, through the enthusiasm of our soldiers, an imposing and formidable aspect.

The island of the Batavi was the appointed rendezvous, because of its easy landing-places, and its convenience for receiving the army and carrying the war across the river. For the Rhine after flowing continuously in a single channel or encircling merely insignificant islands, divides itself, so to say, where the Batavian territory begins, into two rivers, retaining its name and the rapidity of its course in the stream which washes

Germany, till it mingles with the ocean. On the Gallic bank, its flow is broader and gentler; it is called by an altered name, the Vahal, by the inhabitants of its shore. Soon that name too is changed for the Mosa river, through whose vast mouth it empties itself into the same ocean.

Caesar, however, while the vessels were coming up, ordered Silius, his lieutenant-general, to make an inroad on the Chatti with a flying column. He himself, on hearing that a fort on the river Luppia was being besieged, led six legions to the spot. Silius owing to sudden rains did nothing but carry off a small booty, and the wife and daughter of Arpus, the chief of the Chatti. And Caesar had no opportunity of fighting given him by the besiegers, who dispersed on the rumour of his advance. They had, however, destroyed the barrow lately raised in memory of Varus's legions, and the old altar of Drusus. The prince restored the altar, and himself with his legions celebrated funeral games in his father's honour. To raise a new barrow was not thought necessary. All the country between the fort Aliso and the Rhine was thoroughly secured by new barriers and earthworks.

By this time the fleet had arrived, and Caesar, having sent on his supplies and assigned vessels for the legions and the allied troops, entered "Drusus's fosse," as it was called. He prayed Drusus his father to lend him, now that he was venturing on the same enterprise, the willing and favourable aid of the example and wi memory of his counsels and achievements, and he arrived after a prosperous voyage through the lakes and the ocean as far as the river Amisia. His fleet remained there on the left bank of the stream, and it was a blunder that he did not have it brought up the river. He disembarked the troops, which were to be marched to the country on the right, and thus several days were wasted in the construction of bridges. The cavalry and the legions fearlessly crossed the first estuaries in which the tide had not yet risen. The rear of the auxiliaries, and the Batavi among the number, plunging recklessly into the water and displaying their skill in swimming, fell into disorder, and some were drowned. While Caesar was measuring out his camp, he was told of a revolt of the Angrivarii in his rear. He at once despatched Stertinius with some cavalry and a light armed force, who punished their perfidy with fire and sword.

The waters of the Visurgis flowed between the Romans and the Cherusci. On its banks stood Arminius with the other chiefs. He asked whether Caesar had arrived, and on the reply that he was present, he begged leave to have an interview with his brother. That brother, surnamed Flavus, was with our army, a man famous for his loyalty, and for having lost an eye by a wound, a few years ago, when Tiberius was in command. The permission was then given, and he stepped forth and was saluted by Arminius, who had removed his guards to a distance and required that the bowmen ranged on our bank should retire. When they had gone away, Arminius asked his brother whence came the scar which disfigured his face, and on being told the particular place and battle, he inquired what reward he had received. Flavus spoke of increased pay, of a neck chain, a crown, and other military gifts, while Arminius jeered at such a paltry recompense for slavery.

Then began a controversy. The one spoke of the greatness of Rome, the resources of Caesar, the dreadful punishment in store for the vanquished, the ready mercy for him who surrenders, and the fact that neither Arminius's wife nor his son were treated as enemies; the other, of the claims of fatherland, of ancestral freedom, of the gods of the homes of Germany, of the mother who shared his prayers, that Flavus might not choose to be the deserter and betrayer rather than the ruler of his kinsfolk and relatives, and indeed of his own people.

By degrees they fell to bitter words, and even the river between them would not have hindered them from joining combat, had not Stertinius hurried up and put his hand on Flavus, who in the full tide of his fury was demanding his weapons and his charger. Arminius was seen facing him, full of menaces and challenging him to conflict. Much of what he said was in Roman speech, for he had served in our camp as leader of his fellow-countrymen.

Next day the German army took up its position on the other side of the Visurgis. Caesar, thinking that without bridges and troops to guard them, it would not be good generalship to expose the legions to danger, sent the cavalry across the river by the fords. It was commanded by Stertinius and Aemilius, one of the first rank centurions, who attacked at widely different points so as to distract the enemy. Chariovalda, the Batavian chief, dashed to the charge where the stream is most rapid. The Cherusci, by a pretended flight, drew him into a plain surrounded by forest-passes. Then bursting on him in a sudden attack from all points they thrust aside all who resisted, pressed fiercely on their retreat, driving them before them, when they rallied in compact array, some by close fighting, others by missiles from a distance. Chariovalda, after long sustaining the enemy's fury, cheered on his men to break by a dense formation the onset of their bands, while he himself, plunging into the thickest of the battle, fell amid a shower of darts with his horse pierced under him, and round him many noble chiefs. The rest were rescued from the peril by their own strength, or by the cavalry which came up with Stertinius and Aemilius.

Caesar on crossing the Visurgis learnt by the information of a deserter that Arminius had chosen a battle-field, that other tribes too had assembled in a forest sacred to Hercules, and would venture on a night attack on his camp. He put faith in this intelligence, and, besides, several watchfires were seen. Scouts also, who had crept close up to the enemy, reported that they had heard the neighing of horses and the hum of a huge and tumultuous host. And so as the decisive crisis drew near, that he ought thoroughly to sound the temper of his soldiers, he considered with himself how this was to be accomplished with a genuine result. Tribunes and centurions, he knew, oftener reported what was welcome than what was true; freedmen had slavish spirits, friends a love of flattery. If an assembly were called, there too the lead of a few was followed by the shout of the many. He must probe their inmost thoughts, when they were uttering their hopes and fears at the military mess, among themselves, and unwatched.

At nightfall, leaving his tent of augury by a secret exit, unknown to the sentries, with one companion, his shoulders covered with a wild beast's skin, he visited the camp streets, stood by the tents, and enjoyed the men's talk about himself, as one extolled his noble rank, another, his handsome person, nearly all of them, his endurance, his gracious manner and the evenness of his temper, whether he was jesting or was serious, while they acknowledged that they ought to repay him with their gratitude in battle, and at the same time sacrifice to a glorious vengeance the perfidious violators of peace. Meanwhile one of the enemy, acquainted with the Roman tongue, spurred his horse up to the entrenchments, and in a loud voice promised in the name of Arminius to all deserters wives and lands with daily pay of a hundred sesterces as long as war lasted. The insult fired the wrath of the legions. "Let daylight come," they said, "let battle be given. The soldiers will possess themselves of the lands of the Germans and will carry off their wives. We hail the omen; we mean the women and riches of the enemy to be our spoil."

About midday there was a skirmishing attack on our camp, without any discharge of missiles, when they saw the cohorts in close array before the lines and no sign of carelessness.

The same night brought with it a cheering dream to Germanicus. He saw himself engaged in sacrifice, and his robe being sprinkled with the sacred blood, another more beautiful was given him by the hands of his grandmother Augusta. Encouraged by the omen and finding the auspices favourable, he called an assembly, and explained the precautions which wisdom suggested as suitable for the impending battle. "It is not," he said, "plains only which are good for the fighting of Roman soldiers, but woods and forest passes, if science be used. For the huge shields and unwieldly lances of the barbarians cannot, amid trunks of trees and brushwood that springs from the ground, be so well managed as our javelins and swords and closefitting armour. Shower your blows thickly; strike at the face with your swords' points. The German has neither cuirass nor helmet; even his shield is not strengthened with leather or steel, but is of osiers woven together or of thin and painted board. If their first line is armed with spears, the rest have only weapons hardened by fire or very short. Again, though their frames are terrible to the eye and formidable in a brief onset, they have no capacity of enduring wounds; without, any shame at the disgrace, without any regard to their leaders, they quit the field and flee; they quail under disaster, just as in success they forget alike divine and human laws. If in your weariness of land and sea you desire an end of service, this battle prepares the way to it. The Elbe is now nearer than the Rhine, and there is no war beyond, provided only you enable me, keeping close as I do to my father's and my uncle's footsteps, to stand a conqueror on the same spot."

The general's speech was followed by enthusiasm in the soldiers, and the signal for battle was given. Nor were Arminius and the other German chiefs slow to call their respective clansmen to witness that "these Romans were the most cowardly fugitives out of Varus's army, men who rather than endure war had taken to mutiny. Half of them have their backs covered with wounds; half are once again exposing limbs battered by waves and storms to a foe full of fury, and to hostile deities, with no hope of advantage. They have, in fact, had recourse to a fleet and to a trackless ocean, that their coming might be unopposed, their flight unpursued. But when once they have joined conflict with us, the help of winds or oars will be unavailing to the vanquished. Remember only their greed, their cruelty, their pride. Is anything left for us but to retain our freedom or to die before we are enslaved?

When they were thus roused and were demanding battle, their chiefs led them down into a plain named Idistavisus. It winds between the Visurgis and a hill range, its breadth varying as the river banks recede or the spurs of the hills project on it. In their rear rose a forest, with the branches rising to a great height, while there were clear spaces between the trunks. The barbarian army occupied the plain and the outskirts of the wood. The Cherusci were posted by themselves on the high ground, so as to rush down on the Romans during the battle.

Our army advanced in the following order. The auxiliary Gauls and Germans were in the van, then the foot-archers, after them, four legions and Caesar himself with two praetorian cohorts and some picked cavalry. Next came as many other legions, and light-armed troops with horse-bowmen, and the remaining cohorts of the allies. The men were quite ready and prepared to form in line of battle according to their marching order.

Caesar, as soon as he saw the Cheruscan bands which in their impetuous spirit had rushed to the attack, ordered the finest of his cavalry to charge them in flank, Stertinius with the other squadrons to make a detour and fall on their rear, promising himself to come up in good time. Meanwhile there was a most encouraging augury. Eight eagles, seen to fly towards the woods and to enter them, caught the general's eye. "Go," he exclaimed, "follow the Roman birds, the true deities of our legions." At the same moment the infantry charged, and the cavalry which had been sent on in advance dashed on the rear and the flanks. And, strange to relate, two columns of the enemy fled in opposite directions, that, which had occupied the wood, rushing into the open, those who had been drawn up on the plains, into the wood. The Cherusci, who were between them, were dislodged from the hills, while Arminius, conspicuous among them by gesture, voice, and a wound he had received, kept up the fight. He had thrown himself on our archers and was on the point of breaking through them, when the cohorts of the Raeti, Vendelici, and Gauls faced his attack. By a strong bodily effort, however, and a furious rush of his horse, he made his way through them, having smeared his face with his blood, that he might not be known. Some have said that he was recognised by Chauci serving among the Roman auxiliaries, who let him go.

Inguiomerus owed his escape to similar courage or treachery. The rest were cut down in every direction. Many in attempting to swim across the Visurgis were overwhelmed under a storm of missiles or by the force of the current, lastly, by the rush of fugitives and the falling in of the banks. Some in their ignominious flight climbed the tops of trees, and as they were hiding themselves in the boughs, archers were brought up and they were shot for sport. Others were dashed to the ground by the felling of the trees.

It was a great victory and without bloodshed to us. From nine in the morning to nightfall the enemy were slaughtered, and ten miles were covered with arms and dead bodies, while there were found amid the plunder the chains which the Germans had brought with them for the Romans, as though the issue were certain. The soldiers on the battle field hailed Tiberius as Imperator, and raised a mound on which arms were piled in the style of a trophy, with the names of the conquered tribes inscribed beneath them.

That sight caused keener grief and rage among the Germans than their wounds, their mourning, and their losses. Those who but now were preparing to quit their settlements and to retreat to the further side of the Elbe, longed for battle and flew to arms. Common people and chiefs, young and old, rushed on the Roman army, and spread disorder. At last they chose a spot closed in by a river and by forests, within which was a narrow swampy plain. The woods too were surrounded by a bottomless morass, only on one side of it the Angrivarii had raised a broad earthwork, as a boundary between themselves and the Cherusci. Here their infantry was ranged. Their cavalry they concealed in neighbouring woods, so as to be on the legions' rear, as soon as they entered the forest.

All this was known to Caesar. He was acquainted with their plans, their positions, with what met the eye, and what was hidden, and he prepared to turn the enemy's stratagems to their own destruction. To Seius Tubero, his chief officer, he assigned the cavalry and the plain. His infantry he drew up so that part might advance on level ground into the forest, and part clamber up the earthwork which confronted them. He charged himself with what was the specially difficult operation, leaving the rest to his officers. Those who had the level ground easily forced a passage. Those who had to assault the earthwork encountered heavy blows from above, as if they were scaling a wall. The general saw how unequal this close fighting was, and having withdrawn his legions to a little distance, ordered the slingers and artillerymen to discharge a volley of missiles and scatter the enemy. Spears were hurled from the engines, and the more conspicuous were the defenders of the position, the more the wounds with which they were driven from it.

Caesar with some praetorian cohorts was the first, after the storming of the ramparts, to dash into the woods. There they fought at close quarters. A morass was in the enemy's rear, and the Romans were hemmed in by the river or by the hills. Both were in a desperate plight from their position; valour was their only hope, victory their only safety.

The Germans were equally brave, but they were beaten by the nature of the fighting and of the weapons, for their vast host in so confined a space could neither thrust out nor recover their immense lances, or avail themselves of their nimble movements and lithe frames, forced as they were to a close engagement. Our soldiers, on the other hand, with their shields pressed to their breasts, and their hands grasping their sword-hilts, struck at the huge limbs and exposed faces of the barbarians, cutting a passage through the slaughtered enemy, for Arminius was now less active, either from incessant perils, or because he was partially disabled by his recent wound. As for Inguiomerus, who flew hither and thither over the battlefield, it was fortune rather than courage which forsook him. Germanicus, too, that he might be the better known, took his helmet off his head and begged his men to follow up the slaughter, as they wanted not prisoners, and the utter destruction of the nation would be the only conclusion of the war. And now, late in the day, he withdrew one of his legions from the field, to intrench a camp, while the rest till nightfall glutted themselves with the enemy's blood. Our cavalry fought with indecisive success.

Having publicly praised his victorious troops, Caesar raised a pile of arms with the proud inscription, "The army of Tiberius Caesar, after thoroughly conquering the tribes between the Rhine and the Elbe, has dedicated this monument to Mars, Jupiter, and Augustus." He added nothing about himself, fearing jealousy, or thinking that the conciousness of the achievement was enough. Next he charged Stertinius with making war on the Angrivarii, but they hastened to surrender. And, as suppliants, by refusing nothing, they obtained a full pardon.

When, however, summer was at its height some of the legions were sent back overland into winter-quarters, but most of them Caesar put on board the fleet and brought down the river Amisia to the ocean. At first the calm waters merely sounded with the oars of a thousand vessels or were ruffled by the sailing ships. Soon, a hailstorm bursting from a black mass of clouds, while the waves rolled hither and thither under tempestuous gales from every quarter, rendered clear sight impossible, and the steering difficult, while our soldiers, terrorstricken and without any experience of disasters on the sea, by embarrassing the sailors or giving them clumsy aid, neutralized the services of the skilled crews. After a while, wind and wave shifted wholly to the south, and from the hilly lands and deep rivers of Germany came with a huge line of rolling clouds, a strong blast, all the more frightful from the frozen north which was so near to them, and instantly caught and drove the ships hither and thither into the open ocean, or on islands with steep cliffs or which hidden shoals made perilous. these they just escaped, with difficulty, and when the tide changed and bore them the same way as the wind, they could not hold to their anchors or bale out the water which rushed in upon them. Horses, beasts of burden, baggage, were thrown overboard, in order to lighten the hulls which leaked copiously through their sides, while the waves too dashed over them.

As the ocean is stormier than all other seas, and as Germany is conspicuous for the terrors of its climate, so in novelty and extent did this disaster transcend every other, for all around were hostile coasts, or an expanse so vast and deep that it is thought to be the remotest shoreless sea. Some of the vessels were swallowed up; many were wrecked on distant islands, and the soldiers, finding there no form of human life, perished of hunger, except some who supported existence on carcases of horses washed on the same shores. Germanicus's trireme alone reached the country of the Chauci. Day and night, on those rocks and promontories he would incessantly exclaim that he was himself responsible for this awful ruin, and friends scarce restrained him from seeking death in the same sea.

At last, as the tide ebbed and the wind blew favourably, the shattered vessels with but few rowers, or clothing spread as sails, some towed by the more powerful, returned, and Germanicus, having speedily repaired them, sent them to search the islands. Many by that means were recovered. The Angrivarii, who had lately been admitted to our alliance, restored to us several had ransomed from the inland tribes. Some had been carried to Britain and were sent back by the petty chiefs. Every one, as he returned from some far-distant region, told of wonders, of violent hurricanes, and unknown birds, of monsters of the sea, of forms half-human, half beast-like, things they had really seen or in their terror believed.

Meanwhile the rumoured loss of the fleet stirred the Germans to hope for war, as it did Caesar to hold them down. He ordered Caius Silius with thirty thousand infantry and three thousand cavalry to march against the Chatti. He himself, with a larger army, invaded the Marsi, whose leader, Mallovendus, whom we had lately admitted to surrender, pointed out a neighbouring wood, where, he said, an eagle of one of Varus's legions was buried and guarded only by a small force. Immediately troops were despatched to draw the enemy from his position by appearing in his front, others, to hem in his rear and open the ground. Fortune favoured both. So Germanicus, with increased energy, advanced into the country, laying it waste, and utterly ruining a foe who dared not encounter him, or who was instantly defeated wherever he resisted, and, as we learnt from prisoners, was never more panic-stricken. The Romans, they declared, were invincible, rising superior to all calamities; for having thrown away a fleet, having lost their arms, after strewing the shores with the carcases of horses and of men, they had rushed to the attack with the same courage, with equal spirit, and, seemingly, with augmented numbers.

The soldiers were then led back into winter-quarters, rejoicing in their hearts at having been compensated for their disasters at sea by a successful expedition. They were helped too by Caesar's bounty, which made good whatever loss any one declared he had suffered. It was also regarded as a certainty that the enemy were wavering and consulting on negotiations for peace, and that, with an additional campaign next summer the war might be ended. Tiberius, however, in repeated letters advised Germanicus to return for the triumph decreed him. "He had now had enough of success, enough of disaster. He had fought victorious battles on a great scale; he should also remember those losses which the winds and waves had inflicted, and which, though due to no fault of the general, were still grievous and shocking. He, Tiberius, had himself been sent nine times by Augustus into Germany, and had done more by policy than by arms. By this means the submission of the Sugambri had been secured, and the Suevi with their king Maroboduus had been forced into peace. The Cherusci too and the other insurgent tribes, since the vengeance of Rome had been satisfied, might be left to their internal feuds."

When Germanicus requested a year for the completion of his enterprise, Tiberius put a severer pressure on his modesty by offering him a second consulship, the functions of which he was to discharge in person. He also added that if war must still be waged, he might as well leave some materials for renown to his brother Drusus, who, as there was then no other enemy, could win only in Germany the imperial title and the triumphal laurel. Germanicus hesitated no longer, though he saw that this was a pretence, and that he was hurried away through jealousy from the glory he had already acquired.

About the same time Libo Drusus, of the family of Scribonii, was accused of revolutionary schemes. I will explain, somewhat minutely, the beginning, progress, and end of this affair, since then first were originated those practices which for so many years have eaten into the heart of the State. Firmius Catus, a senator, an intimate friend of Libo's, prompted the young man, who was thoughtless and an easy prey to delusions, to resort to astrologers' promises, magical rites, and interpreters of dreams, dwelling ostentatiously on his great-grandfather Pompeius, his aunt Scribonia, who had formerly been wife of Augustus, his imperial cousins, his house crowded with ancestral busts, and urging him to extravagance and debt, himself the companion of his profligacy and desperate embarrassments, thereby to entangle him in all the more proofs of guilt.

As soon as he found enough witnesses, with some slaves who knew the facts, he begged an audience of the emperor, after first indicating the crime and the criminal through Flaccus Vescularius, a Roman knight, who was more intimate with Tiberius than himself. Caesar, without disregarding the information, declined an interview, for the communication, he said, might be conveyed to him through the same messenger, Flaccus. Meanwhile he conferred the praetorship on Libo and often invited him to his table, showing no unfriendliness in his looks or anger in his words (so thoroughly had he concealed his resentment); and he wished to know all his saying and doings, though it was in his power to stop them, till one Junius, who had been tampered with by Libo for the purpose of evoking by incantations spirits of the dead, gave information to Fulcinius Trio. Trio's ability was conspicuous among informers, as well as his eagerness for an evil notoriety. He at once pounced on the accused, went to the consuls, and demanded an inquiry before the Senate. The Senators were summoned, with a special notice that they must consult on a momentous and terrible matter.

Libo meanwhile, in mourning apparel and accompanied by ladies of the highest rank, went to house after house, entreating his relatives, and imploring some eloquent voice to ward off his perils; which all refused, on different pretexts, but from the same apprehension. On the day the Senate met, jaded with fear and mental anguish, or, as some have related, feigning illness, he was carried in a litter to the doors of the Senate House, and leaning on his brother he raised his hands and voice in supplication to Tiberius, who received him with unmoved countenance. The emperor then read out the charges and the accusers' names, with such calmness as not to seem to soften or aggravate the accusations.

Besides Trio and Catus, Fonteius Agrippa and Caius Vibius were among his accusers, and claimed with eager rivalry the privilege of conducting the case for the prosecution, till Vibius, as they would not yield one to the other, and Libo had entered without counsel, offered to state the charges against him singly, and produced an extravagantly absurd accusation, according to which Libo had consulted persons whether he would have such wealth as to be able to cover the Appian road as far as Brundisium with money. There were other questions of the same sort, quite senseless and idle; if leniently regarded, pitiable. But there was one paper in Libo's handwriting, so the prosecutor alleged, with the names of Caesars and of Senators, to which marks were affixed of dreadful or mysterious significance. When the accused denied this, it was decided that his slaves who recognised the writing should be examined by torture. As an ancient statute of the Senate forbade such inquiry in a case affecting a master's life, Tiberius, with his cleverness in devising new law, ordered Libo's slaves to be sold singly to the State-agent, so that, forsooth, without an infringement of the Senate's decree, Libo might be tried on their evidence. As a consequence, the defendant asked an adjournment till next day, and having gone home he charged his kinsman, Publius Quirinus, with his last prayer to the emperor.

The answer was that he should address himself to the Senate. Meanwhile his house was surrounded with soldiers; they crowded noisily even about the entrance, so that they could be heard and seen; when Libo, whose anguish drove him from the very banquet he had prepared as his last gratification, called for a minister of death, grasped the hands of his slaves, and thrust a sword into them. In their confusion, as they shrank back, they overturned the lamp on the table at his side, and in the darkness, now to him the gloom of death, he aimed two blows at a vital part. At the groans of the falling man his freedmen hurried up, and the soldiers, seeing the bloody deed, stood aloof. Yet the prosecution was continued in the Senate with the same persistency, and Tiberius declared on oath that he would have interceded for his life, guilty though he was, but for his hasty suicide.

His property was divided among his accusers, and praetorships out of the usual order were conferred on those who were of senators' rank. Cotta Messalinus then proposed that Libo's bust should not be carried in the funeral procession of any of his descendants; and Cneius Lentulus, that no Scribonius should assume the surname of Drusus. Days of public thanksgiving were appointed on the suggestion of Pomponius Flaccus. Offerings were given to Jupiter, Mars, and Concord, and the 13th day of September, on which Libo had killed himself, was to be observed as a festival, on the motion of Gallus Asinius, Papius Mutilus, and Lucius Apronius. I have mentioned the proposals and sycophancy of these men, in order to bring to light this old-standing evil in the State.

Decrees of the Senate were also passed to expel from Italy astrologers and magicians. One of their number, Lucius Pituanius, was hurled from the Rock. Another, Publius Marcius, was executed, according to ancient custom, by the consuls outside the Esquiline Gate, after the trumpets had been bidden to sound.

On the next day of the Senate's meeting much was said against the luxury of the country by Quintus Haterius, an ex-consul, and by Octavius Fronto, an ex-praetor. It was decided that vessels of solid gold should not be made for the serving of food, and that men should not disgrace themselves with silken clothing from the East. Fronto went further, and insisted on restrictions being put on plate, furniture, and household establishments. It was indeed still usual with the Senators, when it was their turn to vote, to suggest anything they thought for the State's advantage. Gallus Asinius argued on the other side. "With the growth of the empire private wealth too," he said, "had increased, and there was nothing new in this, but it accorded with the fashions of the earliest antiquity. Riches were one thing with the Fabricii, quite another with the Scipios. The State was the standard of everything; when it was poor, the homes of the citizens were humble; when it reached such magnificence, private grandeur increased. In household establishments, and plate, and in whatever was provided for use, there was neither excess nor parsimony except in relation to the fortune of the possessor. A distinction had been made in the assessments of Senators and knights, not because they differed naturally, but that the superiority of the one class in places in the theatre, in rank and in honour, might be also maintained in everything else which insured mental repose and bodily recreation, unless indeed men in the highest position were to undergo more anxieties and more dangers, and to be at the same time deprived of all solace under those anxieties and dangers." Gallus gained a ready assent, under these specious phrases, by a confession of failings with which his audience symphathised. And Tiberius too had added that this was not a time for censorship, and that if there were any declension in manners, a promoter of reform would not be wanting.

During this debate Lucius Piso, after exclaiming against the corruption of the courts, the bribery of judges, the cruel threats of accusations from hired orators, declared that he would depart and quit the capital, and that he meant to live in some obscure and distant rural retreat. At the same moment he rose to leave the Senate House. Tiberius was much excited, and though he pacified Piso with gentle words, he also strongly urged his relatives to stop his departure by their influence or their entreaties.

Soon afterwards this same Piso gave an equal proof of a fearless sense of wrong by suing Urgulania, whom Augusta's friendship had raised above the law. Neither did Urgulania obey the summons, for in defiance of Piso she went in her litter to the emperor's house; nor did Piso give way, though Augusta complained that she was insulted and her majesty slighted. Tiberius, to win popularity by so humouring his mother as to say that he would go to the praetor's court and support Urgulania, went forth from the palace, having ordered soldiers to follow him at a distance. He was seen, as the people thronged about him, to wear a calm face, while he prolonged his time on the way with various conversations, till at last when Piso's relatives tried in vain to restrain him, Augusta directed the money which was claimed to be handed to him. This ended the affair, and Piso, in consequence, was not dishonoured, and the emperor rose in reputation. Urgulania's influence, however, was so formidable to the State, that in a certain cause which was tried by the Senate she would not condescend to appear as a witness. The praetor was sent to question her at her own house, although the Vestal virgins, according to ancient custom, were heard in the courts, before judges, whenever they gave evidence.

I should say nothing of the adjournment of public business in this year, if it were not worth while to notice the conflicting opinions of Cneius Piso and Asinius Gallus on the subject. Piso, although the emperor had said that he would be absent, held that all the more ought the business to be transacted, that the State might have honour of its Senate and knights being able to perform their duties in the sovereign's absence. Gallus, as Piso had forestalled him in the display of freedom, maintained that nothing was sufficiently impressive or suitable to the majesty of the Roman people, unless done before Caesar and under his very eyes, and that therefore the gathering from all Italy and the influx from the provinces ought to be reserved for his presence. Tiberius listened to this in silence, and the matter was debated on both sides in a sharp controversy. The business, however, was adjourned.

A dispute then arose between Gallus and the emperor. Gallus proposed that the elections of magistrates should be held every five years, and that the commanders of the legions who before receiving a praetorship discharged this military service should at once become praetorselect, the emperor nominating twelve candidates every year. It was quite evident that this motion had a deeper meaning and was an attempt to explore the secrets of imperial policy. Tiberius, however, argued as if his power would be thus increased. "It would," he said, "be trying to his moderation to have to elect so many and to put off so many. He scarcely avoided giving offence from year to year, even though a candidate's rejection was solaced by the near prospect of office. What hatred would be incurred from those whose election was deferred for five years! How could he foresee through so long an interval what would be a man's temper, or domestic relations, or estate? Men became arrogant even with this annual appointment. What would happen if their thoughts were fixed on promotion for five years? It was in fact a multiplying of the magistrates five-fold, and a subversion of the laws which had prescribed proper periods for the exercise of the candidate's activity and the seeking or securing office. With this seemingly conciliatory speech he retained the substance of power.

He also increased the incomes of some of the Senators. Hence it was the more surprising that he listened somewhat disdainfully to the request of Marcus Hortalus, a youth of noble rank in conspicuous poverty. He was the grandson of the orator Hortensius, and had been induced by Augustus, on the strength of a gift of a million sesterces, to marry and rear children, that one of our most illustrious families might not become extinct. Accordingly, with his four sons standing at the doors of the Senate House, the Senate then sitting in the palace, when it was his turn to speak he began to address them as follows, his eyes fixed now on the statue of Hortensius which stood among those of the orators, now on that of Augustus:—"Senators, these whose numbers and boyish years you behold I have reared, not by my own choice, but because the emperor advised me. At the same time, my ancestors deserved to have descendants. For myself, not having been able in these altered times to receive or acquire wealth or popular favour, or that eloquence which has been the hereditary possession of our house, I was satisfied if my narrow means were neither a disgrace to myself nor burden to others. At the emperor's bidding I married. Behold the offspring and progeny of a succession of consuls and dictators. Not to excite odium do I recall such facts, but to win compassion. While you prosper, Caesar, they will attain such promotion as you shall bestow. Meanwhile save from penury the great-grandsons of Quintus Hortensius, the foster-children of Augustus."

The Senate's favourable bias was an incitement to Tiberius to offer prompt opposition, which he did in nearly these words:—"If all poor men begin to come here and to beg money for their children, individuals will never be satisfied, and the State will be bankrupt. Certainly our ancestors did not grant the privilege of occasionally proposing amendments or of suggesting, in our turn for speaking, something for the general advantage in order that we might in this house increase our private business and property, thereby bringing odium on the Senate and on emperors whether they concede or refuse their bounty. In fact, it is not a request, but an importunity, as utterly unreasonable as it is unforeseen, for a senator, when the house has met on other matters, to rise from his place and, pleading the number and age of his children, put a pressure on the delicacy of the Senate, then transfer the same constraint to myself, and, as it were, break open the exchequer, which, if we exhaust it by improper favouritism, will have to be replenished by crimes. Money was given you, Hortalus, by Augustus, but without solicitation, and not on the condition of its being always given. Otherwise industry will languish and idleness be encouraged, if a man has nothing to fear, nothing to hope from himself, and every one, in utter recklessness, will expect relief from others, thus becoming useless to himself and a burden to me."

These and like remarks, though listened to with assent by those who make it a practice to eulogise everything coming from sovereigns, both good and bad, were received by the majority in silence or with suppressed murmurs. Tiberius perceived it, and having paused a while, said that he had given Hortalus his answer, but that if the senators thought it right, he would bestow two hundred thousand sesterces on each of his children of the male sex. The others thanked him; Hortalus said nothing, either from alarm or because even in his reduced fortunes he clung to his hereditary nobility. Nor did Tiberius afterwards show any pity, though the house of Hortensius sank into shameful poverty.

That same year the daring of a single slave, had it not been promptly checked, would have ruined the State by discord and civil war. A servant of Postumus Agrippa, Clemens by name, having ascertained that Augustus was dead, formed a design beyond a slave's conception, of going to the island of Planasia and seizing Agrippa by craft or force and bringing him to the armies of Germany. The slowness of a merchant vessel thwarted his bold venture. Meanwhile the murder of Agrippa had been perpetrated, and then turning his thoughts to a greater and more hazardous enterprise, he stole the ashes of the deceased, sailed to Cosa, a promontory of Etruria, and there hid himself in obscure places till his hair and beard were long. In age and figure he was not unlike his master. Then through suitable emissaries who shared his secret, it was rumoured that Agrippa was alive, first in whispered gossip, soon, as is usual with forbidden topics, in vague talk which found its way to the credulous ears of the most ignorant people or of restless and revolutionary schemers. He himself went to the towns, as the day grew dark, without letting himself be seen publicly or remaining long in the same places, but, as he knew that truth gains strength by notoriety and time, falsehood by precipitancy and vagueness, he would either withdraw himself from publicity or else forestall it.

It was rumoured meanwhile throughout Italy, and was believed at Rome, that Agrippa had been saved by the blessing of Heaven. Already at Ostia, where he had arrived, he was the centre of interest to a vast concourse as well as to secret gatherings in the capital, while Tiberius was distracted by the doubt whether he should crush this slave of his by military force or allow time to dissipate a silly credulity. Sometimes he thought that he must overlook nothing, sometimes that he need not be afraid of everything, his mind fluctuating between shame and terror. At last he entrusted the affair to Sallustius Crispus, who chose two of his dependants (some say they were soldiers) and urged them to go to him as pretended accomplices, offering money and promising faithful companionship in danger. They did as they were bidden; then, waiting for an unguarded hour of night, they took with them a sufficient force, and having bound and gagged him, dragged him to the palace. When Tiberius asked him how he had become Agrippa, he is said to have replied, "As you became Caesar." He could not be forced to divulge his accomplices. Tiberius did not venture on a public execution, but ordered him to be slain in a private part of the palace and his body to be secretly removed. And although many of the emperor's household and knights and senators were said to have supported him with their wealth and helped him with their counsels, no inquiry was made.

At the close of the year was consecrated an arch near the temple of Saturn to commemorate the recovery of the standards lost with Varus, under the leadership of Germanicus and the auspices of Tiberius; a temple of Fors Fortuna, by the Tiber, in the gardens which Caesar, the dictator, bequeathed to the Roman people; a chapel to the Julian family, and statues at Bovillae to the Divine Augustus.

In the consulship of Caius Caecilius and Lucius Pomponius, Germanicus Caesar, on the 26th day of May, celebrated his triumph over the Cherusci, Chatti, and Angrivarii, and the other tribes which extend as far as the Elbe. There were borne in procession spoils, prisoners, representations of the mountains, the rivers and battles; and the war, seeing that he had been forbidden to finish it, was taken as finished. The admiration of the beholders was heightened by the striking comeliness of the general and the chariot which bore his five children. Still, there was a latent dread when they remembered how unfortunate in the case of Drusus, his father, had been the favour of the crowd; how his uncle Marcellus, regarded by the city populace with passionate enthusiasm, had been snatched from them while yet a youth, and how short-lived and ill-starred were the attachments of the Roman people.

Tiberius meanwhile in the name of Germanicus gave every one of the city populace three hundred sesterces, and nominated himself his colleague in the consulship. Still, failing to obtain credit for sincere affection, he resolved to get the young prince out of the way, under pretence of conferring distinction, and for this he invented reasons, or eagerly fastened on such as chance presented.

King Archelaus had been in possession of Cappadocia for fifty years, and Tiberius hated him because he had not shown him any mark of respect while he was at Rhodes. This neglect of Archelaus was not due to pride, but was suggested by the intimate friends of Augustus, because, when Caius Caesar was in his prime and had charge of the affairs of the East, Tiberius's friendship was thought to be dangerous. When, after the extinction of the family of the Caesars, Tiberius acquired the empire, he enticed Archelaus by a letter from his mother, who without concealing her son's displeasure promised mercy if he would come to beg for it. Archelaus, either quite unsuspicious of treachery, or dreading compulsion, should it be thought that he saw through it, hastened to Rome. There he was received by a pitiless emperor, and soon afterwards was arraigned before the Senate. In his anguish and in the weariness of old age, and from being unused, as a king, to equality, much less to degradation, not, certainly, from fear of the charges fabricated against him, he ended his life, by his own act or by a natural death. His kingdom was reduced into a province, and Caesar declared that, with its revenues, the one per cent. tax could be lightened, which, for the future, he fixed at one-half per cent.

During the same time, on the deaths of Antiochus and Philopator, kings respectively of the Commageni and Cilicians, these nations became excited, a majority desiring the Roman rule, some, that of their kings. The provinces too of Syria and Judaea, exhausted by their burdens, implored a reduction of tribute.

Tiberius accordingly discussed these matters and the affairs of Armenia, which I have already related, before the Senate. "The commotions in the East," he said, "could be quieted only by the wisdom, of Germanicus; own life was on the decline, and Drusus had not yet reached his maturity." Thereupon, by a decree of the Senate, the provinces beyond sea were entrusted to Germanicus, with greater powers wherever he went than were given to those who obtained their provinces by lot or by the emperor's appointment.

Tiberius had however removed from Syria Creticus Silanus, who was connected by a close tie with Germanicus, his daughter being betrothed to Nero, the eldest of Germanicus's children. He appointed to it Cneius Piso, a man of violent temper, without an idea of obedience, with indeed a natural arrogance inherited from his father Piso, who in the civil war supported with the most energetic aid against Caesar the reviving faction in Africa, then embraced the cause of Brutus and Cassius, and, when suffered to return, refrained from seeking promotion till, he was actually solicited to accept a consulship offered by Augustus. But beside the father's haughty temper there was also the noble rank and wealth of his wife Plancina, to inflame his ambition. He would hardly be the inferior of Tiberius, and as for Tiberius's children, he looked down on them as far beneath him. He thought it a certainty that he had been chosen to govern Syria in order to thwart the aspirations of Germanicus. Some believed that he had even received secret instructions from Tiberius, and it was beyond a question that Augusta, with feminine jealousy, had suggested to Plancina calumnious insinuations against Agrippina. For there was division and discord in the court, with unexpressed partialities towards either Drusus or Germanicus. Tiberius favoured Drusus, as his. son and born of his own blood. As for

Germanicus, his uncle's estrangement had increased the affection which all others felt for him, and there was the fact too that he had an advantage in the illustrious rank of his mother's family, among whom he could point to his grandfather Marcus Antonius and to his great-uncle Augustus. Drusus, on the other hand, had for his great-grandfather a Roman knight, Pomponius Atticus, who seemed to disgrace the ancestral images of the Claudii. Again, the consort of Germanicus, Agrippina, in number of children and in character, was superior to Livia, the wife of Drusus. Yet the brothers were singularly united, and were wholly unaffected by the rivalries of their kinsfolk.

Soon afterwards Drusus was sent into Illyricum to be familiarised with military service, and to win the goodwill of the army. Tiberius also thought that it was better for the young prince, who was being demoralised by the luxury of the capital, to serve in a camp, while he felt himself the safer with both his sons in command of legions. However, he made a pretext of the Suevi, who were imploring help against the Cherusci. For when the Romans had departed and they were free from the fear of an invader, these tribes, according to the custom of the race, and then specially as rivals in fame, had turned their arms against each other. The strength of the two nations, the valour of their chiefs were equal. But the title of king rendered Maroboduus hated among his countrymen, while Arminius was regarded with favour as the champion of freedom.

Thus it was not only the Cherusci and their allies, the old soldiers of Arminius, who took up arms, but even the Semnones and Langobardi from the kingdom of Maroboduus revolted to that chief. With this addition he must have had an overwhelming superiority, had not Inguiomerus deserted with a troop of his dependants to Maroboduus, simply for the reason that the aged uncle scorned to obey a brother's youthful son. The armies were drawn up, with equal confidence on both sides, and there were not those desultory attacks or irregular bands, formerly so common with the Germans. Prolonged warfare against us had accustomed them to keep close to their standards, to have the support of reserves, and to take the word of command from their generals. On this occasion Arminius, who reviewed the whole field on horseback, as he rode up to each band, boasted of regained freedom, of slaughtered legions, of spoils and weapons wrested from the Romans, and still in the hands of many of his men. As for Maroboduus, he called him a fugitive, who had no experience of battles, who had sheltered himself in the recesses of the Hercynian forest and then with presents and embassies sued for a treaty; a traitor to his country, a satellite of Caesar, who deserved to be driven out, with rage as furious as that with which they had slain Quintilius Varus. They should simply remember their many battles, the result of which, with the final expulsion of the Romans, sufficiently showed who could claim the crowning success in war.

Nor did Maroboduus abstain from vaunts about himself or from revilings of the foe. Clasping the hand of Inguiomerus, he protested "that in the person before them centred all the renown of the Cherusci, that to his counsels was due whatever had ended successfully. Arminius in his infatuation and ignorance was taking to himself the glory which belonged to another, for he had treacherously surprised three unofficered legions and a general who had not an idea of perfidy, to the great hurt of Germany and to his own disgrace, since his wife and his son were still enduring slavery. As for himself, he had been attacked by twelve legions led by Tiberius, and had preserved untarnished the glory of the Germans, and then on equal terms the armies had parted. He was by no means sorry that they had the matter in their own hands, whether they preferred to war with all their might against Rome, or to accept a bloodless peace."

To these words, which roused the two armies, was added the stimulus of special motives of their own. The Cherusci and Langobardi were fighting for ancient renown or newly-won freedom; the other side for the increase of their dominion. Never at any time was the shock of battle more tremendous or the issue more doubtful, as the right wings of both armies were routed. Further fighting was expected, when Maroboduus withdrew his camp to the hills. This was a sign of discomfiture. He was gradually stripped of his strength by desertions, and, having fled to the Marcomanni, he sent envoys to Tiberius with entreaties for help. The answer was that he had no right to invoke the aid of Roman arms against the Cherusci, when he had rendered no assistance to the Romans in their conflict with the same enemy. Drusus, however, was sent as I have related, to establish peace.

That same year twelve famous cities of Asia fell by an earthquake in the night, so that the destruction was all the more unforeseen and fearful. Nor were there the means of escape usual in, such a disaster, by rushing out into the open country, for there people were swallowed up by the yawning earth. Vast mountains, it is said, collapsed; what had been level ground seemed to be raised aloft, and fires blazed out amid the ruin. The calamity fell most fatally on the inhabitants of Sardis, and it attracted to them the largest share of sympathy. The emperor promised ten million sesterces, and remitted for five years all they paid to the exchequer or to the emperor's purse. Magnesia, under Mount Sipylus, was considered to come next in loss and in need of help. The people of Temnus, Philadelpheia, Aegae, Apollonis, the Mostenians, and Hyrcanian Macedonians, as they were called, with the towns of Hierocaesarea, Myrina, Cyme, and Tmolus, were; it was decided, to be exempted from tribute for the same time, and some one was to be sent from the Senate to examine their actual condition and to relieve them. Marcus Aletus, one of the expraetors, was chosen, from a fear that, as an exconsul was governor of Asia, there might be rivalry between men of equal rank, and consequent embarrassment.

To his splendid public liberality the emperor added bounties no less popular. The property of Aemilia Musa, a rich woman who died intestate, on which the imperial treasury had a claim, he handed over to Aemilius Lepidus, to whose family she appeared to belong; and the estate of Patuleius, a wealthy Roman knight, though he was himself left in part his heir, he gave to Marcus Servilius, whose name he discovered in an earlier and unquestioned will. In both these cases he said that noble rank ought to have the support of wealth. Nor did he accept a legacy from any one unless he had earned it by friendship. Those who were strangers to him, and who, because they were at enmity with others, made the emperor their heir, he kept at a distance. While, however, he relieved the honourable poverty of the virtuous, he expelled from the Senate or suffered voluntarily to retire spendthrifts whose vices had brought them to penury, like Vibidius Varro, Marius Nepos, Appius Appianus, Cornelius Sulla, and Quintus Vitellius.

About the same time he dedicated some temples of the gods, which had perished from age or from fire, and which Augustus had begun to restore. These were temples to Liber, Libera, and Ceres, near the Great Circus, which last Aulus Postumius, when Dictator, had vowed; a temple to Flora in the same place, which had been built by Lucius and Marcus Publicius, aediles, and a temple to Janus, which had been erected in the vegetable market by Caius Duilius, who was the first to make the Roman power successful at sea and to win a naval triumph over the Carthaginians. A temple to Hope was consecrated by Germanicus; this had been vowed by Atilius in that same war.

Meantime the law of treason was gaining strength. Appuleia Varilia, grand-niece of Augustus, was accused of treason by an informer for having ridiculed the Divine

Augustus, Tiberius, and Tiberius's mother, in some insulting remarks, and for having been convicted of adultery, allied though she was to Caesar's house. Adultery, it was thought, was sufficiently guarded against by the Julian law. As to the charge of treason, the emperor insisted that it should be taken separately, and that she should be condemned if she had spoken irreverently of Augustus. Her insinuations against himself he did not wish to be the subject of judicial inquiry. When asked by the consul what he thought of the unfavourable speeches she was accused of having uttered against his mother, he said nothing. Afterwards, on the next day of the Senate's meeting, he even begged in his mother's name that no words of any kind spoken against her might in any case be treated as criminal. He then acquitted Appuleia of treason. For her adultery, he deprecated the severer penalty, and advised that she should be removed by her kinsfolk, after the example of our forefathers, to more than two hundred miles from Rome. Her paramour, Manlius, was forbidden to live in Italy or Africa.

A contest then arose about the election of a praetor in the room of Vipstanus Gallus, whom death had removed. Germanicus and Drusus (for they were still at Rome) supported Haterius Agrippa, a relative of Germanicus. Many, on the other hand, endeavoured to make the number of children weigh most in favour of the candidates. Tiberius rejoiced to see a strife in the Senate between his sons and the law. Beyond question the law was beaten, but not at once, and only by a few votes, in the same way as laws were defeated even when they were in force.

In this same year a war broke out in Africa, where the enemy was led by Tacfarinas. A Numidian by birth, he had served as an auxiliary in the Roman camp, then becoming a deserter, he at first gathered round him a roving band familiar with robbery, for plunder and for rapine. After a while, he marshalled them like regular soldiers, under standards and in troops, till at last he was regarded as the leader, not of an undisciplined rabble, but of the Musulamian people. This powerful tribe, bordering on the deserts of Africa, and even then with none of the civilisation of cities, took up arms and drew their Moorish neighbours into the war. These too had a leader, Mazippa. The army was so divided that Tacfarinas kept the picked men who were armed in Roman fashion within a camp, and familiarised them with a commander's authority, while Mazippa, with light troops, spread around him fire, slaughter, and consternation. They had forced the Ciniphii, a far from contemptible tribe, into their cause, when Furius Camillus, proconsul of Africa, united in one force a legion and all the regularly enlisted allies, and, with an army insignificant indeed compared with the multitude of the Numidians and Moors, marched against the enemy. There was nothing however which he strove so much to avoid as their eluding an engagement out of fear. It was by the hope of victory that they were lured on only to be defeated. The legion was in the army's centre; the light cohorts and two cavalry squadrons on its wings. Nor did Tacfarinas refuse battle. The Numidians were routed, and after a number of years the name of Furius won military renown. Since the days of the famous deliverer of our city and his son Camillus, fame as a general had fallen to the lot of other branches of the family, and the man of whom I am now speaking was regarded as an inexperienced soldier. All the more willingly did Tiberius commemorate his achievements in the Senate, and the Senators voted him the ornaments of triumph, an honour which Camillus, because of his unambitious life, enjoyed without harm.

In the following year Tiberius held his third, Germanicus his second, consulship. Germanicus, however, entered on the office at Nicopolis, a city of Achaia, whither he had arrived by the coast of Illyricum, after having seen his brother Drusus, who was then in Dalmatia, and endured a stormy voyage through the Adriatic and afterwards the Ionian

Sea. He accordingly devoted a few days to the repair of his fleet, and, at the same time, in remembrance of his ancestors, he visited the bay which the victory of Actium had made famous, the spoils consecrated by Augustus, and the camp of Antonius. For, as I have said, Augustus was his great-uncle, Antonius his grandfather, and vivid images of disaster and success rose before him on the spot. Thence he went to Athens, and there, as a concession to our treaty with an allied and ancient city, he was attended only by a single lictor. The Greeks welcomed him with the most elaborate honours, and brought forward all the old deeds and sayings of their countrymen, to give additional dignity to their flattery.

Thence he directed his course to Euboea and crossed to Lesbos, where Agrippina for the last time was confined and gave birth to Julia. He then penetrated to the remoter parts of the province of Asia, visited the Thracian cities, Perinthus and Byzantium; next, the narrow strait of the Propontis and the entrance of the Pontus, from an anxious wish to become acquainted with those ancient and celebrated localities. He gave relief, as he went, to provinces which had been exhausted by internal feuds or by the oppressions of governors. In his return he attempted to see the sacred mysteries of the Samothracians, but north winds which he encountered drove him aside from his course. And so after visiting Ilium and surveying a scene venerable from the vicissitudes of fortune and as the birth-place of our people, he coasted back along Asia, and touched at Colophon, to consult the oracle of the Clarian Apollo. There, it is not a woman, as at Delphi, but a priest chosen from certain families, generally from Miletus, who ascertains simply the number and the names of the applicants. Then descending into a cave and drinking a draught from a secret spring, the man, who is commonly ignorant of letters and of poetry, utters a response in verse answering to the thoughts conceived in the mind of any inquirer. It was said that he prophesied to Germanicus, in dark hints, as oracles usually do, an early doom.

Cneius Piso meanwhile, that he might the sooner enter on his design, terrified the citizens of Athens by his tumultuous approach, and then reviled them in a bitter speech, with indirect reflections on Germanicus, who, he said, had derogated from the honour of the Roman name in having treated with excessive courtesy, not the people of Athens, who indeed had been exterminated by repeated disasters, but a miserable medley of tribes. As for the men before him, they had been Mithridates's allies against Sulla, allies of Antonius against the Divine Augustus. He taunted them too with the past, with their ill-success against the Macedonians, their violence to their own countrymen, for he had his own special grudge against this city, because they would not spare at his intercession one Theophilus whom the Areopagus had condemned for forgery. Then, by sailing rapidly and by the shortest route through the Cyclades, he overtook Germanicus at the island of Rhodes. The prince was not ignorant of the slanders with which he had been assailed, but his good nature was such that when a storm arose and drove Piso on rocks, and his enemy's destruction could have been referred to chance, he sent some triremes, by the help of which he might be rescued from danger. But this did not soften Piso's heart. Scarcely allowing a day's interval, he left Germanicus and hastened on in advance. When he reached Syria and the legions, he began, by bribery and favouritism, to encourage the lowest of the common soldiers, removing the old centurions and the strict tribunes and assigning their places to creatures of his own or to the vilest of the men, while he allowed idleness in the camp, licentiousness in the towns, and the soldiers to roam through the country and take their pleasure. He went such lengths in demoralizing them, that he was spoken of in their vulgar talk as the father of the legions.

Plancina too, instead of keeping herself within the proper limits of a woman, would be present at the evolutions of the cavalry and the manoeuvres of the cohorts, and would fling insulting remarks at Agrippina and Germanicus. Some even of the good soldiers were inclined to a corrupt compliance, as a whispered rumour gained ground that the emperor was not averse to these proceedings. Of all this Germanicus was aware, but his most pressing anxiety was to be first in reaching Armenia.

This had been of old an unsettled country from the character of its people and from its geographical position, bordering, as it does, to a great extent on our provinces and stretching far away to Media. It lies between two most mighty empires, and is very often at strife with them, hating Rome and jealous of Parthia. It had at this time no king, Vonones having been expelled, but the nation's likings inclined towards Zeno, son of Polemon, king of Pontus, who from his earliest infancy had imitated Armenian manners and customs, loving the chase, the banquet, and all the popular pastimes of barbarians, and who had thus bound to himself chiefs and people alike. Germanicus accordingly, in the city of Artaxata, with the approval of the nobility, in the presence of a vast multitude, placed the royal diadem on his head. All paid him homage and saluted him as King Artaxias, which name they gave him from the city.

Cappadocia meanwhile, which had been reduced to the form of a province, received as its governor Quintus Veranius. Some of the royal tributes were diminished, to inspire hope of a gentler rule under Rome. Quintus Servaeus was appointed to Commagene, then first put under a praetor's jurisdiction.

Successful as was this settlement of all the interests of our allies, it gave Germanicus little joy because of the arrogance of Piso. Though he had been ordered to march part of the legions into Armenia under his own or his son's command, he had neglected to do either. At length the two met at Cyrrhus, the winter-quarters of the tenth legion, each controlling his looks, Piso concealing his fears, Germanicus shunning the semblance of menace. He was indeed, as I have said, a kind-hearted man. But friends who knew well how to inflame a quarrel, exaggerated what was true and added lies, alleging various charges against Piso, Plancina, and their sons.

At last, in the presence of a few intimate associates, Germanicus addressed him in language such as suppressed resentment suggests, to which Piso replied with haughty apologies. They parted in open enmity. After this Piso was seldom seen at Caesar's tribunal, and if he ever sat by him, it was with a sullen frown and a marked display of opposition. He was even heard to say at a banquet given by the king of the Nabataeans, when some golden crowns of great weight were presented to Caesar and Agrippina and light ones to Piso and the rest, that the entertainment was given to the son of a Roman emperor, not of a Parthian king. At the same time he threw his crown on the ground, with a long speech against luxury, which, though it angered Germanicus, he still bore with patience.

Meantime envoys arrived from Artabanus, king of the Parthians. He had sent them to recall the memory of friendship and alliance, with an assurance that he wished for a renewal of the emblems of concord, and that he would in honour of Germanicus yield the point of advancing to the bank of the Euphrates. He begged meanwhile that Vonones might not be kept in Syria, where, by emissaries from an easy distance, he might draw the chiefs of the tribes into civil strife. Germanicus' answer as to the alliance between Rome and Parthia was dignified; as to the king's visit and the respect shown to himself, it was graceful and modest. Vonones was removed to Pompeiopolis, a city on the coast of Cilicia. This was not merely a concession to the request of Artabanus, but was meant as an affront to Piso, who had a special liking for Vonones, because of the many attentions and presents by which he had won Plancina's favour.

In the consulship of Marcus Silanus and Lucius Norbanus, Germanicus set out for Egypt to study its antiquities. His ostensible motive however was solicitude for the province. He reduced the price of corn by opening the granaries, and adopted many practices pleasing to the multitude. He would go about without soldiers, with sandalled feet, and apparelled after the Greek fashion, in imitation of Publius Scipio, who, it is said, habitually did the same in Sicily, even when the war with Carthage was still raging. Tiberius having gently expressed disapproval of his dress and manners, pronounced a very sharp censure on his visit to Alexandria without the emperor's leave, contrary to the regulations of Augustus. That prince, among other secrets of imperial policy, had forbidden senators and Roman knights of the higher rank to enter Egypt except by permission, and he had specially reserved the country, from a fear that any one who held a province containing the key of the land and of the sea, with ever so small a force against the mightiest army, might distress Italy by famine.

Germanicus, however, who had not yet learnt how much he was blamed for his expedition, sailed up the Nile from the city of Canopus as his starting-point. Spartans founded the place because Canopus, pilot of one of their ships, had been buried there, when Menelaus on his return to Greece was driven into a distant sea and to the shores of Libya. Thence he went to the river's nearest mouth, dedicated to a Hercules who, the natives say, was born in the country and was the original hero, others, who afterwards showed like valour, having received his name. Next he visited the vast ruins of ancient Thebes. There yet remained on the towering piles Egyptian inscriptions, with a complete account of the city's past grandeur. One of the aged priests, who was desired to interpret the language of his country, related how once there had dwelt in Thebes seven hundred thousand men of military age, and how with such an army king Rhamses conquered Libya, Ethiopia, Media, Persia, Bactria, and Scythia, and held under his sway the countries inhabited by the Syrians, Armenians, and their neighbours, the Cappadocians, from the Bithynian to the Lycian sea. There was also to be read what tributes were imposed on these nations, the weight of silver and gold, the tale of arms and horses, the gifts of ivory and of perfumes to the temples, with the amount of grain and supplies furnished by each people, a revenue as magnificent as is now exacted by the might of Parthia or the power of Rome.

But Germanicus also bestowed attention on other wonders. Chief of these were the stone image of Memnon, which, when struck by the sun's rays, gives out the sound of a human voice; the pyramids, rising up like mountains amid almost impassable wastes of shifting sand, raised by the emulation and vast wealth of kings; the lake hollowed out of the earth to be a receptacle for the Nile's overflow; and elsewhere the river's narrow channel and profound depth which no line of the explorer can penetrate. He then came to Elephantine and Syene, formerly the limits of the Roman empire, which now extends to the Red Sea.

While Germanicus was spending the summer in visits to several provinces, Drusus gained no little glory by sowing discord among the Germans and urging them to complete the destruction of the now broken power of Maroboduus. Among the Gotones was a youth of noble birth, Catualda by name, who had formerly been driven into exile by the might of Maroboduus, and who now, when the king's fortunes were declining, ventured on revenge. He entered the territory of the Marcomanni with a strong force, and, having corruptly won over the nobles to join him, burst into the palace and into an adjacent fortress. There he found the long-accumulated plunder of the Suevi and camp followers and traders from our provinces who had been attracted to an enemy's land, each from their various homes, first by the freedom of commerce, next by the desire of amassing wealth, finally by forgetfulness of their fatherland.

Maroboduus, now utterly deserted, had no resource but in the mercy of Caesar. Having crossed the Danube where it flows by the province of Noricum, he wrote to Tiberius, not like a fugitive or a suppliant, but as one who remembered his past greatness. When as a most famous king in former days he received invitations from many nations, he had still, he said, preferred the friendship of Rome. Caesar replied that he should have a safe and honourable home in Italy, if he would remain there, or, if his interests required something different, he might leave it under the same protection under which he had come. But in the Senate he maintained that Philip had not been so formidable to the Athenians, or Pyrrhus or Antiochus to the Roman people, as was Maroboduus. The speech is extant, and in it he magnifies the man's power, the ferocity of the tribes under his sway, his proximity to Italy as a foe, finally his own measures for his overthrow. The result was that Maroboduus was kept at Ravenna, where his possible return was a menace to the Suevi, should they ever disdain obedience. But he never left Italy for eighteen years, living to old age and losing much of his renown through an excessive clinging to life.

Catualda had a like downfall and no better refuge. Driven out soon afterwards by the overwhelming strength of the Hermundusi led by Vibilius, he was received and sent to Forum Julii, a colony of Narbonensian Gaul. The barbarians who followed the two kings, lest they might disturb the peace of the provinces by mingling with the population, were settled beyond the Danube between the rivers Marus and Cusus, under a king, Vannius, of the nation of the Quadi.

Tidings having also arrived of Artaxias being made king of Armenia by Germanicus, the Senate decreed that both he and Drusus should enter the city with an ovation. Arches too were raised round the sides of the temple of Mars the Avenger, with statues of the two Caesars. Tiberius was the more delighted at having established peace by wise policy than if he had finished a war by battle. And so next he planned a crafty scheme against Rhescuporis, king of Thrace. That entire country had been in the possession of Rhoemetalces, after whose death Augustus assigned half to the king's brother Rhescuporis, half to his son Cotys. In this division the cultivated lands, the towns, and what bordered on Greek territories, fell to Cotys; the wild and barbarous portion, with enemies on its frontier, to Rhescuporis. The kings too themselves differed, Cotys having a gentle and kindly temper, the other a fierce and ambitious spirit, which could not brook a partner. Still at first they lived in a hollow friendship, but soon Rhescuporis overstepped his bounds and appropriated to himself what had been given to Cotys, using force when he was resisted, though somewhat timidly under Augustus, who having created both kingdoms would, he feared, avenge any contempt of his arrangement. When however he heard of the change of emperor, he let loose bands of freebooters and razed the fortresses, as a provocation to war.

Nothing made Tiberius so uneasy as an apprehension of the disturbance of any settlement. He commissioned a centurion to tell the kings not to decide their dispute by arms. Cotys at once dismissed the forces which he had prepared. Rhescuporis, with assumed modesty, asked for a place of meeting where, he said, they might settle their differences by an interview. There was little hesitation in fixing on a time, a place, finally on terms, as every point was mutually conceded and accepted, by the one out of good nature, by the other with a treacherous intent. Rhescuporis, to ratify the treaty, as he said, further proposed a banquet; and when their mirth had been prolonged far into the night, and Cotys amid the feasting and the wine was unsuspicious of danger, he loaded him with chains, though he appealed, on perceiving the perfidy, to the sacred character of a king, to the gods of their common house, and to the hospitable board. Having possessed himself of all Thrace, he wrote word to Tiberius that a plot had been formed against him, and that he had forestalled the plotter. Meanwhile, under pretext of a war against the Bastarnian and Scythian tribes, he was strengthening himself with fresh forces of infantry and cavalry.

He received a conciliatory answer. If there was no treachery in his conduct, he could rely on his innocence, but neither the emperor nor the Senate would decide on the right or wrong of his cause without hearing it. He was therefore to surrender Cotys, come in person transfer from himself the odium of the charge.

This letter Latinius Pandus, propraetor of Moesia, sent to Thrace, with soldiers to whose custody Cotys was to be delivered. Rhescuporis, hesitating between fear and rage, preferred to be charged with an accomplished rather than with an attempted crime. He ordered Cotys to be murdered and falsely represented his death as self-inflicted. Still the emperor did not change the policy which he had once for all adopted. On the death of Pandus, whom Rhescuporis accused of being his personal enemy, he appointed to the government of Moesia Pomponius Flaccus, a veteran soldier, specially because of his close intimacy with the king and his consequent ability to entrap him.

Flaccus on arriving in Thrace induced the king by great promises, though he hesitated and thought of his guilty deeds, to enter the Roman lines. He then surrounded him with a strong force under pretence of showing him honour, and the tribunes and centurions, by counsel, by persuasion, and by a more undisguised captivity the further he went, brought him, aware at last of his desperate plight, to Rome. He was accused before the Senate by the wife of Cotys, and was condemned to be kept a prisoner far away from his kingdom. Thrace was divided between his son Rhoemetalces, who, it was proved, had opposed his father's designs, and the sons of Cotys. As these were still minors, Trebellienus Rufus, an expraetor, was appointed to govern the kingdom in the meanwhile, after the precedent of our ancestors who sent Marcus Lepidus into Egypt as guardian to Ptolemy's children. Rhescuporis was removed to Alexandria, and there attempting or falsely charged with attempting escape, was put to death.

About the same time, Vonones, who, as I have related, had been banished to Cilicia, endeavoured by bribing his guards to escape into Armenia, thence to Albania and Heniochia, and to his kinsman, the king of Scythia. Quitting the sea-coast on the pretence of a hunting expedition, he struck into trackless forests, and was soon borne by his swift steed to the river Pyramus, the bridges over which had been broken down by the natives as soon as they heard of the king's escape. Nor was there a ford by which it could be crossed. And so on the river's bank he was put in chains by Vibius Fronto, an officer of cavalry; and then Remmius, an enrolled pensioner, who had previously been entrusted with the king's custody, in pretended rage, pierced him with his sword. Hence there was more ground for believing that the man, conscious of guilty complicity and fearing accusation, had slain Vonones.

Germanicus meanwhile, as he was returning from Egypt, found that all his directions to the legions and to the various cities had been repealed or reversed. This led to grievous insults on Piso, while he as savagely assailed the prince. Piso then resolved to quit Syria. Soon he was detained there by the failing health of Germanicus, but when he heard of his recovery, while people were paying the vows they had offered for his safety, he went attended by his lictors, drove away the victims placed by the altars with all the preparations for sacrifice, and the festal gathering of the populace of Antioch. Then he left for Seleucia and awaited the result of the illness which had again attacked Germanicus. The terrible intensity of the malady was increased by the belief that he had been poisoned by Piso. And certainly there were found hidden in the floor and in the walls disinterred remains of human bodies, incantations and spells, and the name of Germanicus inscribed on leaden tablets, half-burnt cinders smeared with blood, and other horrors by which in popular belief souls are devoted so the infernal deities. Piso too was accused of sending emissaries to note curiously every unfavourable symptom of the illness.

Germanicus heard of all this with anger, no less than with fear. "If my doors," he said, "are to be besieged, if I must gasp out my last breath under my enemies' eyes, what will then be the lot of my most unhappy wife, of my infant children? Poisoning seems tedious; he is in eager haste to have the sole control of the province and the legions. But Germanicus is not yet fallen so low, nor will the murderer long retain the reward of the fatal deed."

He then addressed a letter to Piso, renouncing his friendship, and, as many also state, ordered him to quit the province. Piso without further delay weighed anchor, slackening his course that he might not have a long way to return should Germanicus' death leave Syria open to him.

For a brief space the prince's hopes rose; then his frame became exhausted, and, as his end drew near, he spoke as follows to the friends by his side:—

"Were I succumbing to nature, I should have just ground of complaint even against the gods for thus tearing me away in my youth by an untimely death from parents, children, country. Now, cut off by the wickedness of Piso and Plancina, I leave to your hearts my last entreaties. Describe to my father and brother, torn by what persecutions, entangled by what plots, I have ended by the worst of deaths the most miserable of lives. If any were touched by my bright prospects, by ties of blood, or even by envy towards me while I lived, they will weep that the once prosperous survivor of so many wars has perished by a woman's treachery. You will have the opportunity of complaint before the Senate, of an appeal to the laws. It is not the chief duty of friends to follow the dead with unprofitable laments, but to remember his wishes, to fulfil his commands. Tears for Germanicus even strangers will shed; vengeance must come from you, if you loved the man more than his fortune. Show the people of Rome her who is the granddaughter of the Divine Augustus, as well as my consort; set before them my six children. Sympathy will be on the side of the accusers, and to those who screen themselves under infamous orders belief or pardon will be refused."

His friends clasped the dying man's right hand, and swore that they would sooner lose life than revenge.

He then turned to his wife and implored her by the memory of her husband and by their common offspring to lay aside her high spirit, to submit herself to the cruel blows of fortune, and not, when she returned to Rome, to enrage by political rivalry those who were stronger than herself. This was said openly; other words were whispered, pointing, it was supposed, to his fears from Tiberius. Soon afterwards he expired, to the intense sorrow of the province and of the neighbouring peoples. Foreign nations and kings grieved over him, so great was his courtesy to allies, his humanity to enemies. He inspired reverence alike by look and voice, and while he maintained the greatness and dignity of the highest rank, he had escaped the hatred that waits on arrogance.

His funeral, though it lacked the family statues and procession, was honoured by panegyrics and a commemoration of his virtues. Some there were who, as they thought of his beauty, his age, and the manner of his death, the vicinity too of the country where he died, likened his end to that of Alexander the Great. Both had a graceful person and were of noble birth; neither had much exceeded thirty years of age, and both fell by the treachery of their own people in strange lands. But Germanicus was gracious to his friends, temperate in his pleasures, the husband of one wife, with only legitimate children. He was too no less a warrior, though rashness he had none, and, though after having cowed Germany by his many victories, he was hindered from crushing it into subjection. Had he had the sole control of affairs, had he possessed the power and title of a king, he would have attained military glory as much more easily as he had excelled Alexander in clemency, in self-restraint, and in all other virtues.

As to the body which, before it was burnt, lay bare in the forum at Antioch, its destined place of burial, it is doubtful whether it exhibited the marks of poisoning. For men according as they pitied Germanicus and were prepossessed with suspicion or were biased by partiality towards Piso, gave conflicting accounts.

Then followed a deliberation among the generals and other senators present about the appointment of a governor to Syria. The contest was slight among all but Vibius Marsus and Cneius Sentius, between whom there was a long dispute. Finally Marsus yielded to Sentius as an older and keener competitor. Sentius at once sent to Rome a woman infamous for poisonings in the province and a special favourite of Plancina, Martina by name, on the demand of Vitellius and Veranius and others, who were preparing the charges and the indictment as if a prosecution had already been commenced.

Agrippina meantime, worn out though she was with sorrow and bodily weakness, yet still impatient of everything which might delay her vengeance, embarked with the ashes of Germanicus and with her children, pitied by all. Here indeed was a woman of the highest nobility, and but lately because of her splendid union wont to be seen amid an admiring and sympathizing throng, now bearing in her bosom the mournful relics of death, with an uncertain hope of revenge, with apprehensions for herself, repeatedly at fortune's mercy by reason of the ill-starred fruitfulness of her marriage. Piso was at the island of Coos when tidings reached him that Germanicus was dead. He received the news with extravagant joy, slew victims, visited the temples, with no moderation in his transports; while Plancina's insolence increased, and she then for the first time exchanged for the gayest attire the mourning she had worn for her lost sister.

Centurions streamed in, and hinted to Piso that he had the sympathy of the legions at his command. "Go back," they said, "to the province which has not been rightfully taken from you, and is still vacant." While he deliberated what he was to do, his son, Marcus Piso, advised speedy return to Rome. "As yet," he said, "you have not contracted any inexpiable guilt, and you need not dread feeble suspicions or vague rumours. Your strife with Germanicus deserved hatred perhaps, but not punishment, and by your having been deprived of the province, your enemies have been fully satisfied. But if you return, should Sentius resist you, civil war is begun, and you will not retain on your side the centurions and soldiers, who are powerfully swayed by the yet recent memory of their general and by a deep-rooted affection for the Caesars."

Against this view Domitius Celer, one of Piso's intimate friends, argued that he ought to profit by the opportunity. "It was Piso, not Sentius, who had been appointed to Syria. It was to Piso that the symbols of power and a praetor's jurisdiction and the legions had been given. In case of a hostile menace, who would more rightfully confront it by arms than the man who had received the authority and special commission of a governor? And as for rumours, it is best to leave time in which they may die away. Often the innocent cannot stand against the first burst of unpopularity. But if Piso possesses himself of the army, and increases his resources, much which cannot be foreseen will haply turn out in his favour. Are we hastening to reach Italy along with the ashes of Germanicus, that, unheard and undefended, you may be hurried to ruin by the wailings of Agrippina and the first gossip of an ignorant mob? You have on your side the complicity of Augusta and the emperor's favour, though in secret, and none mourn more ostentatiously over the death of Germanicus than those who most rejoice at it."

Without much difficulty Piso, who was ever ready for violent action, was led into this view. He sent a letter to Tiberius accusing Germanicus of luxury and arrogance, and asserting that, having been driven away to make room for revolution, he had resumed the command of the army in the same loyal spirit in which he had before held it. At the same time he put Domitius on board a trireme, with an order to avoid the coast and to push on to Syria through the open sea away from the islands. He formed into regular companies the deserters who flocked to him, armed the camp-followers, crossed with his ships to the mainland, intercepted a detachment of new levies on their way to Syria, and wrote word to the petty kings of Cilicia that they were to help him with auxiliaries, the young Piso actively assisting in all the business of war, though he had advised against undertaking it.

And so they coasted along Lycia and Pamphylia, and on meeting the fleet which conveyed Agrippina, both sides in hot anger at first armed for battle, and then in mutual fear confined themselves to revilings, Marsus Vibius telling Piso that he was to go to Rome to defend himself. Piso mockingly replied that he would be there as soon as the praetor who had to try poisoning cases had fixed a day for the accused and his prosecutors.

Meanwhile Domitius having landed at Laodicea, a city of Syria, as he was on his way to the winter-quarters of the sixth legion, which was, he believed, particularly open to revolutionary schemes, was anticipated by its commander Pacuvius. Of this Sentius informed Piso in a letter, and warned him not to disturb the armies by agents of corruption or the province by war. He gathered round him all whom he knew to cherish the memory of Germanicus, and to be opposed to his enemies, dwelling repeatedly on the greatness of the general, with hints that the State was being threatened with an armed attack, and he put himself at the head of a strong force, prepared for battle.

Piso, too, though his first attempts were unsuccessful, did not omit the safest precautions under present circumstances, but occupied a very strongly fortified position in Cilicia, named, Celenderis. He had raised to the strength of a legion the Cilician auxiliaries which the petty kings had sent, by mixing with them some deserters, and the lately intercepted recruits with his own and Plancina's slaves. And he protested that he, though Caesar's legate, was kept out of the province which Caesar had given him, not by the legions (for he had come at their invitation) but by Sentius, who was veiling private animosity under lying charges. "Only," he said, "stand in battle array, and the soldiers will not fight when they see that Piso whom they themselves once called 'father,' is the stronger, if right is to decide; if arms, is far from powerless."

He then deployed his companies before the lines of the fortress on a high and precipitous hill, with the sea surrounding him on every other side. Against him were the veteran troops drawn up in ranks and with reserves, a formidable soldiery on one side, a formidable position on the other. But his men had neither heart nor hope, and only rustic weapons, extemporised for sudden use. When they came to fighting, the result was doubtful only while the Roman cohorts were struggling up to level ground; then, the Cilicians turned their backs and shut themselves up within the fortress.

Meanwhile Piso vainly attempted an attack on the fleet which waited at a distance; he then went back, and as he stood before the walls, now smiting his breast, now calling on individual soldiers by name, and luring them on by rewards, sought to excite a mutiny. He had so far roused them that a standard bearer of the sixth legion went over to him with his standard. Thereupon Sentius ordered the horns and trumpets to be sounded, the rampart to be assaulted, the scaling ladders to be raised, all the bravest men to mount on them, while others were to discharge from the engines spears, stones, and brands. At last Piso's obstinacy was overcome, and he begged that he might remain in the fortress on surrendering his arms, while the emperor was being consulted about the appointment of a governor to Syria. The proposed terms were refused, and all that was granted him were some ships and a safe return to Rome.

There meantime, when the illness of Germanicus was universally known, and all news, coming, as it did, from a distance, exaggerated the danger, there was grief and indignation. There was too an outburst of complaint. "Of course this was the meaning," they said, "of banishing him to the ends of the earth, of giving Piso the province; this was the drift of Augusta's secret interviews with Plancina. What elderly men had said of Drusus was perfectly true, that rulers disliked a citizen-like temper in their sons, and the young princes had been put out of the way because they had the idea of comprehending in a restored era of freedom the Roman people under equal laws."

This popular talk was so stimulated by the news of Germanicus's death that even before the magistrate's proclamation or the Senate's resolution, there was a voluntary suspension of business, the public courts were deserted, and private houses closed. Everywhere there was a silence broken only by groans; nothing was arranged for mere effect. And though they refrained not from the emblems of the mourner, they sorrowed yet the more deeply in their hearts.

It chanced that some merchants who left Syria while Germanicus was still alive, brought more cheering tidings about his health. These were instantly believed, instantly published. Every one passed on to others whom he met the intelligence, ill-authenticated as it was, and they again to many more, with joyous exaggeration. They ran to and fro through the city and broke open the doors of the temples. Night assisted their credulity, and amid the darkness confident assertion was comparatively easy. Nor did Tiberius check the false reports till by lapse of time they died away.

And so the people grieved the more bitterly as though Germanicus was again lost to them. New honours were devised and decreed, as men were inspired by affection for him or by genius. His name was to be celebrated in the song of the Salii; chairs of state with oaken garlands over them were to be set up in the places assigned to the priesthood of the Augustales; his image in ivory was to head the procession in the games of the circus; no flamen or augur, except from the Julian family, was to be chosen in the room of Germanicus. Triumphal arches were erected at Rome, on the banks of the Rhine, and on mount Amanus in Syria, with an inscription recording his achievements, and how he had died in the public service. A cenotaph was raised at Antioch, where the body was burnt, a lofty mound at Epidaphna, where he had ended his life. The number of his statues, or of the places in which they were honoured, could not easily be computed. When a golden shield of remarkable size was voted him as a leader among orators, Tiberius declared that he would dedicate to him one of the usual kind, similar to the rest, for in eloquence, he said, there was no distinction of rank, and it was a sufficient glory for him to be classed among ancient writers. The knights called the seats in the theatre known as "the juniors," Germanicus's benches, and arranged that their squadrons were to ride in procession behind his effigy on the fifteenth of July. Many of these honours still remain; some were at once dropped, or became obsolete with time.

While men's sorrow was yet fresh, Germanicus's sister Livia, who was married to Drusus, gave birth to twin sons. This, as a rare event, causing joy even in humble homes, so delighted the emperor that he did not refrain from boasting before the senators that to no Roman of the same rank had twin offspring ever before been born. In fact, he would turn to his own glory every incident, however casual. But at such a time, even this brought grief to the people, who thought that the increase of Drusus's family still further depressed the house of Germanicus.

That same year the profligacy of women was checked by stringent enactments, and it was provided that no woman whose grandfather, father, or husband had been a Roman knight should get money by prostitution. Vistilia, born of a praetorian family, had actually published her name with this object on the aedile's list, according to a recognised custom of our ancestors, who considered it a sufficient punishment on unchaste women to have to profess their shame. Titidius Labeo, Vistilia's husband, was judicially called on to say why with a wife whose guilt was manifest he had neglected to inflict the legal penalty. When he pleaded that the sixty days given for deliberation had not yet expired, it was thought sufficient to decide Vistilia's case, and she was banished out of sight to the island of Seriphos.

There was a debate too about expelling the Egyptian and Jewish worship, and a resolution of the Senate was passed that four thousand of the freedmen class who were infected with those superstitions and were of military age should be transported to the island of Sardinia, to quell the brigandage of the place, a cheap sacrifice should they die from the pestilential climate. The rest were to quit Italy, unless before a certain day they repudiated their impious rites.

Next the emperor brought forward a motion for the election of a Vestal virgin in the room of Occia, who for fifty-seven years had presided with the most immaculate virtue over the Vestal worship. He formally thanked Fonteius Agrippa and Domitius Pollio for offering their daughters and so vying with one another in zeal for the commonwealth. Pollio's daughter was preferred, only because her mother had lived with one and the same husband, while Agrippa had impaired the honour of his house by a divorce. The emperor consoled his daughter, passed over though she was, with a dowry of a million sesterces.

As the city populace complained of the cruel dearness of corn, he fixed a price for grain to be paid by the purchaser, promising himself to add two sesterces on every peck for the traders. But he would not therefore accept the title of "father of the country" which once before too had been offered him, and he sharply rebuked those who called his work "divine" and himself "lord." Consequently, speech was restricted and perilous under an emperor who feared freedom while he hated sycophancy.

I find it stated by some writers and senators of the period that a letter from Adgandestrius, chief of the Chatti, was read in the Senate, promising the death of Arminius, if poison were sent for the perpetration of the murder, and that the reply was that it was not by secret treachery but openly and by arms that the people of Rome avenged themselves on their enemies. A noble answer, by which Tiberius sought to liken himself to those generals of old who had forbidden and even denounced the poisoning of king Pyrrhus.

Arminius, meanwhile, when the Romans retired and Maroboduus was expelled, found himself opposed in aiming at the throne by his countrymen's independent spirit. He was assailed by armed force, and while fighting with various success, fell by the treachery of his kinsmen. Assuredly he was the deliverer of Germany, one too who had defied Rome, not in her early rise, as other kings and generals, but in the height of her empire's glory, had fought, indeed, indecisive battles, yet in war remained unconquered. He completed thirty-seven years of life, twelve years of power, and he is still a theme of song among barbarous nations, though to Greek historians, who admire only their own achievements, he is unknown, and to Romans not as famous as he should be, while we extol the past and are indifferent to our own times.

BOOK III, A.D. 20-22

Without pausing in her winter voyage Agrippina arrived at the island of Corcyra, facing the shores of Calabria. There she spent a few days to compose her mind, for she was wild with grief and knew not how to endure. Meanwhile on hearing of her arrival, all her intimate friends and several officers, every one indeed who had served under Germanicus, many strangers too from the neighbouring towns, some thinking it respectful to the emperor, and still more following their example, thronged eagerly to Brundisium, the nearest and safest landing place for a voyager.

As soon as the fleet was seen on the horizon, not only the harbour and the adjacent shores, but the city walls too and the roofs and every place which commanded the most distant prospect were filled with crowds of mourners, who incessantly asked one another, whether, when she landed, they were to receive her in silence or with some utterance of emotion. They were not agreed on what befitted the occasion when the fleet slowly approached, its crew, not joyous as is usual, but wearing all a studied expression of grief. When Agrippina descended from the vessel with her two children, clasping the funeral urn, with eyes riveted to the earth, there was one universal groan. You could not distinguish kinsfolk from strangers, or the laments of men from those of women; only the attendants of Agrippina, worn out as they were by long sorrow, were surpassed by the mourners who now met them, fresh in their grief.

The emperor had despatched two praetorian cohorts with instructions that the magistrates of Calabria, Apulia, and Campania were to pay the last honours to his son's memory. Accordingly tribunes and centurions bore Germanicus's ashes on their shoulders. They were preceded by the standards unadorned and the faces reversed. As they passed colony after colony, the populace in black, the knights in their state robes, burnt vestments and perfumes with other usual funeral adjuncts, in proportion to the wealth of the place. Even those whose towns were out of the route, met the mourners, offered victims and built altars to the dead, testifying their grief by tears and wailings. Drusus went as far as Tarracina with Claudius, brother of Germanicus, and had been at Rome. Marcus Valerius and Caius Aurelius, the consuls, who had already entered on office, and a great number of the people thronged the road in scattered groups, every one weeping as he felt inclined. Flattery there was none, for all knew that Tiberius could scarcely dissemble his joy at the death of Germanicus.

Tiberius Augusta refrained from showing themselves, thinking it below their dignity to shed tears in public, or else fearing that, if all eyes scrutinised their faces, their hypocrisy would be revealed. I do not find in any historian or in the daily register that Antonia, Germanicus's mother, rendered any conspicuous honour to the deceased, though besides Agrippina, Drusus, and Claudius, all his other kinsfolk are mentioned by name. She may either have been hindered by illness, or with a spirit overpowered by grief she may not have had the heart to endure the sight of so great an affliction. But I can more easily believe that Tiberius and Augusta, who did not leave the palace, kept her within, that their sorrow might seem equal to hers, and that the grandmother and uncle might be thought to follow the mother's example in staying at home.

The day on which the remains were consigned to the tomb of Augustus, was now desolate in its silence, now distracted by lamentations. The streets of the city were crowded; torches were blazing throughout the Campus Martius. There the soldiers under arms, the magistrates without their symbols of office, the people in the tribes, were all incessantly exclaiming that the commonwealth was ruined, that not a hope remained, too boldly and openly to let one think that they remembered their rulers. But nothing impressed Tiberius more deeply than the enthusiasm kindled in favor of Agrippina, whom men spoke of as the glory of the country, the sole surviving off spring of Augustus, the solitary example of the old times, while looking up to heaven and the gods they prayed for the safety of her children and that they might outlive their oppressors.

Some there were who missed the grandeur of a state-funeral, and contrasted the splendid honours conferred by Augustus on Drusus, the father of Germanicus. "Then the emperor himself," they said, "went in the extreme rigour of winter as far as Ticinum, and never leaving the corpse entered Rome with it. Round the funeral bier were ranged the images of the Claudii and the Julii; there was weeping in the forum, and a panegyric before the rostra; every honour devised by our ancestors or invented by their descendants was heaped on him. But as for Germanicus, even the customary distinctions due to any noble had not fallen to his lot. Granting that his body, because of the distance of tie journey, was burnt in any fashion in foreign lands, still all the more honours ought to have been afterwards paid him, because at first chance had denied them. His brother had gone but one day's journey to meet him; his uncle, not even to the city gates. Where were all those usages of the past, the image at the head of the bier, the lays composed in commemoration of worth, the eulogies and laments, or at least the semblance of grief?"

All this was known to Tiberius, and, to silence popular talk, he reminded the people in a proclamation that many eminent Romans had died for their country and that none had been honoured with such passionate regret. This regret was a glory both to himself and to all, provided only a due mean were observed; for what was becoming in humble homes and communities, did not befit princely personages and an imperial people. Tears and the solace found in mourning were suitable enough for the first burst of grief; but now they must brace their hearts to endurance, as in former days the Divine Julius after the loss of his only daughter, and the Divine Augustus when he was bereft of his grandchildren, had thrust away their sorrow. There was no need of examples from the past, showing how often the Roman people had patiently endured the defeats of armies, the destruction of generals, the total extinction of noble families. Princes were mortal; the State was everlasting. Let them then return to their usual pursuits, and, as the shows of the festival of the Great Goddess were at hand, even resume their amusements.

The suspension of business then ceased, and men went back to their occupations. Drusus was sent to the armies of Illyricum, amidst an universal eagerness to exact vengeance on Piso, and ceaseless complaints that he was meantime roaming through the delightful regions of Asia and Achaia, and was weakening the proofs of his guilt by an insolent and artful procrastination. It was indeed widely rumoured that the notorius poisoner Martina, who, as I have related, had been despatched to Rome by Cneius Sentius, had died suddenly at Brundisium; that poison was concealed in a knot of her hair, and that no symptoms of suicide were discovered on her person.

Piso meanwhile sent his son on to Rome with a message intended to pacify the emperor, and then made his way to Drusus, who would, he hoped, be not so much infuriated at his brother's death as kindly disposed towards himself in consequence of a rival's removal. Tiberius, to show his impartiality, received the youth courteously, and enriched him with the liberality he usually bestowed on the sons of noble families. Drusus replied to Piso that if certain insinuations were true, he must be foremost in his resentment, but he preferred to believe that they were false and groundless, and that Germanicus's death need be the ruin of no one. This he said openly, avoiding anything like secrecy. Men did not doubt that his answer prescribed him by Tiberius, inasmuch as one who had generally all the simplicity and candour of youth, now had recourse to the artifices of old age.

Piso, after crossing the Dalmatian sea and leaving his ships at Ancona, went through Picenum and along the Flaminian road, where he overtook a legion which was marching from Pannonia to Rome and was then to garrison Africa. It was a matter of common talk how he had repeatedly displayed himself to the soldiers on the road during the march. From Narnia, to avoid suspicion or because the plans of fear are uncertain, he sailed down the Nar, then down the Tiber, and increased the fury of the populace by bringing his vessel to shore at the tomb of the Caesars. In broad daylight, when the river-bank was thronged, he himself with a numerous following of dependents, and Plancina with a retinue of women, moved onward with joy in their countenances. Among other things which provoked men's anger was his house towering above the forum, gay with festal decorations, his banquets and his feasts, about which there was no secrecy, because the place was so public.

Next day, Fulcinius Trio asked the consul's leave to prosecute Piso. It was contended against him by Vitellius and Veranius and the others who had been the companions of Germanicus, that this was not Trio's proper part, and that they themselves meant to report their instructions from Germanicus, not as accusers, but as deponents and witnesses to facts. Trio, abandoning the prosecution on this count, obtained leave to accuse Piso's previous career, and the emperor was requested to undertake the inquiry. This even the accused did not refuse, fearing, as he did, the bias of the people and of the Senate; while Tiberius, he knew, was resolute enough to despise report, and was also entangled in his mother's complicity. Truth too would be more easily distinguished from perverse misrepresentation by a single judge, where a number would be swayed by hatred and ill-will.

Tiberius was not unaware of the formidable difficulty of the inquiry and of the rumours by which he was himself assailed. Having therefore summoned a few intimate friends, he listened to the threatening speeches of the prosecutors and to the pleadings of the accused, and finally referred the whole case to the Senate.

Drusus meanwhile, on his return from Illyricum, though the Senate had voted him an ovation for the submission of Maroboduus and the successes of the previous summer, postponed the honour and entered Rome. Then the defendant sought the advocacy of Lucius Arruntius, Marcus Vinicius, Asinius Gallus, Aeserninus Marcellus and Sextus

Pompeius, and on their declining for different reasons, Marcus Lepidus, Lucius Piso, and Livineius Regulus became his counsel, amid the excitement of the whole country, which wondered how much fidelity would be shown by the friends of Germanicus, on what the accused rested his hopes, and how far Tiberius would repress and hide his feelings. Never were the people more keenly interested; never did they indulge themselves more freely in secret whispers against the emperor or in the silence of suspicion.

On the day the Senate met, Tiberius delivered a speech of studied moderation. "Piso," he said, "was my father's representative and friend, and was appointed by myself, on the advice of the Senate, to assist Germanicus in the administration of the East. Whether he there had provoked the young prince by wilful opposition and rivalry, and had rejoiced at his death or wickedly destroyed him, is for you to determine with minds unbiassed. Certainly if a subordinate oversteps the bounds of duty and of obedience to his commander, and has exulted in his death and in my affliction, I shall hate him and exclude him from my house, and I shall avenge a personal quarrel without resorting to my power as emperor. If however a crime is discovered which ought to be punished, whoever the murdered man may be, it is for you to give just reparation both to the children of Germanicus and to us, his parents.

"Consider this too, whether Piso dealt with the armies in a revolutionary and seditious spirit; whether he sought by intrigue popularity with the soldiers; whether he attempted to repossess himself of the province by arms, or whether these are falsehoods which his accusers have published with exaggeration. As for them, I am justly angry with their intemperate zeal. For to what purpose did they strip the corpse and expose it to the pollution of the vulgar gaze, and circulate a story among foreigners that he was destroyed by poison, if all this is still doubtful and requires investigation? For my part, I sorrow for my son and shall always sorrow for him; still I would not hinder the accused from producing all the evidence which can relieve his innocence or convict Germanicus of any unfairness, if such there was. And I implore you not to take as proven charges alleged, merely because the case is intimately bound up with my affliction. Do you, whom ties of blood or your own true-heartedness have made his advocates, help him in his peril, every one of you, as far as each man's eloquence and diligence can do so. To like exertions and like persistency I would urge the prosecutors. In this, and in this only, will we place Germanicus above the laws, by conducting the inquiry into his death in this house instead of in the forum, and before the Senate instead of before a bench of judges. In all else let the case be tried as simply as others. Let no one heed the tears of Drusus or my own sorrow, or any stories invented to our discredit."

Two days were then assigned for the bringing forward of the charges, and after six days' interval, the prisoner's defence was to occupy three days. Thereupon Fulcinius Trio began with some old and irrelevant accusations about intrigues and extortion during Piso's government of Spain. This, if proved, would not have been fatal to the defendant, if he cleared himself as to his late conduct, and, if refuted, would not have secured his acquittal, if he were convicted of the greater crimes. Next, Servaeus, Veranius, and Vitellius, all with equal earnestness, Vitellius with striking eloquence, alleged against Piso that out of hatred of Germanicus and a desire of revolution he had so corrupted the common soldiers by licence and oppression of the allies that he was called by the vilest of them "father of the legions" while on the other hand to all the best men, especially to the companions and friends of Germanicus, he had been savagely cruel. Lastly, he had, they said, destroyed Germanicus himself by sorceries and poison, and hence came those ceremonies and horrible sacrifices made by himself and Plancina; then he had threatened the State with war, and had been defeated in battle, before he could be tried as a prisoner.

On all points but one the defence broke down. That he had tampered with the soldiers, that his province had been at the mercy of the vilest of them, that he had even insulted his chief, he could not deny. It was only the charge of poisoning from which he seemed to have cleared himself. This indeed the prosecutors did not adequately sustain by merely alleging that at a banquet given by Germanicus, his food had been tainted with poison by the hands of Piso who sat next above him. It seemed absurd to suppose that he would have dared such an attempt among strange servants, in the sight of so many bystanders, and under Germanicus's own eyes. And, besides, the defendant offered his slaves to the torture, and insisted on its application to the attendants on that occasion. But the judges for different reasons were merciless, the emperor, because war had been made on a province, the Senate because they could not be sufficiently convinced that there had been no treachery about the death of Germanicus.

At the same time shouts were heard from the people in front of the Senate House, threatening violence if he escaped the verdict of the Senators. They had actually dragged Piso's statues to the Gemonian stairs, and were breaking them in pieces, when by the emperor's order they were rescued and replaced. Piso was then put in a litter and attended by a tribune of one of the Praetorian cohorts, who followed him, so it was variously rumoured, to guard his person or to be his executioner.

Plancina was equally detested, but had stronger interest. Consequently it was considered a question how far the emperor would be allowed to go against her. While Piso's hopes were in suspense, she offered to share his lot, whatever it might be, and in the worst event, to be his companion in death. But as soon as she had secured her pardon through the secret intercessions of Augusta, she gradually withdrew from her husband and separated her defence from his. When the prisoner saw that this was fatal to him, he hesitated whether he should still persist, but at the urgent request of his sons braced his courage and once more entered the Senate. There he bore patiently the renewal of the accusation, the furious voices of the Senators, savage opposition indeed from every quarter, but nothing daunted him so much as to see Tiberius, without pity and without anger, resolutely closing himself against any inroad of emotion. He was conveyed back to his house, where, seemingly by way of preparing his defence for the next day, he wrote a few words, sealed the paper and handed it to a freedman. Then he bestowed the usual attention on his person; after a while, late at night, his wife having left his chamber, he ordered the doors to be closed, and at daybreak was found with his throat cut and a sword lying on the ground.

I remember to have heard old men say that a document was often seen in Piso's hands, the substance of which he never himself divulged, but which his friends repeatedly declared contained a letter from Tiberius with instructions referring to Germanicus, and that it was his intention to produce it before the Senate and upbraid the emperor, had he not been deluded by vain promises from Sejanus. Nor did he perish, they said, by his own hand, but by that of one sent to be his executioner. Neither of these statements would I positively affirm; still it would not have been right for me to conceal what was related by those who lived up to the time of my youth.

The emperor, assuming an air of sadness, complained in the Senate that the purpose of such a death was to bring odium on himself, and he asked with repeated questionings how Piso had spent his last day and night. Receiving answers which were mostly judicious, though in part somewhat incautious, he read out a note written by Piso, nearly to the following effect:—

"Crushed by a conspiracy of my foes and the odium excited by a lying charge, since my truth and innocence find no place here, I call the immortal gods to witness that towards you Caesar, I have lived loyally, and with like dutiful respect towards your mother. And I implore you to think of my children, one of whom, Cneius is in way implicated in my career, whatever it may have been, seeing that all this time he has been at Rome, while the other, Marcus Piso, dissuaded me from returning to Syria. Would that I had yielded to my young son rather than he to his aged father! And therefore I pray the more earnestly that the innocent may not pay the penalty of my wickedness. By forty-five years of obedience, by my association with you in the consulate, as one who formerly won the esteem of the Divine Augustus, your father, as one who is your friend and will never hereafter ask a favour, I implore you to save my unhappy son." About Plancina he added not a word.

Tiberius after this acquitted the young Piso of the charge of civil war on the ground that a son could not have refused a father's orders, compassionating at the same time the high rank of the family and the terrible downfall even of Piso himself, however he might have deserved it. For Plancina he spoke with shame and conscious disgrace, alleging in excuse the intercession of his mother, secret complaints against whom from all good men were growing more and more vehement. "So it was the duty of a grandmother," people said, "to look a grandson's murderess in the face, to converse with her and rescue her from the Senate. What the laws secure on behalf of every citizen, had to Germanicus alone been denied. The voices of a Vitellius and Veranius had bewailed a Caesar, while the emperor and Augusta had defended Plancina. She might as well now turn her poisonings, and her devices which had proved so successful, against Agrippina and her children, and thus sate this exemplary grandmother and uncle with the blood of a most unhappy house."

Two days were frittered away over this mockery of a trial, Tiberius urging Piso's children to defend their mother. While the accusers and their witnesses pressed the prosecution with rival zeal, and there was no reply, pity rather than anger was on the increase. Aurelius Cotta, the consul, who was first called on for his vote (for when the emperor put the question, even those in office went through the duty of voting), held that Piso's name ought to be erased from the public register, half of his property confiscated, half given up to his son, Cneius Piso, who was to change his first name; that Marcus Piso, stript of his rank, with an allowance of five million sesterces, should be banished for ten years, Plancina's life being spared in consideration of Augusta's intercession.

Much of the sentence was mitigated by the emperor. The name of Piso was not to be struck out of the public register, since that of Marcus Antonius who had made war on his country, and that of Julius Antonius who had dishonoured the house of Augustus, still remained. Marcus Piso too he saved from degradation, and gave him his father's property, for he was firm enough, as I have often related, against the temptation of money, and now for very shame at Plancina's acquittal, he was more than usually merciful. Again, when Valerius Messalinus and Caecina Severus proposed respectively the erection of a golden statue in the temple of Mars the Avenger and of an altar to Vengeance, he interposed, protesting that victories over the foreigner were commemorated with such monuments, but that domestic woes ought to be shrouded in silent grief.

There was a further proposal of Messalinus, that Tiberius, Augusta, Antonia, Agrippina and Drusus ought to be publicly thanked for having avenged Germanicus. He omitted all mention of Claudius. Thereupon he was pointedly asked by Lucius Asprenas before the Senate, whether the omission had been intentional, and it was only then that the name of Claudius was added. For my part, the wider the scope of my reflection on the present and the past, the more am I impressed by their mockery of human plans in every transaction. Clearly, the very last man marked out for empire by public opinion, expectation and general respect was he whom fortune was holding in reserve as the emperor of the future.

A few days afterwards the emperor proposed to the Senate to confer the priesthood on Vitellius, Veranius and Servaeus. To Fulcinius he promised his support in seeking promotion, but warned him not to ruin his eloquence by rancour. This was the end of avenging the death of Germanicus, a subject of conflicting rumours not only among the people then living but also in after times. So obscure are the greatest events, as some take for granted any hearsay, whatever its source, others turn truth into falsehood, and both errors find encouragement with posterity.

Drusus meanwhile quitted Rome to resume his command and soon afterwards re-entered the city with an ovation. In the course of a few days his mother Vipsania died, the only one of all Agrippa's children whose death was without violence. As for the rest, they perished, some it is certain by the sword, others it was believed by poison or starvation.

That same year Tacfarinas who had been defeated, as I have related, by Camillus in the previous summer, renewed hostilities in Africa, first by mere desultory raids, so swift as to be unpunished; next, by destroying villages and carrying off plunder wholesale. Finally, he hemmed in a Roman cohort near the river Pagyda. The position was commanded by Decrius, a soldier energetic in action and experienced in war, who regarded the siege as a disgrace. Cheering on his men to offer battle in the open plain, he drew up his line in front of his intrenchments. At the first shock, the cohort was driven back, upon which he threw himself fearlessly amid the missiles in the path of the fugitives and cried shame on the standard-bearers for letting Roman soldiers show their backs to a rabble of deserters. At the same moment he was covered with wounds, and though pierced through the eye, he resolutely faced the enemy and ceased not to fight till he fell deserted by his men.

On receiving this information, Lucius Apronius, successor to Camillus, alarmed more by the dishonour of his own men than by the glory of the enemy, ventured on a deed quite exceptional at that time and derived from old tradition. He flogged to death every tenth man drawn by lot from the disgraced cohort. So beneficial was this rigour that a detachment of veterans, numbering not more than five hundred, routed those same troops of Tacfarinas on their attacking a fortress named Thala. In this engagement Rufus Helvius, a common soldier, won the honour of saving a citizen's life, and was rewarded by Apronius with a neck-chain and a spear. To these the emperor added the civic crown, complaining, but without anger, that Apronius had not used his right as proconsul to bestow this further distinction.

Tacfarinas, however, finding that the Numidians were cowed and had a horror of siege-operations, pursued a desultory warfare, retreating when he was pressed, and then again hanging on his enemy's rear. While the barbarian continued these tactics, he could safely insult the baffled and exhausted Romans. But when he marched away towards the coast and, hampered with booty, fixed himself in a regular camp, Caesianus was despatched by his father Apronius with some cavalry and auxiliary infantry, reinforced by the most active of the legionaries, and, after a successful battle with the Numidians, drove them into the desert.

At Rome meanwhile Lepida, who beside the glory of being one of the Aemilii was the great-granddaughter of Lucius Sulla and Cneius Pompeius, was accused of pretending to be a mother by Publius Quirinus, a rich and childless man. Then, too, there were charges of adulteries, of poisonings, and of inquiries made through astrologers concerning the imperial house. The accused was defended by her brother Manius Lepidus. Quirinus by his relentless enmity even after his divorce, had procured for her some sympathy, infamous and guilty as she was. One could not easily perceive the emperor's feelings at her trial; so effectually did he interchange and blend the outward signs of resentment and compassion. He first begged the Senate not to deal with the charges of treason, and subsequently induced Marcus Servilius, an ex-consul, to divulge what he had seemingly wished to suppress. He also handed over to the consuls Lepida's slaves, who were in military custody, but would not allow them to be examined by torture on matters referring to his own family. Drusus too, the consul-elect, he released from the necessity of having to speak first to the question. Some thought this a gracious act, done to save the rest of the Senators from a compulsory assent, while others ascribed it to malignity, on the ground that he would have yielded only where there was a necessity of condemning.

On the days of the games which interrupted the trial, Lepida went into the theatre with some ladies of rank, and as she appealed with piteous wailings to her ancestors and to that very Pompey, the public buildings and statues of whom stood there before their eyes, she roused such sympathy that people burst into tears and shouted, without ceasing, savage curses on Quirinus, "to whose childless old-age and miserably obscure family, one once destined to be the wife of Lucius Caesar and the daughter-in-law of the Divine Augustus was being sacrificed." Then, by the torture of the slaves, her infamies were brought to light, and a motion of Rubellius Blandus was carried which outlawed her. Drusus supported him, though others had proposed a milder sentence. Subsequently, Scaurus, who had had daughter by her, obtained as a concession that her property should not be confiscated. Then at last Tiberius declared that he had himself too ascertained from the slaves of Publius Quirinus that Lepida had attempted their master's life by poison.

It was some compensation for the misfortunes of great houses (for within a short interval the Calpurnii had lost Piso and the Aemilii Lepida) that Decimus Silanus was now restored to the Junian family. I will briefly relate his downfall.

Though the Divine Augustus in his public life enjoyed unshaken prosperity, he was unfortunate at home from the profligacy of his daughter and granddaughter, both of whom he banished from Rome, and punished their paramours with death or exile. Calling, as he did, a vice so habitual among men and women by the awful name of sacrilege and treason, he went far beyond the indulgent spirit of our ancestors, beyond indeed his own legislation. But I will relate the deaths of others with the remaining events of that time, if after finishing the work I have now proposed to myself, I prolong my life for further labours.

Decimus Silanus, the paramour of the granddaughter of Augustus, though the only severity he experienced was exclusion from the emperor's friendship, saw clearly that it meant exile; and it was not till Tiberius's reign that he ventured to appeal to the Senate and to the prince, in reliance on the influence of his brother Marcus Silanus, who was conspicuous both for his distinguished rank and eloquence. But Tiberius, when Silanus thanked him, replied in the Senate's presence, "that he too rejoiced at the brother's return from his long foreign tour, and that this was justly allowable, inasmuch as he had been banished not by a decree of the Senate or under any law. Still, personally," he said, "he felt towards him his father's resentment in all its force, and the return of Silanus had not cancelled the intentions of Augustus." Silanus after this lived at Rome without attaining office.

It was next proposed to relax the Papia Poppaea law, which Augustus in his old age had passed subsequently to the Julian statutes, for yet further enforcing the penalties on celibacy and for enriching the exchequer. And yet, marriages and the rearing of children did not become more frequent, so powerful were the attractions of a childless state. Meanwhile there was an increase in the number of persons imperilled, for every household was undermined by the insinuations of informers; and now the country suffered from its laws, as it had hitherto suffered from its vices. This suggests to me a fuller discussion of the origin of law and of the methods by which we have arrived at the present endless multiplicity and variety of our statutes.

Mankind in the earliest age lived for a time without a single vicious impulse, without shame or guilt, and, consequently, without punishment and restraints. Rewards were not needed when everything right was pursued on its own merits; and as men desired nothing against morality, they were debarred from nothing by fear. When however they began to throw off equality, and ambition and violence usurped the place of self-control and modesty, despotisms grew up and became perpetual among many nations. Some from the beginning, or when tired of kings, preferred codes of laws. These were at first simple, while men's minds were unsophisticated. The most famous of them were those of the Cretans, framed by Minos; those of the Spartans, by Lycurgus, and, subsequently, those which Solan drew up for the Athenians on a more elaborate and extensive scale. Romulus governed us as he pleased; then Numa united our people by religious ties and a constitution of divine origin, to which some additions were made by Tullus and Ancus. But Servius Tullius was our chief legislator, to whose laws even kings were to be subject.

After Tarquin's expulsion, the people, to check cabals among the Senators, devised many safeguards for freedom and for the establishment of unity. Decemvirs were appointed; everything specially admirable elsewhere was adopted, and the Twelve Tables drawn up, the last specimen of equitable legislation. For subsequent enactments, though occasionally directed against evildoers for some crime, were oftener carried by violence amid class dissensions, with a view to obtain honours not as yet conceded, or to banish distinguished citizens, or for other base ends. Hence the Gracchi and Saturnini, those popular agitators, and Drusus too, as flagrant a corrupter in the Senate's name; hence, the bribing of our allies by alluring promises and the cheating them by tribunes vetoes. Even the Italian and then the Civil war did not pass without the enactment of many conflicting laws, till Lucius Sulla, the Dictator, by the repeal or alteration of past legislation and by many additions, gave us a brief lull in this process, to be instantly followed by the seditious proposals of Lepidus, and soon afterwards by the tribunes recovering their license to excite the people just as they chose. And now bills were passed, not only for national objects but for individual cases, and laws were most numerous when the commonwealth was most corrupt.

Cneius Pompeius was then for the third time elected consul to reform public morals, but in applying remedies more terrible than the evils and repealing the legislation of which he had himself been the author, he lost by arms what by arms he had been maintaining. Then followed twenty years of continuous strife; custom or law there was none; the vilest deeds went unpunished, while many noble acts brought ruin. At last, in his sixth consulship, Caesar Augustus, feeling his power secure, annulled the decrees of his triumvirate, and gave us a constitution which might serve us in peace under a monarchy. Henceforth our chains became more galling, and spies were set over us, stimulated by rewards under the Papia Poppaea law, so that if men shrank from the privileges of fatherhood, the State, as universal parent, might possess their ownerless properties. But this espionage became too searching, and Rome and Italy and Roman citizens everywhere fell into its clutches. Many men's fortunes were ruined, and over all there hung a terror till Tiberius, to provide a remedy, selected by lot five ex-consuls, five ex-praetors, and five senators, by whom most of the legal knots were disentangled and some light temporary relief afforded.

About this same time he commended to the Senate's favour, Nero, Germanicus's son, who was just entering on manhood, and asked them, not without smiles of ridicule from his audience, to exempt him from serving as one of the Twenty Commissioners, and let him be a candidate for quaestorship five years earlier than the law allowed. His excuse was that a similar decree had been made for himself and his brother at the request of Augustus. But I cannot doubt that even then there were some who secretly laughed at such a petition, though the Caesars were but in the beginning of their grandeur, and ancient usage was more constantly before men's eyes, while also the tie between stepfather and stepson was weaker than that between grandfather and grandchild. The pontificate was likewise conferred on Nero, and on the day on which he first entered the forum, a gratuity was given to the city-populace, who greatly rejoiced at seeing a son of Germanicus now grown to manhood. Their joy was further increased by Nero's marriage to Julia, Drusus's daughter. This news was met with favourable comments, but it was heard with disgust that Sejanus was to be the father-in-law of the son of Claudius. The emperor was thought to have polluted the nobility of his house and to have yet further elevated Sejanus, whom they already suspected of overweening ambition.

Two remarkable men died at the end of the year, Lucius Volusius and Sallustius Crispus. Volusius was of an old family, which had however never risen beyond the praetorship. He brought into it the consulship; he also held the office of censor for arranging the classes of the knights, and was the first to pile up the wealth which that house enjoyed to a boundless extent.

Crispus was of equestrian descent and grandson of a sister of Caius Sallustius, that most admirable Roman historian, by whom he was adopted and whose name he took. Though his road to preferment was easy, he chose to emulate Maecenas, and without rising to a senator's rank, he surpassed in power many who had won triumphs and consulships. He was a contrast to the manners of antiquity in his elegance and refinement, and in the sumptuousness of his wealth he was almost a voluptuary. But beneath all this was a vigorous mind, equal to the greatest labours, the more active in proportion as he made a show of sloth and apathy. And so while Maecenas lived, he stood next in favour to him, and was afterwards the chief depository of imperial secrets, and accessory to the murder of Postumus Agrippa, till in advanced age he retained the shadow rather than the substance of the emperor's friendship. The same too had happened to Maecenas, so rarely is it the destiny of power to be lasting, or perhaps a sense of weariness steals over princes when they have bestowed everything, or over favourites, when there is nothing left them to desire.

Next followed Tiberius's fourth, Drusus's second consulship, memorable from the fact that father and son were colleagues. Two years previously the association of Germanicus and Tiberius in the same honour had not been agreeable to the uncle, nor had it the link of so close a natural tie.

At the beginning of this year Tiberius, avowedly to recruit his health, retired to Campania, either as a gradual preparation for long and uninterrupted seclusion, or in order that Drusus alone in his father's absence might discharge the duties of the consulship. It happened that a mere trifle which grew into a sharp contest gave the young prince the means of acquiring popularity. Domitius Corbulo, an ex-praetor, complained to the Senate that Lucius Sulla, a young noble, had not given place to him at a gladiatorial show. Corbulo had age, national usage and the feelings of the older senators in his favour. Against him Mamercus Scaurus, Lucius Arruntius and other kinsmen of Sulla strenuously exerted themselves. There was a keen debate, and appeal was made to the precedents of our ancestors, as having censured in severe decrees disrespect on the part of the young, till Drusus argued in a strain calculated to calm their feelings. Corbulo too received an apology from Mamercus, who was Sulla's uncle and stepfather, and the most fluent speaker of that day.

It was this same Corbulo, who, after raising a cry that most of the roads in Italy were obstructed or impassable through the dishonesty of contractors and the negligence of officials, himself willingly undertook the complete management of the business. This proved not so beneficial to the State as ruinous to many persons, whose property and credit he mercilessly attacked by convictions and confiscations.

Soon afterwards Tiberius informed the Senate by letter that Africa was again disturbed by an incursion of Tacfarinas, and that they must use their judgment in choosing as proconsul an experienced soldier of vigorous constitution, who would be equal to the war. Sextus Pompeius caught at this opportunity of venting his hatred against Lepidus, whom he condemned as a poor-spirited and needy man, who was a disgrace to his ancestors, and therefore deserved to lose even his chance of the province of Asia. But the Senate were against him, for they thought Lepidus gentle rather than cowardly, and that his inherited poverty, with the high rank in which he had lived without a blot, ought to be considered a credit to instead of a reproach. And so he was sent to Asia, and with respect to Africa it was decided that the emperor should choose to whom it was to be assigned.

During this debate Severus Caecina proposed that no magistrate who had obtained a province should be accompanied by his wife. He began by recounting at length how harmoniously he had lived with his wife, who had borne him six children, and how in his own home he had observed what he was proposing for the public, by having kept her in Italy, though he had himself served forty campaigns in various provinces. "With good reason," he said, "had it been formerly decided that women were not to be taken among our allies or into foreign countries. A train of women involves delays through luxury in peace and through panic in war, and converts a Roman army on the march into the likeness of a barbarian progress. Not only is the sex feeble and unequal to hardship, but, when it has liberty, it is spiteful, intriguing and greedy of power. They show themselves off among the soldiers and have the centurions at their beck. Lately a woman had presided at the drill of the cohorts and the evolutions of the legions. You should yourselves bear in mind that, whenever men are accused of extortion, most of the charges are directed against the wives. It is to these that the vilest of the provincials instantly attach themselves; it is they who undertake and settle business; two persons receive homage when they appear; there are two centres of government, and the women's orders are the more despotic and intemperate. Formerly they were restrained by the Oppian and other laws; now, loosed from every bond, they rule our houses, our tribunals, even our armies."

A few heard this speech with approval, but the majority clamorously objected that there was no proper motion on the subject, and that Caecina was no fit censor on so grave an issue. Presently Valerius Messalinus, Messala's son, in whom the father's eloquence was reproduced, replied that much of the sternness of antiquity had been changed into a better and more genial system. "Rome," he said, "is not now, as formerly, beset with wars, nor are the provinces hostile. A few concessions are made to the wants of women, but such as are not even a burden to their husbands homes, much less to the allies. In all other respects man and wife share alike, and this arrangement involves no trouble in peace. War of course requires that men should be unincumbered, but when they return what worthier solace can they have after their hardships than a wife's society? But some wives have abandoned themselves to scheming and rapacity. Well; even among our magistrates, are not many subject to various passions? Still, that is not a reason for sending no one into a province. Husbands have often been corrupted by the vices of their wives. Are then all unmarried men blameless? The Oppian laws were formerly adopted to meet the political necessities of the time, and subsequently there was some remission and mitigation of them on grounds of expediency. It is idle to shelter our own weakness under other names; for it is the husband's fault if the wife transgresses propriety. Besides, it is wrong that because of the imbecility of one or two men, all husbands should be cut off from their partners in prosperity and adversity. And further, a sex naturally weak will be thus left to itself and be at the mercy of its own voluptuousness and the passions of others. Even with the husband's personal vigilance the marriage tie is scarcely preserved inviolate. What would happen were it for a number of years to be forgotten, just as in a divorce? You must not check vices abroad without remembering the scandals of the capital."

Drusus added a few words on his own experience as a husband. "Princes," he said, "must often visit the extremities of their empire. How often had the Divine Augustus travelled to West and to the East accompanied by Livia? He had himself gone to Illyricum and, should it be expedient, he would go to other countries, not always however with a contented mind, if he had to tear himself from a much loved wife, the mother of his many children."

Caecina's motion was thus defeated. At the Senate's next meeting came a letter from Tiberius, which indirectly censured them for throwing on the emperor every political care, and named Marcus Lepidus and Junius Blaesus, one of whom was to be chosen pro-consul of Africa. Both spoke on the subject, and Lepidus begged earnestly to be excused. He alleged ill-health, his children's tender age, his having a daughter to marry, and something more of which he said nothing, was well understood, the fact that Blaesus was uncle of Sejanus and so had very powerful interest. Blaesus replied with an affectation of refusal, but not with the same persistency, nor was he backed up by the acquiescence of flatterers.

Next was exposed an abuse, hitherto the subject of many a whispered complaint. The vilest wretches used a growing freedom in exciting insult and obloquy against respectable citizens, and escaped punishment by clasping some statue of the emperor. The very freedman or slave was often an actual terror to his patron or master whom he would menace by word and gesture. Accordingly Caius Cestius, a senator, argued that "though princes were like deities, yet even the gods listened only to righteous prayers from their suppliants, and that no one fled to the Capitol or any other temple in Rome to use it as an auxiliary in crime. There was an end and utter subversion of all law when, in the forum and on the threshold of the Senate House, Annia Rufilla, whom he had convicted of fraud before a judge, assailed him with insults and threats, while he did not himself dare to try legal proceedings, because he was confronted by her with the emperor's image." There rose other clamorous voices, with even more flagrant complaints, and all implored Drusus to inflict exemplary vengeance, till he ordered Rufilla to be summoned, and on her conviction to be confined in the common prison.

Considius Aequus too and Coelius Cursor, Roman knights, were punished on the emperor's proposal, by a decree of the Senate, for having attacked the praetor, Magius Caecilianus, with false charges of treason. Both these results were represented as an honour to Drusus. By moving in society at Rome, amid popular talk, his father's dark policy, it was thought, was mitigated. Even voluptuousness in one so young gave little offence. Better that he should incline that way, spend his days in architecture, his nights in banquets, than that he should live in solitude, cut off from every pleasure, and absorbed in a gloomy vigilance and mischievous schemes.

Tiberius indeed and the informers were never weary. Ancharius Priscus had prosecuted Caesius Cordus, proconsul of Crete, for extortion, adding a charge of treason, which then crowned all indictments. Antistius Vetus, one of the chief men of Macedonia, who had been acquitted of adultery, was recalled by the emperor himself, with a censure on the judges, to be tried for treason, as a seditious man who had been implicated in the designs of Rhescuporis, when that king after the murder of his brother Cotys had meditated war against us. The accused was accordingly outlawed, with the further sentence that he was to be confined in an island from which neither Macedonia nor Thrace were conveniently accessible.

As for Thrace, since the division of the kingdom between Rhoemetalces and the children of Cotys, who because of their tender age were under the guardianship of Trebellienus Rufus, it was divided against itself, from not being used to our rule, and blamed Rhoemetalces no less than Trebellienus for allowing the wrongs of his countrymen to go unpunished. The Coelaletae, Odrusae and Dii, powerful tribes, took up arms, under different leaders, all on a level from their obscurity. This hindered them from combining in a formidable war. Some roused their immediate neighbourhood; others crossed Mount Haemus, to stir up remote tribes; most of them, and the best disciplined, besieged the king in the city of Philippopolis, founded by the Macedonian Philip.

When this was known to Publius Vellaeus who commanded the nearest army, he sent some allied cavalry and light infantry to attack those who were roaming in quest of plunder or of reinforcements, while he marched in person with the main strength of the foot to raise the siege. Every operation was at the same moment successful; the pillagers were cut to pieces; dissensions broke out among the besiegers, and the king made a well-timed sally just as the legion arrived. A battle or even a skirmish it did not deserve to be called, in which merely half-armed stragglers were slaughtered without bloodshed on our side.

That same year, some states of Gaul, under the pressure of heavy debts, attempted a revolt. Its most active instigators were Julius Florus among the Treveri and Julius Sacrovir among the Aedui. Both could show noble birth and signal services rendered by ancestors, for which Roman citizenship had formerly been granted them, when the gift was rare and a recompense only of merit. In secret conferences to which the fiercest spirits were admitted, or any to whom poverty or the fear of guilt was an irresistible stimulus to crime, they arranged that Florus was to rouse the Belgae, Sacrovir the Gauls nearer home. These men accordingly talked sedition before small gatherings and popular assemblies about the perpetual tributes, the oppressive usury, the cruelty and arrogance of their governors, hinting too that there was disaffection among our soldiers, since they had heard of the murder of Germanicus. "It was," they said, "a grand opportunity for the recovery of freedom, if only they would contrast their own vigour with the exhaustion of Italy, the unwarlike character of the city populace, and the utter weakness of Rome's armies in all but their foreign element."

Scarcely a single community was untouched by the germs of this commotion. First however in actual revolt were the Andecavi and Turoni. Of these the former were put down by an officer, Acilius Aviola, who had summoned a cohort which was on garrison duty at Lugdunum. The Turoni were quelled by some legionary troops sent by Visellius Varro who commanded in Lower Germany, and led by the same Aviola and some Gallic chieftains who brought aid, in order that they might disguise their disaffection and exhibit it at a better opportunity. Sacrovir too was conspicuous, with head uncovered, cheering on his men to fight for Rome, to display, as he said, his valour. But the prisoners asserted that he sought recognition that he might not be a mark for missiles. Tiberius when consulted on the matter disdained the information, and fostered the war by his irresolution.

Florus meanwhile followed up his designs and tried to induce a squadron of cavalry levied among the Treveri, trained in our service and discipline, to begin hostilities by a massacre of the Roman traders. He corrupted a few of the men, but the majority were steadfast in their allegiance. A host however of debtors and dependents took up arms, and they were on their way to the forest passes known as the Arduenna, when they were stopped by legions which Visellius and Silius had sent from their respective armies, by opposite routes, to meet them. Julius Indus from the same state, who was at feud with Florus and therefore particularly eager to render us a service, was sent on in advance with a picked force, and dispersed the undisciplined rabble. Florus after eluding the conquerors by hiding himself in one place after another, at last when he saw some soldiers who had barred every possible escape, fell by his own hand. Such was the end of the rebellion of the Treveri.

A more formidable movement broke out among the Aedui, proportioned to the greater wealth of the state and the distance of the force which should repress it. Sacrovir with some armed cohorts had made himself master of Augustodunum, the capital of the tribe, with the noblest youth of Gaul, there devoting themselves to a liberal education, and with such hostages he proposed to unite in his cause their parents and kinsfolk. He also distributed among the youth arms which he had had secretly manufactured. There were forty thousand, one fifth armed like our legionaries; the rest had spears and knives and other weapons used in the chase. In addition were some slaves who were being trained for gladiators, clad after the national fashion in a complete covering of steel. They were called crupellarii, and though they were ill-adapted for inflicting wounds, they were impenetrable to them. This army was continually increased, not yet by any open combination of the neighbouring states, but by zealous individual enthusiasm, as well as by strife between the Roman generals, each of whom claimed the war for himself. Varro after a while, as he was infirm and aged, yielded to Silius who was in his prime.

At Rome meanwhile people said that it was not only the Treveri and Aedui who had revolted, but sixty-four states of Gaul with the Germans in alliance, while Spain too was disaffected; anything in fact was believed, with rumour's usual exaggeration. All good men were saddened by anxiety for the country, but many in their loathing of the present system and eagerness for change, rejoiced at their very perils and exclaimed against Tiberius for giving attention amid such political convulsions to the calumnies of informers. "Was Sacrovir too," they asked, "to be charged with treason before the Senate? We have at last found men to check those murderous missives by the sword. Even war is a good exchange for a miserable peace." Tiberius all the more studiously assumed an air of unconcern. He changed neither his residence nor his look, but kept up his usual demeanour during the whole time, either from the profoundness of his reserve; or was it that he had convinced himself that the events were unimportant and much more insignificant than the rumours represented?

Silius meantime was advancing with two legions, and having sent forward some auxiliary troops was ravaging those villages of the Sequani, which, situated on the border, adjoin the Aedui, and were associated with them in arms. He then pushed on by forced marches to Augustodunum, his standard-bearers vying in zeal, and even the privates loudly protesting against any halt for their usual rest or during the hours of night. "Only," they said, "let us have the foe face to face; that will be enough for victory." Twelve miles from Augustodunum they saw before them Sacrovir and his army in an open plain. His men in armour he had posted in the van, his light infantry on the wings, and the half-armed in the rear. He himself rode amid the foremost ranks on a splendid charger, reminding them of the ancient glories of the Gauls, of the disasters they had inflicted on the Romans, how grand would be the freedom of the victorious, how more intolerable than ever the slavery of a second conquest.

His words were brief and heard without exultation. For now the legions in battle array were advancing, and the rabble of townsfolk who knew nothing of war had their faculties of sight and hearing quite paralysed. Silius, on the one hand, though confident hope took away any need for encouragement, exclaimed again and again that it was a shame to the conquerors of Germany to have to be led against Gauls, as against an enemy. "Only the other day the rebel Turoni had been discomfited by a single cohort, the Treveri by one cavalry squadron, the Sequani by a few companies of this very army. Prove to these Aedui once for all that the more they abound in wealth and luxury, the more unwarlike are they, but spare them when they flee."

Then there was a deafening cheer; the cavalry threw itself on the flanks, and the infantry charged the van. On the wings there was but a brief resistance. The men in mail were somewhat of an obstacle, as the iron plates did not yield to javelins or swords; but our men, snatching up hatchets and pickaxes, hacked at their bodies and their armour as if they were battering a wall. Some beat down the unwieldy mass with pikes and forked poles, and they were left lying on the ground, without an effort to rise, like dead men. Sacrovir with his most trustworthy followers hurried first to Augustodunum and then, from fear of being surrendered, to an adjacent country house. There by his own hand he fell, and his comrades by mutually inflicted wounds. The house was fired over their heads, and with it they were all consumed.

Then at last Tiberius informed the Senate by letter of the beginning and completion of the war, without either taking away from or adding to the truth, but ascribing the success to the loyalty and courage of his generals, and to his own policy. He also gave the reasons why neither he himself nor Drusus had gone to the war; he magnified the greatness of the empire, and said it would be undignified for emperors, whenever there was a commotion in one or two states, to quit the capital, the centre of all government. Now, as he was not influenced by fear, he would go to examine and settle matters.

The Senate decreed vows for his safe return, with thanksgivings and other appropriate ceremonies. Cornelius Dolabella alone, in endeavouring to outdo the other Senators, went the length of a preposterous flattery by proposing that he should enter

Rome from Campania with an ovation. Thereupon came a letter from the emperor, declaring that he was not so destitute of renown as after having subdued the most savage nations and received or refused so many triumphs in his youth, to covet now that he was old an unmeaning honour for a tour in the neighbourhood of Rome.

About the same time he requested the Senate to let the death of Sulpicius Quirinus be celebrated with a public funeral. With the old patrician family of the Sulpicii this Quirinus, who was born in the town of Lanuvium, was quite unconnected. An indefatigable soldier, he had by his zealous services won the consulship under the Divine Augustus, and subsequently the honours of a triumph for having stormed some fortresses of the Homonadenses in Cilicia. He was also appointed adviser to Caius Caesar in the government of Armenia, and had likewise paid court to Tiberius, who was then at Rhodes. The emperor now made all this known to the Senate, and extolled the good offices of Quirinus to himself, while he censured Marcus Lollius, whom he charged with encouraging Caius Caesar in his perverse and quarrelsome behaviour. But people generally had no pleasure in the memory of Quirinus, because of the perils he had brought, as I have related, on Lepida, and the meanness and dangerous power of his last years.

At the close of the year, Caius Lutorius Priscus, a Roman knight, who, after writing a popular poem bewailing the death of Germanicus, had received a reward in money from the emperor, was fastened on by an informer, and charged with having composed another during the illness of Drusus, which, in the event of the prince's death, might be published with even greater profit to himself. He had in his vanity read it in the house of Publius Petronius before Vitellia, Petronius's mother-in-law, and several ladies of rank. As soon as the accuser appeared, all but Vitellia were frightened into giving evidence. She alone swore that she had heard not a word. But those who criminated him fatally were rather believed, and on the motion of Haterius Agrippa, the consul-elect, the last penalty was invoked on the accused.

Marcus Lepidus spoke against the sentence as follows:—"Senators, if we look to the single fact of the infamous utterance with which Lutorius has polluted his own mind and the ears of the public, neither dungeon nor halter nor tortures fit for a slave would be punishment enough for him. But though vice and wicked deeds have no limit, penalties and correctives are moderated by the clemency of the sovereign and by the precedents of your ancestors and yourselves. Folly differs from wickedness; evil words from evil deeds, and thus there is room for a sentence by which this offence may not go unpunished, while we shall have no cause to regret either leniency or severity. Often have I heard our emperor complain when any one has anticipated his mercy by a self-inflicted death. Lutorius's life is still safe; if spared, he will be no danger to the State; if put to death, he will be no warning to others. His productions are as empty and ephemeral as they are replete with folly. Nothing serious or alarming is to be apprehended from the man who is the betrayer of his own shame and works on the imaginations not of men but of silly women. However, let him leave Rome, lose his property, and be outlawed. That is my proposal, just as though he were convicted under the law of treason."

Only one of the ex-consuls, Rubellius Blandus, supported Lepidus. The rest voted with Agrippa. Priscus was dragged off to prison and instantly put to death. Of this Tiberius complained to the Senate with his usual ambiguity, extolling their loyalty in so sharply avenging the very slightest insults to the sovereign, though he deprecated such hasty punishment of mere words, praising Lepidus and not censuring Agrippa. So the Senate passed a resolution that their decrees should not be registered in the treasury till nine days had expired, and so much respite was to be given to condemned persons. Still the Senate had not liberty to alter their purpose, and lapse of time never softened Tiberius.

Caius Sulpicius and Didius Haterius were the next consuls. It was a year free from commotions abroad, while at home stringent legislation was apprehended against the luxury which had reached boundless excess in everything on which wealth is lavished. Some expenses, though very serious, were generally kept secret by a concealment of the real prices; but the costly preparations for gluttony and dissipation were the theme of incessant talk, and had suggested a fear that a prince who clung to old-fashioned frugality would be too stern in his reforms. In fact, when the aedile Caius Bibulus broached the topic, all his colleagues had pointed out that the sumptuary laws were disregarded, that prohibited prices for household articles were every day on the increase, and that moderate measures could not stop the evil.

The Senate on being consulted had, without handling the matter, referred it to the emperor. Tiberius, after long considering whether such reckless tastes could be repressed, whether the repression of them would not be still more hurtful to the State, also, how undignified it would be to meddle with what he could not succeed in, or what, if effected, would necessitate the disgrace and infamy of men of distinction, at last addressed a letter to the Senate to the following purport:—

Perhaps in any other matter, Senators, it would be more convenient that I should be consulted in your presence, and then state what I think to be for the public good. In this debate it was better that my eyes should not be on you, for while you were noting the anxious faces of individual senators charged with shameful luxury, I too myself might observe them and, as it were, detect them. Had those energetic men, our aediles, first taken counsel with me, I do not know whether I should not have advised them to let alone vices so strong and so matured, rather than merely attain the result of publishing what are the corruptions with which we cannot cope. They however have certainly done their duty, as I would wish all other officials likewise to fulfil their parts. For myself, it is neither seemly to keep silence nor is it easy to speak my mind, as I do not hold the office of aedile, praetor, or consul. Something greater and loftier is expected of a prince, and while everybody takes to himself the credit of right policy, one alone has to bear the odium of every person's failures. For what am I first to begin with restraining and cutting down to the old standard? The vast dimensions of country houses? The number of slaves of every nationality? The masses of silver and gold? The marvels in bronze and painting? The apparel worn indiscriminately by both sexes, or that peculiar luxury of women which, for the sake of jewels, diverts our wealth to strange or hostile nations?

I am not unaware that people at entertainments and social gatherings condemn all this and demand some restriction. But if a law were to be passed and a penalty imposed, those very same persons will cry out that the State is revolutionised, that ruin is plotted against all our most brilliant fashion, that not a citizen is safe from incrimination. Yet as even bodily disorders of long standing and growth can be checked only by sharp and painful treatment, so the fever of a diseased mind, itself polluted and a pollution to others, can be quenched only by remedies as strong as the passions which inflame it. Of the many laws devised by our ancestors, of the many passed by the Divine Augustus, the first have been forgotten, while his (all the more to our disgrace) have become obsolete through contempt, and this has made luxury bolder than ever. The truth is, that when one craves something not yet forbidden, there is a fear that it may be forbidden; but when people once transgress prohibitions with impunity, there is no longer any fear or any shame.

Why then in old times was economy in the ascendant? Because every one practised self-control; because we were all members of one city. Nor even afterwards had we the same temptations, while our dominion was confined to Italy. Victories over the foreigner taught us how to waste the substance of others; victories over ourselves, how to squander our own. What a paltry matter is this of which the aediles are reminding us! What a mere trifle if you look at everything else! No one represents to the Senate that Italy requires supplies from abroad, and that the very existence of the people of Rome is daily at the mercy of uncertain waves and storms. And unless masters, slaves, and estates have the resources of the provinces as their mainstay, our shrubberies, forsooth, and our country houses will have to support us.

Such, Senators, are the anxieties which the prince has to sustain, and the neglect of them will be utter ruin to the State. The cure for other evils must be sought in our own hearts. Let us be led to amendment, the poor by constraint, the rich by satiety. Or if any of our officials give promise of such energy and strictness as can stem the corruption, I praise the man, and I confess that I am relieved of a portion of my burdens. But if they wish to denounce vice, and when they have gained credit for so doing they arouse resentments and leave them to me, be assured, Senators, that I too am by no means eager to incur enmities, and though for the public good I encounter formidable and often unjust enmities, yet I have a right to decline such as are unmeaning and purposeless and will be of use neither to myself nor to you.

When they had heard the emperor's letter, the aediles were excused from so anxious a task, and that luxury of the table which from the close of the war ended at Actium to the armed revolution in which Servius Galba rose to empire, had been practised with profuse expenditure, gradually went out of fashion. It is as well that I should trace the causes of this change.

Formerly rich or highly distinguished noble families often sank into ruin from a passion for splendour. Even then men were still at liberty to court and be courted by the city populace, by our allies and by foreign princes, and every one who from his wealth, his mansion and his establishment was conspicuously grand, gained too proportionate lustre by his name and his numerous *clientèle*. After the savage massacres in which greatness of renown was fatal, the survivors turned to wiser ways. The new men who were often admitted into the Senate from the towns, colonies and even the provinces, introduced their household thrift, and though many of them by good luck or energy attained an old age of wealth, still their former tastes remained. But the chief encourager of strict manners was Vespasian, himself old-fashioned both in his dress and diet. Henceforth a respectful feeling towards the prince and a love of emulation proved more efficacious than legal penalties or terrors. Or possibly there is in all things a kind of cycle, and there may be moral revolutions just as there are changes of seasons. Nor was everything better in the past, but our own age too has produced many specimens of excellence and culture for posterity to imitate. May we still keep up with our ancestors a rivalry in all that is honourable!

Tiberius having gained credit for forbearance by the check he had given to the growing terror of the informers, wrote a letter to the Senate requesting the tribunitian power for Drusus. This was a phrase which Augustus devised as a designation of supremacy, so that without assuming the name of king or dictator he might have some title to mark his elevation above all other authority. He then chose Marcus Agrippa to be his associate in this power, and on Agrippa's death, Tiberius Nero, that there might be no uncertainty as to the succession. In this manner he thought to check the perverse ambition of others, while he had confidence in Nero's moderation and in his own greatness.

Following this precedent, Tiberius now placed Drusus next to the throne, though while Germanicus was alive he had maintained an impartial attitude towards the two princes. However in the beginning of his letter he implored heaven to prosper his plans on behalf of the State, and then added a few remarks, without falsehood or exaggeration, on the character of the young prince. He had, he reminded them, a wife and three children, and his age was the same as that at which he had himself been formerly summoned by the Divine Augustus to undertake this duty. Nor was it a precipitate step; it was only after an experience of eight years, after having quelled mutinies and settled wars, after a triumph and two consulships, that he was adopted as a partner in trials already familiar to him.

The senators had anticipated this message and hence their flattery was the more elaborate. But they could devise nothing but voting statues of the two princes, shrines to certain deities, temples, arches and the usual routine, except that Marcus Silanus sought to honour the princes by a slur on the consulate, and proposed that on all monuments, public or private, should be inscribed, to mark the date, the names, not of the consuls, but of those who were holding the tribunitian power. Quintus Haterius, when he brought forward a motion that the decrees passed that day should be set up in the Senate House in letters of gold, was laughed at as an old dotard, who would get nothing but infamy out of such utterly loathsome sycophancy.

Meantime Junius Blaesus received an extension of his government of Africa, and Servius Maluginensis, the priest of Jupiter, demanded to have Asia allotted to him. "It was," he asserted, "a popular error that it was not lawful for the priests of Jupiter to leave Italy; in fact, his own legal position differed not from that of the priests of Mars and of Quirinus. If these latter had provinces allotted to them, why was it forbidden to the priests of Jupiter? There were no resolutions of the people or anything to be found in the books of ceremonies on the subject. Pontiffs had often performed the rites to Jupiter when his priest was hindered by illness or by public duty. For seventy-five years after the suicide of Cornelius Merula no successor to his office had been appointed; yet religious rites had not ceased. If during so many years it was possible for there to be no appointment without any prejudice to religion, with what comparative ease might he be absent for one year's proconsulate? That these priests in former days were prohibited by the pontiff from going into the provinces, was the result of private feuds. Now, thank heaven, the supreme pontiff was also the supreme man, and was influenced by no rivalry, hatred or personal feeling."

As the augur Lentulus and others argued on various grounds against this view, the result was that they awaited the decision of the supreme pontiff. Tiberius deferred any investigation into the priest's legal position, but he modified the ceremonies which had been decreed in honour of Drusus's tribunitian power with special censure on the extravagance of the proposed inscription in gold, so contrary to national usage. Letters also from Drusus were read, which, though studiously modest in expression, were taken to be extremely supercilious. "We have fallen so low," people said, "that even a mere youth who has received so high an honour does not go as a worshipper to the city's gods, does not enter the Senate, does not so much as take the auspices on his country's soil. There is a war, forsooth, or he is kept from us in some remote part of the world. Why, at this very moment, he is on a tour amid the shores and lakes of Campania. Such is the training of the future ruler of mankind; such the lesson he first learns from his father's counsels. An aged emperor may indeed shrink from the citizen's gaze, and plead the weariness of declining years and the toils of the past. But, as for Drusus, what can be his hindrance but pride?"

Tiberius meantime, while securing to himself the substance of imperial power, allowed the Senate some shadow of its old constitution by referring to its investigation certain demands of the provinces. In the Greek cities license and impunity in establishing sanctuaries were on the increase. Temples were thronged with the vilest of the slaves; the same refuge screened the debtor against his creditor, as well as men suspected of capital offences. No authority was strong enough to check the turbulence of a people which protected the crimes of men as much as the worship of the gods.

It was accordingly decided that the different states were to send their charters and envoys to Rome. Some voluntarily relinquished privileges which they had groundlessly usurped; many trusted to old superstitions, or to their services to the Roman people. It was a grand spectacle on that day, when the Senate examined grants made by our ancestors, treaties with allies, even decrees of kings who had flourished before Rome's ascendancy, and the forms of worship of the very deities, with full liberty as in former days, to ratify or to alter.

First of all came the people of Ephesus. They declared that Diana and Apollo were not born at Delos, as was the vulgar belief. They had in their own country a river Cenchrius, a grove Ortygia, where Latona, as she leaned in the pangs of labour on an olive still standing, gave birth to those two deities, whereupon the grove at the divine intimation was consecrated. There Apollo himself, after the slaughter of the Cyclops, shunned the wrath of Jupiter; there too father Bacchus, when victorious in war, pardoned the suppliant Amazons who had gathered round the shrine. Subsequently by the permission of Hercules, when he was subduing Lydia, the grandeur of the temple's ceremonial was augmented, and during the Persian rule its privileges were not curtailed. They had afterwards been maintained by the Macedonians, then by ourselves.

Next the people of Magnesia relied on arrangements made by Lucius Scipio and Lucius Sulla. These generals, after respectively defeating Antiochus and Mithridates, honoured the fidelity and courage of the Magnesians by allowing the temple of Diana of the White Brow to be an inviolable sanctuary. Then the people of Aphrodisia produced a decree of the dictator Caesar for their old services to his party, and those of Stratonicea, one lately passed by the Divine Augustus, in which they were commended for having endured the Parthian invasion without wavering in their loyalty to the Roman people. Aphrodisia maintained the worship of Venus; Stratonicea, that of Jupiter and of Diana of the Cross Ways.

Hierocaesarea went back to a higher antiquity, and spoke of having a Persian Diana, whose fane was consecrated in the reign of Cyrus. They quoted too the names of Perperna, Isauricus, and many other generals who had conceded the same sacred character not only to the temple but to its precincts for two miles. Then came the Cyprians on behalf of three shrines, the oldest of which had been set up by their founder Aerias to the Paphian Venus, the second by his son Amathus to Venus of Amathus, and the last to Jupiter of Salamis, by Teucer when he fled from the wrath of his father Telamon.

Audience was also given to embassies from other states. The senators wearied by their multiplicity and seeing the party spirit that was being roused, intrusted the inquiry to the consuls, who were to sift each title and see if it involved any abuse, and then refer back the entire matter to the Senate. Besides the states already mentioned, the consuls reported that they had ascertained that at Pergamus there was a sanctuary of Aesculapius, but that the rest relied on an origin lost in the obscurity of antiquity. For example, the people of Smyrna quoted an oracle of Apollo, which had commanded them to dedicate a temple to Venus Stratonicis; and the islanders of Tenos, an utterance from the same deity, bidding them consecrate a statue and a fane to Neptune. Sardis preferred a more modern claim, a grant from the victorious Alexander. So again Miletus relied on king Darius. But in each case their religious worship was that of Diana or Apollo. The Cretans too demanded a like privilege for a statue of the Divine Augustus. Decrees of the Senate were passed, which though very respectful, still prescribed certain limits, and the petitioners were directed to set up bronze tablets in each temple, to be a sacred memorial and to restrain them from sinking into selfish aims under the mask of religion.

About this time Julia Augusta had an alarming illness, which compelled the emperor to hasten his return to Rome, for hitherto there had been a genuine harmony between the mother and son, or a hatred well concealed. Not long before, for instance, Julia in dedicating a statue to the Divine Augustus near the theatre of Marcellus had inscribed the name of Tiberius below her own, and it was surmised that the emperor, regarding this as a slight on a sovereign's dignity, had brooded over it with deep and disguised resentment. However the Senate now decreed supplications to the gods and the celebration of the Great Games, which were to be exhibited by the pontiffs, augurs, the colleges of the Fifteen and of the Seven, with the Augustal Brotherhood. Lucius Apronius moved that the heralds too should preside over these Games. This the emperor opposed, distinguishing the peculiar privileges of the sacred guilds, and quoting precedents. Never, he argued, had the heralds this dignity. "The Augustal priests were included expressly because their sacred office was specially attached to the family for which vows were being performed."

My purpose is not to relate at length every motion, but only such as were conspicuous for excellence or notorious for infamy. This I regard as history's highest function, to let no worthy action be uncommemorated, and to hold out the reprobation of posterity as a terror to evil words and deeds. So corrupted indeed and debased was that age by sycophancy that not only the foremost citizens who were forced to save their grandeur by servility, but every exconsul, most of the ex-praetors and a host of inferior senators would rise in eager rivalry to propose shameful and preposterous motions. Tradition says that Tiberius as often as he left the Senate-House used to exclaim in Greek, "How ready these men are to be slaves." Clearly, even he, with his dislike of public freedom, was disgusted at the abject abasement of his creatures.

From unseemly flatteries they passed by degrees to savage acts. Caius Silanus, pro-consul of Asia, was accused by our allies of extortion; whereupon Mamercus Scaurus, an ex-consul, Junius Otho, a praetor, Brutidius Niger, an aedile, simultaneously fastened on him and charged him with sacrilege to the divinity of Augustus, and contempt of the majesty of Tiberius, while Mamercus Scaurus quoted old precedents, the prosecutions of Lucius Cotta by Scipio Africanus, of Servius Galba by Cato the Censor and of Publius Rutilius by Scaurus. As if indeed Scipio's and Cato's vengeance fell on such offences, or that of the famous Scaurus, whom his great grandson, a blot on his ancestry, this Mamercus was now disgracing by his infamous occupation. Junius Otho's old employment had been the keeping of a preparatory school. Subsequently, becoming a senator by the influence of Sejanus, he shamed his origin, low as it was, by his unblushing effronteries. Brutidius who was rich in excellent accomplishments, and was sure, had he pursued a path of virtue, to reach the most brilliant distinction, was goaded on by an eager impatience, while he strove to outstrip his equals, then his superiors, and at last even his own aspirations. Many have thus perished, even good men, despising slow and safe success and hurrying on even at the cost of ruin to premature greatness.

Gellius Publicola and Marcus Paconius, respectively quaestor and lieutenant of Silanus, swelled the number of the accusers. No doubt was felt as to the defendant's conviction for oppression and extortion, but there was a combination against him, that must have been perilous even to an innocent man. Besides a host of adverse Senators there were the most accomplished orators of all Asia, who, as such, had been retained for the prosecution, and to these he had to reply alone, without any experience in pleading, and under that personal apprehension which is enough to paralyse even the most practised eloquence. For Tiberius did not refrain from pressing him with angry voice and look, himself putting incessant questions, without allowing him to rebut or evade them, and he had often even to make admissions, that the questions might not have been asked in vain. His slaves too were sold by auction to the state-agent, to be examined by torture. And that not a friend might help him in his danger, charges of treason were added, a binding guarantee for sealed lips. Accordingly he begged a few days' respite, and at last abandoned his defence, after venturing on a memorial to the emperor, in which he mingled reproach and entreaty.

Tiberius, that his proceedings against Silanus might find some justification in precedent, ordered the Divine Augustus's indictment of Volesus Messala, also a proconsul of Asia, and the Senate's sentence on him to be read. He then asked Lucius Piso his opinion. After a long preliminary eulogy on the prince's clemency, Piso pronounced that Silanus ought to be outlawed and banished to the island of Gyarus. The rest concurred, with the exception of Cneius Lentulus, who, with the assent of Tiberius, proposed that the property of Silanus's mother, as she was very different from him, should be exempted from confiscation, and given to the son.

Cornelius Dolabella however, by way of carrying flattery yet further, sharply censured the morals of Silanus, and then moved that no one of disgraceful life and notorious infamy should be eligible for a province, and that of this the emperor should be judge. "Laws, indeed," he said, "punish crimes committed; but how much more merciful would it be to individuals, how much better for our allies, to provide against their commission."

The emperor opposed the motion. "Although," he said, "I am not ignorant of the reports about Silanus, still we must decide nothing by hearsay. Many a man has behaved in a province quite otherwise than was hoped or feared of him. Some are roused to higher things by great responsibility; others are paralysed by it. It is not possible for a prince's knowledge to embrace everything, and it is not expedient that he should be exposed to the ambitious schemings of others. Laws are ordained to meet facts, inasmuch as the future is uncertain. It was the rule of our ancestors that, whenever there was first an offence, some penalty should follow. Let us not revolutionise a wisely devised and ever approved system. Princes have enough burdens, and also enough power. Rights are invariably abridged, as despotism increases; nor ought we to fall back on imperial authority, when we can have recourse to the laws."

Such constitutional sentiments were so rare with Tiberius, that they were welcomed with all the heartier joy. Knowing, as he did, how to be forbearing, when he was not under the stimulus of personal resentment, he further said that Gyarus was a dreary and uninhabited island, and that, as a concession to the Junian family and to a man of the same order as themselves, they might let him retire by preference to Cythnus. This, he added, was also the request of Torquata, Silanus's sister, a vestal of primitive purity. The motion was carried after a division.

Audience was next given to the people of Cyrene, and on the prosecution of Ancharius Priscus, Caesius Cordus was convicted of extortion. Lucius Ennius, a Roman knight, was accused of treason, for having converted a statue of the emperor to the common use of silver plate; but the emperor forbade his being put upon his trial, though Ateius Capito openly remonstrated, with a show of independence. "The Senate," he said, "ought not to have wrested from it the power of deciding a question, and such a crime must not go unpunished. Granted that the emperor might be indifferent to a personal grievance, still he should not be generous in the case of wrongs to the commonwealth." Tiberius interpreted the remark according to its drift rather than its mere expression, and persisted in his veto. Capito's disgrace was the more conspicuous, for, versed as he was in the science of law, human and divine, he had now dishonoured a brilliant public career as well as a virtuous private life.

Next came a religious question, as to the temple in which ought to be deposited the offering which the Roman knights had vowed to Fortune of the Knights for the recovery of Augusta. Although that Goddess had several shrines in Rome, there was none with this special designation. It was ascertained that there was a temple so called at Antium, and that all sacred rites in the towns of Italy as well as temples and images of deities were under the jurisdiction and authority of Rome. Accordingly the offering was placed at Antium.

As religious questions were under discussion, the emperor now produced his answer to Servius Maluginensis, Jupiter's priest, which he had recently deferred, and read the pontifical decree, prescribing that whenever illness attacked a priest of Jupiter, he might, with the supreme pontiff's permission, be absent more than two nights, provided it was not during the days of public sacrifice or more than twice in the same year. This regulation of the emperor Augustus sufficiently proved that a year's absence and a provincial government were not permitted to the priests of Jupiter. There was also cited the precedent of Lucius Metellus, supreme pontiff, who had detained at Rome the priest Aulus Postumius. And so Asia was allotted to the exconsul next in seniority to Maluginensis.

About the same time Lepidus asked the Senate's leave to restore and embellish, at his own expense, the basilica of Paulus, that monument of the Aemilian family. Public-spirited munificence was still in fashion, and Augustus had not hindered Taurus, Philippus, or Balbus from applying the spoils of war or their superfluous wealth to adorn the capital and to win the admiration of posterity. Following these examples, Lepidus, though possessed of a moderate fortune, now revived the glory of his ancestors.

Pompeius's theatre, which had been destroyed by an accidental fire, the emperor promised to rebuild, simply because no member of the family was equal to restoring it, but Pompeius's name was to be retained. At the same time he highly extolled Sejanus on the ground that it was through his exertions and vigilance that such fury of the flames had been confined to the destruction of a single building. The Senate voted Sejanus a statue, which was to be placed in Pompeius's theatre. And soon afterwards the emperor in honouring Junius Blaesus proconsul of Africa, with triumphal distinctions, said that he granted them as a compliment to Sejanus, whose uncle Blaesus was.

Still the career of Blaesus merited such a reward. For Tacfarinas, though often driven back, had recruited his resources in the interior of Africa, and had become so insolent as to send envoys to Tiberius, actually demanding a settlement for himself and his army, or else threatening us with an interminable war. Never, it is said, was the emperor so exasperated by an insult to himself and the Roman people as by a deserter and brigand assuming the character of a belligerent. "Even Spartacus when he had destroyed so many consular armies and was burning Italy with impunity, though the State was staggering under the tremendous wars of Sertorius and Mithridates, had not the offer of an honourable surrender on stipulated conditions; far less, in Rome's most glorious height of power, should a robber like Tacfarinas be bought off by peace and concessions of territory." He intrusted the affair to Blaesus, who was to hold out to the other rebels the prospect of laying down their arms without hurt to themselves, while he was by any means to secure the person of the chief. Many surrendered themselves on the strength of this amnesty. Before long the tactics of Tacfarinas were encountered in a similar fashion.

Unequal to us in solid military strength, but better in a war of surprises, he would attack, would elude pursuit, and still arrange ambuscades with a multitude of detachments. And so we prepared three expeditions and as many columns. One of the three under the command of Cornelius Scipio, Blaesus's lieutenant, was to stop the enemy's forays on the Leptitani and his retreat to the Garamantes. In another quarter, Blaesus's son led a separate force of his own, to save the villages of Cirta from being ravaged with impunity. Between the two was the general himself with some picked troops. By establishing redoubts and fortified lines in commanding positions, he had rendered the whole country embarrassing and perilous to the foe, for, whichever way he turned, a body of Roman soldiers was in his face, or on his flank, or frequently in the rear. Many were thus slain or surprised.

Blaesus then further divided his triple army into several detachments under the command of centurions of tried valour. At the end of the summer he did not, as was usual, withdraw his troops and let them rest in winter-quarters in the old province; but, forming a chain of forts, as though he were on the threshold of a campaign, he drove Tacfarinas by flying columns well acquainted with the desert, from one set of huts to another, till he captured the chief's brother, and then returned, too soon however for the welfare of our allies, as there yet remained those who might renew hostilities.

Tiberius however considered the war as finished, and awarded Blaesus the further distinction of being hailed "Imperator" by the legions, an ancient honour conferred on generals who for good service to the State were saluted with cheers of joyful enthusiasm by a victorious army. Several men bore the title at the same time, without pre-eminence above their fellows. Augustus too granted the name to certain persons; and now, for the last time, Tiberius gave it to Blaesus.

Two illustrious men died that year. One was Asinius Saloninus, distinguished as the grandson of Marcus Agrippa, and Asinius Pollio, as the brother of Drusus and the intended husband of the emperor's granddaughter. The other was Capito Ateius, already mentioned, who had won a foremost position in the State by his legal attainments, though his grandfather was but a centurion in Sulla's army, his father having been a praetor. He was prematurely advanced to the consulship by Augustus, so that he might be raised by the honour of this promotion above Labeo Antistius, a conspicuous member of the same profession. That age indeed produced at one time two brilliant ornaments of peace. But while Labeo was a man of sturdy independence and consequently of wider fame, Capito's obsequiousness was more acceptable to those in power. Labeo, because his promotion was confined to the praetorship, gained in public favour through the wrong; Capito, in obtaining the consulship, incurred the hatred which grows out of envy.

Junia too, the niece of Cato, wife of Caius Cassius and sister of Marcus Brutus, died this year, the sixty-fourth after the battle of Philippi. Her will was the theme of much popular criticism, for, with her vast wealth, after having honourably mentioned almost every nobleman by name, she passed over the emperor. Tiberius took the omission graciously and did not forbid a panegyric before the Rostra with the other customary funeral honours. The busts of twenty most illustrious families were borne in the procession, with the names of Manlius, Quinctius, and others of equal rank. But Cassius and Brutus outshone them all, from the very fact that their likenesses were not to be seen.

BOOK IV, A.D. 23-28

The year when Caius Asinius and Caius Antistius were consuls was the ninth of Tiberius's reign, a period of tranquillity for the State and prosperity for his own house, for he counted Germanicus's death a happy incident. Suddenly fortune deranged everything; the emperor became a cruel tyrant, as well as an abettor of cruelty in others. Of this the cause and origin was Aelius Sejanus, commander of the praetorian cohorts, of whose influence I have already spoken. I will now fully describe his extraction, his character, and the daring wickedness by which he grasped at power.

Born at Vulsinii, the son of Seius Strabo, a Roman knight, he attached himself in his early youth to Caius Caesar, grandson of the Divine Augustus, and the story went that he had sold his person to Apicius, a rich debauchee. Soon afterwards he won the heart of Tiberius so effectually by various artifices that the emperor, ever dark and mysterious towards others, was with Sejanus alone careless and freespoken. It was not through his craft, for it was by this very weapon that he was overthrown; it was rather from heaven's wrath against Rome, to whose welfare his elevation and his fall were alike disastrous. He had a body which could endure hardships, and a daring spirit. He was one who screened himself, while he was attacking others; he was as cringing as he was imperious; before the world he affected humility; in his heart he lusted after supremacy, for the sake of which he sometimes lavish and luxurious, but oftener energetic and watchful, qualities quite as mischievous when hypocritically assumed for the attainment of sovereignty.

He strengthened the hitherto moderate powers of his office by concentrating the cohorts scattered throughout the capital into one camp, so that they might all receive orders at the same moment, and that the sight of their numbers and strength might give confidence to themselves, while it would strike terror into the citizens. His pretexts were the demoralisation incident to a dispersed soldiery, the greater effectiveness of simultaneous action in the event of a sudden peril, and the stricter discipline which would be insured by the establishment of an encampment at a distance from the temptations of the city. As soon as the camp was completed, he crept gradually into the affections of the soldiers by mixing with them and addressing them by name, himself selecting the centurions and tribunes. With the Senate too he sought to ingratiate himself, distinguishing his partisans with offices and provinces, Tiberius readily yielding, and being so biassed that not only in private conversation but before the senators and the people he spoke highly of him as the partner of his toils, and allowed his statues to be honoured in theatres, in forums, and at the head-quarters of our legions.

There were however obstacles to his ambition in the imperial house with its many princes, a son in youthful manhood and grown-up grandsons. As it would be unsafe to sweep off such a number at once by violence, while craft would necessitate successive intervals in crime, he chose, on the whole, the stealthier way and to begin with Drusus, against whom he had the stimulus of a recent resentment. Drusus, who could not brook a rival and was somewhat irascible, had, in a casual dispute, raised his fist at Sejanus, and, when he defended himself, had struck him in the face. On considering every plan Sejanus thought his easiest revenge was to turn his attention to Livia, Drusus's wife. She was a sister of Germanicus, and though she was not handsome as a girl, she became a woman of surpassing beauty. Pretending an ardent passion for her, he seduced her, and having won his first infamous triumph, and assured that a woman after having parted with her virtue will hesitate at nothing, he lured her on to thoughts of marriage, of a share in sovereignty, and of her husband's destruction. And she, the niece of Augustus, the daughter-in-law of Tiberius, the mother of children by Drusus, for a provincial paramour, foully disgraced herself, her ancestors, and her descendants, giving up honour and a sure position for prospects as base as they were uncertain. They took into their confidence Eudemus, Livia's friend and physician, whose profession was a pretext for frequent secret interviews. Sejanus, to avert his mistress's jealousy, divorced his wife Apicata, by whom he had had three children. Still the magnitude of the crime caused fear and delay, and sometimes a conflict of plans.

Meanwhile, at the beginning of this year, Drusus, one of the children of Germanicus, assumed the dress of manhood, with a repetition of the honours decreed by the Senate to his brother Nero. The emperor added a speech with warm praise of his son for sharing a father's affection to his brother's children. Drusus indeed, difficult as it is for power and mutual harmony to exist side by side, had the character of being kindly disposed or at least not unfriendly towards the lads. And now the old plan, so often insincerely broached, of a progress through the provinces, was again discussed. The emperor's pretext was the number of veterans on the eve of discharge and the necessity of fresh levies for the army. Volunteers were not forthcoming, and even if they were sufficiently numerous, they had not the same bravery and discipline, as it is chiefly the needy and the homeless who adopt by their own choice a soldier's life. Tiberius also rapidly enumerated the legions and the provinces which they had to garrison. I too ought, I think, to go through these details, and thus show what forces Rome then had under arms, what kings were our allies, and how much narrower then were the limits of our empire.

Italy on both seas was guarded by fleets, at Misenum and at Ravenna, and the contiguous coast of Gaul by ships of war captured in the victory of Actium, and sent by Augustus powerfully manned to the town of Forojulium. But chief strength was on the Rhine, as a defence alike against Germans and Gauls, and numbered eight legions. Spain, lately subjugated, was held by three. Mauretania was king Juba's, who had received it as a gift from the Roman people. The rest of Africa was garrisoned by two legions, and Egypt by the same number. Next, beginning with Syria, all within the entire tract of country stretching as far as the Euphrates, was kept in restraint by four legions, and on this frontier were Iberian, Albanian, and other kings, to whom our greatness was a protection against any foreign power. Thrace was held by Rhoemetalces and the children of Cotys; the bank of the Danube by two legions in Pannonia, two in Moesia, and two also were stationed in Dalmatia, which, from the situation of the country, were in the rear of the other four, and, should Italy suddenly require aid, not to distant to be summoned. But the capital was garrisoned by its own special soldiery, three city, nine praetorian cohorts, levied for the most part in Etruria and Umbria, or ancient Latium and the old Roman colonies. There were besides, in commanding positions in the provinces, allied fleets, cavalry and light infantry, of but little inferior strength. But any detailed account of them would be misleading, since they moved from place to place as circumstances required, and had their numbers increased and sometimes diminished.

It is however, I think, a convenient opportunity for me to review the hitherto prevailing methods of administration in the other departments of the State, inasmuch as that year brought with it the beginning of a change for the worse in Tiberius's policy. In the first place, public business and the most important private matters were managed by the Senate: the leading men were allowed freedom of discussion, and when they stooped to flattery, the emperor himself checked them. He bestowed honours with regard to noble ancestry, military renown, or brilliant accomplishments as a civilian, letting it be clearly seen that there were no better men to choose. The consul and the praetor retained their prestige; inferior magistrates exercised their authority; the laws too, with the single exception of cases of treason, were properly enforced.

As to the duties on corn, the indirect taxes and other branches of the public revenue, they were in the hands of companies of Roman knights. The emperor intrusted his own property to men of the most tried integrity or to persons known only by their general reputation, and once appointed they were retained without any limitation, so that most of them grew old in the same employments. The city populace indeed suffered much from high prices, but this was no fault of the emperor, who actually endeavoured to counteract barren soils and stormy seas with every resource of wealth and foresight. And he was also careful not to distress the provinces by new burdens, and to see that in bearing the old they were safe from any rapacity or oppression on the part of governors. Corporal punishments and confiscations of property were unknown.

The emperor had only a few estates in Italy, slaves on a moderate scale, and his household was confined to a few freedmen. If ever he had a dispute with a private person, it was decided in the law courts. All this, not indeed with any graciousness, but in a blunt fashion which often alarmed, he still kept up, until the death of Drusus changed everything. While he lived, the system continued, because Sejanus, as yet only in the beginning of his power, wished to be known as an upright counsellor, and there was one whose vengeance he dreaded, who did not conceal his hatred and incessantly complained "that a stranger was invited to assist in the government while the emperor's son was alive. How near was the step of declaring the stranger a colleague! Ambition at first had a steep path before it; when once the way had been entered, zealous adherents were forthcoming. Already, at the pleasure of the commander of the guards, a camp had been established; the soldiers given into his hands; his statues were to be seen among the monuments of Cneius Pompeius; his grandsons would be of the same blood as the family of the Drusi. Henceforth they must pray that he might have self-control, and so be contented." So would Drusus talk, not unfrequently, or only in the hearing of a few persons. Even his confidences, now that his wife had been corrupted, were betrayed.

Sejanus accordingly thought that he must be prompt, and chose a poison the gradual working of which might be mistaken for a natural disorder. It was given to Drusus by Lygdus, a eunuch, as was ascertained eight years later. As for Tiberius, he went to the Senate house during the whole time of the prince's illness, either because he was not afraid, or to show his strength of mind, and even in the interval between his death and funeral. Seeing the consuls, in token of their grief, sitting on the ordinary benches, he reminded them of their high office and of their proper place; and when the Senate burst into tears, suppressing a groan, he revived their spirits with a fluent speech. "He knew indeed that he might be reproached for thus encountering the gaze of the Senate after so recent an affliction. Most mourners could hardly bear even the soothing words of kinsfolk or to look on the light of day. And such were not to be condemned as weak. But he had sought a more manly consolation in the bosom of the commonwealth."

Then deploring the extreme age of Augusta, the childhood of his grandsons, and his own declining years, he begged the Senate to summon Germanicus's children, the only comfort under their present misery. The consuls went out, and having encouraged the young princes with kind words, brought them in and presented them to the emperor. Taking them by the hand he said: "Senators, when these boys lost their father, I committed them to their uncle, and begged him, though he had children of his own, to cherish and rear them as his own offspring, and train them for himself and for posterity. Drusus is now lost to us, and I turn my prayers to you, and before heaven and your country I adjure you to receive into your care and guidance the great-grandsons of Augustus, descendants of a most noble ancestry. So fulfil your duty and mine. To you, Nero and Drusus, these senators are as fathers. Such is your birth that your prosperity and adversity must alike affect the State."

There was great weeping at these words, and then many a benediction. Had the emperor set bounds to his speech, he must have filled the hearts of his hearers with sympathy and admiration. But he now fell back on those idle and often ridiculed professions about restoring the republic, and the wish that the consuls or some one else might undertake the government, and thus destroyed belief even in what was genuine and noble.

The same honours were decreed to the memory of Drusus as to that of Germanicus, and many more were added. Such is the way with flattery, when repeated. The funeral with its procession of statues was singularly grand. Aeneas, the father of the Julian house, all the Alban kings, Romulus, Rome's founder, then the Sabine nobility, Attus Clausus, and the busts of all the other Claudii were displayed in a long train.

In relating the death of Drusus I have followed the narrative of most of the best historians. But I would not pass over a rumour of the time, the strength of which is not even yet exhausted. Sejanus, it is said, having seduced Livia into crime, next secured, by the foulest means, the consent of Lygdus, the eunuch, as from his youth and beauty he was his master's favourite, and one of his principal attendants. When those who were in the secret had decided on the time and place of the poisoning, Sejanus, with the most consummate daring, reversed his plan, and, whispering an accusation against Drusus of intending to poison his father, warned Tiberius to avoid the first draught offered him as he was dining at his son's house. Thus deceived, the old emperor, on sitting down to the banquet, took the cup and handed it to Drusus. His suspicions were increased when Drusus, in perfect unconsciousness, drank it off with youthful eagerness, apparently, out of fear and shame, bringing on himself the death which he had plotted against his father.

These popular rumours, over and above the fact that they are not vouched for by any good writer, may be instantly refuted. For who, with moderate prudence, far less Tiberius with his great experience, would have thrust destruction on a son, without even hearing him, with his own hand too, and with an impossibility of returning to better thoughts. Surely he would rather have had the slave who handed the poison, tortured, have sought to discover the traitor, in short, would have been as hesitating and tardy in the case of an only son hitherto unconvicted of any crime, as he was naturally even with strangers. But as Sejanus had the credit of contriving every sort of wickedness, the fact that he was the emperor's special favourite, and that both were hated by the rest of the world, procured belief for any monstrous fiction, and rumour too always has a dreadful side in regard to the deaths of men in power. Besides, the whole process of the crime was betrayed by

Apicata, Sejanus's wife, and fully divulged, under torture, by Eudemus and Lygdus. No writer has been found sufficiently malignant to fix the guilt on Tiberius, though every circumstance was scrutinized and exaggerated. My object in mentioning and refuting this story is, by a conspicuous example, to put down hearsay, and to request all into whose hands my work shall come, not to catch eagerly at wild and improbable rumours in preference to genuine history which has not been perverted into romance.

Tiberius pronounced a panegyric on his son before the Rostra, during which the Senate and people, in appearance rather than in heart, put on the expression and accents of sorrow, while they inwardly rejoiced at the brightening future of the family of Germanicus. This beginning of popularity and the ill-concealed ambition of their mother Agrippina, hastened its downfall. Sejanus when he saw that the death of Drusus was not avenged on the murderers and was no grief to the people, grew bold in wickedness, and, now that his first attempt had succeeded, speculated on the possibility of destroying the children of Germanicus, whose succession to the throne was a certainty. There were three, and poison could not be distributed among them, because of the singular fidelity of their guardians and the unassailable virtue of Agrippina. So Sejanus inveighed against Agrippina's arrogance, and worked powerfully on Augusta's old hatred of her and on Livia's consciousness of recent guilt, and urged both these women to represent to the emperor that her pride as a mother and her reliance on popular enthusiasm were leading her to dream of empire. Livia availed herself of the cunning of accusers, among whom she had selected Julius Postumus, a man well suited to her purpose, as he had an intrigue with Mutilia Prisca, and was consequently in the confidence of Augusta, over whose mind Prisca had great influence. She thus made her aged grandmother, whose nature it was to tremble for her power, irreconcilably hostile to her grandson's widow. Agrippina's friends too were induced to be always inciting her proud spirit by mischievous talk.

Tiberius meanwhile, who did not relax his attention to business, and found solace in his work, occupied himself with the causes of citizens at Rome and with petitions from allies. Decrees of the Senate were passed at his proposal for relieving the cities of Cibyra and Aegium in Asia and Achaia, which had suffered from earthquakes, by a remission of three years' tribute. Vibius Serenus too, proconsul of Further Spain, was condemned for violence in his official capacity, and was banished to the island of Amorgus for his savage temper. Carsidius Sacerdos, accused of having helped our enemy Tacfarinas with supplies of grain, was acquitted, as was also Caius Gracchus on the same charge. Gracchus's father, Sempronius, had taken him when a mere child to the island of Cercina to be his companion in exile. There he grew up among outcasts who knew nothing of a liberal education, and after a while supported himself in Africa and Sicily by petty trade. But he did not escape the dangers of high rank. Had not his innocence been protected by Aelius Lamia and Lucius Apronius, successive governors of Africa, the splendid fame of that ill-starred family and the downfall of his father would have dragged him to ruin.

This year too brought embassies from the Greek communities. The people of Samos and Cos petitioned for the confirmation of the ancient right of sanctuary for the respective temples of Juno and Aesculapius. The Samians relied on a decree of the Amphictyonic Council, which had the supreme decision of all questions when the Greeks, through the cities they had founded in Asia, had possession of the sea-coast. Cos could boast equal antiquity, and it had an additional claim connected with the place. Roman citizens had been admitted to the temple of Aesculapius, when king Mithridates ordered a general massacre of them throughout all the islands and cities of Asia.

Next, after various and usually fruitless complaints from the praetors, the emperor finally brought forward a motion about the licentious behaviour of the players. "They had often," he said, "sought to disturb the public peace, and to bring disgrace on private families, and the old Oscan farce, once a wretched amusement for the vulgar, had become at once so indecent and so popular, that it must be checked by the Senate's authority. The players, upon this, were banished from Italy.

That same year also brought fresh sorrow to the emperor by being fatal to one of the twin sons of Drusus, equally too by the death of an intimate friend. This was Lucilius Longus, the partner of all his griefs and joys, the only senator who had been the companion of his retirement in Rhodes. And so, though he was a man of humble origin, the Senate decreed him a censor's funeral and a statue in the forum of Augustus at the public expense. Everything indeed was as yet in the hands of the Senate, and consequently Lucilius Capito, procurator of Asia, who was impeached by his province, was tried by them, the emperor vehemently asserting "that he had merely given the man authority over the slaves and property of the imperial establishments; that if he had taken upon himself the powers of a praetor and used military force, he had disregarded his instructions; therefore they must hear the provincials." So the case was heard and the accused condemned. The cities of Asia, gratified by this retribution and the punishment inflicted in the previous year on Caius Silanus, voted a temple to Tiberius, his mother, and the Senate, and were permitted to build it. Nero thanked the Senators and his grandfather on their behalf and carried with him the joyful sympathies of his audience, who, with the memory of Germanicus fresh in their minds, imagined that it was his face they saw, his voice they heard. The youth too had a modesty and a grace of person worthy of a prince, the more charming because of his peril from the notorious enmity of Sejanus.

About the same time the emperor spoke on the subject of electing a priest of Jupiter in the room of Servius Maluginensis, deceased, and of the enactment of a new law. "It was," he said, "the old custom to nominate together three patricians, sons of parents wedded according to the primitive ceremony, and of these one was to be chosen. Now however there was not the same choice as formerly, the primitive form of marriage having been given up or being observed only by a few persons." For this he assigned several reasons, the chief being men's and women's indifference; then, again, the ceremony itself had its difficulties, which were purposely avoided; and there was the objection that the man who obtained this priesthood was emancipated from the father's authority, as also was his wife, as passing into the husband's control. So the Senate, Tiberius argued, ought to apply some remedy by a decree of a law, as Augustus had accommodated certain relics of a rude antiquity to the modern spirit.

It was then decided, after a discussion of religious questions, that the institution of the priests of Jupiter should remain unchanged. A law however was passed that the priestess, in regard to her sacred functions, was to be under the husband's control, but in other respects to retain the ordinary legal position of women. Maluginensis, the son, was chosen successor to his father. To raise the dignity of the priesthood and to inspire the priests with more zeal in attending to the ceremonial, a gift of two million sesterces was decreed to the Vestal Cornelia, chosen in the room of Scantia; and, whenever Augusta entered the theatre, she was to have a place in the seats of the Vestals.

In the consulship of Cornelius Cethegus and Visellius Varro, the pontiffs, whose example was followed by the other priests in offering prayers for the emperor's health, commended also Nero and Drusus to the same deities, not so much out of love for the young princes as out of sycophancy, the absence and excess of which in a corrupt age are alike dangerous. Tiberius indeed, who was never friendly to the house of Germanicus, was then vexed beyond endurance at their youth being honoured equally with his declining years. He summoned the pontiffs, and asked them whether it was to the entreaties or the threats of Agrippina that they had made this concession. And though they gave a flat denial, he rebuked them but gently, for many of them were her own relatives or were leading men in the State. However he addressed a warning to the Senate against encouraging pride in their young and excitable minds by premature honours. For Sejanus spoke vehemently, and charged them with rending the State almost by civil war. "There were those," he said, "who called themselves the party of Agrippina, and, unless they were checked, there would be more; the only remedy for the increasing discord was the overthrow of one or two of the most enterprising leaders."

Accordingly he attacked Caius Silius and Titius Sabinus. The friendship of Germanicus was fatal to both. As for Silius, his having commanded a great army for seven years, and won in Germany the distinctions of a triumph for his success in the war with Sacrovir, would make his downfall all the more tremendous and so spread greater terror among others. Many thought that he had provoked further displeasure by his own presumption and his extravagant boasts that his troops had been steadfastly loyal, while other armies were falling into mutiny, and that Tiberius's throne could not have lasted had his legions too been bent on revolution. All this the emperor regarded as undermining his own power, which seemed to be unequal to the burden of such an obligation. For benefits received are a delight to us as long as we think we can requite them; when that possibility is far exceeded, they are repaid with hatred instead of gratitude.

Silius had a wife, Sosia Galla, whose love of Agrippina made her hateful to the emperor. The two, it was decided, were to be attacked, but Sabinus was to be put off for a time. Varro, the consul, was let loose on them, who, under colour of a hereditary feud, humoured the malignity of Sejanus to his own disgrace. The accused begged a brief respite, until the prosecutor's consulship expired, but the emperor opposed the request. "It was usual," he argued, "for magistrates to bring a private citizen to trial, and a consul's authority ought not to be impaired, seeing that it rested with his vigilance to guard the commonwealth from loss." It was characteristic of Tiberius to veil new devices in wickedness under ancient names. And so, with a solemn appeal, he summoned the Senate, as if there were any laws by which Silius was being tried, as if Varro were a real consul, or Rome a commonwealth. The accused either said nothing, or, if he attempted to defend himself, hinted, not obscurely, at the person whose resentment was crushing him. A long concealed complicity in Sacrovir's rebellion, a rapacity which sullied his victory, and his wife Sosia's conduct, were alleged against him. Unquestionably, they could not extricate themselves from the charge of extortion. The whole affair however was conducted as a trial for treason, and Silius forestalled impending doom by a self-inflicted death.

Yet there was a merciless confiscation of his property, though not to refund their money to the provincials, none of whom pressed any demand. But Augustus's bounty was wrested from him, and the claims of the imperial exchequer were computed in detail. This was the first instance on Tiberius's part of sharp dealing with the wealth of others. Sosia was banished on the motion of Asinius Gallus, who had proposed that half her estate should be confiscated, half left to the children. Marcus Lepidus, on the contrary, was for giving a fourth to the prosecutors, as the law required, and the remainder to the children.

This Lepidus, I am satisfied, was for that age a wise and high-principled man. Many a cruel suggestion made by the flattery of others he changed for the better, and yet he did not want tact, seeing that he always enjoyed an uniform prestige, and also the favour of Tiberius. This compels me to doubt whether the liking of princes for some men and their antipathy to others depend, like other contingencies, on a fate and destiny to which we are born, or, to some degree, on our own plans; so that it is possible to pursue a course between a defiant independence and a debasing servility, free from ambition and its perils. Messalinus Cotta, of equally illustrious ancestry as Lepidus, but wholly different in disposition, proposed that the Senate should pass a decree providing that even innocent governors who knew nothing of the delinquencies of others should be punished for their wives' offences in the provinces as much as for their own.

Proceedings were then taken against Calpurnius Piso, a high-spirited nobleman. He it was, as I have related, who had exclaimed more than once in the Senate that he would quit Rome because of the combinations of the informers, and had dared in defiance of Augusta's power, to sue Urgulania and summon her from the emperor's palace. Tiberius submitted to this at the time not ungraciously, but the remembrance of it was vividly impressed on a mind which brooded over its resentments, even though the first impulse of his displeasure had subsided.

Quintus Granius accused Piso of secret treasonable conversation, and added that he kept poison in his house and wore a dagger whenever he came into the Senate. This was passed over as too atrocious to be true. He was to be tried on the other charges, a multitude of which were heaped on him, but his timely death cut short the trial.

Next was taken the case of Cassius Severus' an exile. A man of mean origin and a life of crime, but a powerful pleader, he had brought on himself, by his persistent quarrelsomeness, a decision of the Senate, under oath, which banished him to Crete. There by the same practices he drew on himself, fresh odium and revived the old; stripped of his property and outlawed, he wore out his old age on the rock of Seriphos.

About the same time Plautius Silvanus, the praetor, for unknown reasons, threw his wife Apronia out of a window. When summoned before the emperor by Lucius Apronius, his father-in-law, he replied incoherently, representing that he was in a sound sleep and consequently knew nothing, and that his wife had chosen to destroy herself. Without a moment's delay Tiberius went to the house and inspected the chamber, where were seen the marks of her struggling and of her forcible ejection. He reported this to the Senate, and as soon as judges had been appointed, Urgulania, the grandmother of Silvanus, sent her grandson a dagger. This was thought equivalent to a hint from the emperor, because of the known intimacy between Augusta and Urgulania. The accused tried the steel in vain, and then allowed his veins to be opened. Shortly afterwards Numantina, his former wife, was charged with having caused her husband's insanity by magical incantations and potions, but she was acquitted.

This year at last released Rome from her long contest with the Numidian Tacfarinas. Former generals, when they thought that their successes were enough to insure them triumphal distinctions, left the enemy to himself. There were now in Rome three laurelled statues, and yet Tacfarinas was still ravaging Africa, strengthened by reinforcements from the Moors, who, under the boyish and careless rule of Ptolemaeus, Juba's son, had chosen war in preference to the despotism of freedmen and slaves. He had the king of the Garamantes to receive his plunder and to be the partner of his raids, not indeed with a regular army, but with detachments of light troops whose strength, as they came from a distance, rumour exaggerated. From the province itself every needy and restless adventurer hurried to join him, for the emperor, as if not an enemy remained in Africa after the achievements of Blaesus, had ordered the ninth legion home, and Publius Dolabella, proconsul that year, had not dared to retain it, because he feared the sovereign's orders more than the risks of war.

Tacfarinas accordingly spread rumours; that elsewhere also nations were rending the empire of Rome and that therefore her soldiers were gradually retiring from Africa, and that the rest might be cut off by a strong effort on the part of all who loved freedom more than slavery. He thus augmented his force, and having formed a camp, he besieged the town of Thubuscum. Dolabella meanwhile collecting all the troops on the spot, raised the siege at his first approach, by the terror of the Roman name and because the Numidians cannot stand against the charge of infantry. He then fortified suitable positions, and at the same time beheaded some chiefs of the Musulamii, who were on the verge of rebellion. Next, as several expeditions against Tacfarinas had proved the uselessness of following up the enemy's desultory movements with the attack of heavy troops from a single point, he summoned to his aid king Ptolemaeus and his people, and equipped four columns, under the command of his lieutenants and tribunes. Marauding parties were also led by picked Moors, Dolabella in person directing every operation.

Soon afterwards news came that the Numidians had fixed their tents and encamped near a half-demolished fortress, by name Auzea, to which they had themselves formerly set fire, and on the position of which they relied, as it was inclosed by vast forests. Immediately the light infantry and cavalry, without knowing whither they were being led, were hurried along at quick march. Day dawned, and with the sound of trumpets and fierce shouts, they were on the half-asleep barbarians, whose horses were tethered or roaming over distant pastures. On the Roman side, the infantry was in close array, the cavalry in its squadrons, everything prepared for an engagement, while the enemy, utterly surprised, without arms, order, or plan, were seized, slaughtered, or captured like cattle. The infuriated soldiers, remembering their hardships and how often the longed-for conflict had been eluded, sated themselves to a man with vengeance and bloodshed. The word went through the companies that all were to aim at securing Tacfarinas, whom, after so many battles, they knew well, as there would be no rest from war except by the destruction of the enemy's leader. Tacfarinas, his guards slain round him, his son a prisoner, and the Romans bursting on him from every side, rushed on the darts, and by a death which was not unavenged, escaped captivity.

This ended the war. Dolabella asked for triumphal distinctions, but was refused by Tiberius, out of compliment to Sejanus, the glory of whose uncle Blaesus he did not wish to be forgotten. But this did not make Blaesus more famous, while the refusal of the honour heightened Dolabella's renown. He had, in fact, with a smaller army, brought back with him illustrious prisoners and the fame of having slain the enemy's leader and terminated the war. In his train were envoys from the Garamantes, a rare spectacle in Rome. The nation, in its terror at the destruction of Tacfarinas, and innocent of any guilty intention, had sent them to crave pardon of the Roman people. And now that this war had proved the zealous loyalty of Ptolemaeus, a custom of antiquity was revived, and one of the Senators was sent to present him with an ivory sceptre and an embroidered robe, gifts anciently bestowed by the Senate, and to confer on him the titles of king, ally, and friend.

The same summer, the germs of a slave war in Italy were crushed by a fortunate accident. The originator of the movement was Titus Curtisius, once a soldier of the praetorian guard. First, by secret meetings at Brundisium and the neighbouring towns, then by placards publicly exhibited, he incited the rural and savage slave-population of the remote forests to assert their freedom. By divine providence, three vessels came to land for the use of those who traversed that sea. In the same part of the country too was Curtius Lupus, the quaestor, who, according to ancient precedent, had had the charge of the "woodland pastures" assigned to him. Putting in motion a force of marines, he broke up the seditious combination in its very first beginnings. The emperor at once sent Staius, a tribune, with a strong detachment, by whom the ringleader himself, with his most daring followers, were brought prisoners to Rome where men already trembled at the vast scale of the slave-establishments, in which there was an immense growth, while the freeborn populace daily decreased.

That same consulship witnessed a horrible instance of misery and brutality. A father as defendant, a son as prosecutor, (Vibius Serenus was the name of both) were brought before the Senate; the father, dragged from exile in filth and squalor now stood in irons, while the son pleaded for his guilt. With studious elegance of dress and cheerful looks, the youth, at once accuser and witness, alleged a plot against the emperor and that men had been sent to Gaul to excite rebellion, further adding that Caecilius Cornutus, an ex-praetor, had furnished money. Cornutus, weary of anxiety and feeling that peril was equivalent to ruin, hastened to destroy himself. But the accused with fearless spirit, looked his son in the face, shook his chains, and appealed to the vengeance of the gods, with a prayer that they would restore him to his exile, where he might live far away from such practices, and that, as for his son, punishment might sooner or later overtake him. He protested too that Cornutus was innocent and that his terror was groundless, as would easily be perceived, if other names were given up; for he never would have plotted the emperor's murder and a revolution with only one confederate.

Upon this the prosecutor named Cneius Lentulus and Seius Tubero, to the great confusion of the emperor, at finding a hostile rebellion and disturbance of the public peace charged on two leading men in the state, his own intimate friends, the first of whom was in extreme old age and the second in very feeble health. They were, however, at once acquitted. As for the father, his slaves were examined by torture, and the result was unfavourable to the accuser. The man, maddened by remorse, and terror-stricken by the popular voice, which menaced him with the dungeon, the rock, or a parricide's doom, fled from Rome. He was dragged back from Ravenna, and forced to go through the prosecution, during which Tiberius did not disguise the old grudge he bore the exile Serenus. For after Libo's conviction, Serenus had sent the emperor a letter, upbraiding him for not having rewarded his special zeal in that trial, with further hints more insolent than could be safely trusted to the easily offended ears of a despot. All this Tiberius revived eight years later, charging on him various misconduct during that interval, even though the examination by torture, owing to the obstinacy of the slaves, had contradicted his guilt.

The Senate then gave their votes that Serenus should be punished according to ancient precedent, when the emperor, to soften the odium of the affair, interposed with his veto. Next, Gallus Asinius proposed that he should be confined in Gyaros or Donusa, but this he rejected, on the ground that both these islands were deficient in water, and that he whose life was spared, ought to be allowed the necessaries of life. And so Serenus was conveyed back to Amorgus.

In consequence of the suicide of Cornutus, it was proposed to deprive informers of their rewards whenever a person accused of treason put an end to his life by his own act before the completion of the trial. The motion was on the point of being carried when the emperor, with a harshness contrary to his manner, spoke openly for the informers, complaining that the laws would be ineffective, and the State brought to the verge of ruin. "Better," he said, "to subvert the constitution than to remove its guardians." Thus the informers, a class invented to destroy the commonwealth, and never enough controlled even by legal penalties, were stimulated by rewards.

Some little joy broke this long succession of horrors. Caius Cominius, a Roman knight, was spared by the emperor, against whom he was convicted of having written libellous verses, at the intercession of his brother, who was a Senator. Hence it seemed the more amazing that one who knew better things and the glory which waits on mercy, should prefer harsher courses. He did not indeed err from dulness, and it is easy to see when the acts of a sovereign meet with genuine, and when with fictitious popularity. And even he himself, though usually artificial in manner, and though his words escaped him with a seeming struggle, spoke out freely and fluently whenever he came to a man's rescue.

In another case, that of Publius Suillius, formerly quaestor to Germanicus, who was to be expelled from Italy on a conviction of having received money for a judicial decision, he held that the man ought to be banished to an island, and so intensely strong was his feeling that he bound the Senate by an oath that this was a State necessity. The act was thought cruel at the moment, but subsequently it redounded to his honour when Suillius returned from exile. The next age saw him in tremendous power and a venal creature of the emperor Claudius, whose friendship he long used, with success, never for good.

The same punishment was adjudged to Catus Firmius, a Senator, for having (it was alleged) assailed his sister with a false charge of treason. Catus, as I have related, had drawn Libo into a snare and then destroyed him by an information. Tiberius remembering this service, while he alleged other reasons, deprecated a sentence of exile, but did not oppose his expulsion from the Senate.

Much what I have related and shall have to relate, may perhaps, I am aware, seem petty trifles to record. But no one must compare my annals with the writings of those who have described Rome in old days. They told of great wars, of the storming of cities, of the defeat and capture of kings, or whenever they turned by preference to home affairs, they related, with a free scope for digression, the strifes of consuls with tribunes, land and corn-laws, and the struggles between the commons and the aristocracy. My labours are circumscribed and inglorious; peace wholly unbroken or but slightly disturbed, dismal misery in the capital, an emperor careless about the enlargement of the empire, such is my theme. Still it will not be useless to study those at first sight trifling events out of which the movements of vast changes often take their rise.

All nations and cities are ruled by the people, the nobility, or by one man. A constitution, formed by selection out of these elements, it is easy to commend but not to produce; or, if it is produced, it cannot be lasting. Formerly, when the people had power or when the patricians were in the ascendant, the popular temper and the methods of controlling it, had to be studied, and those who knew most accurately the spirit of the Senate and aristocracy, had the credit of understanding the age and of being wise men. So now, after a revolution, when Rome is nothing but the realm of a single despot, there must be good in carefully noting and recording this period, for it is but few who have the foresight to distinguish right from wrong or what is sound from what is hurtful, while most men learn wisdom from the fortunes of others. Still, though this is instructive, it gives very little pleasure. Descriptions of countries, the various incidents of battles, glorious deaths of great generals, enchain and refresh a reader's mind. I have to present in succession the merciless biddings of a tyrant, incessant prosecutions, faithless friendships, the ruin of innocence, the same causes issuing in the same results, and I am everywhere confronted by a wearisome monotony in my subject matter. Then, again, an ancient historian has but few disparagers, and no one cares whether you praise more heartily the armies of Carthage or Rome. But of many who endured punishment or disgrace under Tiberius, the descendants yet survive; or even though the families themselves may be now extinct, you will find those who, from a resemblance of character, imagine that the evil deeds of others are a reproach to themselves. Again, even honour and virtue make enemies, condemning, as they do, their opposites by too close a contrast. But I return to my work.

In the year of the consulship of Cornelius Cossus and Asinius Agrippa, Cremutius Cordus was arraigned on a new charge, now for the first time heard. He had published a history in which he had praised Marcus Brutus and called Caius Cassius the last of the Romans. His accusers were Satrius Secundus and Pinarius Natta, creatures of Sejanus. This was enough to ruin the accused; and then too the emperor listened with an angry frown to his defence, which Cremutius, resolved to give up his life, began thus:—

"It is my words, Senators, which are condemned, so innocent am I of any guilty act; yet these do not touch the emperor or the emperor's mother, who are alone comprehended under the law of treason. I am said to have praised Brutus and Cassius, whose careers many have described and no one mentioned without eulogy. Titus Livius, pre-eminently famous for eloquence and truthfulness, extolled Cneius Pompeius in such a panegyric that Augustus called him Pompeianus, and yet this was no obstacle to their friendship. Scipio, Afranius, this very Cassius, this same Brutus, he nowhere describes as brigands and traitors, terms now applied to them, but repeatedly as illustrious men. Asinius Pollio's writings too hand down a glorious memory of them, and Messala Corvinus used to speak with pride of Cassius as his general. Yet both these men prospered to the end with wealth and preferment. Again, that book of Marcus Cicero, in which he lauded Cato to the skies, how else was it answered by Caesar the dictator, than by a written oration in reply, as if he was pleading in court? The letters Antonius, the harangues of Brutus contain reproaches against Augustus, false indeed, but urged with powerful sarcasm; the poems which we read of Bibaculus and Catullus are crammed with invectives on the Caesars. Yet the Divine Julius, the Divine Augustus themselves bore all this and let it pass, whether in forbearance or in wisdom I cannot easily say. Assuredly what is despised is soon forgotten; when you resent a thing, you seem to recognise it."

"Of the Greeks I say nothing; with them not only liberty, but even license went unpunished, or if a person aimed at chastising, he retaliated on satire by satire. It has, however, always been perfectly open to us without any one to censure, to speak freely of those whom death has withdrawn alike from the partialities of hatred or esteem. Are Cassius and Brutus now in arms on the fields of Philippi, and am I with them rousing the people by harangues to stir up civil war? Did they not fall more than seventy years ago, and as they are known to us by statues which even the conqueror did not destroy, so too is not some portion of their memory preserved for us by historians? To every man posterity gives his due honour, and, if a fatal sentence hangs over me, there will be those who will remember me as well as Cassius and Brutus."

He then left the Senate and ended his life by starvation. His books, so the Senators decreed, were to be burnt by the aediles; but some copies were left which were concealed and afterwards published. And so one is all the more inclined to laugh at the stupidity of men who suppose that the despotism of the present can actually efface the remembrances of the next generation. On the contrary, the persecution of genius fosters its influence; foreign tyrants, and all who have imitated their oppression, have merely procured infamy for themselves and glory for their victims.

That year was such a continuous succession of prosecutions that on the days of the Latin festival when Drusus, as city-prefect, had ascended his tribunal for the inauguration of his office, Calpurnius Salvianus appeared before him against Sextus Marius. This the emperor openly censured, and it caused the banishment of Salvianus. Next, the people of Cyzicus were accused of publicly neglecting the established worship of the Divine Augustus, and also of acts of violence to Roman citizens. They were deprived of the franchise which they had earned during the war with Mithridates, when their city was besieged, and when they repulsed the king as much by their own bravery as by the aid of Lucullus. Then followed the acquittal of Fonteius Capito, the late proconsul of Asia, on proof that charges brought against him by Vibius Serenus were fictitious. Still this did not injure Serenus, to whom public hatred was actually a protection. Indeed any conspicuously restless informer was, so to say, inviolable; only the insignificant and undistinguished were punished.

About the same time Further Spain sent a deputation to the Senate, with a request to be allowed, after the example of Asia, to erect a temple to Tiberius and his mother. On this occasion, the emperor, who had generally a strong contempt for honours, and now thought it right to reply to the rumour which reproached him with having yielded to vanity, delivered the following speech:—

"I am aware, Senators, that many deplore my want of firmness in not having opposed a similar recent petition from the cities of Asia. I will therefore both explain the grounds of my previous silence and my intentions for the future. Inasmuch as the Divine Augustus did not forbid the founding of a temple at Pergamos to himself and to the city of Rome, I who respect as law all his actions and sayings, have the more readily followed a precedent once approved, seeing that with the worship of myself was linked an expression of reverence towards the Senate. But though it may be pardonable to have allowed this once, it would be a vain and arrogant thing to receive the sacred honour of images representing the divine throughout all the provinces, and the homage paid to Augustus will disappear if it is vulgarised by indiscriminate flattery.

"For myself, Senators, I am mortal and limited to the functions of humanity, content if I can adequately fill the highest place; of this I solemnly assure you, and would have posterity remember it. They will more than sufficiently honour my memory by believing me to have been worthy of my ancestry, watchful over your interests, courageous in danger, fearless of enmity, when the State required it. These sentiments of your hearts are my temples, these my most glorious and abiding monuments. Those built of stone are despised as mere tombs, if the judgment of posterity passes into hatred. And therefore this is my prayer to our allies, our citizens, and to heaven itself; to the last, that, to my life's close, it grant me a tranquil mind, which can discern alike human and divine claims; to the first, that, when I die, they honour my career and the reputation of my name with praise and kindly remembrance."

Henceforth Tiberius even in private conversations persisted in showing contempt for such homage to himself. Some attributed this to modesty; many to self-distrust; a few to a mean spirit. "The noblest men," it was said, "have the loftiest aspirations, and so Hercules and Bacchus among the Greeks and Quirinus among us were enrolled in the number of the gods. Augustus, did better, seeing that he had aspired. All other things princes have as a matter of course; one thing they ought insatiably to pursue, that their memory may be glorious. For to despise fame is to despise merit."

Sejanus meanwhile, dazed by his extravagant prosperity and urged on too by a woman's passion, Livia now insisting on his promise of marriage, addressed a memorial to the emperor. For it was then the custom to apply to him by writing, even though he was at Rome. This petition was to the following effect:—The kindness of Augustus, the father, and then the many favourable testimonies of Tiberius, the son, had engendered the habit of confiding his hopes and wishes to the ears of emperors as readily as to those of the gods. The splendour of high distinctions he had never craved; he had rather chosen watchings and hardships, like one of the common soldiers, for the emperor's safety. But there was one most glorious honour he had won, the reputation of being worthy of an alliance with a Caesar. This was the first motive of his ambition. As he had heard that Augustus, in marrying his daughter, had even entertained some thoughts of Roman knights, so if a husband were sought for Livia, he hoped Tiberius would bear in mind a friend who would find his reward simply in the glory of the alliance. He did not wish to rid himself of the duties imposed on him; he thought it enough for his family to be secured against the unjust displeasure of Agrippina, and this for the sake of his children. For, as for himself, enough and more than enough for him would be a life completed while such a sovereign still reigned.

Tiberius, in reply, after praising the loyal sentiments of Sejanus and briefly enumerating the favours he had bestowed on him, asked time for impartial consideration, adding that while other men's plans depended on their ideas of their own interest, princes, who had to regulate their chief actions by public opinion, were in a different position. "Hence," he said, "I do not take refuge in an answer which it would be easy to return, that Livia can herself decide whether she considers that, after Drusus, she ought again to marry or rather to endure life in the same home, and that she has in her mother and grandmother counsellors nearer and dearer to her. I will deal more frankly. First, as to the enmity of Agrippina, I maintain that it will blaze out more fiercely if Livia's marriage rends, so to say, the house of the Caesars into two factions. Even as it is, feminine jealousies break out, and my grandsons are torn asunder by the strife. What will happen if the rivalry is rendered more intense by such a marriage? For you are mistaken, Sejanus, if you think that you will then remain in the same position, and that Livia, who has been the wife of Caius Caesar and afterwards of Drusus, will have the inclination to pass her old age with a mere Roman knight. Though I might allow it, do you imagine it would be tolerated by those who have seen her brother, her father, and our ancestors in the highest offices of state? You indeed desire to keep within your station; but those magistrates and nobles who intrude on you against your wishes and consult you on all matters, openly give out that you have long overstepped the rank of a knight and gone far beyond my father's friendships, and from their dislike of you they also condemn me. But, you say, Augustus had thoughts of giving his daughter to a Roman knight. Is it surprising that, with so many distracting cares, foreseeing too the immense elevation to which a man would be raised above others by such an alliance, he talked of Caius Proculeius and certain persons of singularly quiet life, wholly free from political entanglements? Still, if the hesitation of Augustus is to influence us, how much stronger is the fact that he bestowed his daughter on Marcus Agrippa, then on myself. All this, as a friend, I have stated without reserve, but I will not oppose your plans or those of Livia. My own earnest thoughts and the ties with which I am still purposing to unite you to myself, I shall for the present forbear to explain. This only I will declare, that nothing is too grand to be deserved by your merits and your goodwill towards me. When an opportunity presents itself, either in the Senate, or in a popular assembly, I shall not be silent."

Sejanus, no longer thinking of his marriage but filled with a deeper alarm, rejoined by deprecating the whispers of suspicion, popular rumour and the gathering storm of odium. That he might not impair his influence by closing his doors on the throngs of his many visitors or strengthen the hands of accusers by admitting them, he made it his aim to induce Tiberius to live in some charming spot at a distance from Rome. In this he foresaw several advantages. Access to the emperor would be under his own control, and letters, for the most part being conveyed by soldiers, would pass through his hands. Caesar too, who was already in the decline of life, would soon, when enervated by retirement, more readily transfer to him the functions of empire; envy towards himself would be lessened when there was an end to his crowded levies and the reality of power would be increased by the removal of its empty show. So he began to declaim against the laborious life of the capital, the bustling crowds and streaming multitudes, while he praised repose and solitude, with their freedom from vexations and misunderstandings, and their special opportunities for the study of the highest questions.

It happened that the trial at this time of Votienus Montanus, a popular wit, convinced the hesitating Tiberius that he ought to shun all assemblies of the Senate, where speeches, often true and offensive, were flung in his very face. Votienus was charged with insulting expressions towards the emperor, and while the witness, Aemilius, a military man, in his eagerness to prove the case, repeated the whole story and amid angry clamour struggled on with loud assertion, Tiberius heard the reproaches by which he was assailed in secret, and was so deeply impressed that he exclaimed that he would clear himself either at once or on a legal inquiry, and the entreaties of friends, with the flattery of the whole assembly, hardly restored his composure. As for Votienus, he suffered the penalty of treason; but the emperor, clinging all the more obstinately to the harshness with which he had been reproached in regard to accused persons, punished Aquilia with exile for the crime of adultery with Varius Ligur, although Lentulus Gaetulicus, the consul-elect, had proposed that she should be sentenced under the Julian law. He next struck off Apidius Merula from the register of the Senate for not having sworn obedience to the legislation of the Divine Augustus.

Then a hearing was given to embassies from the Lacedaemonians and Messenians on the question of the temple of Diana in the Marshes. The Lacedaemonians asserted that it had been dedicated by their ancestors and in their territory, and appealed to the records of their history and the hymns of poets, but it had been wrested from, they said, by the arms of the Macedonian Philip, with whom they had fought, and subsequently restored by the decision of Caius Caesar and Marcus Antonius. The Messenians, on the contrary, alleged the ancient division of the Peloponnesus among the descendants of Hercules, in which the territory of Denthelia (where the temple stood) had fallen to their king. Records of this event still existed, engraven on stone and ancient bronze. But if they were asked for the testimony of poetry and of history, they had it, they said, in greater abundance and authenticity. Philip had not decided arbitrarily, but according to fact, and king Antigonus, as also the general Mummius, had pronounced the same judgment. Such too had been the award of the Milesians to whom the arbitration had been publicly entrusted, and, finally, of Atidius Geminus, the praetor of Achaia. And so the question was decided in favour of the Messenians.

Next the people of Segesta petitioned for the restoration of the temple of Venus at Mount Eryx, which had fallen to ruin from its antiquity. They repeated the well-known story of its origin, which delighted Tiberius. He undertook the work willingly, as being a kinsman of the goddess. After this was discussed a petition from the city of Massilia, and sanction given to the precedent of Publius Rutilius, who having been legally banished from Rome, had been adopted as a citizen by the people of Smyrna. Volcatius Moschus, also an exile, had been received with a similar privilege by the inhabitants of Massilia, and had left his property to their community, as being now his own country.

Two men of noble rank died in that year, Cneius Lentulus and Lucius Domitius. It had been the glory of Lentulus, to say nothing of his consulship and his triumphal distinctions over the Gaetuli, to have borne poverty with a good grace, then to have attained great wealth, which had been blamelessly acquired and was modestly enjoyed. Domitius derived lustre from a father who during the civil war had been master of the sea, till he united himself to the party of Antonius and afterwards to that of Caesar. His grandfather had fallen in the battle of Pharsalia, fighting for the aristocracy. He had himself been chosen to be the husband of the younger Antonia, daughter of Octavia, and subsequently led an army across the Elbe, penetrating further into Germany than any Roman before him. For this achievement he gained triumphal honours.

Lucius Antonius too then died, of a most illustrious but unfortunate family. His father, Julius Antonius, was capitally punished for adultery with Julia, and the son, when a mere youth, was banished by Augustus, whose sister's grandson he was, to the city of Massilia, where the name of exile might be masked under that of student. Yet honour was paid him in death, and his bones, by the Senate's decree, were consigned to the sepulchre of the Octavii.

While the same consuls were in office, an atrocious crime was committed in Nearer Spain by a peasant of the Termestine tribe. Suddenly attacking the praetor of the province, Lucius Piso, as he was travelling in all the carelessness of peace, he killed him with a single wound. He then fled on a swift horse, and reached a wooded country, where he parted with his steed and eluded pursuit amid rocky and pathless wilds. But he was soon discovered. The horse was caught and led through the neighbouring villages, and its owner ascertained. Being found and put to the torture that he might be forced to reveal his accomplices, he exclaimed in a loud voice, in the language of his country, that it was in vain to question him; his comrades might stand by and look on, but that the most intense agony would not wring the truth from him. Next day, when he was dragged back to torture, he broke loose from his guards and dashed his head against a stone with such violence that he instantly fell dead. It was however believed that Piso was treacherously murdered by the Termestini. Some public money had been embezzled, and he was pressing for its payment too rigorously for the patience of barbarians.

In the consulship of Lentulus Gaetulicus and Caius Calvisius, triumphal distinctions were decreed to Poppaeus Sabinus, for a crushing defeat of some Thracian tribes, whose wild life in the highlands of a mountainous country made them unusually fierce. Besides their natural ferocity, the rebellion had its origin in their scornful refusal to endure levies and to supply our armies with their bravest men. Even native princes they would obey only according to their caprice, and if they sent aid, they used to appoint their own leaders and fight only against their neighbours. A rumour had then spread itself among them that, dispersed and mingled with other tribes, they were to be dragged away to distant countries. Before however they took up arms, they sent envoys with assurances of their friendship and loyalty, which, they said, would continue, if they were not tried by any fresh burden. But if they were doomed to slavery as a conquered people, they had swords and young warriors and a spirit bent on freedom or resigned to death. As they spoke, they pointed to fortresses amid rocks whither they had conveyed their parents and their wives, and threatened us with a difficult, dangerous and sanguinary war.

Sabinus meantime, while he was concentrating his troops, returned gentle answers; but on the arrival of Pomponius Labeo with a legion from Moesia and of king Rhoemetalces with some reinforcements from his subjects, who had not thrown off their allegiance, with these and the force he had on the spot, he advanced on the enemy, who were drawn up in some wooded defiles. Some ventured to show themselves on the open hills; these the Roman general approached in fighting order and easily dislodged them, with only a small slaughter of the barbarians, who had not far to flee. In this position he soon established a camp, and held with a strong detachment a narrow and unbroken mountain ridge, stretching as far as the next fortress, which was garrisoned by a large force of armed soldiers along with some irregulars. Against the boldest of these, who after the manner of their country were disporting themselves with songs and dances in front of the rampart, he sent some picked archers, who, discharging distant volleys, inflicted many wounds without loss to themselves. As they advanced, a sudden sortie put them to the rout, and they fell back on the support of a Sugambrian cohort, drawn up at no great distance by the Roman general, ready for any emergency and as terrible as the foe, with the noise of their war songs and the clashing of their arms.

He then moved his camp near to the enemy, leaving in his former entrenchments the Thracians who, as I have mentioned, were with us. These had permission to ravage, burn, and plunder, provided they confined their forays to daylight, and passed the night securely and vigilantly in their camp. This at first they strictly observed. Soon they resigned themselves to enjoyment, and, enriched by plunder, they neglected their guards, and amid feasts and mirth sank down in the carelessness of the banquet, of sleep and of wine. So the enemy, apprised of their heedlessness, prepared two detachments, one of which was to attack the plunderers, the other, to fall on the Roman camp, not with the hope of taking it, but to hinder the din of the other battle from being heard by our soldiers, who, with shouts and missiles around them, would be all intent on their own peril. Night too was chosen for the movement to increase the panic. Those however who tried to storm the entrenchment of the legions were easily repulsed; the Thracian auxiliaries were dismayed by the suddenness of the onset, for though some were lying close to their lines, far more were straggling beyond them, and the massacre was all the more savage, inasmuch as they were taunted with being fugitives and traitors and bearing arms for their own and their country's enslavement.

Next day Sabinus displayed his forces in the plain, on the chance of the barbarians being encouraged by the night's success to risk an engagement. Finding that they did not quit the fortress and the adjoining hills, he began a siege by means of the works which he had opportunely began to construct; then he drew a fosse and stockade enclosing an extent of four miles, and by degrees contracted and narrowed his lines, with the view of cutting off their water and forage. He also threw up a rampart, from which to discharge stones, darts, and brands on the enemy, who was now within range. It was thirst however which chiefly distressed them, for there was only one spring for the use of a vast multitude of soldiers and non-combatants. Their cattle too, penned up close to them, after the fashion of barbarians, were dying of want of fodder; near them lay human bodies which had perished from wounds or thirst, and the whole place was befouled with rotting carcases and stench and infection. To their confusion was added the growing misery of discord, some thinking of surrender, others of destruction by mutual blows. Some there were who suggested a sortie instead of an unavenged death, and these were all men of spirit, though they differed in their plans.

One of their chiefs, Dinis, an old man who well knew by long experience both the strength and clemency of Rome, maintained that they must lay down their arms, this being the only remedy for their wretched plight, and he was the first to give himself up with his wife and children to the conqueror. He was followed by all whom age or sex unfitted for war, by all too who had a stronger love of life than of renown. The young were divided between Tarsa and Turesis, both of whom had resolved to fall together with their freedom. Tarsa however kept urging them to speedy death and to the instant breaking off of all hope and fear, and, by way of example, plunged his sword into his heart. And there were some who chose the same death. Turesis and his band waited for night, not without the knowledge of our general. Consequently, the sentries were strengthened with denser masses of troops. Night was coming on with a fierce storm, and the foe, one moment with a tumultuous uproar, another in awful silence, had perplexed the besiegers, when Sabinus went round the camp, entreating the men not to give a chance to their stealthy assailants by heeding embarrassing noises or being deceived by quiet, but to keep, every one, to his post without moving or discharging their darts on false alarms.

The barbarians meanwhile rushed down with their bands, now hurling at the entrenchments stones such as the hand could grasp, stakes with points hardened by fire, and boughs lopped from oaks; now filling up the fosses with bushes and hurdles and dead bodies, while others advanced up to the breastwork with bridges and ladders which they had constructed for the occasion, seized it, tore it down, and came to close quarters with the defenders. Our soldiers on the other side drove them back with missiles, repelled them with their shields, and covered them with a storm of long siege-javelins and heaps of stones. Success already gained and the more marked disgrace which would follow repulse, were a stimulus to the Romans, while the courage of the foe was heightened by this last chance of deliverance and the presence of many mothers and wives with mournful cries. Darkness, which increased the daring of some and the terror of others, random blows, wounds not foreseen, failure to recognise friend or enemy, echoes, seemingly in their rear, from the winding mountain valleys, spread such confusion that the Romans abandoned some of their lines in the belief that they had been stormed. Only however a very few of the enemy had broken through them; the rest, after their bravest men had been beaten back or wounded, were towards daybreak pushed back to the upper part of the fortress and there at last compelled to surrender. Then the immediate neighbourhood, by the voluntary action of the inhabitants, submitted. The early and severe winter of Mount Haemus saved the rest of the population from being reduced by assault or blockade.

At Rome meanwhile, besides the shocks already sustained by the imperial house, came the first step towards the destruction of Agrippina, Claudia Pulchra, her cousin, being prosecuted by Domitius Afer. Lately a praetor, a man of but moderate position and eager to become notorious by any sort of deed, Afer charged her with unchastity, with having Furnius for her paramour, and with attempts on the emperor by poison and sorcery. Agrippina, always impetuous, and now kindled into fury by the peril of her kinswoman, went straight to Tiberius and found him, as it happened, offering a sacrifice to his father. This provoked an indignant outburst. "It is not," she exclaimed, "for the same man to slay victims to the Divine Augustus and to persecute his posterity. The celestial spirit has not transferred itself to the mute statue; here is the true image, sprung of heavenly blood, and she perceives her danger, and assumes its mournful emblems. Pulchra's name is a mere blind; the only reason for her destruction is that she has, in utter folly, selected Agrippina for her admiration, forgetting that Sosia was thereby ruined." These words wrung from the emperor one of the rare utterances of that inscrutable breast; he rebuked Agrippina with a Greek verse, and reminded her that "she was not wronged because she was not a queen." Pulchra and Furnius were condemned. Afer was ranked with the foremost orators, for the ability which he displayed, and which won strong praise from Tiberius, who pronounced him a speaker of natural genius. Henceforward as a counsel for the defence or the prosecution he enjoyed the fame of eloquence rather than of virtue, but old age robbed him of much of his speaking power, while, with a failing intellect, he was still impatient of silence.

Agrippina in stubborn rage, with the grasp of disease yet on her, when the emperor came to see her, wept long and silently, and then began to mingle reproach and supplication. She begged him "to relieve her loneliness and provide her with a husband; her youth still fitted her for marriage, which was a virtuous woman's only solace, and there were citizens in Rome who would not disdain to receive the wife of Germanicus and his children." But the emperor, who perceived the political aims of her request, but did not wish to show displeasure or apprehension, left her, notwithstanding her urgency, without an answer. This incident, not mentioned by any historian, I have found in the memoirs of the younger Agrippina, the mother of the emperor Nero, who handed down to posterity the story of her life and of the misfortunes of her family.

Sejanus meanwhile yet more deeply alarmed the sorrowing and unsuspecting woman by sending his agents, under the guise of friendship, with warnings that poison was prepared for her, and that she ought to avoid her father-in-law's table. Knowing not how to dissemble, she relaxed neither her features nor tone of voice as she sat by him at dinner, nor did she touch a single dish, till at last Tiberius noticed her conduct, either casually or because he was told of it. To test her more closely, he praised some fruit as it was set on the table and passed it with his own hand to his daughter-in-law. This increased the suspicions of Agrippina, and without putting the fruit to her lips she gave it to the slaves. Still no remark fell from Tiberius before the company, but he turned to his mother and whispered that it was not surprising if he had decided on harsh treatment against one who implied that he was a poisoner. Then there was a rumour that a plan was laid for her destruction, that the emperor did not dare to attempt it openly, and was seeking to veil the deed in secrecy.

Tiberius, to divert people's talk, continually attended the Senate, and gave an audience of several days to embassies from Asia on a disputed question as to the city in which the temple before mentioned should be erected. Eleven cities were rivals for the honour, of which they were all equally ambitious, though they differed widely in resources. With little variation they dwelt on antiquity of race and loyalty to Rome throughout her wars with Perseus, Aristonicus, and other kings. But the people of Hypaepa, Tralles, Laodicaea, and Magnesia were passed over as too insignificant; even Ilium, though it boasted that Troy was the cradle of Rome, was strong only in the glory of its antiquity. There was a little hesitation about Halicarnassus, as its inhabitants affirmed that for twelve hundred years their homes had not been shaken by an earthquake and that the foundations of their temple were on the living rock. Pergamos, it was thought, had been sufficiently honoured by having a temple of Augustus in the city, on which very fact they relied. The Ephesians and Milesians had, it seemed, wholly devoted their respective towns to the worships of Apollo and Diana. And so the question lay between Sardis and

Smyrna. The envoys from Sardis read a decree of the Etrurians, with whom they claimed kindred. "Tyrrhenus and Lydus," it was said, "the sons of King Atys, divided the nation between them because of its multitude; Lydus remained in the country of his fathers; Tyrrhenus had the work assigned him of establishing new settlements, and names, taken from the two leaders, were given to the one people in Asia and to the other in Italy. The resources of the Lydians were yet further augmented by the immigration of nations into that part of Greece which afterwards took its name from Pelops." They spoke too of letters from Roman generals, of treaties concluded with us during the Macedonian war, and of their copious rivers, of their climate, and the rich countries round them.

The envoys from Smyrna, after tracing their city's antiquity back to such founders as either Tantalus, the son of Jupiter, or Theseus, also of divine origin, or one of the Amazons, passed on to that on which they chiefly relied, their services to the Roman people, whom they had helped with naval armaments, not only in wars abroad, but in those under which we struggled in Italy. They had also been the first, they said, to build a temple in honour of Rome, during the consulship of Marcus Porcius Cato, when Rome's power indeed was great, but not yet raised to the highest point, inasmuch as the Punic capital was still standing and there were mighty kings in Asia. They appealed too to the of Lucius Sulla, whose army was once in terrible jeopardy from a severe winter and want of clothing, and this having been announced at Smyrna in a public assembly, all who were present stript their clothes off their backs and sent them to our legions. And so the Senate, when the question was put, gave the preference to Smyrna. Vibius Marsus moved that Marcus Lepidus, to whom the province of Asia had been assigned, should have under him a special commissioner to undertake the charge of this temple. As Lepidus himself, out of modesty, declined to appoint, Valerius Naso, one of the ex-praetors, was chosen by lot and sent out.

Meanwhile, after long reflection on his purpose and frequent deferment of it, the emperor retired into Campania to dedicate, as he pretended, a temple to Jupiter at Capua and another to Augustus at Nola, but really resolved to live at a distance from Rome. Although I have followed most historians in attributing the cause of his retirement to the arts of Sejanus, still, as he passed six consecutive years in the same solitude after that minister's destruction, I am often in doubt whether it is not to be more truly ascribed to himself, and his wish to hide by the place of his retreat the cruelty and licentiousness which he betrayed by his actions. Some thought that in his old age he was ashamed of his personal appearance. He had indeed a tall, singularly slender and stooping figure, a bald head, a face full of eruptions, and covered here and there with plasters. In the seclusion of Rhodes he had habituated himself to shun society and to hide his voluptuous life. According to one account his mother's domineering temper drove him away; he was weary of having her as his partner in power, and he could not thrust her aside, because he had received this very power as her gift. For Augustus had had thoughts of putting the Roman state under Germanicus, his sister's grandson, whom all men esteemed, but yielding to his wife's entreaties he left Germanicus to be adopted by Tiberius and adopted Tiberius himself. With this Augusta would taunt her son, and claim back what she had given.

His departure was attended by a small retinue, one senator, who was an ex-consul, Cocceius Nerva, learned in the laws, one Roman knight, besides Sejanus, of the highest order, Curtius Atticus, the rest being men of liberal culture, for the most part Greeks, in whose conversation he might find amusement. It was said by men who knew the stars that the motions of the heavenly bodies when Tiberius left Rome were such as to forbid the possibility of his return. This caused ruin for many who conjectured that his end was near and spread the rumour; for they never foresaw the very improbable contingency of his voluntary exile from his home for eleven years. Soon afterwards it was clearly seen what a narrow margin there is between such science and delusion and in what obscurity truth is veiled. That he would not return to Rome was not a mere random assertion; as to the rest, they were wholly in the dark, seeing that he lived to extreme old age in the country or on the coast near Rome and often close to the very walls of the city.

It happened at this time that a perilous accident which occurred to the emperor strengthened vague rumours and gave him grounds for trusting more fully in the friendship and fidelity of Sejanus. They were dining in a country house called "The Cave," between the gulf of Amuclae and the hills of Fundi, in a natural grotto. The rocks at its entrance suddenly fell in and crushed some of the attendants; there upon panic seized the whole company and there was a general flight of the guests. Sejanus hung over the emperor, and with knee, face, and hand encountered the falling stones; and was found in this attitude by the soldiers who came to their rescue. After this he was greater than ever, and though his counsels were ruinous, he was listened to with confidence, as a man who had no care for himself. He pretended to act as a judge towards the children of Germanicus, after having suborned persons to assume the part of prosecutors and to inveigh specially against Nero, next in succession to the throne, who, though he had proper youthful modesty, often forgot present expediency, while freedmen and clients, eager to get power, incited him to display vigour and self-confidence. "This," they said, "was what the Roman people wished, what the armies desired, and Sejanus would not dare to oppose it, though now he insulted alike the tame spirit of the old emperor and the timidity of the young prince."

Nero, while he listened to this and like talk, was not indeed inspired with any guilty ambition, but still occasionally there would break from him wilful and thoughtless expressions which spies about his person caught up and reported with exaggeration, and this he had no opportunity of rebutting. Then again alarms under various forms were continually arising. One man would avoid meeting him; another after returning his salutation would instantly turn away; many after beginning a conversation would instantly break it off, while Sejanus's friends would stand their ground and laugh at him. Tiberius indeed wore an angry frown or a treacherous smile. Whether the young prince spoke or held his tongue, silence and speech were alike criminal. Every night had its anxieties, for his sleepless hours, his dreams and sighs were all made known by his wife to her mother Livia and by Livia to Sejanus. Nero's brother Drusus Sejanus actually drew into his scheme by holding out to him the prospect of becoming emperor through the removal of an elder brother, already all but fallen. The savage temper of Drusus, to say nothing of lust of power and the usual feuds between brothers, was inflamed with envy by the partiality of the mother Agrippina towards Nero. And yet Sejanus, while he favoured Drusus, was not without thoughts of sowing the seeds of his future ruin, well knowing how very impetuous he was and therefore the more exposed to treachery.

Towards the close of the year died two distinguished men, Asinius Agrippa and Quintus Haterius. Agrippa was of illustrious rather than ancient ancestry, which his career did not disgrace; Haterius was of a senatorian family and famous for his eloquence while he lived, though the monuments which remain of his genius are not admired as of old. The truth is he succeeded more by vehemence than by finish of style. While the research and labours of other authors are valued by an after age, the harmonious fluency of Haterius died with him.

In the year of the consulship of Marcus Licinius and Lucius Calpurnius, the losses of a great war were matched by an unexpected disaster, no sooner begun than ended. One Atilius, of the freedman class, having undertaken to build an amphitheatre at Fidena for the exhibition of a show of gladiators, failed to lay a solid foundation to frame the wooden superstructure with beams of sufficient strength; for he had neither an abundance of wealth, nor zeal for public popularity, but he had simply sought the work for sordid gain. Thither flocked all who loved such sights and who during the reign of Tiberius had been wholly debarred from such amusements; men and women of every age crowding to the place because it was near Rome. And so the calamity was all the more fatal. The building was densely crowded; then came a violent shock, as it fell inwards or spread outwards, precipitating and burying an immense multitude which was intently gazing on the show or standing round. Those who were crushed to death in the first moment of the accident had at least under such dreadful circumstances the advantage of escaping torture. More to be pitied were they who with limbs torn from them still retained life, while they recognised their wives and children by seeing them during the day and by hearing in the night their screams and groans. Soon all the neighbours in their excitement at the report were bewailing brothers, kinsmen or parents. Even those whose friends or relatives were away from home for quite a different reason, still trembled for them, and as it was not yet known who had been destroyed by the crash, suspense made the alarm more widespread.

As soon as they began to remove the debris, there was a rush to see the lifeless forms and much embracing and kissing. Often a dispute would arise, when some distorted face, bearing however a general resemblance of form and age, had baffled their efforts at recognition. Fifty thousand persons were maimed or destroyed in this disaster. For the future it was provided by a decree of the Senate that no one was to exhibit a show of gladiators, whose fortune fell short of four hundred thousand sesterces, and that no amphitheatre was to be erected except on a foundation, the solidity of which had been examined. Atilius was banished. At the moment of the calamity the nobles threw open houses and supplied indiscriminately medicines and physicians, so that Rome then, notwithstanding her sorrowful aspect, wore a likeness to the manners of our forefathers who after a great battle always relieved the wounded with their bounty and attentions.

This disaster was not forgotten when a furious conflagration damaged the capital to an unusual extent, reducing Mount Caelius to ashes. "It was an ill-starred year," people began to say, "and the emperor's purpose of leaving Rome must have been formed under evil omens." They began in vulgar fashion to trace ill-luck to guilt, when Tiberius checked them by distributing money in proportion to losses sustained. He received a vote of thanks in the Senate from its distinguished members, and was applauded by the populace for having assisted with his liberality, without partiality or the solicitations of friends, strangers whom he had himself sought out. And proposals were also made that Mount Caelius should for the future be called Mount Augustus, inasmuch as when all around was in flames only a single statue of Tiberius in the house of one Junius, a senator, had remained uninjured. This, it was said, had formerly happened to Claudia Quinta; her statue, which had twice escaped the violence of fire, had been dedicated by our ancestors in the temple of the Mother of Gods; hence the Claudii had been accounted sacred and numbered among deities, and so additional sanctity ought to be given to a spot where heaven showed such honour to the emperor.

It will not be uninteresting to mention that Mount Caelius was anciently known by the name of Querquetulanus, because it grew oak timber in abundance and was afterwards called Caelius by Caeles Vibenna, who led the Etruscan people to the aid of

Rome and had the place given him as a possession by Tarquinius Priscus or by some other of the kings. As to that point historians differ; as to the rest, it is beyond a question that Vibenna's numerous forces established themselves in the plain beneath and in the neighbourhood of the forum, and that the Tuscan street was named after these strangers.

But though the zeal of the nobles and the bounty of the prince brought relief to suffering, yet every day a stronger and fiercer host of informers pursued its victims, without one alleviating circumstance. Quintilius Varus, a rich man and related to the emperor, was suddenly attacked by Domitius Afer, the successful prosecutor of Claudia Pulchra, his mother, and no one wondered that the needy adventurer of many years who had squandered his lately gotten recompense was now preparing himself for fresh iniquities. That Publius Dolabella should have associated himself in the prosecution was a marvel, for he was of illustrious ancestry, was allied to Varus, and was now himself seeking to destroy his own noble race, his own kindred. The Senate however stopped the proceeding, and decided to wait for the emperor, this being the only means of escaping for a time impending horrors.

Caesar, meanwhile, after dedicating the temples in Campania, warned the public by an edict not to disturb his retirement and posted soldiers here and there to keep off the throngs of townsfolk. But he so loathed the towns and colonies and, in short, every place on the mainland, that he buried himself in the island of Capreae which is separated by three miles of strait from the extreme point of the promontory of Sorrentum. The solitude of the place was, I believe, its chief attraction, for a harbourless sea surrounds it and even for a small vessel it has but few safe retreats, nor can any one land unknown to the sentries. Its air in winter is soft, as it is screened by a mountain which is a protection against cutting winds. In summer it catches the western breezes, and the open sea round it renders it most delightful. It commanded too a prospect of the most lovely bay, till Vesuvius, bursting into flames, changed the face of the country. Greeks, so tradition says, occupied those parts and Capreae was inhabited by the Teleboi. Tiberius had by this time filled the island with twelve country houses, each with a grand name and a vast structure of its own. Intent as he had once been on the cares of state, he was now for thoroughly unbending himself in secret profligacy and a leisure of malignant schemes. For he still retained that rash proneness to suspect and to believe, which even at Rome Sejanus used to foster, and which he here excited more keenly, no longer concealing his machinations against Agrippina and Nero. Soldiers hung about them, and every message, every visit, their public and their private life were I may say regularly chronicled. And persons were actually suborned to advise them to flee to the armies of Germany, or when the Forum was most crowded, to clasp the statue of statue of the Divine Augustus and appeal to the protection of the people and Senate. These counsels they disdained, but they were charged with having had thoughts of acting on them.

The year of the consulship of Silanus and Silius Nerva opened with a foul beginning. A Roman knight of the highest rank, Titius Sabinus, was dragged to prison because he had been a friend of Germanicus. He had indeed persisted in showing marked respect towards his wife and children, as their visitor at home, their companion in public, the solitary survivor of so many clients, and he was consequently esteemed by the good, as he was a terror to the evil-minded. Latinius Latiaris, Porcius Cato, Petitius Rufus, and Marcus Opsius, ex-praetors, conspired to attack him, with an eye to the consulship, to which there was access only through Sejanus, and the good will of Sejanus was to be gained only by a crime. They arranged amongst themselves that Latiaris, who had some slight acquaintance with Sabinus, should devise the plot, that the rest should be present as witnesses, and that then they should begin the prosecution. Accordingly Latiaris, after first dropping some casual remarks, went on to praise the fidelity of Sabinus in not having, like others, forsaken after its fall the house of which he had been the friend in its prosperity. He also spoke highly of Germanicus and compassionately of Agrippina. Sabinus, with the natural softness of the human heart under calamity, burst into tears, which he followed up with complaints, and soon with yet more daring invective against Sejanus, against his cruelty, pride and ambition. He did not spare even Tiberius in his reproaches. That conversation, having united them, as it were, in an unlawful secret, led to a semblance of close intimacy. Henceforward Sabinus himself sought Latiaris, went continually to his house, and imparted to him his griefs, as to a most faithful friend.

The men whom I have named now consulted how these conversations might fall within the hearing of more persons. It was necessary that the place of meeting should preserve the appearance of secrecy, and, if witnesses were to stand behind the doors, there was a fear of their being seen or heard, or of suspicion casually arising. Three senators thrust themselves into the space between the roof and ceiling, a hiding-place as shameful as the treachery was execrable. They applied their ears to apertures and crevices. Latiaris meanwhile having met Sabinus in the streets, drew him to his house and to the room, as if he was going to communicate some fresh discoveries. There he talked much about past and impending troubles, a copious topic indeed, and about fresh horrors. Sabinus spoke as before and at greater length, as sorrow, when once it has broken into utterance, is the harder to restrain. Instantly they hastened to accuse him, and having despatched a letter to the emperor, they informed him of the order of the plot and of their own infamy. Never was Rome more distracted and terror-stricken. Meetings, conversations, the ear of friend and stranger were alike shunned; even things mute and lifeless, the very roofs and walls, were eyed with suspicion.

The emperor in his letter on the first of January, after offering the usual prayers for the new year, referred to Sabinus, whom he reproached with having corrupted some of his freedmen and having attempted his life, and he claimed vengeance in no obscure language. It was decreed without hesitation, and the condemned man was dragged off, exclaiming as loudly as he could, with head covered and throat tightly bound, "that this was inaugurating the year; these were the victims slain to Sejanus." Wherever he turned his eyes, wherever his words fell, there was flight and solitude; the streets and public places were forsaken. A few retraced their steps and again showed themselves, shuddering at the mere fact that they had betrayed alarm. "What day," they asked, "will be without some execution, when amid sacrifices and prayers, a time when it is usual to refrain even from a profane word, the chain and halter are introduced? Tiberius has not incurred such odium blindly; this is a studied device to make us believe that there is no reason why the new magistrates should not open the dungeons as well as the temple and the altars." Thereupon there came a letter of thanks to them for having punished a bitter foe to the State, and the emperor further added that he had an anxious life, that he apprehended treachery from enemies, but he mentioned no one by name. Still there was no question that this was aimed at Nero and Agrippina.

But for my plan of referring each event to its own year, I should feel a strong impulse to anticipate matters and at once relate the deaths by which Latinius and Opsius and the other authors of this atrocious deed perished, some after Caius became emperor, some even while Tiberius yet ruled. For although he would not have the instruments of his wickedness destroyed by others, he frequently, when he was tired of them, and fresh ones offered themselves for the same services, flung off the old, now become a mere incubus. But these and other punishments of guilty men I shall describe in due course.

Asinius Gallus, to whose children Agrippina was aunt, then moved that the emperor should be requested to disclose his apprehensions to the Senate and allow their removal. Of all his virtues, as he counted them, there was none on which Tiberius so prided himself as his ability to dissemble, and he was therefore the more irritated at an attempt to expose what he was hiding. Sejanus however pacified him, not out of love for Gallus, but rather to wait the result of the emperor's wavering mood, knowing, as he did, that, though slow in forming his purpose, yet having once broken through his reserve, he would follow up harsh words with terrible deeds.

About the same time Julia died, the granddaughter of Augustus. He had condemned her on a conviction of adultery and had banished her to the island of Trimerus, not far from the shores of Apulia. There she endured a twenty years' exile, in which she was supported by relief from Augusta, who having overthrown the prosperity of her step-children by secret machinations, made open display of her compassion to the fallen family.

That same year the Frisii, a nation beyond the Rhine, cast off peace, more because of our rapacity than from their impatience of subjection. Drusus had imposed on them a moderate tribute, suitable to their limited resources, the furnishing of ox hides for military purposes. No one ever severely scrutinized the size or thickness till Olennius, a first-rank centurion, appointed to govern the Frisii, selected hides of wild bulls as the standard according to which they were to be supplied. This would have been hard for any nation, and it was the less tolerable to the Germans, whose forests abound in huge beasts, while their home cattle are undersized. First it was their herds, next their lands, last, the persons of their wives and children, which they gave up to bondage. Then came angry remonstrances, and when they received no relief, they sought a remedy in war. The soldiers appointed to collect the tribute were seized and gibbeted. Olennius anticipated their fury by flight, and found refuge in a fortress, named Flevum, where a by no means contemptible force of Romans and allies kept guard over the shores of the ocean.

As soon as this was known to Lucius Apronius, propraetor of Lower Germany, he summoned from the Upper province the legionary veterans, as well as some picked auxiliary infantry and cavalry. Instantly conveying both armies down the Rhine, he threw them on the Frisii, raising at once the siege of the fortress and dispersing the rebels in defence of their own possessions. Next, he began constructing solid roads and bridges over the neighbouring estuaries for the passage of his heavy troops, and meanwhile having found a ford, he ordered the cavalry of the Canninefates, with all the German infantry which served with us, to take the enemy in the rear. Already in battle array, they were beating back our auxiliary horse as well as that of the legions sent to support them, when three light cohorts, then two more, and after a while the entire cavalry were sent to the attack. They were strong enough, had they charged altogether, but coming up, as they did, at intervals, they did not give fresh courage to the repulsed troops and were themselves carried away in the panic of the fugitives. Apronius entrusted the rest of the auxiliaries to Cethegus Labeo, the commander of the fifth legion, but he too, finding his men's position critical and being in extreme peril, sent messages imploring the whole strength of the legions. The soldiers of the fifth sprang forward, drove back the enemy in a fierce encounter, and saved our cohorts and cavalry, who were exhausted by their wounds. But the Roman general did not attempt vengeance or even bury the dead, although many tribunes, prefects, and first-rank centurions had fallen. Soon afterwards it was ascertained from deserters that nine hundred Romans had been cut to pieces in a wood called Braduhenna's, after prolonging the fight to the next day, and that another body of four hundred, which had taken possession of the house of one Cruptorix, once a soldier in our pay, fearing betrayal, had perished by mutual slaughter.

The Frisian name thus became famous in Germany, and Tiberius kept our losses a secret, not wishing to entrust any one with the war. Nor did the Senate care whether dishonour fell on the extreme frontiers of the empire. Fear at home had filled their hearts, and for this they sought relief in sycophancy. And so, although their advice was asked on totally different subjects, they decreed an altar to Clemency, an altar to Friendship, and statues round them to Caesar and Sejanus, both of whom they earnestly begged with repeated entreaties to allow themselves to be seen in public. Still, neither of them would visit Rome or even the neighbourhood of Rome; they thought it enough to quit the island and show themselves on the opposite shores of Campania. Senators, knights, a number of the city populace flocked thither, anxiously looking to Sejanus, approach to whom was particularly difficult and was consequently sought by intrigue and by complicity in his counsels. It was sufficiently clear that his arrogance was increased by gazing on this foul and openly displayed servility. At Rome indeed hurrying crowds are a familiar sight, from the extent of the city no one knows on what business each citizen is bent; but there, as they lounged in promiscuous crowds in the fields or on the shore, they had to bear day and night alike the patronising smiles and the supercilious insolence of hall-porters, till even this was forbidden them, and those whom Sejanus had not deigned to accost or to look on, returned to the capital in alarm, while some felt an evil joy, though there hung over them the dreadful doom of that ill-starred friendship.

Tiberius meanwhile having himself in person bestowed the hand of his granddaughter Agrippina, Germanicus's daughter, on Cneius Domitius, directed the marriage to be celebrated at Rome. In selecting Domitius he looked not only to his ancient lineage, but also to his alliance with the blood of the Caesars, for he could point to Octavia as his grandmother and through her to Augustus as his great-uncle.

BOOK V, A.D. 29-31

In the consulship of Rubellius and Fufius, both of whom had the surname Geminus, died in an advanced old age Julia Augusta. A Claudia by birth and by adoption a Livia and a Julia, she united the noblest blood of Rome. Her first marriage, by which she had children, was with Tiberius Nero, who, an exile during the Perusian war, returned to Rome when peace had been concluded between Sextus Pompeius and the triumvirs. After this Caesar, enamoured of her beauty, took her away from her husband, whether against her wish is uncertain. So impatient was he that he brought her to his house actually pregnant, not allowing time for her confinement. She had no subsequent issue, but allied as she was through the marriage of Agrippina and Germanicus to the blood of Augustus, her great-grandchildren were also his. In the purity of her home life she was of the ancient type, but was more gracious than was thought fitting in ladies of former days. An imperious mother and an amiable wife, she was a match for the diplomacy of her husband and the dissimulation of her son. Her funeral was simple, and her will long remained unexecuted. Her panegyric was pronounced from the Rostra by her great-grandson, Caius Caesar, who afterwards succeeded to power.

Tiberius however, making no change in his voluptuous life, excused himself by letter for his absence from his last duty to his mother on the ground of the pressure of business.

He even abridged, out of moderation, as it seemed, the honours which the Senate had voted on a lavish scale to her memory, allowing only a very few, and adding that no religious worship was to be decreed, this having been her own wish. In a part of the same letter he sneered at female friendships, with an indirect censure on the consul Fufius, who had risen to distinction through Augusta's partiality. Fufius was indeed a man well fitted to win the affection of a woman; he was witty too, and accustomed to ridicule Tiberius with those bitter jests which the powerful remember so long.

This at all events was the beginning of an unmitigated and grinding despotism. As long indeed as Augusta lived, there yet remained a refuge, for with Tiberius obedience to his mother was the habit of a life, and Sejanus did not dare to set himself above a parent's authority. Now, so to say, they threw off the reins and let loose their fury. A letter was sent, directed against Agrippina and Nero, which was popularly believed to have been long before forwarded and to have been kept back by Augusta, as it was publicly read soon after her death. It contained expressions of studied harshness, yet it was not armed rebellion or a longing for revolution, but unnatural passions and profligacy which the emperor imputed to his grandson. Against his daughter-in-law he did not dare to invent this much; he merely censured her insolent tongue and defiant spirit, amid the panic-stricken silence of the Senate, till a few who had no hope from merit (and public calamities are ever used by individuals for interested purposes) demanded that the question should be debated. The most eager was Cotta Messalinus, who made a savage speech. Still, the other principal senators, and especially the magistrates, were perplexed, for Tiberius, notwithstanding his furious invective, had left everything else in doubt.

There was in the Senate one Junius Rusticus, who having been appointed by the emperor to register its debates was therefore supposed to have an insight into his secret purposes. This man, whether through some fatal impulse (he had indeed never before given any evidence of courage) or a misdirected acuteness which made him tremble at the uncertain future, while he forgot impending perils, attached himself to the waverers, and warned the consuls not to enter on the debate. He argued that the highest issues turned on trivial causes, and that the fall of the house of Germanicus might one day move the old man's remorse. At the same moment the people, bearing the images of Agrippina and Nero, thronged round the Senate-house, and, with words of blessing on the emperor, kept shouting that the letter was a forgery and that it was not by the prince's will that ruin was being plotted against his house. And so that day passed without any dreadful result.

Fictitious speeches too against Sejanus were published under the names of ex-consuls, for several persons indulged, all the more recklessly because anonymously, the caprice of their imaginations. Consequently the wrath of Sejanus was the more furious, and he had ground for alleging that the Senate disregarded the emperor's trouble; that the people were in revolt; that speeches in a new style and new resolutions were being heard and read. What remained but to take the sword and chose for their generals and emperors those whose images they had followed as standards.

Upon this the emperor, after repeating his invectives against his grandson and his daughter-in-law and reprimanding the populace in an edict complained to the Senate that by the trick of one senator the imperial dignity had been publicly flouted, and he insisted that, after all, the whole matter should be left to his exclusive decision. Without further deliberation, they proceeded, not indeed to pronounce the final sentence (for this was forbidden), but to declare that they were prepared for vengeance, and were restrained only by the strong hand of the sovereign.

[The remainder of the fifth book and the beginning of the sixth, recounting Sejanus' marriage and fall and covering a space of nearly three years, are lost. Newer editions of Tacitus mark the division between the fifth and sixth books at this point rather than at the end of section 11; but references are regularly made to the older numbering, and so it has been retained here. The beginning of section 6 is obviously fragmentary.]

.... forty-four speeches were delivered on this subject, a few of which were prompted by fear, most by the habit of flattery...

"There is now a change of fortune, and even he who chose Sejanus to be his colleague and his son-in-law excuses his error. As for the rest, the man whom they encouraged by shameful baseness, they now wickedly revile. Which is the most pitiable, to be accused for friendship's sake or to have to accuse a friend, I cannot decide. I will not put any man's cruelty or compassion to the test, but, while I am free and have a clear conscience, I will anticipate peril. I implore you to cherish my memory with joy rather than with sorrow, numbering me too with those who by noble death have fled from the miseries of our country."

Then detaining those of his friends who were minded to stay with him and converse, or, if otherwise, dismissing them, he thus spent part of the day, and with a numerous circle yet round him, all gazing on his fearless face, and imagining that there was still time to elapse before the last scene, he fell on a sword which he had concealed in his robe. The emperor did not pursue him after his death with either accusation or reproach, although he had heaped a number of foul charges on Blaesus.

Next were discussed the cases of Publius Vitellius and Pomponius Secundus. The first was charged by his accusers with having offered the keys of the treasury, of which he was prefect, and the military chest in aid of a revolution. Against the latter, Considius, an ex-praetor, alleged intimacy with Aelius Gallus, who, after the punishment of Sejanus, had fled to the gardens of Pomponius, as his safest refuge. They had no resource in their peril but in the courageous firmness of their brothers who became their sureties. Soon, after several adjournments, Vitellius, weary alike of hope and fear, asked for a penknife, avowedly, for his literary pursuits, and inflicted a slight wound in his veins, and died at last of a broken heart. Pomponius, a man of refined manners and brilliant genius, bore his adverse fortune with resignation, and outlived Tiberius.

It was next decided to punish the remaining children of Sejanus, though the fury of the populace was subsiding, and people generally had been appeased by the previous executions. Accordingly they were carried off to prison, the boy, aware of his impending doom, and the little girl, who was so unconscious that she continually asked what was her offence, and whither she was being dragged, saying that she would do so no more, and a childish chastisement was enough for her correction. Historians of the time tell us that, as there was no precedent for the capital punishment of a virgin, she was violated by the executioner, with the rope on her neck. Then they were strangled and their bodies, mere children as they were, were flung down the Gemoniae.

About the same time Asia and Achaia were alarmed by a prevalent but short-lived rumour that Drusus, the son of Germanicus, had been seen in the Cyclades and subsequently on the mainland. There was indeed a young man of much the same age, whom some of the emperor's freedmen pretended to recognise, and to whom they attached themselves with a treacherous intent. The renown of the name attracted the ignorant, and the Greek mind eagerly fastens on what is new and marvellous. The story indeed, which they no sooner invented than believed, was that Drusus had escaped from custody, and was on his way to the armies of his father, with the design of invading

Egypt or Syria. And he was now drawing to himself a multitude of young men and much popular enthusiasm, enjoying the present and cherishing idle hopes of the future, when Poppaeus Sabinus heard of the affair. At the time he was chiefly occupied with Macedonia, but he also had the charge of Achaia. So, to forestall the danger, let the story be true or false, he hurried by the bays of Torone and Thermae, then passed on to Euboea, an island of the Aegaean, to Piraeus, on the coast of Attica, thence to the shores of Corinth and the narrow Isthmus, and having arrived by the other sea at Nicopolis, a Roman colony, he there at last ascertained that the man, when skilfully questioned, had said that he was the son of Marcus Silanus, and that, after the dispersion of a number of his followers' he had embarked on a vessel, intending, it seemed, to go to Italy. Sabinus sent this account to Tiberius, and of the origin and issue of the affair nothing more is known to me.

At the close of the year a long growing feud between the consuls broke out. Trio, a reckless man in incurring enmities and a practised lawyer, had indirectly censured Regulus as having been half-hearted in crushing the satellites of Sejanus. Regulus, who, unless he was provoked, loved quietness, not only repulsed his colleague's attack, but was for dragging him to trial as a guilty accomplice in the conspiracy. And though many of the senators implored them to compose a quarrel likely to end fatally, they continued their enmity and their mutual menaces till they retired from office.

BOOK VI, A.D. 32-37

Cneius Domitius and Camillus Scribonianus had entered on the consulship when the emperor, after crossing the channel which divides Capreae from Surrentum, sailed along Campania, in doubt whether he should enter Rome, or, possibly, simulating the intention of going thither, because he had resolved otherwise. He often landed at points in the neighborhood, visited the gardens by the Tiber, but went back again to the cliffs and to the solitude of the sea shores, in shame at the vices and profligacies into which he had plunged so unrestrainedly that in the fashion of a despot he debauched the children of free-born citizens. It was not merely beauty and a handsome person which he felt as an incentive to his lust, but the modesty of childhood in some, and noble ancestry in others. Hitherto unknown terms were then for the first time invented, derived from the abominations of the place and the endless phases of sensuality. Slaves too were set over the work of seeking out and procuring, with rewards for the willing, and threats to the reluctant, and if there was resistance from a relative or a parent, they used violence and force, and actually indulged their own passions as if dealing with captives.

At Rome meanwhile, in the beginning of the year, as if Livia's crimes had just been discovered and not also long ago punished, terrible decrees were proposed against her very statues and memory, and the property of Sejanus was to be taken from the exchequer and transferred to the imperial treasury; as if there was any difference. The motion was being urged with extreme persistency, in almost the same or with but slightly changed language, by such men as Scipio, Silanus, and Cassius, when suddenly Togonius Gallus intruding his own obscurity among illustrious names, was heard with ridicule. He begged the emperor to select a number of senators, twenty out of whom should be chosen by lot to wear swords and to defend his person, whenever he entered the Senate House. The man had actually believed a letter from him in which he asked the protection of one of the consuls, so that he might go in safety from Capreae to Rome. Tiberius however, who usually combined jesting and seriousness, thanked the senators for their goodwill, but asked who could be rejected, who could be chosen? "Were they always to be the same, or was there to be a succession? Were they to be men who had held office or youths, private citizens or officials? Then, again, what a scene would be presented by persons grasping their swords on the threshold of the Senate House? His life was not of so much worth if it had to be defended by arms." This was his answer to Togonius, guarded in its expression, and he urged nothing beyond the rejection of the motion.

Junius Gallio however, who had proposed that the praetorian soldiers, after having served their campaigns, should acquire the privilege of sitting in the fourteen rows of the theatre, received a savage censure. Tiberius, just as if he were face to face with him, asked what he had to do with the soldiers, who ought to receive the emperor's orders or his rewards except from the emperor himself? He had really discovered something which the Divine Augustus had not foreseen. Or was not one of Sejanus's satellites rather seeking to sow discord and sedition, as a means of prompting ignorant minds, under the pretence of compliment, to ruin military discipline? This was Gallio's recompense for his carefully prepared flattery, with immediate expulsion from the Senate, and then from Italy. And as men complained that he would endure his exile with equanimity, since he had chosen the famous and lovely island of Lesbos, he was dragged back to Rome, and confined in the houses of different officials.

The emperor in the same letter crushed Sextius Paconianus, an ex-praetor, to the great joy of the senators, as he was a daring, mischievous man, who pryed into every person's secrets, and had been the chosen instrument of Sejanus in his treacherous designs against Caius Caesar. When this fact was divulged, there came an outburst of long-concealed hatreds, and there must have been a sentence of capital punishment, had he not himself volunteered a disclosure.

As soon as he named Latinius Latiaris, accuser and accused, both alike objects of execration, presented a most welcome spectacle. Latiaris, as I have related, had been foremost in contriving the ruin of Titius Sabinus, and was now the first to pay the penalty. By way of episode, Haterius Agrippa inveighed against the consuls of the previous year for now sitting silent after their threats of impeaching one another. "It must be fear," he said, "and a guilty conscience which are acting as a bond of union. But the senators must not keep back what they have heard." Regulus replied that he was awaiting the opportunity for vengeance, and meant to press it in the emperor's presence. Trio's answer was that it was best to efface the memory of rivalries between colleagues, and of any words uttered in quarrels. When Agrippa still persisted, Sanquinius Maximus, one of the ex-consuls, implored the Senate not to increase the emperor's anxieties by seeking further occasions of bitterness, as he was himself competent to provide remedies. This secured the safety of Regulus and the postponement of Trio's ruin. Haterius was hated all the more. Wan with untimely slumbers and nights of riot, and not fearing in his indolence even the cruellest of princes, he yet plotted amid his gluttony and lust the destruction of illustrious men.

Several charges were next brought, as soon as the opportunity offered, against Cotta Messalinus, the author of every unusually cruel proposal, and consequently, regarded with inveterate hatred. He had spoken, it was said, of Caius Caesar, as if it were a question whether he was a man, and of an entertainment at which he was present on Augusta's birthday with the priests, as a funeral banquet. In remonstrating too against the influence of Marcus Lepidus and Lucius Arruntius, with whom he had disputes on many matters, he had added the remark, "They will have the Senate's support; I shall have that of my darling Tiberius." But the leading men of the State failed to convict him on all the charges. When they pressed the case, he appealed to the emperor. Soon afterwards, a letter arrived, in which Tiberius traced the origin of the friendship between himself and Cotta, enumerated his frequent services, and then requested that words perversely misrepresented and the freedom of table talk might not be construed into a crime.

The beginning of the emperor's letter seemed very striking. It opened thus: "May all the gods and goddesses destroy me more miserably than I feel myself to be daily perishing, if I know at know at this moment what to write to you, Senators, how to write it, or what, in short, not to write." So completely had his crimes and infamies recoiled, as a penalty, on himself. With profound meaning was it often affirmed by the greatest teacher of philosophy that, could the minds of tyrants be laid bare, there would be seen gashes and wounds; for, as the body is lacerated by scourging, so is the spirit by brutality, by lust and by evil thoughts. Assuredly Tiberius was not saved by his elevation or his solitude from having to confess the anguish of his heart and his self-inflicted punishment.

Authority was then given to the Senate to decide the case of Caecilianus, one of its members, the chief witness against Cotta, and it was agreed that the same penalty should be inflicted as on Aruseius and Sanquinius, the accusers of Lucius Arruntius. Nothing ever happened to Cotta more to his distinction. Of noble birth, but beggared by extravagance and infamous for his excesses, he was now by dignity of his revenge, raised to a level with the stainless virtues of Arruntius.

Quintus Servaeus and Minucius Thermus were next arraigned. Servaeus was an ex-praetor, and had formerly been a companion of Germanicus; Minucius was of equestrian rank, and both had enjoyed, though discreetly, the friendship of Sejanus. Hence they were the more pitied. Tiberius, on the contrary, denounced them as foremost in crime, and bade Caius Cestius, the elder, tell the Senate what he had communicated to the emperor by letter. Cestius undertook the prosecution. And this was the most dreadful feature of the age, that leading members of the Senate, some openly, some secretly employed themselves in the very lowest work of the informer. One could not distinguish between aliens and kinsfolk, between friends and strangers, or say what was quite recent, or what half-forgotten from lapse of time. People were incriminated for some casual remark in the forum or at the dinner-table, for every one was impatient to be the first to mark his victim, some to screen themselves, most from being, as it were, infected with the contagion of the malady.

Minucius and Servaeus, on being condemned, went over to the prosecution, and then Julius Africanus with Seius Quadratus were dragged into the same ruin. Africanus was from the Santones, one of the states of Gaul; the origin of Quadratus I have not ascertained. Many authors, I am well aware, have passed over the perils and punishments of a host of persons, sickened by the multiplicity of them, or fearing that what they had themselves found wearisome and saddening would be equally fatiguing to their readers. For myself, I have lighted on many facts worth knowing, though other writers have not recorded them.

A Roman knight, Marcus Terentius, at the crisis when all others had hypocritically repudiated the friendship of Sejanus, dared, when impeached on that ground, to cling to it by the following avowal to the Senate: "In my position it is perhaps less to my advantage to acknowledge than to deny the charge. Still, whatever is to be the issue of the matter, I shall admit that I was the friend of Sejanus, that I anxiously sought to be such, and was delighted when I was successful. I had seen him his father's colleague in the command of the praetorian cohorts, and subsequently combining the duties of civil and military life. His kinsfolk and connections were loaded with honours; intimacy with Sejanus was in every case a powerful recommendation to the emperor's friendship. Those, on the contrary, whom he hated, had to struggle with danger and humiliation. I take no individual as an instance. All of us who had no part in his last design, I mean to defend at the peril of myself alone. It was really not Sejanus of Vulsinii, it was a member of the Claudian and Julian houses, in which he had taken a position by his marriage-alliance, it was your son-in-law, Caesar, your partner in the consulship, the man who administered your political functions, whom we courted. It is not for us to criticise one whom you may raise above all others, or your motives for so doing. Heaven has intrusted you with the supreme decision of affairs, and for us is left the glory of obedience. And, again, we see what takes place before our eyes, who it is on whom you bestow riches and honours, who are the most powerful to help or to injure. That Sejanus was such, no one will deny. To explore the prince's secret thoughts, or any of his hidden plans, is a forbidden, a dangerous thing, nor does it follow that one could reach them.

"Do not, Senators, think only of Sejanus's last day, but of his sixteen years of power. We actually adored a Satrius and a Pomponius. To be known even to his freedmen and hall-porters was thought something very grand. What then is my meaning? Is this apology meant to be offered for all without difference and discrimination? No; it is to be restricted within proper limits. Let plots against the State, murderous designs against the emperor be punished. As for friendship and its obligations, the same principle must acquit both you, Caesar, and us."

The courage of this speech and the fact that there had been found a man to speak out what was in all people's thoughts, had such an effect that the accusers of Terentius were sentenced to banishment or death, their previous offences being taken into account. Then came a letter from Tiberius against Sextus Vestilius, an ex-praetor, whom, as a special favourite of his brother Drusus, the emperor had admitted into his own select circle. His reason for being displeased with Vestilius was that he had either written an attack on Caius Caesar as a profligate, or that Tiberius believed a false charge. For this Vestilius was excluded from the prince's table. He then tried the knife with his aged hand, but again bound up his veins, opening them once more however on having begged for pardon by letter and received a pitiless answer. After him a host of persons were charged with treason, Annius Pollio, Appius Silanus, Scaurus Mamercus, Sabinus Calvisius, Vinicianus too, coupled with Pollio, his father, men all of illustrious descent, some too of the highest political distinction. The senators were panic-stricken, for how few of their number were not connected by alliance or by friendship with this multitude of men of rank! Celsus however, tribune of a city cohort, and now one of the prosecutors, saved Appius and Calvisius from the peril. The emperor postponed the cases of Pollio, Vinicianus, and Scaurus, intending to try them himself with the Senate, not however without affixing some ominous marks to the name of Scaurus.

Even women were not exempt from danger. Where they could not be accused of grasping at political power, their tears were made a crime. Vitia, an aged woman, mother of Fufius Geminus, was executed for bewailing the death of her son. Such were the proceedings in the Senate. It was the same with the emperor. Vescularius Atticus and Julius Marinus were hurried off to execution, two of his oldest friends, men who had followed him to Rhodes and been his inseparable companions at Capreae. Vescularius was his agent in the plot against Libo, and it was with the co-operation of Marinus that Sejanus had ruined Curtius Atticus. Hence there was all the more joy at the recoil of these precedents on their authors.

About the same time Lucius Piso, the pontiff, died a natural death, a rare incident in so high a rank. Never had he by choice proposed a servile motion, and, whenever necessity was too strong for him, he would suggest judicious compromises. His father, as I have related, had been a censor. He lived to the advanced age of eighty, and had won in Thrace the honour of a triumph. But his chief glory rested on the wonderful tact with which as city-prefect he handled an authority, recently made perpetual and all the more galling to men unaccustomed to obey it.

In former days, when the kings and subsequently the chief magistrates went from Rome, an official was temporarily chosen to administer justice and provide for emergencies, so that the capital might not be left without government. It is said that Denter Romulius was appointed by Romulus, then Numa Marcius by Tullus Hostilius, and Spurius Lucretius by Tarquinius Superbus. Afterwards, the consuls made the appointment. The shadow of the old practice still survives, whenever in consequence of the Latin festival some one is deputed to exercise the consul's functions. And Augustus too during the civil wars gave Cilnius Maecenas, a Roman knight, charge of everything in Rome and Italy. When he rose to supreme power, in consideration of the magnitude of the State and the slowness of legal remedies, he selected one of the exconsuls to overawe the slaves and that part of the population which, unless it fears a strong hand, is disorderly and reckless. Messala Corvinus was the first to obtain the office, which he lost within a few days, as not knowing how to discharge it. After him Taurus Statilius, though in advanced years, sustained it admirably; and then Piso, after twenty years of similar credit, was, by the Senate's decree, honoured with a public funeral.

A motion was next brought forward in the Senate by Quintilianus, a tribune of the people, respecting an alleged book of the Sibyl. Caninius Gallus, a book of the College of the Fifteen, had asked that it might be received among the other volumes of the same prophetess by a decree on the subject. This having been carried by a division, the emperor sent a letter in which he gently censured the tribune, as ignorant of ancient usage because of his youth. Gallus he scolded for having introduced the matter in a thin Senate, notwithstanding his long experience in the science of religious ceremonies, without taking the opinion of the College or having the verses read and criticised, as was usual, by its presidents, though their authenticity was very doubtful. He also reminded him that, as many spurious productions were current under a celebrated name, Augustus had prescribed a day within which they should be deposited with the city-praetor, and after which it should not be lawful for any private person to hold them. The same regulations too had been made by our ancestors after the burning of the Capitol in the social war, when there was a search throughout Samos, Ilium, Erythrae, and even in Africa, Sicily and the Italian colonies for the verses of the Sibyl (whether there were but one or more) and the priests were charged with the business of distinguishing, as far as they could by human means, what were genuine. Accordingly the book in question was now also submitted to the scrutiny of the College of the Fifteen.

During the same consulship a high price of corn almost brought on an insurrection. For several days there were many clamorous demands made in the theatre with an unusual freedom of language towards the emperor. This provoked him to censure the magistrates and the Senate for not having used the authority of the State to put down the people. He named too the corn-supplying provinces, and dwelt on the far larger amount of grain imported by himself than by Augustus. So the Senate drew up a decree in the severe spirit of antiquity, and the consuls issued a not less stringent proclamation. The emperor's silence was not, as he had hoped, taken as a proof of patriotism, but of pride.

At the year's close Geminius, Celsus and Pompeius, Roman knights, fell beneath a charge of conspiracy. Of these Caius Geminius, by lavish expenditure and a luxurious life, had been a friend of Sejanus, but with no serious result. Julius Celsus, a tribune, while in confinement, loosened his chain, and having twisted it around him, broke his neck by throwing himself in an opposite direction. Rubrius Fabatus was put under surveillance, on a suspicion that, in despair of the fortunes of Rome, he meant to throw himself on the mercy of the Parthians. He was, at any rate, found near the Straits of the Sicily, and, when dragged back by a centurion, he assigned no adequate reason for his long journey. Still, he lived on in safety, thanks to forgetfulness rather than to mercy.

In the consulship of Servius Galba and Lucius Sulla, the emperor, after having long considered whom he was to choose to be husbands for his granddaughters, now that the maidens were of marriageable age, selected Lucius Cassius and Marcus Vinicius. Vinicius was of provincial descent; he was born at Cales, his father and grandfather having been consuls, and his family, on the other side, being of the rank of knights. He was a man of amiable temper and of cultivated eloquence. Cassius was of an ancient and honourable, though plebeian house, at Rome. Though he was brought up by his father under a severe training, he won esteem more frequently by his good-nature than by his diligence. To him and to Vinicius the emperor married respectively Drusilla and Julia, Germanicus's daughters, and addressed a letter on the subject to the Senate, with a slightly complimentary mention of the young men. He next assigned some very vague reasons for his absence, then passed to more important matters, the ill-will against him originating in his state policy, and requested that Macro, who commanded the praetorians, with a few tribunes and centurions, might accompany him whenever he entered the Senate-house. But though a decree was voted by the Senate on a liberal scale and without any restrictions as to rank or numbers, he never so much as went near the walls of Rome, much less the State-council, for he would often go round and avoid his native city by circuitous routes.

Meanwhile a powerful host of accusers fell with sudden fury on the class which systematically increased its wealth by usury in defiance of a law passed by Caesar the Dictator defining the terms of lending money and of holding estates in Italy, a law long obsolete because the public good is sacrificed to private interest. The curse of usury was indeed of old standing in Rome and a most frequent cause of sedition and discord, and it was therefore repressed even in the early days of a less corrupt morality. First, the Twelve Tables prohibited any one from exacting more than 10 per cent., when, previously, the rate had depended on the caprice of the wealthy. Subsequently, by a bill brought in by the tribunes, interest was reduced to half that amount, and finally compound interest was wholly forbidden. A check too was put by several enactments of the people on evasions which, though continually put down, still, through strange artifices, reappeared. On this occasion, however, Gracchus, the praetor, to whose jurisdiction the inquiry had fallen, felt himself compelled by the number of persons endangered to refer the matter to the Senate. In their dismay the senators, not one of whom was free from similar guilt, threw themselves on the emperor's indulgence. He yielded, and a year and six months were granted, within which every one was to settle his private accounts conformably to the requirements of the law.

Hence followed a scarcity of money, a great shock being given to all credit, the current coin too, in consequence of the conviction of so many persons and the sale of their property, being locked up in the imperial treasury or the public exchequer. To meet this, the Senate had directed that every creditor should have two-thirds his capital secured on estates in Italy. Creditors however were suing for payment in full, and it was not respectable for persons when sued to break faith. So, at first, there were clamorous meetings and importunate entreaties; then noisy applications to the praetor's court. And the very device intended as a remedy, the sale and purchase of estates, proved the contrary, as the usurers had hoarded up all their money for buying land. The facilities for selling were followed by a fall of prices, and the deeper a man was in debt, the more reluctantly did he part with his property, and many were utterly ruined. The destruction of private wealth precipitated the fall of rank and reputation, till at last the emperor interposed his aid by distributing throughout the banks a hundred million sesterces, and allowing freedom to borrow without interest for three years, provided the borrower gave security to the State in land to double the amount. Credit was thus restored, and gradually private lenders were found. The purchase too of estates was not carried out according to the letter of the Senate's decree, rigour at the outset, as usual with such matters, becoming negligence in the end.

Former alarms then returned, as there was a charge of treason against Considius Proculus. While he was celebrating his birthday without a fear, he was hurried before the Senate, condemned and instantly put to death. His sister Sancia was outlawed, on the accusation of Quintus Pomponius, a restless spirit, who pretended that he employed himself in this and like practices to win favour with the sovereign, and thereby alleviate the perils hanging over his brother Pomponius Secundus.

Pompeia Macrina too was sentenced to banishment. Her husband Argolicus and her father-in-law Laco, leading men of Achaia, had been ruined by the emperor. Her father likewise, an illustrious Roman knight, and her brother, an ex-praetor, seeing their doom was near, destroyed themselves. It was imputed to them as a crime that their great-grandfather Theophanes of Mitylene had been one of the intimate friends of Pompey the Great, and that after his death Greek flattery had paid him divine honours.

Sextus Marius, the richest man in Spain, was next accused of incest with his daughter, and thrown headlong from the Tarpeian rock. To remove any doubt that the vastness of his wealth had proved the man's ruin, Tiberius kept his gold-mines for himself, though they were forfeited to the State. Executions were now a stimulus to his fury, and he ordered the death of all who were lying in prison under accusation of complicity with Sejanus. There lay, singly or in heaps, the unnumbered dead, of every age and sex, the illustrious with the obscure. Kinsfolk and friends were not allowed to be near them, to weep over them, or even to gaze on them too long. Spies were set round them, who noted the sorrow of each mourner and followed the rotting corpses, till they were dragged to the Tiber, where, floating or driven on the bank, no one dared to burn or to touch them. The force of terror had utterly extinguished the sense of human fellowship, and, with the growth of cruelty, pity was thrust aside.

About this time Caius Caesar, who became his grandfather's companion on his retirement to Capreae, married Claudia, daughter of Marcus Silanus. He was a man who masked a savage temper under an artful guise of self-restraint, and neither his mother's doom nor the banishment of his brothers extorted from him a single utterance. Whatever the humour of the day with Tiberius, he would assume the like, and his language differed as little. Hence the fame of a clever remark from the orator Passienus, that "there never was a better slave or a worse master."

I must not pass over a prognostication of Tiberius respecting Servius Galba, then consul. Having sent for him and sounded him on various topics, he at last addressed him in Greek to this effect: "You too, Galba, will some day have a taste of empire." He thus hinted at a brief span of power late in life, on the strength of his acquaintance with the art of astrologers, leisure for acquiring which he had had at Rhodes, with Thrasyllus for instructor. This man's skill he tested in the following manner.

Whenever he sought counsel on such matters, he would make use of the top of the house and of the confidence of one freedman, quite illiterate and of great physical strength. The man always walked in front of the person whose science Tiberius had determined to test, through an unfrequented and precipitous path (for the house stood on rocks), and then, if any suspicion had arisen of imposture or of trickery, he hurled the astrologer, as he returned, into the sea beneath, that no one might live to betray the secret. Thrasyllus accordingly was led up the same cliffs, and when he had deeply impressed his questioner by cleverly revealing his imperial destiny and future career, he was asked whether he had also thoroughly ascertained his own horoscope, and the character of that particular year and day. After surveying the positions and relative distances of the stars, he first paused, then trembled, and the longer he gazed, the more was he agitated by amazement and terror, till at last he exclaimed that a perilous and well-nigh fatal crisis impended over him. Tiberius then embraced him and congratulated him on foreseeing his dangers and on being quite safe. Taking what he had said as an oracle, he retained him in the number of his intimate friends.

When I hear of these and like occurrences, I suspend my judgment on the question whether it is fate and unchangeable necessity or chance which governs the revolutions of human affairs. Indeed, among the wisest of the ancients and among their disciples you will find conflicting theories, many holding the conviction that heaven does not concern itself with the beginning or the end of our life, or, in short, with mankind at all; and that therefore sorrows are continually the lot of the good, happiness of the wicked; while others, on the contrary, believe that though there is a harmony between fate and events, yet it is not dependent on wandering stars, but on primary elements, and on a combination of natural causes. Still, they leave us the capacity of choosing our life, maintaining that, the choice once made, there is a fixed sequence of events. Good and evil, again, are not what vulgar opinion accounts them; many who seem to be struggling with adversity are happy; many, amid great affluence, are utterly miserable, if only the first bear their hard lot with patience, and the latter make a foolish use of their prosperity.

Most men, however, cannot part with the belief that each person's future is fixed from his very birth, but that some things happen differently from what has been foretold through the impostures of those who describe what they do not know, and that this destroys the credit of a science, clear testimonies to which have been given both by past ages and by our own. In fact, how the son of this same Thrasyllus predicted Nero's reign I shall relate when the time comes, not to digress too far from my subject.

That same year the death of Asinius Gallus became known. That he died of starvation, there was not a doubt; whether of his own choice or by compulsion, was a question. The emperor was asked whether he would allow him to be buried, and he blushed not to grant the favour, and actually blamed the accident which had proved fatal to the accused before he could be convicted in his presence. Just as if in a three years' interval an opportunity was wanting for the trial of an old ex-consul and the father of a number of ex-consuls.

Next Drusus perished, after having prolonged life for eight days on the most wretched of food, even chewing the stuffing, his bed. According to some writers, Macro had been instructed that, in case of Sejanus attempting an armed revolt, he was to hurry the young prince out of the confinement in which he was detained in the Palace and put him at the head of the people. Subsequently the emperor, as a rumour was gaining ground that he was on the point of a reconciliation with his daughter-in-law and his grandson, chose to be merciless rather than to relent.

He even bitterly reviled him after his death, taunting him with nameless abominations and with a spirit bent on his family's ruin and hostile to the State. And, what seemed most horrible of all, he ordered a daily journal of all that he said and did to be read in public. That there had been spies by his side for so many years, to note his looks, his sighs, and even his whispered thoughts, and that his grandfather could have heard read, and published all, was scarce credible. But letters of Attius, a centurion, and Didymus, a freedman, openly exhibited the names of slave after slave who had respectively struck or scared Drusus as he was quitting his chamber. The centurion had actually added, as something highly meritorious, his own language in all its brutality, and some utterances of the dying man in which, at first feigning loss of reason, he imprecated in seeming madness fearful things on Tiberius, and then, when hope of life was gone, denounced him with a studied and elaborate curse. "As he had slain a daughter-in-law, a brother's son, and son's sons, and filled his whole house with bloodshed, so might he pay the full penalty due to the name and race of his ancestors as well as to future generations."

The Senate clamorously interrupted, with an affectation of horror, but they were penetrated by alarm and amazement at seeing that a hitherto cunning prince, who had shrouded his wickedness in mystery, had waxed so bold as to remove, so to speak, the walls of his house and display his grandson under a centurion's lash, amid the buffetings of slaves, craving in vain the last sustenance of life.

Men's grief at all this had not died away when news was heard of Agrippina. She had lived on, sustained by hope, I suppose, after the destruction of Sejanus, and, when she found no abatement of horrors, had voluntarily perished, though possibly nourishment was refused her and a fiction concocted of a death that might seem self-chosen. Tiberius, it is certain, vented his wrath in the foulest charges. He reproached her with unchastity, with having had Asinius Gallus as a paramour and being driven by his death to loathe existence. But Agrippina, who could not endure equality and loved to domineer, was with her masculine aspirations far removed from the frailties of women. The emperor further observed that she died on the same day on which Sejanus had paid the penalty of his crime two years before, a fact, he said, to be recorded; and he made it a boast that she had not been strangled by the halter and flung down the Gemonian steps. He received a vote of thanks, and it was decreed that on the seventeenth of October, the day on which both perished, through all future years, an offering should be consecrated to Jupiter.

Soon afterwards Cocceius Nerva, a man always at the emperor's side, a master of law both divine and human, whose position was secure and health sound, resolved to die. Tiberius, as soon as he knew it, sat by him and asked his reasons, adding intreaties, and finally protesting that it would be a burden on his conscience and a blot on his reputation, if the most intimate of his friends were to fly from life without any cause for death. Nerva turned away from his expostulations and persisted in his abstinence from all food. Those who knew his thoughts said that as he saw more closely into the miseries of the State, he chose, in anger and alarm, an honourable death, while he was yet safe and unassailed on.

Meanwhile Agrippina's ruin, strange to say, dragged Plancina with it. Formerly the wife of Cneius Piso, and one who had openly exulted at the death of Germanicus, she had been saved, when Piso fell, by the intreaties of Augusta, and not less by the enmity of Agrippina. When hatred and favour had alike passed away, justice asserted itself. Pursued by charges universally notorious, she suffered by her own hand a penalty tardy rather than undeserved.

Amid the many sorrows which saddened Rome, one cause of grief was the marriage of Julia, Drusus's daughter and Nero's late wife, into the humbler family of Rubellius Blandus, whose grandfather many remembered as a Roman knight from Tibur. At the end of the year the death of Aelius Lamia, who, after being at last released from the farce of governing Syria, had become city-prefect, was celebrated with the honours of a censor's funeral. He was a man of illustrious descent, and in a hale old age; and the fact of the province having been withheld gained him additional esteem. Subsequently, on the death of Flaccus Pomponius, propraetor of Syria, a letter from the emperor was read, in which he complained that all the best men who were fit to command armies declined the service, and that he was thus necessarily driven to intreaties, by which some of the ex-consuls might be prevailed on to take provinces. He forgot that Arruntius had been kept at home now for ten years, that he might not go to Spain.

That same year Marcus Lepidus also died. I have dwelt at sufficient length on his moderation and wisdom in my earlier books, and I need not further enlarge on his noble descent. Assuredly the family of the Aemilii has been rich in good citizens, and even the members of that house whose morals were corrupt, still lived with a certain splendour.

During the consulship of Paulus Fabius and Lucius Vitellius, the bird called the phoenix, after a long succession of ages, appeared in Egypt and furnished the most learned men of that country and of Greece with abundant matter for the discussion of the marvellous phenomenon. It is my wish to make known all on which they agree with several things, questionable enough indeed, but not too absurd to be noticed.

That it is a creature sacred to the sun, differing from all other birds in its beak and in the tints of its plumage, is held unanimously by those who have described its nature. As to the number of years it lives, there are various accounts. The general tradition says five hundred years. Some maintain that it is seen at intervals of fourteen hundred and sixty-one years, and that the former birds flew into the city called Heliopolis successively in the reigns of Sesostris, Amasis, and Ptolemy, the third king of the Macedonian dynasty, with a multitude of companion birds marvelling at the novelty of the appearance. But all antiquity is of course obscure. From Ptolemy to Tiberius was a period of less than five hundred years. Consequently some have supposed that this was a spurious phoenix, not from the regions of Arabia, and with none of the instincts which ancient tradition has attributed to the bird. For when the number of years is completed and death is near, the phoenix, it is said, builds a nest in the land of its birth and infuses into it a germ of life from which an offspring arises, whose first care, when fledged, is to bury its father. This is not rashly done, but taking up a load of myrrh and having tried its strength by a long flight, as soon as it is equal to the burden and to the journey, it carries its father's body, bears it to the altar of the Sun, and leaves it to the flames. All this is full of doubt and legendary exaggeration. Still, there is no question that the bird is occasionally seen in Egypt.

Rome meanwhile being a scene of ceaseless bloodshed, Pomponius Labeo, who was, as I have related, governor of Moesia, severed his veins and let his life ebb from him. His wife, Paxaea, emulated her husband. What made such deaths eagerly sought was dread of the executioner, and the fact too that the condemned, besides forfeiture of their property, were deprived of burial, while those who decided their fate themselves, had their bodies interred, and their wills remained valid, a recompense this for their despatch. The emperor, however, argued in a letter to the Senate that it had been the practice of our ancestors, whenever they broke off an intimacy, to forbid the person their house, and so put an end to friendship. "This usage he had himself revived in Labeo's case, but Labeo, being pressed by charges of maladministration in his province and other crimes, had screened his guilt by bringing odium on another, and had groundlessly alarmed his wife, who, though criminal, was still free from danger."

Mamercus Scaurus was then for the second time impeached, a man of distinguished rank and ability as an advocate, but of infamous life. He fell, not through the friendship of Sejanus, but through what was no less powerful to destroy, the enmity of Macro, who practised the same arts more secretly. Macro's information was grounded on the subject of a tragedy written by Scaurus, from which he cited some verses which might be twisted into allusions to Tiberius. But Servilius and Cornelius, his accusers, alleged adultery with Livia and the practice of magical rites. Scaurus, as befitted the old house of the Aemilii, forestalled the fatal sentence at the persuasion of his wife Sextia, who urged him to die and shared his death.

Still the informers were punished when ever an opportunity occurred. Servilius and Cornelius, for example, whom the destruction of Scaurus had made notorious, were outlawed and transported to some islands for having taken money from Varius Ligur for dropping a prosecution. Abudius Ruso too, who had been an aedile, in seeking to imperil Lentulus Gaetulicus, under whom he had commanded a legion, by alleging that he had fixed on a son of Sejanus for his son-in-law, was himself actually condemned and banished from Rome. Gaetulicus at this time was in charge of the legions of Upper Germany, and had won from them singular affection, as a man of unbounded kindliness, moderate in his strictness, and popular even with the neighbouring army through his father-in-law, Lucius Apronius. Hence rumour persistently affirmed that he had ventured to send the emperor a letter, reminding him that his alliance with Sejanus had not originated in his own choice, but in the advice of Tiberius; that he was himself as liable to be deceived as Tiberius, and that the same mistake ought not to be held innocent in the prince and be a source of ruin to others. His loyalty was still untainted and would so remain, if he was not assailed by any plot. A successor he should accept as an announcement of his doom. A compact, so to say, ought to be sealed between them, by which he should retain his province, and the emperor be master of all else. Strange as this story was, it derived credibility from the fact that Gaetulicus alone of all connected with Sejanus lived in safety and in high favour, Tiberius bearing in mind the people's hatred, his own extreme age how his government rested more on prestige than on power.

In the consulship of Caius Cestius and Marcus Servilius, some Parthian nobles came to Rome without the knowledge of their king Artabanus. Dread of Germanicus had made that prince faithful to the Romans and just to his people, but he subsequently changed this behaviour for insolence towards us and tyranny to his subjects. He was elated by the wars which he had successfully waged against the surrounding nations, while he disdained the aged and, as he thought, unwarlike Tiberius, eagerly coveting Armenia, over which, on the death of Artaxias, he placed Arsaces, his eldest son. He further added insult, and sent envoys to reclaim the treasures left by Vonones in Syria and Cilicia. Then too he insisted on the ancient boundaries of Persia and Macedonia, and intimated, with a vainglorious threat, that he meant to seize on the country possessed by Cyrus and afterwards by Alexander.

The chief adviser of the Parthians in sending the secret embassy was Sinnaces, a man of distinguished family and corresponding wealth. Next in influence was Abdus, an eunuch, a class which, far from being despised among barbarians, actually possesses power. These, with some other nobles whom they admitted to their counsels, as there was not a single Arsacid whom they could put on the throne, most of the family having been murdered by Artabanus or being under age, demanded that Phraates, son of king Phraates, should be sent from Rome. "Only a name," they said, "and an authority were wanted; only, in fact, that, with Caesar's consent, a scion of the house of Arsaces should show himself on the banks of the Euphrates."

This suited the wishes of Tiberius. He provided Phraates with what he needed for assuming his father's sovereignty, while he clung to his purpose of regulating foreign affairs by a crafty policy and keeping war at a distance. Artabanus meanwhile, hearing of the treacherous arrangement, was one moment perplexed by apprehension, the next fired with a longing for revenge. With barbarians, indecision is a slave's weakness; prompt action king-like. But now expediency prevailed, and he invited Abdus, under the guise of friendship, to a banquet, and disabled him by a lingering poison; Sinnaces he put off by pretexts and presents, and also by various employments. Phraates meanwhile, on arriving in Syria, where he threw off the Roman fashions to which for so many years he had been accustomed, and adapted himself to Parthian habits, unable to endure the customs of his country, was carried off by an illness. Still, Tiberius did not relinquish his purpose. He chose Tiridates, of the same stock as Artabanus, to be his rival, and the Iberian Mithridates to be the instrument of recovering Armenia, having reconciled him to his brother Pharasmanes, who held the throne of that country. He then intrusted the whole of his eastern policy to Lucius Vitellius. The man, I am aware, had a bad name at Rome, and many a foul story was told of him. But in the government of provinces he acted with the virtue of ancient times. He returned, and then, through fear of Caius Caesar and intimacy with Claudius, he degenerated into a servility so base that he is regarded by an after-generation as the type of the most degrading adulation. The beginning of his career was forgotten in its end, and an old age of infamy effaced the virtues of youth.

Of the petty chiefs Mithridates was the first to persuade Pharasmanes to aid his enterprise by stratagem and force, and agents of corruption were found who tempted the servants of Arsaces into crime by a quantity of gold. At the same instant the Iberians burst into Armenia with a huge host, and captured the city of Artaxata. Artabanus, on hearing this, made his son Orodes the instrument of vengeance. He gave him the Parthian army and despatched men to hire auxiliaries. Pharasmanes, on the other hand, allied himself with the Albanians, and procured aid from the Sarmatae, whose highest chiefs took bribes from both sides, after the fashion of their countrymen, and engaged themselves in conflicting interests. But the Iberians, who were masters of the various positions, suddenly poured the Sarmatae into Armenia by the Caspian route. Meanwhile those who were coming up to the support of the Parthians were easily kept back, all other approaches having been closed by the enemy except one, between the sea and the mountains on the Albanian frontier, which summer rendered difficult, as there the shallows are flooded by the force of the Etesian gales. The south wind in winter rolls back the waves, and when the sea is driven back upon itself, the shallows along the coast, are exposed.

Meantime, while Orodes was without an ally, Pharasmanes, now strengthened by reinforcements, challenged him to battle, taunted him on his refusal, rode up to his camp and harassed his foraging parties. He often hemmed him in with his picquets in the fashion of a blockade, till the Parthians, who were unused to such insults, gathered round the king and demanded battle. Their sole strength was in cavalry; Pharasmanes was also powerful in infantry, for the Iberians and Albanians, inhabiting as they did a densely wooded country, were more inured to hardship and endurance. They claim to have been descended from the Thessalians, at the period when Jason, after the departure of Medea and the children born of her, returned subsequently to the empty palace of Aeetes, and the vacant kingdom of Colchi. They have many traditions connected with his name and with the oracle of Phrixus. No one among them would think of sacrificing a ram, the animal supposed to have conveyed Phrixus, whether it was really a ram or the figure-head of a ship.

Both sides having been drawn up in battle array, the Parthian leader expatiated on the empire of the East, and the renown of the Arsacids, in contrast to the despicable Iberian chief with his hireling soldiery. Pharasmanes reminded his people that they had been free from Parthian domination, and that the grander their aims, the more glory they would win if victorious, the more disgrace and peril they would incur if they turned their backs. He pointed, as he spoke, to his own menacing array, and to the Median bands with their golden embroidery; warriors, as he said, on one side, spoil on the other.

Among the Sarmatae the general's voice was not alone to be heard. They encouraged one another not to begin the battle with volleys of arrows; they must, they said, anticipate attack by a hand to hand charge. Then followed every variety of conflict. The Parthians, accustomed to pursue or fly with equal science, deployed their squadrons, and sought scope for their missiles. The Sarmatae, throwing aside their bows, which at a shorter range are effective, rushed on with pikes and swords. Sometimes, as in a cavalry-action, there would be alternate advances and retreats, then, again, close fighting, in which, breast to breast, with the clash of arms, they repulsed the foe or were themselves repulsed. And now the Albanians and Iberians seized, and hurled the Parthians from their steeds, and embarrassed their enemy with a double attack, pressed as they were by the cavalry on the heights and by the nearer blows of the infantry. Meanwhile Pharasmanes and Orodes, who, as they cheered on the brave and supported the wavering, were conspicuous to all, and so recognised each other, rushed to the combat with a shout, with javelins, and galloping chargers, Pharasmanes with the greater impetuosity, for he pierced his enemy's helmet at a stroke. But he could not repeat the blow, as he was hurried onwards by his horse, and the wounded man was protected by the bravest of his guards. A rumour that he was slain, which was believed by mistake, struck panic into the Parthians, and they yielded the victory.

Artabanus very soon marched with the whole strength of his kingdom, intent on vengeance. The Iberians from their knowledge of the country fought at an advantage. Still Artabanus did not retreat till Vitellius had assembled his legions and, by starting a report that he meant to invade Mesopotamia, raised an alarm of war with Rome. Armenia was then abandoned, and the fortunes of Artabanus were overthrown, Vitellius persuading his subjects to forsake a king who was a tyrant in peace, and ruinously unsuccessful in war. And so Sinnaces, whose enmity to the prince I have already mentioned, drew into actual revolt his father Abdageses and others, who had been secretly in his counsel, and were now after their continued disasters more eager to fight. By degrees, many flocked to him who, having been kept in subjection by fear rather than by goodwill, took courage as soon as they found leaders.

Artabanus had now no resources but in some foreigners who guarded his person, men exiled from their own homes, who had no perception of honour, or any scruple about a base act, mere hireling instruments of crime. With these attendants he hastened his flight into the remote country on the borders of Scythia, in the hope of aid, as he was connected by marriage alliances with the Hyrcanians and Carmanians. Meantime the

Parthians, he thought, indulgent as they are to an absent prince, though restless under his presence, might turn to a better mind.

Vitellius, as soon as Artabanus had fled and his people were inclined to have a new king, urged Tiridates to seize the advantage thus offered, and then led the main strength of the legions and the allies to the banks of the Euphrates. While they were sacrificing, the one, after Roman custom, offering a swine, a ram and a bull; the other, a horse which he had duly prepared as a propitiation to the river-god, they were informed by the neighbouring inhabitants that the Euphrates, without any violent rains, was of itself rising to an immense height, and that the white foam was curling into circles like a diadem, an omen of a prosperous passage. Some explained it with more subtlety, of a successful commencement to the enterprise, which, however, would not be lasting, on the ground, that though a confident trust might be placed in prognostics given in the earth or in the heavens, the fluctuating character of rivers exhibited omens which vanished the same moment.

A bridge of boats having been constructed and the army having crossed, the first to enter the camp was Ornospades, with several thousand cavalry. Formerly an exile, he had rendered conspicuous aid to Tiberius in the completion of the Dalmatic war, and had for this been rewarded with Roman citizenship. Subsequently, he had again sought the friendship of his king, by whom he had been raised to high honour, and appointed governor of the plains, which, being surrounded by the waters of those famous rivers, the Euphrates and Tigris, have received the name of Mesopotamia. Soon afterwards, Sinnaces reinforced the army, and Abdageses, the mainstay of the party, came with the royal treasure and what belonged to the crown. Vitellius thought it enough to have displayed the arms of Rome, and he then bade Tiridates remember his grandfather Phraates, and his foster-father Caesar, and all that was glorious in both of them, while the nobles were to show obedience to their king, and respect for us, each maintaining his honour and his loyalty. This done, he returned with the legions to Syria.

I have related in sequence the events of two summer-campaigns, as a relief to the reader's mind from our miseries at home. Though three years had elapsed since the destruction of Sejanus, neither time, intreaties, nor sated gratification, all which have a soothing effect on others, softened Tiberius, or kept him from punishing doubtful or forgotten offenses as most flagrant and recent crimes. Under this dread, Fulcinius Trio, unwilling to face an onslaught of accusers, inserted in his will several terrible imputations on Macro and on the emperor's principal freedmen, while he taunted the emperor himself with the mental decay of old age, and the virtual exile of continuous retirement. Tiberius ordered these insults, which Trio's heirs had suppressed, to be publicly read, thus showing his tolerance of free speech in others and despising his own shame, or, possibly, because he had long been ignorant of the villanies of Sejanus, and now wished any remarks, however reckless, to published, and so to ascertain, through invective, if it must be so, the truth, which flattery obscures. About the same time Granius Marcianus, a senator, who was accused of treason by Caius Gracchus, laid hands on himself. Tarius Gratianus too, an ex-praetor, was condemned under the same law to capital punishment.

A similar fate befell Trebellienus Rufus and Sextius Paconianus. Trebellienus perished by his own hand; Paconianus was strangled in prison for having there written some lampoons on the emperor. Tiberius received the news, no longer parted by the sea, as he had been once, or through messengers from a distance, but in close proximity to Rome, so that on the same day, or after the interval of a single night, he could reply to the despatches of the consuls, and almost behold the bloodshed as it streamed from house to house, and the strokes of the executioner.

At the year's close Poppaeus Sabinus died, a man of somewhat humble extraction, who had risen by his friendship with two emperors to the consulship and the honours of a triumph. During twenty-four years he had the charge of the most important provinces, not for any remarkable ability, but because he was equal to business and was not too great for it.

Quintus Plautius and Sextus Papinius were the next consuls. The fact that that year Lucius Aruseius was put to death did not strike men as anything horrible, from their familiarity with evil deeds. But there was a panic when Vibulenus Agrippa, a Roman knight, as soon as his accusers had finished their case, took from his robe, in the very Senate-house, a dose of poison, drank it off, and, as he fell expiring, was hurried away to prison by the prompt hands of lictors, where the neck of the now lifeless man was crushed with the halter. Even Tigranes, who had once ruled Armenia and was now impeached, did not escape the punishment of an ordinary citizen on the strength of his royal title.

Caius Galba meanwhile and the Blaesi perished by a voluntary death; Galba, because a harsh letter from the emperor forbade him to have a province allotted to him; while, as for the Blaesi, the priesthoods intended for them during the prosperity of their house, Tiberius had withheld, when that prosperity was shaken, and now conferred, as vacant offices, on others. This they understood as a signal of their doom, and acted on it.

Aemilia Lepida too, whose marriage with the younger Drusus I have already related, who, though she had pursued her husband with ceaseless accusations, remained unpunished, infamous as she was, as long as her father Lepidus lived, subsequently fell a victim to the informers for adultery with a slave. There was no question about her guilt, and so without an attempt at defence she put an end to her life.

At this same time the Clitae, a tribe subject to the Cappadocian Archelaus, retreated to the heights of Mount Taurus, because they were compelled in Roman fashion to render an account of their revenue and submit to tribute. There they defended themselves by means of the nature of the country against the king's unwarlike troops, till Marcus Trebellius, whom Vitellius, the governor of Syria, sent as his lieutenant with four thousand legionaries and some picked auxiliaries, surrounded with his lines two hills occupied by the barbarians, the lesser of which was named Cadra, the other Davara. Those who dared to sally out, he reduced to surrender by the sword, the rest by drought.

Tiridates meanwhile, with the consent of the Parthians, received the submission of Nicephorium, Anthemusias and the other cities, which having been founded by Macedonians, claim Greek names, also of the Parthian towns Halus and Artemita. There was a rivalry of joy among the inhabitants who detested Artabanus, bred as he had been among the Scythians, for his cruelty, and hoped to find in Tiridates a kindly spirit from his Roman training.

Seleucia, a powerful and fortified city which had never lapsed into barbarism, but had clung loyally to its founder Seleucus, assumed the most marked tone of flattery. Three hundred citizens, chosen for wealth or wisdom, form a kind of senate, and the people have powers of their own. When both act in concert, they look with contempt on the Parthians; as soon as they are at discord, and the respective leaders invite aid for themselves against their rivals, the ally summoned to help a faction crushes them all. This had lately happened in the reign of Artabanus, who, for his own interest, put the people at the mercy of the nobles. As a fact, popular government almost amounts to freedom, while the rule of the few approaches closely to a monarch's caprice.

Seleucia now celebrated the arrival of Tiridates with all the honours paid to princes of old and all which modern times, with a more copious inventiveness, have devised. Reproaches were at the same time heaped on Artabanus, as an Arsacid indeed on his mother's side, but as in all else degenerate. Tiridates gave the government of Seleucia to the people. Soon afterwards, as he was deliberating on what day he should inaugurate his reign, he received letters from Phraates and Hiero, who held two very powerful provinces, imploring a brief delay. It was thought best to wait for men of such commanding influence, and meanwhile Ctesiphon, the seat of empire, was their chosen destination. But as they postponed their coming from day to day, the Surena, in the presence of an approving throng, crowned Tiridates, according to the national usage, with the royal diadem.

And now had he instantly made his way to the heart of the country and to its other tribes, the reluctance of those who wavered, would have been overpowered, and all to a man would have yielded. By besieging a fortress into which Artabanus had conveyed his treasure and his concubines, he gave them time to disown their compact. Phraates and Hiero, with others who had not united in celebrating the day fixed for the coronation, some from fear, some out of jealousy of Abdageses, who then ruled the court and the new king, transferred their allegiance to Artabanus. They found him in Hyrcania, covered with filth and procuring sustenance with his bow. He was at first alarmed under the impression that treachery was intended, but when they pledged their honour that they had come to restore to him his dominion, his spirit revived, and he asked what the sudden change meant. Hiero then spoke insultingly of the boyish years of Tiridates, hinting that the throne was not held by an Arsacid, but that a mere empty name was enjoyed by a feeble creature bred in foreign effeminacy, while the actual power was in the house of Abdageses.

An experienced king, Artabanus knew that men do not necessarily feign hatred because they are false in friendship. He delayed only while he was raising auxiliaries in Scythia, and then pushed on in haste, thus anticipating the plots of enemies and the fickleness of friends. Wishing to attract popular sympathy, he did not even cast off his miserable garb. He stooped to wiles and to entreaties, to anything indeed by which he might allure the wavering and confirm the willing.

He was now approaching the neighbourhood of Seleucia with a large force, while Tiridates, dismayed by the rumour. and then by the king's presence in person, was divided in mind, and doubted whether he should march against him or prolong the war by delay. Those who wished for battle with its prompt decision argued that ill-arrayed levies fatigued by a long march could not even in heart be thoroughly united in obedience, traitors and enemies as they had lately been, to the prince whom now again they were supporting. Abdageses, however, advised a retreat into Mesopotamia. There, with a river in their front, they might in the interval summon to their aid the Armenians and Elymaeans and other nations in their rear, and then, reinforced by allies and troops which would be sent by the Roman general, they might try the fortune of war. This advice prevailed, for Abdageses had the chief influence and Tiridates was a coward in the face of danger. But their retreat resembled a flight. The Arabs made a beginning, and then the rest went to their homes or to the camp of Artabanus, till Tiridates returned to Syria with a few followers and thus relieved all from the disgrace of desertion.

That same year Rome suffered from a terrible fire, and part of the circus near the Aventine hill was burnt, as well as the Aventine quarter itself. This calamity the emperor turned to his own glory by paying the values of the houses and blocks of tenements. A hundred million of sesterces was expended in this munificence, a boon all the more acceptable to the populace, as Tiberius was rather sparing in building at his private expense. He raised only two structures even at the public cost, the temple of Augustus and the stage of Pompey's theatre, and when these were completed, he did not dedicate them, either out of contempt for popularity or from his extreme age. Four commissioners, all husbands of the emperor's granddaughters—Cneius Domitius, Cassius Longinus, Marcus Vinicius, Rubellius Blandus—were appointed to assess the damage in each case, and Publius Petronius was added to their number on the nomination of the consuls. Various honours were devised and decreed to the emperor such as each man's ingenuity suggested. It is a question which of these he rejected or accepted, as the end of his life was so near.

For soon afterwards Tiberius's last consuls, Cneius Acerronius and Caius Pontius, entered on office, Macro's power being now excessive. Every day the man cultivated more assiduously than ever the favour of Caius Caesar, which, indeed, he had never neglected, and after the death of Claudia, who had, as I have related, been married to Caius, he had prompted his wife Ennia to inveigle the young prince by a pretence of love, and to bind him by an engagement of marriage, and the lad, provided he could secure the throne, shrank from no conditions. For though he was of an excitable temper, he had thoroughly learnt the falsehoods of hypocrisy under the loving care of his grandfather.

This the emperor knew, and he therefore hesitated about bequeathing the empire, first, between his grandsons. Of these, the son of Drusus was nearest in blood and natural affection, but he was still in his childhood. Germanicus's son was in the vigour of youth and enjoyed the people's favour, a reason for having his grandfather's hatred. Tiberius had even thought of Claudius, as he was of sedate age and had a taste for liberal culture, but a weak intellect was against him. If however he were to seek a successor outside of his house, he feared that the memory of Augustus and the name of the Caesars would become a laughing-stock and a scorn. It was, in fact, not so much popularity in the present for which he cared as for glory in the future.

Perplexed in mind, exhausted in body, he soon left to destiny a question to which he was unequal, though he threw out some hints from which it might be inferred that he foresaw what was to come. He taunted Macro, in no obscure terms, with forsaking the setting and looking to the rising sun. Once too when Caius Caesar in a casual conversation ridiculed Lucius Sulla, he predicted to him that he would have all Sulla's vices and none of his virtues. At the same moment he embraced the younger of his two grandsons with a flood of tears, and, noting the savage face of the other, said, "You will slay this boy, and will be yourself slain by another." But even while his strength was fast failing he gave up none of his debaucheries. In his sufferings he would simulate health, and was wont to jest at the arts of the physician and at all who, after the age of thirty, require another man's advice to distinguish between what is beneficial or hurtful to their constitutions.

At Rome meanwhile were being sown the seeds of bloodshed to come even after Tiberius's death. Acutia, formerly the wife of Publius Vitellius, had been accused of treason by Laelius Balbus. When on her condemnation a reward was being voted to her prosecutor, Junius Otho, tribune of the people, interposed his veto. Hence a feud between Vitellius and Otho, ending in Otho's banishment. Then Albucilla, notorious for the number of her lovers, who had been married to Satrius Secundus, the betrayer of the late conspiracy, was charged with irreverence towards the emperor. With her were involved as her accomplices and paramours Cneius Domitius, Vibius Marsus and Lucius Arruntius. I have already spoken of the illustrious rank of Domitius. Marsus too was distinguished by the honours of his ancestors and by his own attainments. It was, however, stated in the notes of the proceedings furnished to the Senate that Macro had superintended the examination of the witnesses and the torture of the slaves, and the fact that there was no letter from the emperor against the defendants caused a suspicion that, while he was very feeble and possibly ignorant of the matter, the charge was to a great extent invented to gratify Macro's well-known enmity against Arruntius.

And so Domitius and Marsus prolonged their lives, Domitius, preparing his defence, Marsus, having apparently resolved on starvation. Arruntius, when his friends advised delay and temporising, replied that "the same conduct was not becoming in all persons. He had had enough of life, and all he regretted was that he had endured amid scorn and peril an old age of anxious fears, long detested by Sejanus, now by Macro, always, indeed, by some powerful minister, not for any fault, but as a man who could not tolerate gross iniquities. Granted the possibility of passing safely through the few last days of Tiberius. How was he to be secure under the youth of the coming sovereign? Was it probable that, when Tiberius with his long experience of affairs was, under the influence of absolute power, wholly perverted and changed, Caius Caesar, who had hardly completed his boyhood, was thoroughly ignorant and bred under the vilest training, would enter on a better course, with Macro for his guide, who having been selected for his superior wickedness, to crush Sejanus had by yet more numerous crimes been the scourge of the State? He now foresaw a still more galling slavery, and therefore sought to flee alike from the past and from the impending future."

While he thus spoke like a prophet, he opened his veins. What followed will be a proof that Arruntius rightly chose death. Albucilla, having stabbed herself with an ineffectual wound, was by the Senate's order carried off to prison. Those who had ministered to her profligacy, Carsidius Sacerdos, an ex-praetor, and Pontius Fregellanus were sentenced, respectively, to transportation to an island and to loss of a senator's rank. A like punishment was adjudged in the case of Laelius Balbus, and, indeed, with intense satisfaction, as Balbus was noted for his savage eloquence and his eagerness to assail the innocent.

About the same time Sextus Papinius, who belonged to a family of consular rank, chose a sudden and shocking death, by throwing himself from a height. The cause was ascribed to his mother who, having been repeatedly repulsed in her overtures, had at last by her arts and seductions driven him to an extremity from which he could find no escape but death. She was accordingly put on her trial before the Senate, and, although she grovelled at the knees of the senators and long urged a parent's grief, the greater weakness of a woman's mind under such an affliction and other sad and pitiful pleas of the same painful kind, she was after all banished from Rome for ten years, till her younger son would have passed the frail period of youth.

Tiberius's bodily powers were now leaving him, but not his skill in dissembling. There was the same stern spirit; he had his words and looks under strict control, and occasionally would try to hide his weakness, evident as it was, by a forced politeness. After frequent changes of place, he at last settled down on the promontory of Misenum in a country-house once owned by Lucius Lucullus. There it was noted, in this way, that he was drawing near his end. There was a physician, distinguished in his profession, of the name of Charicles, usually employed, not indeed to have the direction of the emperor's varying health, but to put his advice at immediate disposal. This man, as if he were leaving on business his own, clasped his hand, with a show of homage, and touched his pulse. Tiberius noticed it. Whether he was displeased and strove the more to hide his anger, is a question; at any rate, he ordered the banquet to be renewed, and sat at the table longer than usual, by way, apparently, of showing honour to his departing friend. Charicles, however, assured Macro that his breath was failing and that he would not last more than two days. All was at once hurry; there were conferences among those on the spot and despatches to the generals and armies. On the 15th of March, his breath failing, he was believed to have expired, and Caius Caesar was going forth with a numerous throng of congratulating followers to take the first possession of the empire, when suddenly news came that Tiberius was recovering his voice and sight, and calling for persons to bring him food to revive him from his faintness. Then ensued a universal panic, and while the rest fled hither and thither, every one feigning grief or ignorance, Caius Caesar, in silent stupor, passed from the highest hopes to the extremity of apprehension. Macro, nothing daunted, ordered the old emperor to be smothered under a huge heap of clothes, and all to quit the entrance-hall.

And so died Tiberius, in the seventy eighth year of his age. Nero was his father, and he was on both sides descended from the Claudian house, though his mother passed by adoption, first into the Livian, then into the Julian family. From earliest infancy, perilous vicissitudes were his lot. Himself an exile, he was the companion of a proscribed father, and on being admitted as a stepson into the house of Augustus, he had to struggle with many rivals, so long as Marcellus and Agrippa and, subsequently, Caius and Lucius Caesar were in their glory. Again his brother Drusus enjoyed in a greater degree the affection of the citizens. But he was more than ever on dangerous ground after his marriage with Julia, whether he tolerated or escaped from his wife's profligacy. On his return from Rhodes he ruled the emperor's now heirless house for twelve years, and the Roman world, with absolute sway, for about twenty-three. His character too had its distinct periods. It was a bright time in his life and reputation, while under Augustus he was a private citizen or held high offices; a time of reserve and crafty assumption of virtue, as long as Germanicus and Drusus were alive. Again, while his mother lived, he was a compound of good and evil; he was infamous for his cruelty, though he veiled his debaucheries, while he loved or feared Sejanus. Finally, he plunged into every wickedness and disgrace, when fear and shame being cast off, he simply indulged his own inclinations.

BOOK VII—X, A.D. 37, 47

[The four following books and the beginning of Book XI, which are lost, contained the history of a period of nearly ten years, from A.D. 37 to A.D. 47. These years included the reign of Caius Caesar (Caligula), the son of Germanicus by the elder Agrippina, and the first six years of the reign of Claudius. Caius Caesar's reign was three years ten months and eight days in duration. Claudius (Tiberius Claudius Drusus Nero Germanicus), the brother of Germanicus, succeeded him, at the age of fifty, and reigned from A.D. 41 to A.D. 54.

The Eleventh Book of the Annals opens with the seventh year of Claudius's reign. The power of his wife Messalina was then at its height. She was, it seems, jealous of a certain Poppaea Sabina, who is mentioned in Book XIII., as "having surpassed in beauty all the ladies of her day." This Poppaea was the daughter of the Poppaeus Sabinus alluded to in Book VI., and the mother of the more famous Poppaea, afterwards the wife of the emperor Nero. Messalina contrived to involve this lady and her lover, Valerius Asiaticus, in a ruinous charge. Asiaticus had been twice consul, once under Caius Caesar, a second time under Claudius in A.D. 46. He was rich as well as noble. The Eleventh Book, as we have it, begins with the account of his prosecution by means Messalina, who with the help of Lucius Vitellius, Vitellius, father of the Vitellius, afterwards emperor, effected his ruin.]

BOOK XI, A.D. 47, 48

Messalina believed that Valerius Asiaticus, who had been twice consul, was one of Poppaea's old lovers. At the same time she was looking greedily at the gardens which Lucullus had begun and which Asiaticus was now adorning with singular magnificence, and so she suborned Suilius to accuse both him and Poppaea. With Suilius was associated Sosibius, tutor to Britannicus, who was to give Claudius an apparently friendly warning to beware of a power and wealth which threatened the throne. Asiaticus, he said, had been the ringleader in the murder of a Caesar, and then had not feared to face an assembly of the Roman people, to own the deed, and challenge its glory for his own. Thus grown famous in the capital, and with a renown widely spread through the provinces, he was planning a journey to the armies of Germany. Born at Vienna, and supported by numerous and powerful connections, he would find it easy to rouse nations allied to his house. Claudius made no further inquiry, but sent Crispinus, commander of the Praetorians, with troops in hot haste, as though to put down a revolt. Crispinus found him at Baiae, loaded him with chains, and hurried him to Rome.

No hearing before the Senate was granted him. It was in the emperor's chamber, in the presence of Messalina, that he was heard. There Suilius accused him of corrupting the troops, of binding them by bribes and indulgences to share in every crime, of adultery with Poppaea, and finally of unmanly vice. It was at this last that the accused broke silence, and burst out with the words, "Question thy own sons, Suilius; they will own my manhood." Then he entered on his defence. Claudius he moved profoundly, and he even drew tears from Messalina. But as she left the chamber to wipe them away, she warned Vitellius not to let the man escape. She hastened herself to effect Poppaea's destruction, and hired agents to drive her to suicide by the terrors of a prison. Caesar meanwhile was so unconscious that a few days afterwards he asked her husband Scipio, who was dining with him, why he sat down to table without his wife, and was told in reply that she had paid the debt of nature.

When Claudius began to deliberate about the acquittal of Asiaticus, Vitellius, with tears in his eyes, spoke of his old friendship with the accused, and of their joint homage to the emperor's mother, Antonia. He then briefly reviewed the services of Asiaticus to the State, his recent campaign in the invasion of Britain, and everything else which seemed likely to win compassion, and suggested that he should be free to choose his death. Claudius's reply was in the same tone of mercy. Some friends urged on Asiaticus the quiet death of self-starvation, but he declined it with thanks. He took his usual exercise, then bathed and dined cheerfully, and saying that he had better have fallen by the craft of Tiberius or the fury of Caius Caesar than by the treachery of a woman and the shameless mouth of Vitellius, he opened his veins, but not till he had inspected his funeral pyre, and directed its removal to another spot, lest the smoke should hurt the thick foliage of the trees. So complete was his calmness even to the last.

The senators were then convoked, and Suilius proceeded to find new victims in two knights of the first rank who bore the surname of Petra. The real cause of their destruction was that they had lent their house for the meetings of Mnester and Poppaea. But it was a vision of the night that was the actual charge against one of them. He had, it was alleged, beheld Claudius crowned with a garland of wheat, the ears of which were turned downwards, and, from this appearance, he foretold scanty harvests. Some have said that it was a vine-wreath, of which the leaves were white, which he saw, and that he interpreted it to signify the death of the emperor after the turn of autumn. It is, however, beyond dispute that in consequence of some dream, whatever it was, both the man and his brother perished.

Fifteen hundred thousand sesterces and the decorations of the praetorship were voted to Crispinus. Vitellius bestowed a million on Sosibius, for giving Britannicus the benefit of his teaching and Claudius that of his counsels. I may add that when Scipio was called on for his opinion, he replied, "As I think what all men think about the deeds of Poppaea, suppose me to say what all men say." A graceful compromise this between the affection of the husband and the necessities of the senator.

Suilius after this plied his accusations without cessation or pity, and his audacity had many rivals. By assuming to himself all the functions of laws and magistrates, the emperor had left exposed everything which invited plunder, and of all articles of public merchandise nothing was more venal than the treachery of advocates. Thus it happened that one Samius, a Roman knight of the first rank, who had paid four hundred thousand sesterces to Suilius, stabbed himself in the advocate's house, on ascertaining his collusion with the adversary. Upon this, following the lead of Silius, consul-elect, whose elevation and fall I shall in due course relate, the senators rose in a body, and demanded the enforcement of the Cincian law, an old enactment, which forbade any one to receive a fee or a gift for pleading a cause.

When the men, at whom this strong censure was levelled, loudly protested, Silius, who had a quarrel with Suilius, attacked them with savage energy. He cited as examples the orators of old who had thought fame with posterity the fairest recompense of eloquence. And, "apart from this," he said, "the first of noble accomplishments was debased by sordid services, and even good faith could not be upheld in its integrity, when men looked at the greatness of their gains. If law suits turned to no one's profit, there would be fewer of them. As it was, quarrels, accusations, hatreds and wrongs were encouraged, in order that, as the violence of disease brings fees to the physician, so the corruption of the forum might enrich the advocate. They should remember Caius Asinius and Messala, and, in later days, Arruntius and Aeserninus, men raised by a blameless life and by eloquence to the highest honours."

So spoke the consul-elect, and others agreed with him. A resolution was being framed to bring the guilty under the law of extortion, when Suilius and Cossutianus and the rest, who saw themselves threatened with punishment rather than trial, for their guilt was manifest, gathered round the emperor, and prayed forgiveness for the past.

When he had nodded assent, they began to plead their cause. "Who," they asked, "can be so arrogant as to anticipate in hope an eternity of renown? It is for the needs and the business of life that the resource of eloquence is acquired, thanks to which no one for want of an advocate is at the mercy of the powerful. But eloquence cannot be obtained for nothing; private affairs are neglected, in order that a man may devote himself to the business of others. Some support life by the profession of arms, some by cultivating land. No work is expected from any one of which he has not before calculated the profits. It was easy for Asinius and Messala, enriched with the prizes of the conflict between Antony and Augustus, it was easy for Arruntius and Aeserninus, the heirs of wealthy families, to assume grand airs. We have examples at hand. How great were the fees for which Publius Clodius and Caius Curio were wont to speak! We are ordinary senators, seeking in the tranquillity of the State for none but peaceful gains. You must consider the plebeian, how he gains distinction from the gown. Take away the rewards of a profession, and the profession must perish." The emperor thought that these arguments, though less noble, were not without force. He limited the fee which might be taken to ten thousand sesterces, and those who exceeded this limit were to be liable to the penalties of extortion.

About this same time Mithridates, of whom I have before spoken as having ruled Armenia, and having been imprisoned by order of Caius Caesar, made his way back to his kingdom at the suggestion of Claudius and in reliance on the help of Pharasmanes. This Pharasmanes, who was king of the Iberians and Mithridates' brother, now told him that the Parthians were divided, and that the highest questions of empire being uncertain, lesser matters were neglected. Gotarzes, among his many cruelties, had caused the death of his brother Artabanus, with his wife and son. Hence his people feared for themselves and sent for Vardanes. Ever ready for daring achievements, Vardanes traversed 375 miles in two days, and drove before him the surprised and terrified Gotarzes. Without moment's delay, he seized the neighbouring governments, Seleucia alone refusing his rule. Rage against the place, which indeed had also revolted from his father, rather than considerations of policy, made him embarrass himself with the siege of a strong city, which the defence of a river flowing by it, with fortifications and supplies, had thoroughly secured. Gotarzes meanwhile, aided by the resources of the Dahae and Hyrcanians, renewed the war; and Vardanes, compelled to raise the siege of Seleucia, encamped on the plains of Bactria.

Then it was that while the forces of the East were divided, and hesitated which side they should take, the opportunity of occupying Armenia was presented to Mithridates, who had the vigorous soldiers of Rome to storm the fortified heights, while his Iberian cavalry scoured the plain. The Armenians made no resistance after their governor, Demonax, had ventured on a battle and had been routed. Cotys, king of Lesser Armenia, to whom some of the nobles inclined, caused some delay, but he was stopped by a despatch from Claudius, and then everything passed into the hands of Mithridates, who showed more cruelty than was wise in a new ruler. The Parthian princes however, just when they were beginning battle, came to a sudden agreement, on discovering a plot among their people, which Gotarzes revealed to his brother. At first they approached each other with hesitation; then, joining right hands, they promised before the altars of their gods to punish the treachery of their enemies and to yield one to the other. Vardanes seemed more capable of retaining rule. Gotarzes, to avoid all rivalry, retired into the depths of Hyrcania. When Vardanes returned, Seleucia capitulated to him, seven years after its revolt, little to the credit of the Parthians, whom a single city had so long defied.

He then visited the strongest governments, and was eager to recover Armenia, but was stopped by Vibius Marsus, governor of Syria, who threatened war. Meanwhile Gotarzes, who repented of having relinquished his throne, at the solicitation of the nobility, to whom subjection is a special hardship in peace, collected a force. Vardanes marched against him to the river Charinda; a fierce battle was fought over the passage,

Vardanes winning a complete victory, and in a series of successful engagements subduing the intermediate tribes as far as the river Sindes, which is the boundary between the Dahae and the Arians. There his successes terminated. The Parthians, victorious though they were, rebelled against distant service. So after erecting monuments on which he recorded his greatness, and the tribute won from peoples from whom no Arsacid had won it before, he returned covered with glory, and therefore the more haughty and more intolerable to his subjects than ever. They arranged a plot, and slew him when he was off his guard and intent upon the chase. He was still in his first youth, and might have been one of the illustrious few among aged princes, had he sought to be loved by his subjects as much as to be feared by his foes.

The murder of Vardanes threw the affairs of Parthia into confusion, as the people were in doubt who should be summoned to the throne. Many inclined to Gotarzes, some to Meherdates, a descendant of Phraates, who was a hostage in our hands. Finally Gotarzes prevailed. Established in the palace, he drove the Parthians by his cruelty and profligacy to send a secret entreaty to the Roman emperor that Meherdates might be allowed to mount the throne of his ancestors.

It was during this consulship, in the eight hundredth year after the foundation of Rome and the sixty-fourth after their celebration by Augustus that the secular games were exhibited. I say nothing of the calculations of the two princes, which I have sufficiently discussed in my history of the emperor Domitian; for he also exhibited secular games, at which indeed, being one of the priesthood of the Fifteen and praetor at the time, I specially assisted. It is in no boastful spirit that I mention this, but because this duty has immemorially belonged to the College of the Fifteen, and the praetors have performed the chief functions in these ceremonies. While Claudius sat to witness the games of the circus, some of the young nobility acted on horseback the battle of Troy. Among them was Britannicus, the emperor's son, and Lucius Domitius, who became soon afterwards by adoption heir to the empire with the surname of Nero. The stronger popular enthusiasm which greeted him was taken to presage his greatness. It was commonly reported that snakes had been seen by his cradle, which they seemed to guard, a fabulous tale invented to match the marvels of other lands. Nero, never a disparager of himself, was wont to say that but one snake, at most, had been seen in his chamber.

Something however of popular favour was bequeathed to him from the remembrance of Germanicus, whose only male descendant he was, and the pity felt for his mother Agrippina was increased by the cruelty of Messalina, who, always her enemy, and then more furious than ever, was only kept from planning an accusation and suborning informers by a new and almost insane passion. She had grown so frantically enamoured of Caius Silius, the handsomest of the young nobility of Rome, that she drove from his bed Junia Silana, a high-born lady, and had her lover wholly to herself. Silius was not unconscious of his wickedness and his peril; but a refusal would have insured destruction, and he had some hope of escaping exposure; the prize too was great, so he consoled himself by awaiting the future and enjoying the present. As for her, careless of concealment, she went continually with a numerous retinue to his house, she haunted his steps, showered on him wealth and honours, and, at last, as though empire had passed to another, the slaves, the freedmen, the very furniture of the emperor were to be seen in the possession of the paramour.

Claudius meanwhile, who knew nothing about his wife, and was busy with his functions as censor, published edicts severely rebuking the lawlessness of the people in the theatre, when they insulted Caius Pomponius, an ex-consul, who furnished verses for the stage, and certain ladies of rank. He introduced too a law restraining the cruel greed of the usurers, and forbidding them to lend at interest sums repayable on a father's death. He also conveyed by an aqueduct into Rome the waters which flow from the hills of Simbrua. And he likewise invented and published for use some new letters, having discovered, as he said, that even the Greek alphabet had not been completed at once.

It was the Egyptians who first symbolized ideas, and that by the figures of animals. These records, the most ancient of all human history, are still seen engraved on stone. The Egyptians also claim to have invented the alphabet, which the Phoenicians, they say, by means of their superior seamanship, introduced into Greece, and of which they appropriated the glory, giving out that they had discovered what they had really been taught. Tradition indeed says that Cadmus, visiting Greece in a Phoenician fleet, was the teacher of this art to its yet barbarous tribes. According to one account, it was Cecrops of Athens or Linus of Thebes, or Palamedes of Argos in Trojan times who invented the shapes of sixteen letters, and others, chiefly Simonides, added the rest. In Italy the Etrurians learnt them from Demaratus of Corinth, and the Aborigines from the Arcadian Evander. And so the Latin letters have the same form as the oldest Greek characters. At first too our alphabet was scanty, and additions were afterwards made. Following this precedent Claudius added three letters, which were employed during his reign and subsequently disused. These may still be seen on the tablets of brass set up in the squares and temples, on which new statutes are published.

Claudius then brought before the Senate the subject of the college of "haruspices," that, as he said, "the oldest of Italian sciences might not be lost through negligence. It had often happened in evil days for the State that advisers had been summoned at whose suggestion ceremonies had been restored and observed more duly for the future. The nobles of Etruria, whether of their own accord or at the instigation of the Roman Senate, had retained this science, making it the inheritance of distinct families. It was now less zealously studied through the general indifference to all sound learning and to the growth of foreign superstitions. At present all is well, but we must show gratitude to the favour of Heaven, by taking care that the rites observed during times of peril may not be forgotten in prosperity." A resolution of the Senate was accordingly passed, charging the pontiffs to see what should be retained or reformed with respect to the "haruspices."

It was in this same year that the Cherusci asked Rome for a king. They had lost all their nobles in their civil wars, and there was left but one scion of the royal house, Italicus by name, who lived at Rome. On the father's side he was descended from Flavus, the brother of Arminius; his mother was a daughter of Catumerus, chief of the Chatti. The youth himself was of distinguished beauty, a skilful horseman and swordsman both after our fashion and that of his country. So the emperor made him a present of money, furnished him with an escort, and bade him enter with a good heart on the honours of his house. "Never before," he said, "had a native of Rome, no hostage but a citizen, gone to mount a foreign throne." At first his arrival was welcome to the Germans, and they crowded to pay him court, for he was untainted by any spirit of faction, and showed the same hearty goodwill to all, practising sometimes the courtesy and temperance which can never offend, but oftener those excesses of wine and lust in which barbarians delight. He was winning fame among his neighbours and even far beyond them, when some who had found their fortune in party feuds, jealous of his power, fled to the tribes on the border, protesting that Germany was being robbed of her ancient freedom, and that the might of Rome was on the rise. "Is there really," they said, "no native of this country to fill the place of king without raising the son of the spy Flavus above all his fellows? It is idle to put forward the name of Arminius. Had even the son of Arminius come to the throne after growing to manhood on a hostile soil, he might well be dreaded, corrupted as he would be by the bread of dependence, by slavery, by luxury, by all foreign habits. But if Italicus had his father's spirit, no man, be it remembered, had ever waged war against his country and his home more savagely than that father."

By these and like appeals they collected a large force. No less numerous were the partisans of Italicus. "He was no intruder," they said, "on an unwilling people; he had obeyed a call. Superior as he was to all others in noble birth, should they not put his valour to the test, and see whether he showed himself worthy of his uncle Arminius and his grandfather Catumerus? He need not blush because his father had never relinquished the loyalty which, with the consent of the Germans, he had promised to Rome. The name of liberty was a lying pretext in the mouths of men who, base in private, dangerous in public life, had nothing to hope except from civil discord."

The people enthusiastically applauded him. After a fierce conflict among the barbarians, the king was victorious. Subsequently, in his good fortune, he fell into a despot's pride, was dethroned, was restored by the help of the Langobardi, and still, in prosperity or adversity, did mischief to the interests of the Cheruscan nation.

It was during the same period that the Chauci, free, as it happened, from dissension at home and emboldened by the death of Sanquinius, made, while Corbulo was on his way, an inroad into Lower Germany, under the leadership of Gannascus. This man was of the tribe of the Canninefates, had served long as our auxiliary, had then deserted, and, getting some light vessels, had made piratical descents specially on the coast of Gaul, inhabited, he knew, by a wealthy and unwarlike population. Corbulo meanwhile entered the province with careful preparation and soon winning a renown of which that campaign was the beginning, he brought his triremes up the channel of the Rhine and the rest of his vessels up the estuaries and canals to which they were adapted. Having sunk the enemy's flotilla, driven out Gannascus, and brought everything into good order, he restored the discipline of former days among legions which had forgotten the labours and toils of the soldier and delighted only in plunder. No one was to fall out of the line; no one was to fight without orders. At the outposts, on guard, in the duties of day and of night, they were always to be under arms. One soldier, it was said, had suffered death for working at the trenches without his sword, another for wearing nothing as he dug, but his poniard. These extreme and possibly false stories at least had their origin in the general's real severity. We may be sure that he was strict and implacable to serious offences, when such sternness in regard to trifles could be believed of him.

The fear thus inspired variously affected his own troops and the enemy. Our men gained fresh valour; the barbarians felt their pride broken. The Frisians, who had been hostile or disloyal since the revolt which had been begun by the defeat of Lucius Apronius, gave hostages and settled down on territories marked out by Corbulo, who, at the same time, gave them a senate, magistrates, and a constitution. That they might not throw off their obedience, he built a fort among them, while he sent envoys to invite the Greater Chauci to submission and to destroy Gannascus by stratagem. This stealthy attempt on the life of a deserter and a traitor was not unsuccessful, nor was it anything ignoble. Yet the Chauci were violently roused by the man's death, and Corbulo was now sowing the seeds of another revolt, thus getting a reputation which many liked, but of which many thought ill. "Why," men asked, "was he irritating the foe? His disasters will fall on the State. If he is successful, so famous a hero will be a danger to peace, and a formidable subject for a timid emperor." Claudius accordingly forbade fresh attacks on

Germany, so emphatically as to order the garrisons to be withdrawn to the left bank of the Rhine.

Corbulo was actually preparing to encamp on hostile soil when the despatch reached him. Surprised, as he was, and many as were the thoughts which crowded on him, thoughts of peril from the emperor, of scorn from the barbarians, of ridicule from the allies, he said nothing but this, "Happy the Roman generals of old," and gave the signal for retreat. To keep his soldiers free from sloth, he dug a canal of twenty-three miles in length between the Rhine and the Meuse, as a means of avoiding the uncertain perils of the ocean. The emperor, though he had forbidden war, yet granted him triumphal distinctions.

Soon afterwards Curtius Rufus obtained the same honour. He had opened mines in the territory of the Mattiaci for working certain veins of silver. The produce was small and soon exhausted. The toil meanwhile of the legions was only to a loss, while they dug channels for water and constructed below the surface works which are difficult enough in the open air. Worn out by the labour, and knowing that similar hardships were endured in several provinces, the soldiers wrote a secret despatch in the name of the armies, begging the emperor to give in advance triumphal distinctions to one to whom he was about to entrust his forces.

Of the birth of Curtius Rufus, whom some affirm to have been the son of a gladiator, I would not publish a falsehood, while I shrink from telling the truth. On reaching manhood he attached himself to a quaestor to whom Africa had been allotted, and was walking alone at midday in some unfrequented arcade in the town of Adrumetum, when he saw a female figure of more than human stature, and heard a voice, "Thou, Rufus, art the man who will one day come into this province as proconsul." Raised high in hope by such a presage, he returned to Rome, where, through the lavish expenditure of his friends and his own vigorous ability, he obtained the quaestorship, and, subsequently, in competition with well-born candidates, the praetorship, by the vote of the emperor Tiberius, who threw a veil over the discredit of his origin, saying, "Curtius Rufus seems to me to be his own ancestor." Afterwards, throughout a long old age of surly sycophancy to those above him, of arrogance to those beneath him, and of moroseness among his equals, he gained the high office of the consulship, triumphal distinctions, and, at last, the province of Africa. There he died, and so fulfilled the presage of his destiny.

At Rome meanwhile, without any motive then known or subsequently ascertained, Cneius Nonius, a Roman knight, was found wearing a sword amid a crowd who were paying their respects to the emperor. The man confessed his own guilt when he was being torn in pieces by torture, but gave up no accomplices, perhaps having none to hide.

During the same consulship, Publius Dolabella proposed that a spectacle of gladiators should be annually exhibited at the cost of those who obtained the quaestorship. In our ancestors' days this honour had been a reward of virtue, and every citizen, with good qualities to support him, was allowed to compete for office. At first there were no distinctions even of age, which prevented a man in his early youth from becoming a consul or a dictator. The quaestors indeed were appointed while the kings still ruled, and this the revival by Brutus of the *lex curiata* plainly shows. The consuls retained the power of selecting them, till the people bestowed this office as well as others. The first so created were Valerius Potitus and Aemilius Mamercus sixty-three years after the expulsion of the Tarquins, and they were to be attached to the war-department. As the public business increased, two more were appointed to attend to affairs at Rome. This number was again doubled, when to the contributions of Italy was added the tribute of the provinces. Subsequently Sulla, by one of his laws, provided that twenty should be elected to fill up the Senate, to which he had intrusted judicial functions. These functions the knights afterwards recovered, but the quaestorship was obtained, without expense, by merit in the candidates or by the good nature of the electors, till at Dolabella's suggestion it was, so to speak, put up to sale.

In the consulship of Aulus Vitellius and Lucius Vipstanus the question of filling up the Senate was discussed, and the chief men of Gallia Comata, as it was called, who had long possessed the rights of allies and of Roman citizens, sought the privilege of obtaining public offices at Rome. There was much talk of every kind on the subject, and it was argued before the emperor with vehement opposition. "Italy," it was asserted, "is not so feeble as to be unable to furnish its own capital with a senate. Once our native-born citizens sufficed for peoples of our own kin, and we are by no means dissatisfied with the Rome of the past. To this day we cite examples, which under our old customs the Roman character exhibited as to valour and renown. Is it a small thing that Veneti and Insubres have already burst into the Senate-house, unless a mob of foreigners, a troop of captives, so to say, is now forced upon us? What distinctions will be left for the remnants of our noble houses, or for any impoverished senators from Latium? Every place will be crowded with these millionaires, whose ancestors of the second and third generations at the head of hostile tribes destroyed our armies with fire and sword, and actually besieged the divine Julius at Alesia. These are recent memories. What if there were to rise up the remembrance of those who fell in Rome's citadel and at her altar by the hands of these same barbarians! Let them enjoy indeed the title of citizens, but let them not vulgarise the distinctions of the Senate and the honours of office."

These and like arguments failed to impress the emperor. He at once addressed himself to answer them, and thus harangued the assembled Senate. "My ancestors, the most ancient of whom was made at once a citizen and a noble of Rome, encourage me to govern by the same policy of transferring to this city all conspicuous merit, wherever found. And indeed I know, as facts, that the Julii came from Alba, the Coruncanii from Camerium, the Porcii from Tusculum, and not to inquire too minutely into the past, that new members have been brought into the Senate from Etruria and Lucania and the whole of Italy, that Italy itself was at last extended to the Alps, to the end that not only single persons but entire countries and tribes might be united under our name. We had unshaken peace at home; we prospered in all our foreign relations, in the days when Italy beyond the Po was admitted to share our citizenship, and when, enrolling in our ranks the most vigorous of the provincials, under colour of settling our legions throughout the world, we recruited our exhausted empire. Are we sorry that the Balbi came to us from Spain, and other men not less illustrious from Narbon Gaul? Their descendants are still among us, and do not yield to us in patriotism.

"What was the ruin of Sparta and Athens, but this, that mighty as they were in war, they spurned from them as aliens those whom they had conquered? Our founder Romulus, on the other hand, was so wise that he fought as enemies and then hailed as fellow-citizens several nations on the very same day. Strangers have reigned over us. That freedmen's sons should be intrusted with public offices is not, as many wrongly think, a sudden innovation, but was a common practice in the old commonwealth. But, it will be said, we have fought with the Senones. I suppose then that the Volsci and Aequi never stood in array against us. Our city was taken by the Gauls. Well, we also gave hostages to the Etruscans, and passed under the yoke of the Samnites. On the whole, if you review all our wars, never has one been finished in a shorter time than that with the

Gauls. Thenceforth they have preserved an unbroken and loyal peace. United as they now are with us by manners, education, and intermarriage, let them bring us their gold and their wealth rather than enjoy it in isolation. Everything, Senators, which we now hold to be of the highest antiquity, was once new. Plebeian magistrates came after patrician; Latin magistrates after plebeian; magistrates of other Italian peoples after Latin. This practice too will establish itself, and what we are this day justifying by precedents, will be itself a precedent."

The emperor's speech was followed by a decree of the Senate, and the Aedui were the first to obtain the right of becoming senators at Rome. This compliment was paid to their ancient alliance, and to the fact that they alone of the Gauls cling to the name of brothers of the Roman people.

About the same time the emperor enrolled in the ranks of the patricians such senators as were of the oldest families, and such as had had distinguished ancestors. There were now but scanty relics of the Greater Houses of Romulus and of the Lesser Houses of Lucius Brutus, as they had been called, and those too were exhausted which the Dictator Caesar by the Cassian and the emperor Augustus by the Saenian law had chosen into their place. These acts, as being welcome to the State, were undertaken with hearty gladness by the imperial censor. Anxiously considering how he was to rid the Senate of men of notorious infamy, he preferred a gentle method, recently devised, to one which accorded with the sternness of antiquity, and advised each to examine his own case and seek the privilege of laying aside his rank. Permission, he said, would be readily obtained. He would publish in the same list those who had been expelled and those who had been allowed to retire, that by this confounding together of the decision of the censors and the modesty of voluntary resignation the disgrace might be softened.

For this, the consul Vipstanus moved that Claudius should be called "Father of the Senate." The title of "Father of the Country" had, he argued, been indiscriminately bestowed; new services ought to be recognized by unusual titles. The emperor, however, himself stopped the consul's flattery, as extravagant. He closed the lustrum, the census for which gave a total of 5,984,072 citizens. Then too ended his blindness as to his domestic affairs. He was soon compelled to notice and punish his wife's infamies, till he afterwards craved passionately for an unhallowed union.

Messalina, now grown weary of the very facility of her adulteries, was rushing into strange excesses, when even Silius, either through some fatal infatuation or because he imagined that, amid the dangers which hung over him, danger itself was the best safety, urged the breaking off of all concealment. "They were not," he said, "in such an extremity as to have to wait for the emperor's old age. Harmless measures were for the innocent. Crime once exposed had no refuge but in audacity. They had accomplices in all who feared the same fate. For himself, as he had neither wife nor child, he was ready to marry and to adopt Britannicus. Messalina would have the same power as before, with the additional advantage of a quiet mind, if only they took Claudius by surprise, who, though unsuspicious of treachery, was hasty in his wrath."

The suggestion was coldly received, not because the lady loved her husband, but from a fear that Silius, after attaining his highest hopes, would spurn an adulteress, and soon estimate at its true value the crime which in the midst of peril he had approved. But she craved the name of wife, for the sake of the monstrous infamy, that last source of delight to the reckless. She waited only till Claudius set out for Ostia to perform a sacrifice, and then celebrated all the solemnities of marriage.

I am well aware that it will seem a fable that any persons in the world could have been so obtuse in a city which knows everything and hides nothing, much more, that these persons should have been a consul-elect and the emperor's wife; that, on an appointed day, before witnesses duly summoned, they should have come together as if for the purpose of legitimate marriage; that she should have listened to the words of the bridegroom's friends, should have sacrificed to the gods, have taken her place among a company of guests, have lavished her kisses and caresses, and passed the night in the freedom which marriage permits. But this is no story to excite wonder; I do but relate what I have heard and what our fathers have recorded.

The emperor's court indeed shuddered, its powerful personages especially, the men who had much to fear from a revolution. From secret whisperings they passed to loud complaints. "When an actor," they said, "impudently thrust himself into the imperial chamber, it certainly brought scandal on the State, but we were a long way from ruin. Now, a young noble of stately beauty, of vigorous intellect, with the near prospect of the consulship, is preparing himself for a loftier ambition. There can be no secret about what is to follow such a marriage." Doubtless there was thrill of alarm when they thought of the apathy of Claudius, of his devotion to his wife and of the many murders perpetrated at Messalina's bidding. On the other hand, the very good nature of the emperor inspired confident hope that if they could overpower him by the enormity of the charge, she might be condemned and crushed before she was accused. The critical point was this, that he should not hear her defence, and that his ears should be shut even against her confession.

At first Callistus, of whom I have already spoken in connection with the assassination of Caius Caesar, Narcissus, who had contrived the death of Appius, and Pallas, who was then in the height of favour, debated whether they might not by secret threats turn Messalina from her passion for Silius, while they concealed all else. Then fearing that they would be themselves involved in ruin, they abandoned the idea, Pallas out of cowardice, and Callistus, from his experience of a former court, remembering that prudent rather than vigorous counsels insure the maintenance of power. Narcissus persevered, only so far changing his plan as not to make her aware beforehand by a single word what was the charge or who was the accuser. Then he eagerly watched his opportunity, and, as the emperor lingered long at Ostia, he sought two of the mistresses to whose society Claudius was especially partial, and, by gifts, by promises, by dwelling on power increased by the wife's fall, he induced them to undertake the work of the informer.

On this, Calpurnia (that was the woman's name), as soon as she was allowed a private interview, threw herself at the emperor's knees, crying out that Messalina was married to Silius. At the same time she asked Cleopatra, who was standing near and waiting for the question, whether she knew it. Cleopatra nodding assent, she begged that Narcissus might be summoned. Narcissus entreated pardon for the past, for having concealed the scandal while confined to a Vettius or a Plautius. Even now, he said, he would not make charges of adultery, and seem to be asking back the palace, the slaves, and the other belongings of imperial rank. These Silius might enjoy; only, he must give back the wife and annul the act of marriage. "Do you know," he said "of your divorce? The people, the army, the Senate saw the marriage of Silius. Act at once, or the new husband is master of Rome."

Claudius then summoned all his most powerful friends. First he questioned Turranius, superintendent of the corn market; next, Lusius Geta, who commanded the praetorians. When they confessed the truth, the whole company clamoured in concert that he must go to the camp, must assure himself of the praetorian cohorts, must think of safety before he thought of vengeance. It is quite certain that Claudius was so overwhelmed by terror that he repeatedly asked whether he was indeed in possession of the empire, whether Silius was still a subject.

Messalina meanwhile, more wildly profligate than ever, was celebrating in mid-autumn a representation of the vintage in her new home. The presses were being trodden; the vats were overflowing; women girt with skins were dancing, as Bacchanals dance in their worship or their frenzy. Messalina with flowing hair shook the thyrsus, and Silius at her side, crowned with ivy and wearing the buskin, moved his head to some lascivious chorus. It is said that one Vettius Valens climbed a very lofty tree in sport, and when they asked him what he saw, replied, "A terrible storm from Ostia." Possibly such appearance had begun; perhaps, a word dropped by chance became a prophecy.

Meanwhile no mere rumour but messengers from all parts brought the news that everything was known to Claudius, and that he was coming, bent on vengeance. Messalina upon this went to the gardens of Lucullus; Silius, to conceal his fear, to his business in the forum. The other guests were flying in all directions when the centurions appeared and put every one in irons where they found them, either in the public streets or in hiding. Messalina, though her peril took away all power of thought, promptly resolved to meet and face her husband, a course in which she had often found safety; while she bade Britannicus and Octavia hasten to embrace their father. She besought Vibidia, the eldest of the Vestal Virgins, to demand audience of the supreme pontiff and to beg for mercy. Meanwhile, with only three companions, so lonely did she find herself in a moment, she traversed the whole length of the city, and, mounting on a cart used to remove garden refuse, proceeded along the road to Ostia; not pitied, so overpoweringly hideous were her crimes, by a single person.

There was equal alarm on the emperor's side. They put but little trust in Geta, who commanded the praetorians, a man swayed with good case to good or evil. Narcissus in concert with others who dreaded the same fate, declared that the only hope of safety for the emperor lay in his transferring for that one day the command of the soldiers to one of the freedmen, and he offered to undertake it himself. And that Claudius might not be induced by Lucius Vitellius and Largus Caecina to repent, while he was riding into Rome, he asked and took a seat in the emperor's carriage.

It was currently reported in after times that while the emperor broke into contradictory exclamations, now inveighing against the infamies of his wife, and now, returning in thought to the remembrance of his love and of his infant children, Vitellius said nothing but, "What audacity! what wickedness!" Narcissus indeed kept pressing him to clear up his ambiguities and let the truth be known, but still he could not prevail upon him to utter anything that was not vague and susceptible of any meaning which might be put on it, or upon Largus Caecina, to do anything but follow his example. And now Messalina had presented herself, and was insisting that the emperor should listen to the mother of Octavia and Britannicus, when the accuser roared out at her the story of Silius and her marriage. At the same moment, to draw Caesar's eyes away from her, he handed him some papers which detailed her debaucheries. Soon afterwards, as he was entering Rome, his children by Messalina were to have shown themselves, had not Narcissus ordered their removal. Vibidia he could not repel, when, with a vehemently indignant appeal, she demanded that a wife should not be given up to death without a hearing. So Narcissus replied that the emperor would hear her, and that she should have an opportunity of disproving the charge. Meanwhile the holy virgin was to go and discharge her sacred duties.

All throughout, Claudius preserved a strange silence; Vitellius seemed unconscious. Everything was under the freedman's control. By his order, the paramour's house was thrown open and the emperor conducted thither. First, on the threshold, he pointed out the statue of Silius's father, which a decree of the Senate had directed to be destroyed; next, how the heirlooms of the Neros and the Drusi had been degraded into the price of infamy. Then he led the emperor, furious and bursting out in menace, into the camp, where the soldiers were purposely assembled. Claudius spoke to them a few words at the dictation of Narcissus. Shame indeed checked the utterance even of a righteous anger. Instantly there came a shout from the cohorts, demanding the names of the culprits and their punishment. Brought before the tribunal, Silius sought neither defence nor delay, but begged that his death might be hastened. A like courage made several Roman knights of the first rank desirous of a speedy doom. Titius Proculus, who had been appointed to watch Messalina and was now offering his evidence, Vettius Valens, who confessed his guilt, together with Pompeius Urbicus and Saufellus Trogus from among her accomplices, were ordered to execution. Decius Calpurnianus too, commander of the watch, Sulpicius Rufus, who had the charge of the Games, and Juncus Virgilianus, a senator, were similarly punished.

Mnester alone occasioned a pause. Rending off his clothes, he insisted on Claudius looking at the scars of his stripes and remembering his words when he surrendered himself, without reserve, to Messalina's bidding. The guilt of others had been the result of presents or of large promises; his, of necessity. He must have been the first victim had Silius obtained empire.

Caesar was touched by his appeal and inclined to mercy, but his freedmen prevailed on him not to let any indulgence be shown to a player when so many illustrious citizens had fallen. "It mattered not whether he had sinned so greatly from choice or compulsion." Even the defence of Traulus Montanus, a Roman knight, was not admitted. A young man of pure life, yet of singular beauty, he had been summoned and dismissed within the space of one night by Messalina, who was equally capricious in her passions and dislikes. In the cases of Suilius Caesoninus and Plautius Lateranus, the extreme penalty was remitted. The latter was saved by the distinguished services of his uncle; the former by his very vices, having amid that abominable throng submitted to the worst degradation.

Messalina meanwhile, in the gardens of Lucullus, was struggling for life, and writing letters of entreaty, as she alternated between hope arid fury. In her extremity, it was her pride alone which forsook her. Had not Narcissus hurried on her death, ruin would have recoiled on her accuser. Claudius had returned home to an early banquet; then, in softened mood, when the wine had warmed him, he bade some one go and tell the "poor creature" (this is the word which they say he used) to come the morrow and plead her cause. Hearing this, seeing too that his wrath was subsiding and his passion returning, and fearing, in the event of delay, the effect of approaching night and conjugal recollections, Narcissus rushed out, and ordered the centurions and the tribunes, who were on guard, to accomplish the deed of blood. Such, he said, was the emperor's bidding. Evodus, one of the freedmen, was appointed to watch and complete the affair. Hurrying on before with all speed to the gardens, he found Messalina stretched upon the ground, while by her side sat Lepida, her mother, who, though estranged from her daughter in prosperity, was now melted to pity by her inevitable doom, and urged her not to wait for the executioner. "Life," she said, "was over; all that could be looked for was honour in death." But in that heart, utterly corrupted by profligacy, nothing noble remained. She still prolonged her tears and idle complaints, till the gates were forced open by the rush of the new comers, and there stood at her side the tribune, sternly silent, and the freedman, overwhelming her with the copious insults of a servile tongue.

Then for the first time she understood her fate and put her hand to a dagger. In her terror she was applying it ineffectually to her throat and breast, when a blow from the tribune drove it through her. Her body was given up to her mother. Claudius was still at the banquet when they told him that Messalina was dead, without mentioning whether it was by her own or another's hand. Nor did he ask the question, but called for the cup and finished his repast as usual. During the days which followed he showed no sign of hatred or joy or anger or sadness, in a word, of any human emotion, either when he looked on her triumphant accusers or on her weeping children. The Senate assisted his forgetfulness by decreeing that her name and her statues should be removed from all places, public or private. To Narcissus were voted the decorations of the quaestorship, a mere trifle to the pride of one who rose in the height of his power above Pallas and Callistus.

BOOK XII, A.D. 48-54

The destruction of Messalina shook the imperial house; for a strife arose among the freedmen, who should choose a wife for Claudius, impatient as he was of a single life and submissive to the rule of wives. The ladies were fired with no less jealousy. Each insisted on her rank, beauty, and fortune, and pointed to her claims to such a marriage. But the keenest competition was between Lollia Paulina, the daughter of Marcus Lollius, an ex-consul, and Julia Agrippina, the daughter of Germanicus. Callistus favoured the first, Pallas the second. Aelia Paetina however, of the family of the Tuberones, had the support of Narcissus. The emperor, who inclined now one way, now another, as he listened to this or that adviser, summoned the disputants to a conference and bade them express their opinions and give their reasons.

Narcissus dwelt on the marriage of years gone by, on the tie of offspring, for Paetina was the mother of Antonia, and on the advantage of excluding a new element from his household, by the return of a wife to whom he was accustomed, and who would assuredly not look with a stepmother's animosity on Britannicus and Octavia, who were next in her affections to her own children. Callistus argued that she was compromised by her long separation, and that were she to be taken back, she would be supercilious on the strength of it. It would be far better to introduce Lollia, for, as she had no children of her own, she would be free from jealousy, and would take the place of a mother towards her stepchildren.

Pallas again selected Agrippina for special commendation because she would bring with her Germanicus's grandson, who was thoroughly worthy of imperial rank, the scion of a noble house and a link to unite the descendants of the Claudian family. He hoped that a woman who was the mother of many children and still in the freshness of youth, would not carry off the grandeur of the Caesars to some other house.

This advice prevailed, backed up as it was by Agrippina's charms. On the pretext of her relationship, she paid frequent visits to her uncle, and so won his heart, that she was preferred to the others, and, though not yet his wife, already possessed a wife's power. For as soon as she was sure of her marriage, she began to aim at greater things, and planned an alliance between Domitius, her son by Cneius Aenobarbus, and Octavia, the emperor's daughter. This could not be accomplished without a crime, for the emperor had betrothed Octavia to Lucius Silanus, a young man otherwise famous, whom he had brought forward as a candidate for popular favour by the honour of triumphal distinctions and by a magnificent gladiatorial show. But no difficulty seemed to be presented by the temper of a sovereign who had neither partialities nor dislikes, but such as were suggested and dictated to him.

Vitellius accordingly, who used the name of censor to screen a slave's trickeries, and looked forward to new despotisms, already impending, associated himself in Agrippina's plans, with a view to her favour, and began to bring charges against Silanus, whose sister, Junia Calvina, a handsome and lively girl, had shortly before become his daughter-in-law. Here was a starting point for an accuser. Vitellius put an infamous construction on the somewhat incautious though not criminal love between the brother and sister. The emperor listened, for his affection for his daughter inclined him the more to admit suspicions against his son-in-law. Silanus meanwhile, who knew nothing of the plot, and happened that year to be praetor, was suddenly expelled from the Senate by an edict of Vitellius, though the roll of Senators had been recently reviewed and the lustrum closed. Claudius at the same time broke off the connection; Silanus was forced to resign his office, and the one remaining day of his praetorship was conferred on Eprius Marcellus.

In the year of the consulship of Caius Pompeius and Quintus Veranius, the marriage arranged between Claudius and Agrippina was confirmed both by popular rumour and by their own illicit love. Still, they did not yet dare to celebrate the nuptials in due form, for there was no precedent for the introduction of a niece into an uncle's house. It was positively incest, and if disregarded, it would, people feared, issue in calamity to the State. These scruples ceased not till Vitellius undertook the management of the matter in his own way. He asked the emperor whether he would yield to the recommendations of the people and to the authority of the Senate. When Claudius replied that he was one among the citizens and could not resist their unanimous voice, Vitellius requested him to wait in the palace, while he himself went to the Senate. Protesting that the supreme interest of the commonwealth was at stake, he begged to be allowed to speak first, and then began to urge that the very burdensome labours of the emperor in a world-wide administration, required assistance, so that, free from domestic cares, he might consult the public welfare. How again could there be a more virtuous relief for the mind of an imperial censor than the taking of a wife to share his prosperity and his troubles, to whom he might intrust his inmost thoughts and the care of his young children, unused as he was to luxury and pleasure, and wont from his earliest youth to obey the laws.

Vitellius, having first put forward these arguments in a conciliatory speech, and met with decided acquiescence from the Senate, began afresh to point out, that, as they all recommended the emperor's marriage, they ought to select a lady conspicuous for noble rank and purity, herself too the mother of children. "It cannot," he said, "be long a question that Agrippina stands first in nobility of birth. She has given proof too that she is not barren, and she has suitable moral qualities. It is, again, a singular advantage to us, due to divine providence, for a widow to be united to an emperor who has limited himself to his own lawful wives. We have heard from our fathers, we have ourselves seen that married women were seized at the caprice of the Caesars. This is quite alien to the propriety of our day. Rather let a precedent be now set for the taking of a wife by an emperor. But, it will be said, marriage with a brother's daughter is with us a novelty. True; but it is common in other countries, and there is no law to forbid it. Marriages of cousins were long unknown, but after a time they became frequent. Custom adapts itself to expediency, and this novelty will hereafter take its place among recognized usages."

There were some who rushed out of the Senate passionately protesting that if the emperor hesitated, they would use violence. A promiscuous throng assembled, and kept exclaiming that the same too was the prayer of the Roman people. Claudius without further delay presented himself in the forum to their congratulations; then entering the Senate, he asked from them a decree which should decide that for the future marriages between uncles and brothers' daughters should be legal. There was, however, found only one person who desired such a marriage, Alledius Severus, a Roman knight, who, as many said, was swayed by the influence of Agrippina. Then came a revolution in the State, and everything was under the control of a woman, who did not, like Messalina, insult Rome by loose manners. It was a stringent, and, so to say, masculine despotism; there was sternness and generally arrogance in public, no sort of immodesty at home, unless it conduced to power. A boundless greed of wealth was veiled under the pretext that riches were being accumulated as a prop to the throne.

On the day of the marriage Silanus committed suicide, having up to that time prolonged his hope of life, or else choosing that day to heighten the popular indignation. His sister, Calvina, was banished from Italy. Claudius further added that sacrifices after the ordinances of King Tullius, and atonements were to be offered by the pontiffs in the grove of Diana, amid general ridicule at the idea devising penalties and propitiations for incest at such a time. Agrippina, that she might not be conspicuous only by her evil deeds, procured for Annaeus Seneca a remission of his exile, and with it the praetorship. She thought this would be universally welcome, from the celebrity of his attainments, and it was her wish too for the boyhood of Domitius to be trained under so excellent an instructor, and for them to have the benefit of his counsels in their designs on the throne. For Seneca, it was believed, was devoted to Agrippina from a remembrance of her kindness, and an enemy to Claudius from a bitter sense of wrong.

It was then resolved to delay no longer. Memmius Pollio, the consul-elect, was induced by great promises to deliver a speech, praying Claudius to betroth Octavia to Domitius. The match was not unsuitable to the age of either, and was likely to develop still more important results. Pollio introduced the motion in much the same language as Vitellius had lately used. So Octavia was betrothed, and Domitius, besides his previous relationship, became now the emperor's affianced son-in-law, and an equal of Britannicus, through the exertions of his mother and the cunning of those who had been the accusers of Messalina, and feared the vengeance of her son.

About the same time an embassy from the Parthians, which had been sent, as I have stated, to solicit the return of Meherdates, was introduced into the Senate, and delivered a message to the following effect:—"They were not," they said, "unaware of the treaty of alliance, nor did their coming imply any revolt from the family of the Arsacids; indeed, even the son of Vonones, Phraates's grandson, was with them in their resistance to the despotism of Gotarzes, which was alike intolerable to the nobility and to the people. Already brothers, relatives, and distant kin had been swept off by murder after murder; wives actually pregnant, and tender children were added to Gotarzes' victims, while, slothful at home and unsuccessful in war, he made cruelty a screen for his feebleness. Between the Parthians and ourselves there was an ancient friendship, founded on a state alliance, and we ought to support allies who were our rivals in strength, and yet yielded to us out of respect. Kings' sons were given as hostages, in order that when Parthia was tired of home rule, it might fall back on the emperor and the Senate, and receive from them a better sovereign, familiar with Roman habits."

In answer to these and like arguments Claudius began to speak of the grandeur of Rome and the submissive attitude of the Parthians. He compared himself to the Divine Augustus, from whom, he reminded them, they had sought a king, but omitted to mention Tiberius, though he too had sent them sovereigns. He added some advice for Meherdates, who was present, and told him not to be thinking of a despot and his slaves, but rather of a ruler among fellow citizens, and to practise clemency and justice which barbarians would like the more for being unused to them. Then he turned to the envoys and bestowed high praise on the young foster-son of Rome, as one whose self-control had hitherto been exemplary. "Still," he said, "they must bear with the caprices of kings, and frequent revolutions were bad. Rome, sated with her glory, had reached such a height that, she wished even foreign nations to enjoy repose." Upon this Caius Cassius, governor of Syria, was commissioned to escort the young prince to the bank of the Euphrates.

Cassius was at that time pre-eminent for legal learning. The profession of the soldier is forgotten in a quiet period, and peace reduces the enterprising and indolent to an equality. But Cassius, as far as it was possible without war, revived ancient discipline, kept exercising the legions, in short, used as much diligence and precaution as if an enemy were threatening him. This conduct he counted worthy of his ancestors and of the Cassian family which had won renown even in those countries.

He then summoned those at whose suggestion a king had been sought from Rome, and having encamped at Zeugma where the river was most easily fordable and awaited the arrival of the chief men of Parthia and of Acbarus, king of the Arabs, he reminded Meherdates that the impulsive enthusiasm of barbarians soon flags from delay or even changes into treachery, and that therefore he should urge on his enterprise. The advice was disregarded through the perfidy Acbarus, by whom the foolish young prince, who thought that the highest position merely meant self-indulgence, was detained for several days in the town of Edessa. Although a certain Carenes pressed them to come and promised easy success if they hastened their arrival, they did not make for Mesopotamia, which was close to them, but, by a long detour, for Armenia, then ill-suited to their movements, as winter was beginning.

As they approached the plains, wearied with the snows and mountains, they were joined by the forces of Carenes, and having crossed the river Tigris they traversed the country of the Adiabeni, whose king Izates had avowedly embraced the alliance of Meherdates, though secretly and in better faith he inclined to Gotarzes. In their march they captured the city of Ninos, the most ancient capital of Assyria, and a fortress, historically famous, as the spot where the last battle between Darius and Alexander the power of Persia fell. Gotarzes meantime was offering vows to the local divinities on a mountain called Sambulos, with special worship of Hercules, who at a stated time bids the priests in a dream equip horses for the chase and place them near his temple. When the horses have been laden with quivers full of arrows, they scour the forest and at length return at night with empty quivers, panting violently. Again the god in a vision of the night reveals to them the track along which he roamed through the woods, and everywhere slaughtered beasts are found.

Gotarzes, his army not being yet in sufficient force, made the river Corma a line of defence, and though he was challenged to an engagement by taunting messages, he contrived delays, shifted his positions and sent emissaries to corrupt the enemy and bribe them to throw off their allegiance. Izates of the Adiabeni and then Acbarus of the Arabs deserted with their troops, with their countrymen's characteristic fickleness, confirming previous experience, that barbarians prefer to seek a king from Rome than to keep him.

Meherdates, stript of his powerful auxiliaries and suspecting treachery in the rest, resolved, as his last resource, to risk everything and try the issue of a battle. Nor did Gotarzes, who was emboldened by the enemy's diminished strength, refuse the challenge. They fought with terrible courage and doubtful result, till Carenes, who having beaten down all resistance had advanced too far, was surprised by a fresh detachment in his rear. Then Meherdates in despair yielded to promises from Parrhaces, one of his father's adherents, and was by his treachery delivered in chains to the conqueror. Gotarzes taunted him with being no kinsman of his or of the Arsacids, but a foreigner and a Roman, and having cut off his ears, bade him live, a memorial of his own clemency, and a disgrace to us. After this Gotarzes fell ill and died, and Vonones, who then ruled the Medes, was summoned to the throne. He was memorable neither for his good nor bad fortune; he completed a short and inglorious reign, and then the empire of Parthia passed to his son Vologeses.

Mithridates of Bosporus, meanwhile, who had lost his power and was a mere outcast, on learning that the Roman general, Didius, and the main strength of his army had retired, and that Cotys, a young prince without experience, was left in his new kingdom with a few cohorts under Julius Aquila, a Roman knight, disdaining both, roused the neighbouring tribes, and drew deserters to his standard. At last he collected an army, drove out the king of the Dandaridae, and possessed himself of his dominions. When this was known, and the invasion of Bosporus was every moment expected, Aquila and Cotys, seeing that hostilities had been also resumed by Zorsines, king of the Siraci, distrusted their own strength, and themselves too sought the friendship of the foreigner by sending envoys to Eunones, who was then chief of the Adorsi. There was no difficulty about alliance, when they pointed to the power of Rome in contrast with the rebel Mithridates. It was accordingly stipulated that Eunones should engage the enemy with his cavalry, and the Romans undertake the siege of towns.

Then the army advanced in regular formation, the Adorsi in the van and the rear, while the centre was strengthened by the cohorts, and native troops of Bosporus with Roman arms. Thus the enemy was defeated, and they reached Soza, a town in Dandarica, which Mithridates had abandoned, where it was thought expedient to leave a garrison, as the temper of the people was uncertain. Next they marched on the Siraci, and after crossing the river Panda besieged the city of Uspe, which stood on high ground, and had the defence of wall and fosses; only the walls, not being of stone, but of hurdles and wicker-work with earth between, were too weak to resist an assault. Towers were raised to a greater height as a means of annoying the besieged with brands and darts. Had not night stopped the conflict, the siege would have been begun and finished within one day.

Next day they sent an embassy asking mercy for the freeborn, and offering ten thousand slaves. As it would have been inhuman to slay the prisoners, and very difficult to keep them under guard, the conquerors rejected the offer, preferring that they should perish by the just doom of war. The signal for massacre was therefore given to the soldiers, who had mounted the walls by scaling ladders. The destruction of Uspe struck terror into the rest of the people, who thought safety impossible when they saw how armies and ramparts, heights and difficult positions, rivers and cities, alike yielded to their foe. And so Zorsines, having long considered whether he should still have regard to the fallen fortunes of Mithridates or to the kingdom of his fathers, and having at last preferred his country's interests, gave hostages and prostrated himself before the emperor's image, to the great glory of the Roman army, which all men knew to have come after a bloodless victory within three days' march of the river Tanais. In their return however fortune was not equally favourable; some of their vessels, as they were sailing back, were driven on the shores of the Tauri and cut off by the barbarians, who slew the commander of a cohort and several centurions.

Meanwhile Mithridates, finding arms an unavailing resource, considered on whose mercy he was to throw himself. He feared his brother Cotys, who had once been a traitor, then become his open enemy. No Roman was on the spot of authority sufficient to make his promises highly valued. So he turned to Eunones, who had no personal animosity against him, and had been lately strengthened by his alliance with us. Adapting his dress and expression of countenance as much as possible to his present condition, he entered the palace, and throwing himself at the feet of Eunones he exclaimed, "Mithridates, whom the Romans have sought so many years by land and sea, stands before you by his own choice. Deal as you please with the descendant of the great Achaemenes, the only glory of which enemies have not robbed me."

The great name of Mithridates, his reverse, his prayer, full of dignity, deeply affected Eunones. He raised the suppliant, and commended him for having chosen the nation of the Adorsi and his own good faith in suing for mercy. He sent at the same time envoys to Caesar with a letter to this effect, that friendship between emperors of Rome and sovereigns of powerful peoples was primarily based on a similarity of fortune, and that between himself and Claudius there was the tie of a common victory. Wars had glorious endings, whenever matters were settled by an amnesty. The conquered Zorsines had on this principle been deprived of nothing. For Mithridates, as he deserved heavier punishment, he asked neither power nor dominions, only that he might not be led in triumph, and pay the penalty of death.

Claudius, though merciful to foreign princes, was yet in doubt whether it were better to receive the captive with a promise of safety or to claim his surrender by the sword. To this last he was urged by resentment at his wrongs, and by thirst for vengeance. On the other hand it was argued that it would be undertaking a war in a country without roads, on a harbourless sea, against warlike kings and wandering tribes, on a barren soil; that a weary disgust would come of tardy movements, and perils of precipitancy; that the glory of victory would be small, while much disgrace would ensue on defeat. Why should not the emperor seize the offer and spare the exile, whose punishment would be the greater, the longer he lived in poverty?

Moved by these considerations, Claudius wrote to Eunones that Mithridates had certainly merited an extreme and exemplary penalty, which he was not wanting in power to inflict, but it had been the principle of his ancestors to show as much forbearance to a suppliant as they showed persistence against a foe. As for triumphs, they were won over nations and kings hitherto unconquered.

After this, Mithridates was given up and brought to Rome by Junius Cilo, the procurator of Pontus. There in the emperor's presence he was said to have spoken too proudly for his position, and words uttered by him to the following effect became the popular talk: "I have not been sent, but have come back to you; if you do not believe me, let me go and pursue me." He stood too with fearless countenance when he was exposed to the people's gaze near the Rostra, under military guard. To Cilo and Aquila were voted, respectively, the consular and praetorian decorations.

In the same consulship, Agrippina, who was terrible in her hatred and detested Lollia, for having competed with her for the emperor's hand, planned an accusation, through an informer who was to tax her with having consulted astrologers and magicians and the image of the Clarian Apollo, about the imperial marriage. Upon this, Claudius, without hearing the accused, first reminded the Senate of her illustrious rank, that the sister of Lucius Volusius was her mother, Cotta Messalinus her granduncle, Memmius Regulus formerly her husband (for of her marriage to Caius Caesar he purposely said nothing), and then added that she had mischievous designs on the State, and must have the means of crime taken from her. Consequently, her property should be confiscated, and she herself banished from Italy. Thus out of immense wealth only five million sesterces were left to the exile. Calpurnia too, a lady of high rank, was ruined, simply because the emperor had praised her beauty in a casual remark, without any passion for her. And so Agrippina's resentment stopped short of extreme vengeance. A tribune was despatched to Lollia, who was to force her to suicide. Next on the prosecution of the Bithynians, Cadius Rufus, was condemned under the law against extortion.

Narbon Gaul, for its special reverence of the Senate, received a privilege. Senators belonging to the province, without seeking the emperor's approval, were to be allowed to visit their estates, a right enjoyed by Sicily. Ituraea and Judaea, on the death of their kings, Sohaemus and Agrippa, were annexed to the province of Syria.

It was also decided that the augury of the public safety, which for twenty-five years had been neglected, should be revived and henceforth observed. The emperor likewise widened the sacred precincts of the capital, in conformity with the ancient usage, according to which, those who had enlarged the empire were permitted also to extend the boundaries of Rome. But Roman generals, even after the conquest of great nations, had never exercised this right, except Lucius Sulla and the Divine Augustus.

There are various popular accounts of the ambitious and vainglorious efforts of our kings in this matter. Still, I think, it is interesting to know accurately the original plan of the precinct, as it was fixed by Romulus. From the ox market, where we see the brazen statue of a bull, because that animal is yoked to the plough, a furrow was drawn to mark out the town, so as to embrace the great altar of Hercules; then, at regular intervals, stones were placed along the foot of the Palatine hill to the altar of Consus, soon afterwards, to the old Courts, and then to the chapel of Larunda. The Roman forum and the Capitol were not, it was supposed, added to the city by Romulus, but by Titus Tatius. In time, the precinct was enlarged with the growth of Rome's fortunes. The boundaries now fixed by Claudius may be easily recognized, as they are specified in the public records.

In the consulship of Caius Antistius and Marcus Suilius, the adoption of Domitius was hastened on by the influence of Pallas. Bound to Agrippina, first as the promoter of her marriage, then as her paramour, he still urged Claudius to think of the interests of the State, and to provide some support for the tender years of Britannicus. "So," he said, "it had been with the Divine Augustus, whose stepsons, though he had grandsons to be his stay, had been promoted; Tiberius too, though he had offspring of his own, had adopted Germanicus. Claudius also would do well to strengthen himself with a young prince who could share his cares with him."

Overcome by these arguments, the emperor preferred Domitius to his own son, though he was but two years older, and made a speech in the senate, the same in substance as the representations of his freedman. It was noted by learned men, that no previous example of adoption into the patrician family of the Claudii was to be found; and that from Attus Clausus there had been one unbroken line.

However, the emperor received formal thanks, and still more elaborate flattery was paid to Domitius. A law was passed, adopting him into the Claudian family with the name of Nero. Agrippina too was honoured with the title of Augusta. When this had been done, there was not a person so void of pity as not to feel keen sorrow at the position of Britannicus. Gradually forsaken by the very slaves who waited on him, he turned into ridicule the ill-timed attentions of his stepmother, perceiving their insincerity. For he is said to have had by no means a dull understanding; and this is either a fact, or perhaps his perils won him sympathy, and so he possessed the credit of it, without actual evidence.

Agrippina, to show her power even to the allied nations, procured the despatch of a colony of veterans to the chief town of the Ubii, where she was born. The place was named after her. Agrippa, her grandfather, had, as it happened, received this tribe, when they crossed the Rhine, under our protection.

During the same time, there was a panic in Upper Germany through an irruption of plundering bands of Chatti. Thereupon Lucius Pomponius, who was in command, directed the Vangiones and Nemetes, with the allied cavalry, to anticipate the raid, and suddenly to fall upon them from every quarter while they were dispersed. The general's plan was backed up by the energy of the troops. These were divided into two columns; and those who marched to the left cut off the plunderers, just on their return, after a riotous enjoyment of their spoil, when they were heavy with sleep. It added to the men's joy that they had rescued from slavery after forty years some survivors of the defeat of Varus.

The column which took the right-hand and the shorter route, inflicted greater loss on the enemy who met them, and ventured on a battle. With much spoil and glory they returned to Mount Taunus, where Pomponius was waiting with the legions, to see whether the Chatti, in their eagerness for vengeance, would give him a chance of fighting. They however fearing to be hemmed in on one side by the Romans, on the other by the Cherusci, with whom they are perpetually at feud, sent envoys and hostages to Rome. To Pomponius was decreed the honour of a triumph; a mere fraction of his renown with the next generation, with whom his poems constitute his chief glory.

At this same time, Vannius, whom Drusus Caesar had made king of the Suevi, was driven from his kingdom. In the commencement of his reign he was renowned and popular with his countrymen; but subsequently, with long possession, he became a tyrant, and the enmity of neighbours, joined to intestine strife, was his ruin. Vibillius, king of the Hermunduri, and Vangio and Sido, sons of a sister of Vannius, led the movement. Claudius, though often entreated, declined to interpose by arms in the conflict of the barbarians, and simply promised Vannius a safe refuge in the event of his expulsion. He wrote instructions to Publius Atellius Hister, governor of Pannonia, that he was to have his legions, with some picked auxiliaries from the province itself, encamped on the riverbank, as a support to the conquered and a terror to the conqueror, who might otherwise, in the elation of success, disturb also the peace of our empire. For an immense host of Ligii, with other tribes, was advancing, attracted by the fame of the opulent realm which Vannius had enriched during thirty years of plunder and of tribute. Vannius's own native force was infantry, and his cavalry was from the Iazyges of Sarmatia; an army which was no match for his numerous enemy. Consequently, he determined to maintain himself in fortified positions, and protract the war.

But the Iazyges, who could not endure a siege, dispersed themselves throughout the surrounding country and rendered an engagement inevitable, as the Ligii and Hermunduri had there rushed to the attack. So Vannius came down out of his fortresses, and though he was defeated in battle, notwithstanding his reverse, he won some credit by having fought with his own hand, and received wounds on his breast. He then fled to the fleet which was awaiting him on the Danube, and was soon followed by his adherents, who received grants of land and were settled in Pannonia. Vangio and Sido divided his kingdom between them; they were admirably loyal to us, and among their subjects, whether the cause was in themselves or in the nature of despotism, much loved, while seeking to acquire power, and yet more hated when they had acquired it.

Meanwhile, in Britain, Publius Ostorius, the propraetor, found himself confronted by disturbance. The enemy had burst into the territories of our allies with all the more fury, as they imagined that a new general would not march against them with winter beginning and with an army of which he knew nothing. Ostorius, well aware that first events are those which produce alarm or confidence, by a rapid movement of his light cohorts, cut down all who opposed him, pursued those who fled, and lest they should rally, and so an unquiet and treacherous peace might allow no rest to the general and his troops, he prepared to disarm all whom he suspected, and to occupy with encampments the whole country to the Avon and Severn. The Iceni, a powerful tribe, which war had not weakened, as they had voluntarily joined our alliance, were the first to resist. At their instigation the surrounding nations chose as a battlefield a spot walled in by a rude barrier, with a narrow approach, impenetrable to cavalry. Through these defences the Roman general, though he had with him only the allied troops, without the strength of the legions, attempted to break, and having assigned their positions to his cohorts, he equipped even his cavalry for the work of infantry. Then at a given signal they forced the barrier, routing the enemy who were entangled in their own defences. The rebels, conscious of their guilt, and finding escape barred, performed many noble feats. In this battle, Marius Ostorius, the general's son, won the reward for saving a citizen's life.

The defeat of the Iceni quieted those who were hesitating between war and peace. Then the army was marched against the Cangi; their territory was ravaged, spoil taken everywhere without the enemy venturing on an engagement, or if they attempted to harass our march by stealthy attacks, their cunning was always punished. And now Ostorius had advanced within a little distance of the sea, facing the island Hibernia, when feuds broke out among the Brigantes and compelled the general's return, for it was his fixed purpose not to undertake any fresh enterprise till he had consolidated his previous successes. The Brigantes indeed, when a few who were beginning hostilities had been slain and the rest pardoned, settled down quietly; but on the Silures neither terror nor mercy had the least effect; they persisted in war and could be quelled only by legions encamped in their country. That this might be the more promptly effected, a colony of a strong body of veterans was established at Camulodunum on the conquered lands, as a defence against the rebels, and as a means of imbuing the allies with respect for our laws.

The army then marched against the Silures, a naturally fierce people and now full of confidence in the might of Caractacus, who by many an indecisive and many a successful battle had raised himself far above all the other generals of the Britons. Inferior in military strength, but deriving an advantage from the deceptiveness of the country, he at once shifted the war by a stratagem into the territory of the Ordovices, where, joined by all who dreaded peace with us, he resolved on a final struggle. He selected a position for the engagement in which advance and retreat alike would be difficult for our men and comparatively easy for his own, and then on some lofty hills, wherever their sides could be approached by a gentle slope, he piled up stones to serve as a rampart. A river too of varying depth was in his front, and his armed bands were drawn up before his defences.

Then too the chieftains of the several tribes went from rank to rank, encouraging and confirming the spirit of their men by making light of their fears, kindling their hopes, and by every other warlike incitement. As for Caractacus, he flew hither and thither, protesting that that day and that battle would be the beginning of the recovery of their freedom, or of everlasting bondage. He appealed, by name, to their forefathers who had driven back the dictator Caesar, by whose valour they were free from the Roman axe and tribute, and still preserved inviolate the persons of their wives and of their children. While he was thus speaking, the host shouted applause; every warrior bound himself by his national oath not to shrink from weapons or wounds.

Such enthusiasm confounded the Roman general. The river too in his face, the rampart they had added to it, the frowning hilltops, the stern resistance and masses of fighting men everywhere apparent, daunted him. But his soldiers insisted on battle, exclaiming that valour could overcome all things; and the prefects and tribunes, with similar language, stimulated the ardour of the troops. Ostorius having ascertained by a survey the inaccessible and the assailable points of the position, led on his furious men, and crossed the river without difficulty. When he reached the barrier, as long as it was a fight with missiles, the wounds and the slaughter fell chiefly on our soldiers; but when he had formed the military testudo, and the rude, ill-compacted fence of stones was torn down, and it was an equal hand-to-hand engagement, the barbarians retired to the heights. Yet even there, both light and heavy-armed soldiers rushed to the attack; the first harassed the foe with missiles, while the latter closed with them, and the opposing ranks of the Britons were broken, destitute as they were of the defence of breast-plates or helmets. When they faced the auxiliaries, they were felled by the swords and javelins of our legionaries; if they wheeled round, they were again met by the sabres and spears of the auxiliaries. It was a glorious victory; the wife and daughter of Caractacus were captured, and his brothers too were admitted to surrender.

There is seldom safety for the unfortunate, and Caractacus, seeking the protection of Cartismandua, queen of the Brigantes, was put in chains and delivered up to the conquerors, nine years after the beginning of the war in Britain. His fame had spread thence, and travelled to the neighbouring islands and provinces, and was actually celebrated in Italy. All were eager to see the great man, who for so many years had defied our power. Even at Rome the name of Caractacus was no obscure one; and the emperor, while he exalted his own glory, enhanced the renown of the vanquished. The people were summoned as to a grand spectacle; the praetorian cohorts were drawn up under arms in the plain in front of their camp; then came a procession of the royal vassals, and the ornaments and neck-chains and the spoils which the king had won in wars with other tribes, were displayed. Next were to be seen his brothers, his wife and daughter; last of all, Caractacus himself. All the rest stooped in their fear to abject supplication; not so the king, who neither by humble look nor speech sought compassion.

When he was set before the emperor's tribunal, he spoke as follows: "Had my moderation in prosperity been equal to my noble birth and fortune, I should have entered this city as your friend rather than as your captive; and you would not have disdained to receive, under a treaty of peace, a king descended from illustrious ancestors and ruling many nations. My present lot is as glorious to you as it is degrading to myself. I had men and horses, arms and wealth. What wonder if I parted with them reluctantly? If you Romans choose to lord it over the world, does it follow that the world is to accept slavery? Were I to have been at once delivered up as a prisoner, neither my fall nor your triumph would have become famous. My punishment would be followed by oblivion, whereas, if you save my life, I shall be an everlasting memorial of your clemency."

Upon this the emperor granted pardon to Caractacus, to his wife, and to his brothers. Released from their bonds, they did homage also to Agrippina who sat near, conspicuous on another throne, in the same language of praise and gratitude. It was indeed a novelty, quite alien to ancient manners, for a woman to sit in front of Roman standards. In fact, Agrippina boasted that she was herself a partner in the empire which her ancestors had won.

The Senate was then assembled, and speeches were delivered full of pompous eulogy on the capture of Caractacus. It was as glorious, they said, as the display of Syphax by Scipio, or of Perses by Lucius Paulus, or indeed of any captive prince by any of our generals to the people of Rome. Triumphal distinctions were voted to Ostorius, who thus far had been successful, but soon afterwards met with reverses; either because, when Caractacus was out of the way, our discipline was relaxed under an impression that the war was ended, or because the enemy, out of compassion for so great a king, was more ardent in his thirst for vengeance. Instantly they rushed from all parts on the camp-prefect, and legionary cohorts left to establish fortified positions among the Silures, and had not speedy succour arrived from towns and fortresses in the neighbourhood, our forces would then have been totally destroyed. Even as it was, the camp-prefect, with eight centurions, and the bravest of the soldiers, were slain; and shortly afterwards, a foraging party of our men, with some cavalry squadrons sent to their support, was utterly routed.

Ostorius then deployed his light cohorts, but even thus he did not stop the flight, till our legions sustained the brunt of the battle. Their strength equalized the conflict, which after a while was in our favour. The enemy fled with trifling loss, as the day was on the decline. Now began a series of skirmishes, for the most part like raids, in woods and morasses, with encounters due to chance or to courage, to mere heedlessness or to calculation, to fury or to lust of plunder, under directions from the officers, or sometimes even without their knowledge. Conspicuous above all in stubborn resistance were the Silures, whose rage was fired by words rumoured to have been spoken by the Roman general, to the effect, that as the Sugambri had been formerly destroyed or transplanted into Gaul, so the name of the Silures ought to be blotted out. Accordingly they cut off two of our auxiliary cohorts, the rapacity of whose officers let them make incautious forays; and by liberal gifts of spoil and prisoners to the other tribes, they were luring them too into revolt, when Ostorius, worn out by the burden of his anxieties, died, to the joy of the enemy, who thought that a campaign at least, though not a single battle, had proved fatal to general whom none could despise.

The emperor on hearing of the death of his representative appointed Aulus Didius in his place, that the province might not be left without a governor. Didius, though he quickly arrived, found matters far from prosperous, for the legion under the command of Manlius Valens had meanwhile been defeated, and the disaster had been exaggerated by the enemy to alarm the new general, while he again magnified it, that he might win the more glory by quelling the movement or have a fairer excuse if it lasted. This loss too had been inflicted on us by the Silures, and they were scouring the country far and wide, till Didius hurried up and dispersed them. After the capture of Caractacus, Venutius of the Brigantes, as I have already mentioned, was pre-eminent in military skill; he had long been loyal to Rome and had been defended by our arms while he was united in marriage to the queen Cartismandua. Subsequently a quarrel broke out between them, followed instantly by war, and he then assumed a hostile attitude also towards us. At first, however, they simply fought against each other, and Cartismandua by cunning stratagems captured the brothers and kinsfolk of Venutius. This enraged the enemy, who were stung with shame at the prospect of falling under the dominion of a woman. The flower of their youth, picked out for war, invaded her kingdom. This we had foreseen; some cohorts were sent to her aid and a sharp contest followed, which was at first doubtful but had a satisfactory termination.

The legion under the command of Caesius Nasica fought with a similar result. For Didius, burdened with years and covered with honours, was content with acting through his officers and merely holding back the enemy. These transactions, though occurring under two propraetors, and occupying several years, I have closely connected, lest, if related separately, they might be less easily remembered. I now return to the chronological order.

In the fifth consulship of Tiberius Claudius with Sextius Cornelius Orfitus for his colleague, Nero was prematurely invested with the dress of manhood, that he might be thought qualified for political life. The emperor willingly complied with the flatteries of the Senate who wished Nero to enter on the consulship in his twentieth year, and meanwhile, as consul-elect, to have pro-consular authority beyond the limits of the capital with the title of "prince of the youth of Rome." A donative was also given to the soldiery in Nero's name, and presents to the city populace. At the games too of the circus which were then being celebrated to win for him popular favour, Britannicus wore the dress of boyhood, Nero the triumphal robe, as they rode in the procession. The people would thus behold the one with the decorations of a general, the other in a boy's habit, and would accordingly anticipate their respective destinies. At the same time those of the centurions and tribunes who pitied the lot of Britannicus were removed, some on false pretexts, others by way of a seeming compliment. Even of the freedmen, all who were of incorruptible fidelity were discarded on the following provocation. Once when they met, Nero greeted Britannicus by that name and was greeted in return as Domitius. Agrippina reported this to her husband, with bitter complaint, as the beginning of a quarrel, as implying, in fact, contempt of Nero's adoption and a cancelling at home of the Senate's decree and the people's vote. She said, too, that, if the perversity of such malignant suggestions were not checked, it would issue in the ruin of the State. Claudius, enraged by what he took as a grave charge, punished with banishment or death all his son's best instructors, and set persons appointed by his stepmother to have the care of him.

Still Agrippina did not yet dare to attempt her greatest scheme, unless Lusius Geta and Rufius Crispinus were removed from the command of the praetorian cohorts; for she thought that they cherished Messalina's memory and were devoted to her children. Accordingly, as the emperor's wife persistently affirmed that faction was rife among these cohorts through the rivalry of the two officers, and that there would be stricter discipline under one commander, the appointment was transferred to Burrus Afranius, who had a brilliant reputation as a soldier, but knew well to whose wish he owed his promotion. Agrippina, too, continued to exalt her own dignity; she would enter the Capitol in a chariot, a practice, which being allowed of old only to the priests and sacred images, increased the popular reverence for a woman who up to this time was the only recorded instance of one who, an emperor's daughter, was sister, wife, and mother of a sovereign. Meanwhile her foremost champion, Vitellius, in the full tide of his power and in extreme age (so uncertain are the fortunes of the great) was attacked by an accusation of which Junius Lupus, a senator, was the author. He was charged with treason and designs on the throne. The emperor would have lent a ready ear, had not Agrippina, by threats rather than entreaties, induced him to sentence the accuser to outlawry. This was all that Vitellius desired.

Several prodigies occurred in that year. Birds of evil omen perched on the Capitol; houses were thrown down by frequent shocks of earthquake, and as the panic spread, all the weak were trodden down in the hurry and confusion of the crowd. Scanty crops too, and consequent famine were regarded as a token of calamity. Nor were there merely whispered complaints; while Claudius was administering justice, the populace crowded round him with a boisterous clamour and drove him to a corner of the forum, where they violently pressed on him till he broke through the furious mob with a body of soldiers. It was ascertained that Rome had provisions for no more than fifteen days, and it was through the signal bounty of heaven and the mildness of the winter that its desperate plight was relieved. And yet in past days Italy used to send supplies for the legions into distant provinces, and even now it is not a barren soil which causes distress. But we prefer to cultivate Africa and Egypt, and trust the life of the Roman people to ships and all their risks.

In the same year war broke out between the Armenians and Iberians, and was the cause of very serious disturbances between Parthia and Rome. Vologeses was king of the Parthians; on the mother's side, he was the offspring of a Greek concubine, and he obtained the throne by the retirement of his brothers. Pharasmanes had been long in possession of Iberia, and his brother, Mithridates, ruled Armenia with our powerful support. There was a son of Pharasmanes named Rhadamistus, tall and handsome, of singular bodily strength, trained in all the accomplishments of his countrymen and highly renowned among his neighbours. He boasted so arrogantly and persistently that his father's prolonged old age kept back from him the little kingdom of Iberia as to make no concealment of his ambition. Pharasmanes accordingly seeing the young prince had power in his grasp and was strong in the attachment of his people, fearing too his own declining years, tempted him with other prospects and pointed to Armenia, which, as he reminded him, he had given to Mithridates after driving out the Parthians. But open violence, he said, must be deferred; artful measures, which might crush him unawares, were better. So Rhadamistus pretended to be at feud with his father as though his stepmother's hatred was too strong for him, and went to his uncle. While he was treated by him like a son, with excessive kindness, he lured the nobles of Armenia into revolutionary schemes, without the knowledge of Mithridates, who was actually loading him with honours.

He then assumed a show of reconciliation with his father, to whom he returned, telling him all that could be accomplished by treachery was now ready and that he must complete the affair by the sword. Meanwhile Pharasmanes invented pretexts for war; when he was fighting with the king of the Albanians and appealing to the Romans for aid, his brother, he said, had opposed him, and he would now avenge that wrong by his destruction. At the same time he gave a large army to his son, who by a sudden invasion drove Mithridates in terror from the open country and forced him into the fortress of Gorneas, which was strongly situated and garrisoned by some soldiers under the command of Caelius Pollio, a camp-prefect, and Casperius, a centurion.

There is nothing of which barbarians are so ignorant as military engines and the skilful management of sieges, while that is a branch of military science which we especially understand. And so Rhadamistus having attempted the fortified walls in vain or with loss, began a blockade, and, finding that his assaults were despised, tried to bribe the rapacity of the camp-prefect. Casperius protested earnestly against the overthrow of an allied king and of Armenia, the gift of the Roman people, through iniquity and greed of gain. At last, as Pollio pleaded the overpowering numbers of the enemy and

Rhadamistus the orders of his father, the centurion stipulated for a truce and retired, intending, if he could not deter Pharasmanes from further hostilities, to inform Ummidius Quadratus, the governor of Syria, of the state of Armenia.

By the centurion's departure the camp prefect was released, so to say, from surveillance; and he now urged Mithridates to conclude a treaty. He reminded him of the tie of brotherhood, of the seniority in age of Pharasmanes, and of their other bonds of kindred, how he was united by marriage to his brother's daughter, and was himself the father-in-law of Rhadamistus. "The Iberians," he said, "were not against peace, though for the moment they were the stronger; the perfidy of the Armenians was notorious, and he had nothing to fall back on but a fortress without stores; so he must not hesitate to prefer a bloodless negotiation to arms." As Mithridates wavered, and suspected the intentions of the camp-prefect, because he had seduced one of the king's concubines and was reputed a man who could be bribed into any wickedness, Casperius meantime went to Pharasmanes, and required of him that the Iberians should raise the blockade. Pharasmanes, to his face, replied vaguely and often in a conciliatory tone, while by secret messages he recommended Rhadamistus to hurry on the siege by all possible means. Then the price of infamy was raised, and Pollio by secret corruption induced the soldiers to demand peace and to threaten that they would abandon the garrison. Under this compulsion, Mithridates agreed to a day and a place for negotiation and quitted the fortress.

Rhadamistus at first threw himself into his embraces, feigning respect and calling him father-in-law and parent. He swore an oath too that he would do him no violence either by the sword or by poison. At the same time he drew him into a neighbouring grove, where he assured him that the appointed sacrifice was prepared for the confirmation of peace in the presence of the gods. It is a custom of these princes, whenever they join alliance, to unite their right hands and bind together the thumbs in a tight knot; then, when the blood has flowed into the extremities, they let it escape by a slight puncture and suck it in turn. Such a treaty is thought to have a mysterious sanctity, as being sealed with the blood of both parties. On this occasion he who was applying the knot pretended that it had fallen off, and suddenly seizing the knees of Mithridates flung him to the ground. At the same moment a rush was made by a number of persons, and chains were thrown round him. Then he was dragged along by a fetter, an extreme degradation to a barbarian; and soon the common people, whom he had held under a harsh sway, heaped insults on him with menacing gestures, though some, on the contrary, pitied such a reverse of fortune. His wife followed him with his little children, and filled every place with her wailings. They were hidden away in different covered carriages till the orders of Pharasmanes were distinctly ascertained. The lust of rule was more to him than his brother and his daughter, and his heart was steeled to any wickedness. Still he spared his eyes the seeing them slain before his face. Rhadamistus too, seemingly mindful of his oath, neither unsheathed the sword nor used poison against his sister and uncle, but had them thrown on the ground and then smothered them under a mass of heavy clothes. Even the sons of Mithridates were butchered for having shed tears over their parent's murder.

Quadratus, learning that Mithridates had been betrayed and that his kingdom was in the hands of his murderers, summoned a council, and, having informed them of what had occurred, consulted them whether he should take vengeance. Few cared for the honour of the State; most argued in favour of a safe course, saying "that any crime in a foreign country was to be welcomed with joy, and that the seeds of strife ought to be actually sown, on the very principle on which Roman emperors had often under a show of generosity given away this same kingdom of Armenia to excite the minds of the barbarians. Rhadamistus might retain his ill-gotten gains, as long as he was hated and infamous; for this was more to Rome's interest than for him to have succeeded with glory." To this view they assented, but that they might not be thought to have approved the crime and receive contrary orders from the emperor, envoys were sent to Pharasmanes, requiring him to withdraw from Armenian territory and remove his son.

Julius Pelignus was then procurator of Cappadocia, a man despised alike for his feebleness of mind and his grotesque personal appearance. He was however very intimate with Claudius, who, when in private life, used to beguile the dullness of his leisure with the society of jesters. This Pelignus collected some provincial auxiliaries, apparently with the design of recovering Armenia, but, while he plundered allies instead of enemies, finding himself, through the desertion of his men and the raids of the barbarians, utterly defenceless, he went to Rhadamistus, whose gifts so completely overcame him that he positively encouraged him to assume the ensigns of royalty, and himself assisted at the ceremony, authorizing and abetting. When the disgraceful news had spread far and wide, lest the world might judge of other governors by Pelignus, Helvidius Priscus was sent in command of a legion to regulate, according to circumstances, the disordered state of affairs. He quickly crossed Mount Taurus, and had restored order to a great extent more by moderation than by force, when he was ordered to return to Syria, that nothing might arise to provoke a war with Parthia.

For Vologeses, thinking that an opportunity presented itself of invading Armenia, which, though the possession of his ancestors, was now through a monstrous crime held by a foreign prince, raised an army and prepared to establish Tiridates on the throne, so that not a member of his house might be without kingly power. On the advance of the Parthians, the Iberians dispersed without a battle, and the Armenian cities, Artaxata and Tigranocerta, submitted to the yoke. Then a frightful winter or deficient supplies, with pestilence arising from both causes, forced Vologeses to abandon his present plans. Armenia was thus again without a king, and was invaded by Rhadamistus, who was now fiercer than ever, looking on the people as disloyal and sure to rebel on the first opportunity. They however, though accustomed to be slaves, suddenly threw off their tameness and gathered round the palace in arms.

Rhadamistus had no means of escape but in the swiftness of the horses which bore him and his wife away. Pregnant as she was, she endured, somehow or other, out of fear of the enemy and love of her husband, the first part of the flight, but after a while, when she felt herself shaken by its continuous speed, she implored to be rescued by an honourable death from the shame of captivity. He at first embraced, cheered, and encouraged her, now admiring her heroism, now filled with a sickening apprehension at the idea of her being left to any man's mercy. Finally, urged by the intensity of his love and familiarity with dreadful deeds, he unsheathed his scymitar, and having stabbed her, dragged her to the bank of the Araxes and committed her to the stream, so that her very body might be swept away. Then in headlong flight he hurried to Iberia, his ancestral kingdom. Zenobia meanwhile (this was her name), as she yet breathed and showed signs of life on the calm water at the river's edge, was perceived by some shepherds, who inferring from her noble appearance that she was no base-born woman, bound up her wound and applied to it their rustic remedies. As soon as they knew her name and her adventure, they conveyed her to the city of Artaxata, whence she was conducted at the public charge to Tiridates, who received her kindly and treated her as a royal person.

In the consulship of Faustus Sulla and Salvius Otho, Furius Scribonianus was banished on the ground that he was consulting the astrologers about the emperor's death. His mother, Junia, was included in the accusation, as one who still resented the misfortune of exile which she had suffered in the past. His father, Camillus, had raised an armed insurrection in Dalmatia, and the emperor in again sparing a hostile family sought the credit of clemency. But the exile did not live long after this; whether he was cut off by a natural death, or by poison, was matter of conflicting rumours, according to people's belief.

A decree of the Senate was then passed for the expulsion of the astrologers from Italy, stringent but ineffectual. Next the emperor, in a speech, commended all who, from their limited means, voluntarily retired from the Senatorian order, while those were degraded from it who, by retaining their seats, added effrontery to poverty.

During these proceedings he proposed to the Senate a penalty on women who united themselves in marriage to slaves, and it was decided that those who had thus demeaned themselves, without the knowledge of the slave's master, should be reduced to slavery; if with his consent, should be ranked as freedwomen. To Pallas, who, as the emperor declared, was the author of this proposal, were offered on the motion of Barea Soranus, consul-elect, the decorations of the praetorship and fifteen million sesterces. Cornelius Scipio added that he deserved public thanks for thinking less of his ancient nobility as a descendant from the kings of Arcadia, than of the welfare of the State, and allowing himself to be numbered among the emperor's ministers. Claudius assured them that Pallas was content with the honour, and that he limited himself to his former poverty. A decree of the Senate was publicly inscribed on a bronze tablet, heaping the praises of primitive frugality on a freedman, the possessor of three hundred million sesterces.

Not equally moderate was his brother, surnamed Felix, who had for some time been governor of Judaea, and thought that he could do any evil act with impunity, backed up as he was by such power. It is true that the Jews had shown symptoms of commotion in a seditious outbreak, and when they had heard of the assassination of Caius, there was no hearty submission, as a fear still lingered that any of the emperors might impose the same orders. Felix meanwhile, by ill-timed remedies, stimulated disloyal acts; while he had, as a rival in the worst wickedness, Ventidius Cumanus, who held a part of the province, which was so divided that Galilea was governed by Cumanus, Samaria by Felix. The two peoples had long been at feud, and now less than ever restrained their enmity, from contempt of their rulers. And accordingly they plundered each other, letting loose bands of robbers, forming ambuscades, and occasionally fighting battles, and carrying the spoil and booty to the two procurators, who at first rejoiced at all this, but, as the mischief grew, they interposed with an armed force, which was cut to pieces. The flame of war would have spread through the province, but it was saved by Quadratus, governor of Syria. In dealing with the Jews, who had been daring enough to slay our soldiers, there was little hesitation about their being capitally punished. Some delay indeed was occasioned by Cumanus and Felix; for Claudius on hearing the causes of the rebellion had given authority for deciding also the case of these procurators. Quadratus, however, exhibited Felix as one of the judges, admitting him to the bench with the view of cowing the ardour of the prosecutors. And so Cumanus was condemned for the crimes which the two had committed, and tranquillity was restored to the province.

Not long afterwards some tribes of the wild population of Cilicia, known as the Clitae, which had often been in commotion, established a camp, under a leader Troxobor, on their rocky mountains, whence rushing down on the coast, and on the towns, they dared to do violence to the farmers and townsfolk, frequently even to the merchants and shipowners. They besieged the city Anemurium, and routed some troopers sent from Syria to its rescue under the command of Curtius Severus; for the rough country in the neighbourhood, suited as it is for the fighting of infantry, did not allow of cavalry operations. After a time, Antiochus, king of that coast, having broken the unity of the barbarian forces, by cajolery of the people and treachery to their leader, slew Troxobor and a few chiefs, and pacified the rest by gentle measures.

About the same time, the mountain between Lake Fucinus and the river Liris was bored through, and that this grand work might be seen by a multitude of visitors, preparations were made for a naval battle on the lake, just as formerly Augustus exhibited such a spectacle, in a basin he had made this side the Tiber, though with light vessels, and on a smaller scale. Claudius equipped galleys with three and four banks of oars, and nineteen thousand men; he lined the circumference of the lake with rafts, that there might be no means of escape at various points, but he still left full space for the strength of the crews, the skill of the pilots, the impact of the vessels, and the usual operations of a seafight. On the raft stood companies of the praetorian cohorts and cavalry, with a breastwork in front of them, from which catapults and balistas might be worked. The rest of the lake was occupied by marines on decked vessels. An immense multitude from the neighbouring towns, others from Rome itself, eager to see the sight or to show respect to the emperor, crowded the banks, the hills, and mountain tops, which thus resembled a theatre. The emperor, with Agrippina seated near him, presided; he wore a splendid military cloak, she, a mantle of cloth of gold. A battle was fought with all the courage of brave men, though it was between condemned criminals. After much bloodshed they were released from the necessity of mutual slaughter.

When the sight was over, the outlet of the water was opened. The careless execution of the work was apparent, the tunnel not having been bored down so low as the bottom, or middle of the lake. Consequently after an interval the excavations were deepened, and to attract a crowd once more, a show of gladiators was exhibited, with floating pontoons for an infantry engagement. A banquet too was prepared close to the outflow of the lake, and it was the means of greatly alarming the whole company, for the water, in the violence of its outburst, swept away the adjoining parts, shook the more remote, and spread terror with the tremendous crash. At the same time, Agrippina availed herself of the emperor's fright to charge Narcissus, who had been the agent of the work, with avarice and peculation. He too was not silent, but inveighed against the domineering temper of her sex, and her extravagant ambition.

In the consulship of Didius Junius and Quintus Haterius, Nero, now sixteen years of age, married Octavia, the emperor's daughter. Anxious to distinguish himself by noble pursuits, and the reputation of an orator, he advocated the cause of the people of Ilium, and having eloquently recounted how Rome was the offspring of Troy, and Aeneas the founder of the Julian line, with other old traditions akin to myths, he gained for his clients exemption from all public burdens. His pleading too procured for the colony of Bononia, which had been ruined by a fire, a subvention of ten million sesterces. The Rhodians also had their freedom restored to them, which had often been taken away, or confirmed, according to their services to us in our foreign wars, or their seditious misdeeds at home. Apamea, too, which had been shaken by an earthquake, had its tribute remitted for five years.

Claudius, on the other hand, was being prompted to exhibit the worst cruelty by the artifices of the same Agrippina. On the accusation of Tarquitius Priscus, she ruined

Statilius Taurus, who was famous for his wealth, and at whose gardens she cast a greedy eye. Priscus had served under Taurus in his proconsular government of Africa, and after their return charged him with a few acts of extortion, but particularly with magical and superstitious practices. Taurus, no longer able to endure a false accusation and an undeserved humiliation, put a violent end to his life before the Senate's decision was pronounced. Tarquitius was however expelled from the Senate, a point which the senators carried, out of hatred for the accuser, notwithstanding the intrigues of Agrippina.

That same year the emperor was often heard to say that the legal decisions of the commissioners of the imperial treasury ought to have the same force as if pronounced by himself. Lest it might be supposed that he had stumbled inadvertently into this opinion, its principle was also secured by a decree of the Senate on a more complete and ample scale than before. It had indeed already been arranged by the Divine Augustus that the Roman knights who governed Egypt should hear causes, and that their decisions were to be as binding as those of Roman magistrates, and after a time most of the cases formerly tried by the praetors were submitted to the knights. Claudius handed over to them the whole administration of justice for which there had been by sedition or war so many struggles; the Sempronian laws vesting judicial power in the equestrian order, and those of Servilius restoring it to the Senate, while it was for this above everything else that Marius and Sulla fought of old. But those were days of political conflict between classes, and the results of victory were binding on the State. Caius Oppius and Cornelius Balbus were the first who were able, with Caesar's support, to settle conditions of peace and terms of war. To mention after them the Matii, Vedii, and other too influential names of Roman knights would be superfluous, when Claudius, we know, raised freedmen whom he had set over his household to equality with himself and with the laws.

Next the emperor proposed to grant immunity from taxation to the people of Cos, and he dwelt much on their antiquity. "The Argives or Coeus, the father of Latona, were the earliest inhabitants of the island; soon afterwards, by the arrival of Aesculapius, the art of the physician was introduced and was practised with much fame by his descendants." Claudius named them one by one, with the periods in which they had respectively flourished. He said too that Xenophon, of whose medical skill he availed himself, was one of the same family, and that they ought to grant his request and let the people of Cos dwell free from all tribute in their sacred island, as a place devoted to the sole service of their god. It was also certain that many obligations under which they had laid Rome and joint victories with her might have been recounted. Claudius however did not seek to veil under any external considerations a concession he had made, with his usual good nature, to an individual.

Envoys from Byzantium having received audience, in complaining to the Senate of their heavy burdens, recapitulated their whole history. Beginning with the treaty which they concluded with us when we fought against that king of Macedonia whose supposed spurious birth acquired for him the name of the Pseudo Philip, they reminded us of the forces which they had afterwards sent against Antiochus, Perses and Aristonicus, of the aid they had given Antonius in the pirate-war, of their offers to Sulla, Lucullus, and Pompeius, and then of their late services to the Caesars, when they were in occupation of a district peculiarly convenient for the land or sea passage of generals and armies, as well as for the conveyance of supplies.

It was indeed on that very narrow strait which parts Europe from Asia, at Europe's furthest extremity, that the Greeks built Byzantium. When they consulted the Pythian Apollo as to where they should found a city, the oracle replied that they were to seek a home opposite to the blind men's country. This obscure hint pointed to the people of Chalcedon, who, though they arrived there first and saw before others the advantageous position, chose the worse. For Byzantium has a fruitful soil and productive seas, as immense shoals of fish pour out of the Pontus and are driven by the sloping surface of the rocks under water to quit the windings of the Asiatic shore and take refuge in these harbours. Consequently the inhabitants were at first money-making and wealthy traders, but afterwards, under the pressure of excessive burdens, they petitioned for immunity or at least relief, and were supported by the emperor, who argued to the Senate that, exhausted as they were by the late wars in Thrace and Bosporus, they deserved help. So their tribute was remitted for five years.

In the year of the consulship of Marcus Asinius and Manius Acilius it was seen to be portended by a succession of prodigies that there were to be political changes for the worse. The soldiers' standards and tents were set in a blaze by lightning. A swarm of bees settled on the summit of the Capitol; births of monsters, half man, half beast, and of a pig with a hawk's talons, were reported. It was accounted a portent that every order of magistrates had had its number reduced, a quaestor, an aedile, a tribune, a praetor and consul having died within a few months. But Agrippina's terror was the most conspicuous. Alarmed by some words dropped by Claudius when half intoxicated, that it was his destiny to have to endure his wives' infamy and at last punish it, she determined to act without a moment's delay. First she destroyed Lepida from motives of feminine jealousy. Lepida indeed as the daughter of the younger Antonia, as the grandniece of Augustus, the cousin of Agrippina, and sister of her husband Cneius, thought herself of equally high rank. In beauty, youth, and wealth they differed but slightly. Both were shameless, infamous, and intractable, and were rivals in vice as much as in the advantages they had derived from fortune. It was indeed a desperate contest whether the aunt or the mother should have most power over Nero. Lepida tried to win the young prince's heart by flattery and lavish liberality, while Agrippina on the other hand, who could give her son empire but could not endure that he should be emperor, was fierce and full of menace.

It was charged on Lepida that she had made attempts on the Emperor's consort by magical incantations, and was disturbing the peace of Italy by an imperfect control of her troops of slaves in Calabria. She was for this sentenced to death, notwithstanding the vehement opposition of Narcissus, who, as he more and more suspected Agrippina, was said to have plainly told his intimate friends that "his destruction was certain, whether Britannicus or Nero were to be emperor, but that he was under such obligations to Claudius that he would sacrifice life to his welfare. Messalina and Silius had been convicted, and now again there were similar grounds for accusation. If Nero were to rule, or Britannicus succeed to the throne, he would himself have no claim on the then reigning sovereign. Meanwhile, a stepmother's treacherous schemes were convulsing the whole imperial house, with far greater disgrace than would have resulted from his concealment of the profligacy of the emperor's former wife. Even as it was, there was shamelessness enough, seeing that Pallas was her paramour, so that no one could doubt that she held honour, modesty and her very person, everything, in short, cheaper than sovereignty."

This, and the like, he was always saying, and he would embrace Britannicus, expressing earnest wishes for his speedy arrival at a mature age, and would raise his hand, now to heaven, now to the young prince, with entreaty that as he grew up, he would drive out his father's enemies and also take vengeance on the murderers of his mother.

Under this great burden of anxiety, he had an attack of illness, and went to Sinuessa to recruit his strength with its balmy climate and salubrious waters. Thereupon, Agrippina, who had long decided on the crime and eagerly grasped at the opportunity thus offered, and did not lack instruments, deliberated on the nature of the poison to be used. The deed would be betrayed by one that was sudden and instantaneous, while if she chose a slow and lingering poison, there was a fear that Claudius, when near his end, might, on detecting the treachery, return to his love for his son. She decided on some rare compound which might derange his mind and delay death. A person skilled in such matters was selected, Locusta by name, who had lately been condemned for poisoning, and had long been retained as one of the tools of despotism. By this woman's art the poison was prepared, and it was to be administered by an eunuch, Halotus, who was accustomed to bring in and taste the dishes.

All the circumstances were subsequently so well known, that writers of the time have declared that the poison was infused into some mushrooms, a favourite delicacy, and its effect not at the instant perceived, from the emperor's lethargic, or intoxicated condition. His bowels too were relieved, and this seemed to have saved him. Agrippina was thoroughly dismayed. Fearing the worst, and defying the immediate obloquy of the deed, she availed herself of the complicity of Xenophon, the physician, which she had already secured. Under pretence of helping the emperor's efforts to vomit, this man, it is supposed, introduced into his throat a feather smeared with some rapid poison; for he knew that the greatest crimes are perilous in their inception, but well rewarded after their consummation.

Meanwhile the Senate was summoned, and prayers rehearsed by the consuls and priests for the emperor's recovery, though the lifeless body was being wrapped in blankets with warm applications, while all was being arranged to establish Nero on the throne. At first Agrippina, seemingly overwhelmed by grief and seeking comfort, clasped Britannicus in her embraces, called him the very image of his father, and hindered him by every possible device from leaving the chamber. She also detained his sisters, Antonia and Octavia, closed every approach to the palace with a military guard, and repeatedly gave out that the emperor's health was better, so that the soldiers might be encouraged to hope, and that the fortunate moment foretold by the astrologers might arrive.

At last, at noon on the 13th of October, the gates of the palace were suddenly thrown open, and Nero, accompanied by Burrus, went forth to the cohort which was on guard after military custom. There, at the suggestion of the commanding officer, he was hailed with joyful shouts, and set on a litter. Some, it is said, hesitated, and looked round and asked where Britannicus was; then, when there was no one to lead a resistance, they yielded to what was offered them. Nero was conveyed into the camp, and having first spoken suitably to the occasion and promised a donative after the example of his father's bounty, he was unanimously greeted as emperor. The decrees of the Senate followed the voice of the soldiers, and there was no hesitation in the provinces. Divine honours were decreed to Claudius, and his funeral rites were solemnized on the same scale as those of Augustus; for Agrippina strove to emulate the magnificence of her great-grandmother, Livia. But his will was not publicly read, as the preference of the stepson to the son might provoke a sense of wrong and angry feeling in the popular mind.

BOOK XIII, A.D. 54-58

The first death under the new emperor, that of Junius Silanus, proconsul of Asia, was, without Nero's knowledge, planned by the treachery of Agrippina. Not that Silanus had provoked destruction by any violence of temper, apathetic as he was, and so utterly despised under former despotisms, that Caius Caesar used to call him the golden sheep. The truth was that Agrippina, having contrived the murder of his brother Lucius Silanus, dreaded his vengeance; for it was the incessant popular talk that preference ought to be given over Nero, who was scarcely out of his boyhood and had gained the empire by crime, to a man of mature age, of blameless life, of noble birth, and, as a point then much regarded, of the line of the Caesars. Silanus in fact was the son of a great-grandson of Augustus. This was the cause of his destruction. The agents of the deed were Publius Celer, a Roman knight, and Helius, a freedman, men who had the charge of the emperor's domains in Asia. They gave the proconsul poison at a banquet, too openly to escape discovery.

With no less precipitation, Narcissus, Claudius's freedman, whose quarrels with Agrippina I have mentioned, was driven to suicide by his cruel imprisonment and hopeless plight, even against the wishes of Nero, with whose yet concealed vices he was wonderfully in sympathy from his rapacity and extravagance.

And now they had proceeded to further murders but for the opposition of Afranius Burrus and Annaeus Seneca. These two men guided the emperor's youth with an unity of purpose seldom found where authority is shared, and though their accomplishments were wholly different, they had equal influence. Burrus, with his soldier's discipline and severe manners, Seneca, with lessons of eloquence and a dignified courtesy, strove alike to confine the frailty of the prince's youth, should he loathe virtue, within allowable indulgences. They had both alike to struggle against the domineering spirit of Agrippina, who inflamed with all the passions of an evil ascendency had Pallas on her side, at whose suggestion Claudius had ruined himself by an incestuous marriage and a fatal adoption of a son. Nero's temper however was not one to submit to slaves, and Pallas, by a surly arrogance quite beyond a freedman, had provoked disgust. Still every honour was openly heaped on Agrippina, and to a tribune who according to military custom asked the watchword, Nero gave "the best of mothers." The Senate also decreed her two lictors, with the office of priestess to Claudius, and voted to the late emperor a censor's funeral, which was soon followed by deification.

On the day of the funeral the prince pronounced Claudius's panegyric, and while he dwelt on the antiquity of his family and on the consulships and triumphs of his ancestors, there was enthusiasm both in himself and his audience. The praise of his graceful accomplishments, and the remark that during his reign no disaster had befallen Rome from the foreigner, were heard with favour. When the speaker passed on to his foresight and wisdom, no one could refrain from laughter, though the speech, which was composed by Seneca, exhibited much elegance, as indeed that famous man had an attractive genius which suited the popular ear of the time. Elderly men who amuse their leisure with comparing the past and the present, observed that Nero was the first emperor who needed another man's eloquence. The dictator Caesar rivalled the greatest orators, and Augustus had an easy and fluent way of speaking, such as became a sovereign. Tiberius too thoroughly understood the art of balancing words, and was sometimes forcible in the expression of his thoughts, or else intentionally obscure. Even Caius Caesar's disordered intellect did not wholly mar his faculty of speech. Nor did Claudius, when he spoke with preparation, lack elegance. Nero from early boyhood turned his lively genius in other directions; he carved, painted, sang, or practised the management of horses, occasionally composing verses which showed that he had the rudiments of learning.

When he had done with his mimicries of sorrow he entered the Senate, and having first referred to the authority of the senators and the concurrence of the soldiery, he then dwelt on the counsels and examples which he had to guide him in the right administration of empire. "His boyhood," he said, "had not had the taint of civil wars or domestic feuds, and he brought with him no hatreds, no sense of wrong, no desire of vengeance." He then sketched the plan of his future government, carefully avoiding anything which had kindled recent odium. "He would not," he said, "be judge in all cases, or, by confining the accuser and the accused within the same walls, let the power of a few favourites grow dangerously formidable. In his house there should be nothing venal, nothing open to intrigue; his private establishment and the State should be kept entirely distinct. The Senate should retain its ancient powers; Italy and the State-provinces should plead their causes before the tribunals of the consuls, who would give them a hearing from the senators. Of the armies he would himself take charge, as specially entrusted to him."

He was true to his word and several arrangements were made on the Senate's authority. No one was to receive a fee or a present for pleading a cause; the quaestors-elect were not to be under the necessity of exhibiting gladiatorial shows. This was opposed by Agrippina, as a reversal of the legislation of Claudius, but it was carried by the senators who used to be summoned to the palace, in order that she might stand close to a hidden door behind them, screened by a curtain which was enough to shut her out of sight, but not out of hearing. When envoys from Armenia were pleading their nation's cause before Nero, she actually was on the point of mounting the emperor's tribunal and of presiding with him; but Seneca, when every one else was paralysed with alarm, motioned to the prince to go and meet his mother. Thus, by an apparently dutiful act, a scandalous scene was prevented.

With the close of the year came disquieting rumours that the Parthians had again broken their bounds and were ravaging Armenia, from which they had driven Rhadamistus, who, having often possessed himself of the kingdom and as often been thrust out of it, had now relinquished hostilities. Rome with its love of talking began to ask how a prince of scarce seventeen was to encounter and avert this tremendous peril, how they could fall back on one who was ruled by a woman; or whether battles and sieges and the other operations of war could be directed by tutors. "Some, on the contrary, argued that this was better than it would have been, had Claudius in his feeble and spiritless old age, when he would certainly have yielded to the bidding of slaves, been summoned to the hardships of a campaign. Burrus, at least, and Seneca were known to be men of very varied experience, and, as for the emperor himself, how far was he really short of mature age, when Cneius Pompeius and Caesar Octavianus, in their eighteenth and nineteenth years respectively, bore the brunt of civil wars? The highest rank chiefly worked through its prestige and its counsels more than by the sword and hand. The emperor would give a plain proof whether he was advised by good or bad friends by putting aside all jealousy and selecting some eminent general, rather than by promoting out of favouritism, a rich man backed up by interest."

Amidst this and like popular talk, Nero ordered the young recruits levied in the adjacent provinces to be brought up for the supply of the legions of the East, and the legions themselves to take up a position on the Armenian frontier while two princes of old standing, Agrippa and Antiochus, were to prepare a force for the invasion of the Parthian territories. The Euphrates too was to be spanned by bridges; Lesser Armenia was intrusted to Aristobulus, Sophene to Sohaemus, each with the ensigns of royalty. There rose up at this crisis a rival to Vologeses in his son Vardanes, and the Parthians quitted Armenia, apparently intending to defer hostilities.

All this however was described with exaggeration to the Senate, in the speeches of those members who proposed a public thanksgiving, and that on the days of the thanksgiving the prince should wear the triumphal robe and enter Rome in ovation, lastly, that he should have statues on the same scale as those of Mars the Avenger, and in the same temple. To their habitual flattery was added a real joy at his having appointed Domitius Corbulo to secure Armenia, thus opening, as it seemed, a field to merit. The armies of the East were so divided that half the auxiliaries and two legions were to remain in the province of Syria under its governor, Quadratus Ummidius; while Corbulo was to have an equal number of citizen and allied troops, together with the auxiliary infantry and cavalry which were in winter quarters in Cappadocia. The confederate kings were instructed to obey orders, just as the war might require. But they had a specially strong liking for Corbulo. That general, with a view to the prestige which in a new enterprise is supremely powerful, speedily accomplished his march, and at Aegeae, a city of Cilicia, met Quadratus who had advanced to the place under an apprehension that, should Corbulo once enter Armenia to take command of the army, he would draw all eyes on himself, by his noble stature, his imposing eloquence, and the impression he would make, not only by his wisdom and experience, but also by the mere display of showy attributes.

Meantime both sent messages to king Vologeses, advising him to choose peace rather than war, and to give hostages and so continue the habitual reverence of his ancestors towards the people of Rome. Vologeses, wishing to prepare for war at an advantage, or to rid himself of suspected rivals under the name of hostages, delivered up some of the noblest of the Arsacids. A centurion, Insteius, sent perhaps by Ummidius on some previous occasion, received them after an interview with the king. Corbulo, on knowing this, ordered Arrius Varus, commander of a cohort, to go and take the hostages. Hence arose a quarrel between the commander and the centurion, and to stop such a scene before foreigners, the decision of the matter was left to the hostages and to the envoys who conducted them. They preferred Corbulo, for his recent renown, and from a liking which even enemies felt for him. Then there was a feud between the two generals; Ummidius complained that he was robbed of what his prudence had achieved, while Corbulo on the other hand appealed to the fact that Vologeses had not brought himself to offer hostages till his own appointment to the conduct of the war turned the king's hopes into fears. Nero, to compose their differences, directed the issue of a proclamation that for the successes of Quadratus and Corbulo the laurel was to be added to the imperial "fasces." I have closely connected these events, though they extend into another consulship.

The emperor in the same year asked the Senate for a statue to his father Domitius, and also that the consular decorations might be conferred on Asconius Labeo, who had been his guardian. Statues to himself of solid gold and silver he forbade, in opposition to offers made, and although the Senate passed a vote that the year should begin with the month of December, in which he was born, he retained for its commencement, the old sacred associations of the first of January. Nor would he allow the prosecution of Carinas

Celer, a senator, whom a slave accused, or of Julius Densus, a knight, whose partiality for Britannicus was construed into a crime.

In the year of his consulship with Lucius Antistius, when the magistrates were swearing obedience to imperial legislation, he forbade his colleague to extend the oath to his own enactments, for which he was warmly praised by the senators, in the hope that his youthful spirit, elated with the glory won by trifles, would follow on to nobler aspirations. Then came an act of mercy to Plautius Lateranus, who had been degraded from his rank for adultery with Messalina, and whom he now restored, assuring them of his clemency in a number of speeches which Seneca, to show the purity of his teaching or to display his genius, published to the world by the emperor's mouth.

Meanwhile the mother's influence was gradually weakened, as Nero fell in love with a freedwoman, Acte by name, and took into his confidence Otho and Claudius Senecio, two young men of fashion, the first of whom was descended from a family of consular rank, while Senecio's father was one of the emperor's freedmen. Without the mother's knowledge, then in spite of her opposition, they had crept into his favour by debaucheries and equivocal secrets, and even the prince's older friends did not thwart him, for here was a girl who without harm to any one gratified his desires, when he loathed his wife Octavia, high born as she was, and of approved virtue, either from some fatality, or because vice is overpoweringly attractive. It was feared too that he might rush into outrages on noble ladies, were he debarred from this indulgence.

Agrippina, however, raved with a woman's fury about having a freedwoman for a rival, a slave girl for a daughter-in-law, with like expressions. Nor would she wait till her son repented or wearied of his passion. The fouler her reproaches, the more powerfully did they inflame him, till completely mastered by the strength of his desire, he threw off all respect for his mother, and put himself under the guidance of Seneca, one of whose friends, Annaeus Serenus, had veiled the young prince's intrigue in its beginning by pretending to be in love with the same woman, and had lent his name as the ostensible giver of the presents secretly sent by the emperor to the girl. Then Agrippina, changing her tactics, plied the lad with various blandishments, and even offered the seclusion of her chamber for the concealment of indulgences which youth and the highest rank might claim. She went further; she pleaded guilty to an ill-timed strictness, and handed over to him the abundance of her wealth, which nearly approached the imperial treasures, and from having been of late extreme in her restraint of her son, became now, on the other hand, lax to excess. The change did not escape Nero; his most intimate friends dreaded it, and begged him to beware of the arts of a woman, was always daring and was now false.

It happened at this time that the emperor after inspecting the apparel in which wives and mothers of the imperial house had been seen to glitter, selected a jewelled robe and sent it as a gift to his mother, with the unsparing liberality of one who was bestowing by preference on her a choice and much coveted present. Agrippina, however, publicly declared that so far from her wardrobe being furnished by these gifts, she was really kept out of the remainder, and that her son was merely dividing with her what he derived wholly from herself.

Some there were who put even a worse meaning on her words. And so Nero, furious with those who abetted such arrogance in a woman, removed Pallas from the charge of the business with which he had been entrusted by Claudius, and in which he acted, so to say, as the controller of the throne. The story went that as he was departing with a great retinue of attendants, the emperor rather wittily remarked that Pallas was going to swear himself out of office. Pallas had in truth stipulated that he should not be questioned for anything he had done in the past, and that his accounts with the State were to be considered as balanced. Thereupon, with instant fury, Agrippina rushed into frightful menaces, sparing not the prince's ears her solemn protest "that Britannicus was now of full age, he who was the true and worthy heir of his father's sovereignty, which a son, by mere admission and adoption, was abusing in outrages on his mother. She shrank not from an utter exposure of the wickedness of that ill-starred house, of her own marriage, to begin with, and of her poisoner's craft. All that the gods and she herself had taken care of was that her stepson was yet alive; with him she would go to the camp, where on one side should be heard the daughter of Germanicus; on the other, the crippled Burrus and the exile Seneca, claiming, forsooth, with disfigured hand, and a pedant's tongue, the government of the world." As she spoke, she raised her hand in menace and heaped insults on him, as she appealed to the deified Claudius, to the infernal shades of the Silani, and to those many fruitless crimes.

Nero was confounded at this, and as the day was near on which Britannicus would complete his fourteenth year, he reflected, now on the domineering temper of his mother, and now again on the character of the young prince, which a trifling circumstance had lately tested, sufficient however to gain for him wide popularity. During the feast of Saturn, amid other pastimes of his playmates, at a game of lot drawing for king, the lot fell to Nero, upon which he gave all his other companions different orders, and such as would not put them to the blush; but when he told Britannicus to step forward and begin a song, hoping for a laugh at the expense of a boy who knew nothing of sober, much less of riotous society, the lad with perfect coolness commenced some verses which hinted at his expulsion from his father's house and from supreme power. This procured him pity, which was the more conspicuous, as night with its merriment had stript off all disguise. Nero saw the reproach and redoubled his hate. Pressed by Agrippina's menaces, having no charge against his brother and not daring openly to order his murder, he meditated a secret device and directed poison to be prepared through the agency of Julius Pollio, tribune of one of the praetorian cohorts, who had in his custody a woman under sentence for poisoning, Locusta by name, with a vast reputation for crime. That every one about the person of Britannicus should care nothing for right or honour, had long ago been provided for. He actually received his first dose of poison from his tutors and passed it off his bowels, as it was rather weak or so qualified as not at once to prove deadly. But Nero, impatient at such slow progress in crime, threatened the tribune and ordered the poisoner to execution for prolonging his anxiety while they were thinking of the popular talk and planning their own defence. Then they promised that death should be as sudden as if it were the hurried work of the dagger, and a rapid poison of previously tested ingredients was prepared close to the emperor's chamber.

It was customary for the imperial princes to sit during their meals with other nobles of the same age, in the sight of their kinsfolk, at a table of their own, furnished somewhat frugally. There Britannicus was dining, and as what he ate and drank was always tested by the taste of a select attendant, the following device was contrived, that the usage might not be dropped or the crime betrayed by the death of both prince and attendant. A cup as yet harmless, but extremely hot and already tasted, was handed to Britannicus; then, on his refusing it because of its warmth, poison was poured in with some cold water, and this so penetrated his entire frame that he lost alike voice and breath. There was a stir among the company; some, taken by surprise, ran hither and thither, while those whose discernment was keener, remained motionless, with their eyes fixed on Nero, who, as he still reclined in seeming unconsciousness, said that this was a common occurrence, from a periodical epilepsy, with which Britannicus had been afflicted from his earliest infancy, and that his sight and senses would gradually return. As for Agrippina, her terror and confusion, though her countenance struggled to hide it, so visibly appeared, that she was clearly just as ignorant as was Octavia, Britannicus's own sister. She saw, in fact, that she was robbed of her only remaining refuge, and that here was a precedent for parricide. Even Octavia, notwithstanding her youthful inexperience, had learnt to hide her grief, her affection, and indeed every emotion.

And so after a brief pause the company resumed its mirth. One and the same night witnessed Britannicus's death and funeral, preparations having been already made for his obsequies, which were on a humble scale. He was however buried in the Campus Martius, amid storms so violent, that in the popular belief they portended the wrath of heaven against a crime which many were even inclined to forgive when they remembered the immemorial feuds of brothers and the impossibility of a divided throne. It is related by several writers of the period that many days before the murder, Nero had offered the worst insult to the boyhood of Britannicus; so that his death could no longer seem a premature or dreadful event, though it happened at the sacred board, without even a moment for the embraces of his sisters, hurried on too, as it was, under the eyes of an enemy, on the sole surviving offspring of the Claudii, the victim first of dishonour, then of poison. The emperor apologised for the hasty funeral by reminding people that it was the practice of our ancestors to withdraw from view any grievously untimely death, and not to dwell on it with panegyrics or display. For himself, he said, that as he had now lost a brother's help, his remaining hopes centred in the State, and all the more tenderness ought to be shown by the Senate and people towards a prince who was the only survivor of a family born to the highest greatness.

He then enriched his most powerful friends with liberal presents. Some there were who reproached men of austere professions with having on such an occasion divided houses and estates among themselves, like so much spoil. It was the belief of others that a pressure had been put on them by the emperor, who, conscious as he was of guilt, hoped for merciful consideration if he could secure the most important men by wholesale bribery. But his mother's rage no lavish bounty could allay. She would clasp Octavia to her arms, and have many a secret interview with her friends; with more than her natural rapacity, she clutched at money everywhere, seemingly for a reserve, and courteously received tribunes and centurions. She honoured the names and virtues of the nobles who still were left, seeking apparently a party and a leader. Of this Nero became aware, and he ordered the departure of the military guard now kept for the emperor's mother, as it had formerly been for the imperial consort, along with some German troops, added as a further honour. He also gave her a separate establishment, that throngs of visitors might no longer wait on her, and removed her to what had been Antonia's house; and whenever he went there himself, he was surrounded by a crowd of centurions, and used to leave her after a hurried kiss.

Of all things human the most precarious and transitory is a reputation for power which has no strong support of its own. In a moment Agrippina's doors were deserted; there was no one to comfort or to go near her, except a few ladies, whether out of love or malice was doubtful. One of these was Junia Silana, whom Messalina had driven from her husband, Caius Silius, as I have already related. Conspicuous for her birth, her beauty, and her wantonness, she had long been a special favourite of Agrippina, till after a while there were secret mutual dislikes, because Sextius Africanus, a noble youth, had been deterred from marrying Silana by Agrippina, who repeatedly spoke of her as an immodest woman in the decline of life, not to secure Africanus for herself, but to keep the childless and wealthy widow out of a husband's control. Silana having now a prospect of vengeance, suborned as accusers two of her creatures, Iturius and Calvisius, not with the old and often-repeated charges about Agrippina's mourning the death of Britannicus or publishing the wrongs of Octavia, but with a hint that it was her purpose to encourage in revolutionary designs Rubellius Plautus, who his mother's side was as nearly connected as Nero with the Divine Augustus; and then, by marrying him and making him emperor, again seize the control of the State. All this Iturius and Calvisius divulged to Atimetus, a freedman of Domitia, Nero's aunt. Exulting in the opportunity, for Agrippina and Domitia were in bitter rivalry, Atimetus urged Paris, who was himself also a freedman of Domitia, to go at once and put the charge in the most dreadful form.

Night was far advanced and Nero was still sitting over his cups, when Paris entered, who was generally wont at such times to heighten the emperor's enjoyments, but who now wore a gloomy expression. He went through the whole evidence in order, and so frightened his hearer as to make him resolve not only on the destruction of his mother and of Plautus, but also on the removal of Burrus from the command of the guards, as a man who had been promoted by Agrippina's interest, and was now showing his gratitude. We have it on the authority of Fabius Rusticus that a note was written to Caecina Tuscus, intrusting to him the charge of the praetorian cohorts, but that through Seneca's influence that distinguished post was retained for Burrus. According to Plinius and Cluvius, no doubt was felt about the commander's loyalty. Fabius certainly inclines to the praise of Seneca, through whose friendship he rose to honour. Proposing as I do to follow the consentient testimony of historians, I shall give the differences in their narratives under the writers' names. Nero, in his bewilderment and impatience to destroy his mother, could not be put off till Burrus answered for her death, should she be convicted of the crime, but "any one," he said, "much more a parent, must be allowed a defence. Accusers there were none forthcoming; they had before them only the word of a single person from an enemy's house, and this the night with its darkness and prolonged festivity and everything savouring of recklessness and folly, was enough to refute."

Having thus allayed the prince's fears, they went at daybreak to Agrippina, that she might know the charges against her, and either rebut them or suffer the penalty. Burrus fulfilled his instructions in Seneca's presence, and some of the freedmen were present to witness the interview. Then Burrus, when he had fully explained the charges with the authors' names, assumed an air of menace. Instantly Agrippina, calling up all her high spirit, exclaimed, "I wonder not that Silana, who has never borne offspring, knows nothing of a mother's feelings. Parents do not change their children as lightly as a shameless woman does her paramours. And if Iturius and Calvisius, after having wasted their whole fortunes, are now, as their last resource, repaying an old hag for their hire by undertaking to be informers, it does not follow that I am to incur the infamy of plotting a son's murder, or that a Caesar is to have the consciousness of like guilt. As for Domitia's enmity, I should be thankful for it, were she to vie with me in goodwill towards my Nero. Now through her paramour, Atimetus, and the actor, Paris, she is, so to say, concocting a drama for the stage. She at her Baiae was increasing the magnificence of her fishponds, when I was planning in my counsels his adoption with a proconsul's powers and a consul-elect's rank and every other step to empire. Only let the man come forward who can charge me with having tampered with the praetorian cohorts in the capital, with having sapped the loyalty of the provinces, or, in a word, with having bribed slaves and freedmen into any wickedness. Could I have lived with Britannicus in the possession of power? And if Plautus or any other were to become master of the State so as to sit in judgment on me, accusers forsooth would not be forthcoming, to charge me not merely with a few incautious expressions prompted by the eagerness of affection, but with guilt from which a son alone could absolve me."

There was profound excitement among those present, and they even tried to soothe her agitation, but she insisted on an interview with her son. Then, instead of pleading her innocence, as though she lacked confidence, or her claims on him by way of reproach, she obtained vengeance on her accusers and rewards for her friends.

The superintendence of the corn supply was given to Faenius Rufus, the direction of the games which the emperor was preparing, to Arruntius Stella, and the province of Egypt to Caius Balbillus. Syria was to be assigned to Publius Anteius, but he was soon put off by various artifices and finally detained at Rome. Silana was banished; Calvisius and Iturius exiled for a time; Atimetus was capitally punished, while Paris was too serviceable to the emperor's profligacy to allow of his suffering any penalty. Plautus for the present was silently passed over.

Next Pallas and Burrus were accused of having conspired to raise Cornelius Sulla to the throne, because of his noble birth and connection with Claudius, whose son-in-law he was by his marriage with Antonia. The promoter of the prosecution was one Paetus, who had become notorious by frequent purchases of property confiscated to the exchequer and was now convicted clearly of imposture. But the proved innocence of Pallas did Pallas did not please men so much, as his arrogance offended them. When his freedmen, his alleged accomplices, were called, he replied that at home he signified his wishes only by a nod or a gesture, or, if further explanation was required, he used writing, so as not to degrade his voice in such company. Burrus, though accused, gave his verdict as one of the judges. The prosecutor was sentenced to exile, and the account-books in which he was reviving forgotten claims of the exchequer, were burnt.

At the end of the year the cohort usually on guard during the games was withdrawn, that there might be a greater show of freedom, that the soldiery too might be less demoralised when no longer in contact with the licence of the theatre, and that it might be proved whether the populace, in the absence of a guard, would maintain their self-control. The emperor, on the advice of the augurs, purified Rome by a lustration, as the temples of Jupiter and Minerva had been struck by lightning.

In the consulship of Quintus Volusius and Publius Scipio, there was peace abroad, but a disgusting licentiousness at home on the part of Nero, who in a slave's disguise, so as to be unrecognized, would wander through the streets of Rome, to brothels and taverns, with comrades, who seized on goods exposed for sale and inflicted wounds on any whom they encountered, some of these last knowing him so little that he even received blows himself, and showed the marks of them in his face. When it was notorious that the emperor was the assailant, and the insults on men and women of distinction were multiplied, other persons too on the strength of a licence once granted under Nero's name, ventured with impunity on the same practices, and had gangs of their own, till night presented the scenes of a captured city. Julius Montanus, a senator, but one who had not yet held any office, happened to encounter the prince in the darkness, and because he fiercely repulsed his attack and then on recognizing him begged for mercy, as though this was a reproach, forced to destroy himself. Nero was for the future more timid, and surrounded himself with soldiers and a number of gladiators, who, when a fray began on a small scale and seemed a private affair, were to let it alone, but, if the injured persons resisted stoutly, they rushed in with their swords. He also turned the licence of the games and the enthusiasm for the actors into something like a battle by the impunity he allowed, and the rewards he offered, and especially by looking on himself, sometimes concealed, but often in public view, till, with the people at strife and the fear of a worse commotion, the only remedy which could be devised was the expulsion of the offending actors from Italy, and the presence once more of the soldiery in the theatre.

During the same time there was a discussion in the Senate on the misconduct of the freedmen class, and a strong demand was made that, as a check on the undeserving, patrons should have the right of revoking freedom. There were several who supported this. But the consuls did not venture to put the motion without the emperor's knowledge, though they recorded the Senate's general opinion, to see whether he would sanction the arrangement, considering that only a few were opposed to it, while some loudly complained that the irreverent spirit which freedom had fostered, had broken into such excess, that freedmen would ask their patrons' advice as to whether they should treat them with violence, or, as legally, their equals, and would actually threaten them with blows, at the same time recommending them not to punish. "What right," it was asked, "was conceded to an injured patron but that of temporarily banishing the freedman a hundred miles off to the shores of Campania? In everything else, legal proceedings were equal and the same for both. Some weapon ought to be given to the patrons which could not be despised. It would be no grievance for the enfranchised to have to keep their freedom by the same respectful behaviour which had procured it for them. But, as for notorious offenders, they deserved to be dragged back into slavery, that fear might be a restraint where kindness had had no effect."

It was argued in reply that, though the guilt of a few ought to be the ruin of the men themselves, there should be no diminution of the rights of the entire class. "For it was," they contended, "a widely diffused body; from it, the city tribes, the various public functionaries, the establishments of the magistrates and priests were for the most part supplied, as well as the cohorts of the city-guard; very many too of the knights and several of the senators derived their origin from no other source. If freedmen were to be a separate class, the paucity of the freeborn would be conspicuously apparent. Not without good reason had our ancestors, in distinguishing the position of the different orders, thrown freedom open to all. Again, two kinds of enfranchisement had been instituted, so as to leave room for retracting the boon, or for a fresh act of grace. Those whom the patron had not emancipated with the freedom-giving rod, were still held, as it were, by the bonds of slavery. Every master should carefully consider the merits of each case, and be slow to grant what once given could not be taken away."

This view prevailed, and the emperor replied to the Senate that, whenever freedmen were accused by their patrons, they were to investigate each case separately and not to annul any right to their common injury. Soon afterwards, his aunt Domitia had her freedman Paris taken from her, avowedly by civil law, much to the emperor's disgrace, by whose direction a decision that he was freeborn was obtained.

Still there yet remained some shadow of a free state. A contest arose between Vibullius, the praetor, and Antistius, a tribune of the people; for the tribune had ordered the release of some disorderly applauders of certain actors, whom the praetor had imprisoned. The Senate approved the imprisonment, and censured the presumption of Antistius. Tribunes were also forbidden to usurp the authority of praetors and consuls, or to summon from any part of Italy persons liable to legal proceedings. It was further proposed by Lucius Piso, consul-elect, that tribunes were not to try any case in their own houses, that a fine imposed by them was not to be entered on the public books by the officials of the exchequer, till four months had expired, and that in the meantime appeals were to be allowed, which the consuls were to decide.

Restrictions were also put on the powers of the aediles and a limit fixed to the amount of bail or penalty which curule and plebeian aediles could respectively exact. On this, Helvidius Priscus, a tribune of the people, followed up a personal quarrel he had with Obultronius Sabinus, one of the officials of the exchequer, by insinuating that he stretched his right of confiscation with merciless rigour against the poor. The emperor then transferred the charge of the public accounts from these officers to the commissioners.

The arrangement of this business had been variously and frequently altered. Augustus allowed the Senate to appoint commissioners; then, when corrupt practices were suspected in the voting, men were chosen by lot for the office out of the whole number of praetors. This did not last long, as the lot strayed away to unfit persons. Claudius then again appointed quaestors, and that they might not be too lax in their duties from fear of offending, he promised them promotion out of the usual course. But what they lacked was the firmness of mature age, entering, as they did, on this office as their first step, and so Nero appointed ex-praetors of approved competency.

During the same consulship, Vipsanius Laenas was condemned for rapacity in his administration of the province of Sardinia. Cestius Proculus was acquitted of extortion, his accusers dropping the charge. Clodius Quirinalis, having, when in command of the crews at Ravenna, caused grievous distress to Italy by his profligacy and cruelty, just as if it were the most contemptible of countries, forestalled his doom by poison. Caninius Rebilus, one of the first men in legal knowledge and vastness of wealth, escaped the miseries of an old age of broken health by letting the blood trickle from his veins, though men did not credit him with sufficient resolution for a self-inflicted death, because of his infamous effeminacy. Lucius Volusius on the other hand died with a glorious name. There was his long life of ninety-three years, his conspicuous wealth, honourably acquired, and his wise avoidance of the malignity of so many emperors.

During Nero's second consulship with Lucius Piso for his colleague, little occurred deserving mention, unless one were to take pleasure in filling volumes with the praise of the foundations and timber work on which the emperor piled the immense amphitheatre in the Field of Mars. But we have learnt that it suits the dignity of the Roman people to reserve history for great achievements, and to leave such details to the city's daily register. I may mention that the colonies of Nuceria and Capua were strengthened by an addition of veterans; to every member of the city populace four hundred sesterces were given, and forty million paid into the exchequer to maintain the credit of the citizens.

A tax also of four per cent. on the sale of slaves was remitted, an apparent more than a real boon, for as the seller was ordered to pay it, purchasers found that it was added as part of the price. The emperor by an edict forbade any magistrate or procurator in the government of a province to exhibit a show of gladiators, or of wild beasts, or indeed any other public entertainment; for hitherto our subjects had been as much oppressed by such bribery as by actual extortion, while governors sought to screen by corruption the guilty deeds of arbitrary caprice.

The Senate next passed a decree, providing alike for punishment and safety. If a master were murdered by his slaves, all those who were enfranchised by his will and lived under the same roof, were to suffer the capital punishment with his other slaves. Lucius Varius, an ex-consul, who had been crushed in the past under charges of extortion, was restored to his rank as a senator. Pomponia Graecina, a distinguished lady, wife of the Plautius who returned from Britain with an ovation, was accused of some foreign superstition and handed over to her husband's judicial decision. Following ancient precedent, he heard his wife's cause in the presence of kinsfolk, involving, as it did, her legal status and character, and he reported that she was innocent. This Pomponia lived a long life of unbroken melancholy. After the murder of Julia, Drusus's daughter, by Messalina's treachery, for forty years she wore only the attire of a mourner, with a heart ever sorrowful. For this, during Claudius's reign, she escaped unpunished, and it was afterwards counted a glory to her.

The same year saw many impeached. One of these, Publius Celer, prosecuted by the province of Asia, the emperor could not acquit, and so he put off the case till the man died of old age. Celer, as I have related, had murdered Silanus, the pro-consul, and the magnitude of this crime veiled his other enormities. Cossutianus Capito was accused by the people of Cilicia; he was a man stained with the foulest guilt, and had actually imagined that his audacious wickedness had the same rights in a province as he had claimed for it at Rome. But he had to confront a determined prosecution, and at last abandoned his defence. Eprius Marcellus, from whom Lycia demanded compensation, was so powerfully supported by corrupt influence that some of his accusers were punished with exile, as though they had imperilled an innocent man.

Nero entered on his third consulship with Valerius Messala, whose great-grandfather, the orator Corvinus, was still remembered by a few old men, as having been the colleague of the Divine Augustus, Nero's great-grandfather, in the same office. But the honour of a noble house was further increased by an annual grant of five hundred thousand sesterces on which Messala might support virtuous poverty. Aurelius Cotta, too, and Haterius Antonius had yearly stipends assigned them by the emperor, though they had squandered their ancestral wealth in profligacy.

Early in this year a war between Parthia and Rome about the possession of Armenia, which, feebly begun, had hitherto dragged on, was vigorously resumed. For Vologeses would not allow his brother Tiridates to be deprived of a kingdom which he had himself given him, or to hold it as a gift from a foreign power, and Corbulo too thought it due to the grandeur of Rome that he should recover what Lucullus and Pompeius had formerly won. Besides, the Armenians in the fluctuations of their allegiance sought the armed protection of both empires, though by their country's position, by resemblance of manners, and by the ties of intermarriage, they were more connected with the Parthians, to whose subjection, in their ignorance of freedom, they rather inclined.

Corbulo however had more to struggle against in the supineness of his soldiers than in the treachery of the enemy. His legions indeed, transferred as they had been from Syria and demoralised by a long peace, endured most impatiently the duties of a Roman camp. It was well known that that army contained veterans who had never been on piquet duty or on night guard, to whom the rampart and the fosse were new and strange sights, men without helmets or breastplates, sleek money-making traders, who had served all their time in towns. Corbulo having discharged all who were old or in ill-health, sought to supply their places, and levies were held in Galatia and Cappadocia, and to these were added a legion from Germany with its auxiliary cavalry and light infantry. The entire army was kept under canvas, though the winter was so severe that the ground, covered as it was with ice, did not yield a place for the tents without being dug up. Many of the men had their limbs frost-bitten through the intensity of the cold, and some perished on guard. A soldier was observed whose hands mortified as he was carrying a bundle of wood, so that sticking to their burden they dropped off from his arms, now mere stumps. The general, lightly clad, with head uncovered, was continually with his men on the march, amid their labours; he had praise for the brave, comfort for the feeble, and was a good example to all. And then as many shrank from the rigour of the climate and of the service, and deserted, he sought a remedy in strictness of discipline. Not, as in other armies, was a first or second offense condoned, but the soldier, who had quitted his colours, instantly paid the penalty with his life. This was shown by experience to be a wholesome measure, better than mercy; for there were fewer desertions in that camp than in those in which leniency was habitual.

Meanwhile Corbulo kept his legions within the camp till spring weather was fairly established, and having stationed his auxiliary infantry at suitable points, he directed them not to begin an engagement. The charge of these defensive positions he entrusted to Paccius Orfitus, who had held the post of a first-rank centurion. Though this officer had reported that the barbarians were heedless, and that an opportunity for success presented itself, he was instructed to keep within his entrenchments and to wait for a stronger force. But he broke the order, and on the arrival of a few cavalry squadrons from the nearest forts, who in their inexperience insisted on fighting, he engaged the enemy and was routed. Panic-stricken by his disaster, those who ought to have given him support returned in precipitate flight to their respective encampments. Corbulo heard of this with displeasure; he sharply censured Paccius, the officers and soldiers, and ordered them to have their quarters outside the lines. There they were kept in disgrace, and were released only on the intercession of the whole army.

Tiridates meantime who, besides his own dependencies, had the powerful aid of his brother Vologeses, ravaged Armenia, not in stealthy raids as before, but in open war, plundering all whom he thought loyal to Rome, while he eluded an action with any force which was brought against him, and thus flying hither and thither, he spread panic more widely by rumour than by arms. So Corbulo, frustrated in his prolonged efforts to bring on an engagement and compelled, like the enemy, to carry hostilities everywhere, divided his army, so that his generals and officers might attack several points simultaneously. He at the same time instructed king Antiochus to hasten to the provinces on his frontier, as Pharasmanes, after having slain his son Rhadamistus as a traitor to prove his loyalty to us, was following up more keenly than ever his old feud with the Armenians. Then, for the first time, we won the friendship of the Moschi, a nation which became pre-eminently attached to Rome, and they overran the wilds of Armenia. Thus the intended plans of Tiridates were wholly reversed, and he sent envoys to ask on behalf of himself and of the Parthians, why, when hostages had lately been given and a friendship renewed which might open up a way to further acts of good will, he was thus driven from Armenia, his ancient possession. "As yet," he said, "Vologeses had not bestirred himself, simply because they preferred negotiation to violence. Should however war be persisted in, the Arsacids would not want the courage and good fortune which had already been proved more than once by disaster to Rome." Corbulo in reply, when he was certain that Vologeses was detained by the revolt of Hyrcania, advised Tiridates to address a petition to the emperor, assuring him that he might reign securely and without bloodshed by relinquishing a prospect in the remote future for the sake of one more solid within his reach.

As no progress was made towards a final settlement of peace by the interchange of messages, it was at last decided to fix a time and a place for an interview between the leaders. "A thousand troopers," Tiridates said, "would be his escort; what force of every kind was to be with Corbulo, he did not prescribe, provided they came in peaceful fashion, without breastplates and helmets." Any human being, to say nothing of an old and wary general, would have seen through the barbarian's cunning, which assigned a limited number on one side and offered a larger on the other, expressly with a treacherous intent; for, were they to be exposed to a cavalry trained in the use of arrows, with the person undefended, numbers would be unavailing. Corbulo however, pretending not to understand this, replied that they would do better to discuss matters requiring consideration for their common good, in the presence of the entire armies, and he selected a place partly consisting of gently sloping hills, suited for ranks of infantry, partly, of a spreading plain where troops of cavalry could manoeuvre. On the appointed day, arriving first, he posted his allied infantry with the king's auxiliaries on the wings, the sixth legion in the centre, with which he had united three thousand men of the third, brought up in the night from another camp, with one eagle, so as to look like a single legion. Tiridates towards evening showed himself at some distance whence he could be seen rather than heard. And so the Roman general, without any conference, ordered his troops to retire to their respective camps.

The king either suspecting a stratagem from these simultaneous movements in different directions, or intending to cut off our supplies as they were coming up from the sea of Pontus and the town of Trapezus, hastily withdrew. He could not however make any attack on the supplies, as they were brought over mountains in the occupation of our forces. Corbulo, that war might not be uselessly protracted, and also to compel the Armenians to defend their possessions, prepared to destroy their fortresses, himself undertaking the assault on the strongest of all in that province named Volandum. The weaker he assigned to Cornelius Flaccus, his lieutenant, and to Insteius Capito, his camp-prefect. Having then surveyed the defences and provided everything suitable for storming them, he exhorted his soldiers to strip of his home this vagabond foe who was preparing neither for peace nor for war, but who confessed his treachery and cowardice by flight, and so to secure alike glory and spoil. Then forming his army into four divisions, he led one in the dense array of the "testudo" close up to the rampart, to undermine it, while others were ordered to apply scaling ladders to the walls, and many more were to discharge brands and javelins from engines. The slingers and artillerymen had a position assigned them from which to hurl their missiles at a distance, so that, with equal tumult everywhere, no support might be given from any point to such as were pressed. So impetuous were the efforts of the army that within a third part of one day the walls were stripped of their defenders, the barriers of the gates overthrown, the fortifications scaled and captured, and all the adult inhabitants massacred, without the loss of a soldier and with but very few wounded. The nonmilitary population were sold by auction; the rest of the booty fell to the conquerors.

Corbulo's lieutenant and camp-prefect met with similar success; three forts were stormed by them in one day, and the remainder, some from panic, others by the consent of the occupants, capitulated. This inspired them with confidence to attack the capital of the country, Artaxata. The legions however were not marched by the nearest route, for should they cross the river Avaxes which washes the city's walls by a bridge, they would be within missile-range. They passed over it at a distance, where it was broad and shallow.

Meantime Tiridates, ashamed of seeming utterly powerless by not interfering with the siege, and afraid that, in attempting to stop it, he would entangle himself and his cavalry on difficult ground, resolved finally to display his forces and either give battle on the first opportunity, or, by a pretended flight, prepare the way for some stratagem.

Suddenly, he threw himself on the Roman columns, without however surprising our general, who had formed his army for fighting as well as for marching. On the right and left flanks marched the third and sixth legions, with some picked men of the tenth in the centre; the baggage was secured within the lines, and the rear was guarded by a thousand cavalry, who were ordered to resist any close attack of the enemy, but not to pursue his retreat. On the wings were the foot-archers and the remainder of the cavalry, with a more extended line on the left wing, along the base of some hills, so that should the enemy penetrate the centre, he might be encountered both in front and flank. Tiridates faced us in skirmishing order, but not within missile-range, now threatening attack, now seemingly afraid, with the view of loosening our formation and falling on isolated divisions. Finding that there was no breaking of our ranks from rashness, and that only one cavalry officer advanced too boldly, and that he falling pierced with arrows, confirmed the rest in obedience by the warning, he retired on the approach of darkness.

Corbulo then encamped on the spot, and considered whether he should push on his legions without their baggage to Artaxata and blockade the city, on which, he supposed, Tiridates had fallen back. When his scouts reported that the king had undertaken a long march, and that it was doubtful whether Media or Albania was its destination, he waited for daylight, and then sent on his light-armed troops, which were meanwhile to hover round the walls and begin the attack from a distance. The inhabitants however opened the gates of their own accord, and surrendered themselves and their property to the Romans. This saved their lives; the city was fired, demolished and levelled to the ground, as it could not be held without a strong garrison from the extent of the walls, and we had not sufficient force to be divided between adequately garrisoning it and carrying on the war. If again the place were left untouched and unguarded, no advantage or glory would accrue from its capture. Then too there was a wonderful occurrence, almost a divine interposition. While the whole space outside the town, up to its buildings, was bright with sunlight, the enclosure within the walls was suddenly shrouded in a black cloud, seamed with lightning-flashes, and thus the city was thought to be given up to destruction, as if heaven was wroth against it.

For all this Nero was unanimously saluted emperor, and by the Senate's decree a thanksgiving was held; statues also, arches and successive consulships were voted to him, and among the holy days were to be included the day on which the victory was won, that on which it was announced, and that on which the motion was brought forward. Other proposals too of a like kind were carried, on a scale so extravagant, that Caius Cassius, after having assented to the rest of the honours, argued that if the gods were to be thanked for the bountiful favours of fortune, even a whole year would not suffice for thanksgivings, and therefore there ought to be a classification of sacred and business-days, that so they might observe divine ordinances and yet not interfer with human affairs.

A man who had struggled with various calamities and earned the hate of many, was then impeached and condemned, but not without angry feelings towards Seneca. This was Publius Suilius. He had been terrible and venal, while Claudius reigned, and when times were changed, he was not so much humbled as his enemies wished, and was one who would rather seem a criminal than a suppliant. With the intent of crushing him, so men believed, a decree of the Senate was revived, along with the penalty of the Cincian law against persons who had pleaded for hire. Suilius spared not complaint or indignant remonstrance; freespoken because of his extreme age as well as from his insolent temper, he taunted Seneca with his savage enmity against the friends of Claudius, under whose reign he had endured a most righteously deserved exile. "The man," he said, "familiar as he was only with profitless studies, and with the ignorance of boyhood, envied those who employed a lively and genuine eloquence in the defence of their fellow-citizens. He had been Germanicus's quaestor, while Seneca had been a paramour in his house. Was it to be thought a worse offence to obtain a reward for honest service with the litigant's consent, than to pollute the chambers of the imperial ladies? By what kind of wisdom or maxims of philosophy had Seneca within four years of royal favour amassed three hundred million sesterces? At Rome the wills of the childless were, so to say, caught in his snare while Italy and the provinces were drained by a boundless usury. His own money, on the other hand, had been acquired by industry and was not excessive. He would suffer prosecutions, perils, anything indeed rather than make an old and self-learned position of honour to bow before an upstart prosperity."

Persons were not wanting to report all this to Seneca, in the exact words, or with a worse sense put on it. Accusers were also found who alleged that our allies had been plundered, when Suilius governed the province of Asia, and that there had been embezzlement of public monies. Then, as an entire year had been granted to them for inquiries, it seemed a shorter plan to begin with his crimes at Rome, the witnesses of which were on the spot. These men charged Suilius with having driven Quintus Pomponius by a relentless prosecution into the extremity of civil war, with having forced Julia, Drusus's daughter, and Sabina Poppaea to suicide, with having treacherously ruined Valerius Asiaticus, Lusius Saturninus and Cornelius Lupus, in fact, with the wholesale conviction of troops of Roman knights, and with all the cruelty of Claudius. His defence was that of all this he had done nothing on his own responsibility but had simply obeyed the emperor, till Nero stopped such pleadings, by stating that he had ascertained from his father's notebooks that he had never compelled the prosecution of a single person.

Suilius then sheltered himself under Messalina's orders, and the defence began to collapse. "Why," it was asked, "was no one else chosen to put his tongue at the service of that savage harlot? We must punish the instruments of atrocious acts, when, having gained the rewards of wickedness, they impute the wickedness to others."

And so, with the loss of half his property, his son and granddaughter being allowed to retain the other half, and what they had inherited under their mother's or grandmother's will being also exempted from confiscation, Suilius was banished to the Balearic isles. Neither in the crisis of his peril nor after his condemnation did he quail in spirit. Rumour said that he supported that lonely exile by a life of ease and plenty. When the accusers attacked his son Nerullinus on the strength of men's hatred of the father and of some charges of extortion, the emperor interposed, as if implying that vengeange was fully satisfied.

About the same time Octavius Sagitta, a tribune of the people, who was enamoured to frenzy of Pontia, a married woman, bribed her by most costly presents into an intrigue and then into abandoning her husband. He had offered her marriage and had won her consent. But as soon as she was free, she devised delays, pretended that her father's wishes were against it, and having secured the prospect of a richer husband, she repudiated her promises. Octavius, on the other hand, now remonstrated, now threatened; his good name, he protested, was lost, his means exhausted, and as for his life, which was all that was left to him, he surrendered it to her mercy. When she spurned him, he asked the solace of one night, with which to soothe his passion, that he might set bounds to it for the future. A night was fixed, and Pontia intrusted the charge of her chamber to a female slave acquainted with her secret. Octavius attended by one freedman entered with a dagger concealed under his dress. Then, as usual in lovers' quarrels, there were chidings, entreaties, reproaches, excuses, and some period of the darkness was given up to passion; then, when seemingly about to go, and she was fearing nothing, he stabbed her with the steel, and having wounded and scared away the slave girl who was hurrying to her, rushed out of the chamber. Next day the murder was notorious, and there was no question as to the murderer, for it was proved that he had passed some time with her. The freedman, however, declared the deed was his, that he had, in fact, avenged his patron's wrongs. He had made some impression by the nobleness of his example, when the slave girl recovered and revealed the truth. Octavius, when he ceased to be tribune, was prosecuted before the consuls by the father of the murdered woman, and was condemned by the sentence of the Senate under "the law concerning assassins."

A profligacy equally notorious in that same year proved the beginning of great evils to the State. There was at Rome one Sabina Poppaea; her father was Titus Ollius, but she had assumed the name of her maternal grandfather Poppaeus Sabinus, a man of illustrious memory and pre-eminently distinguished by the honours of a consulship and a triumph. As for Ollius, before he attained promotion, the friendship of Sejanus was his ruin. This Poppaea had everything but a right mind. Her mother, who surpassed in personal attractions all the ladies of her day, had bequeathed to her alike fame and beauty. Her fortune adequately corresponded to the nobility of her descent. Her conversation was charming and her wit anything but dull. She professed virtue, while she practised laxity. Seldom did she appear in public, and it was always with her face partly veiled, either to disappoint men's gaze or to set off her beauty. Her character she never spared, making no distinction between a husband and a paramour, while she was never a slave to her own passion or to that of her lover. Wherever there was a prospect of advantage, there she transferred her favours. And so while she was living as the wife of Rufius Crispinus, a Roman knight, by whom she had a son, she was attracted by the youth and fashionable elegance of Otho, and by the fact too that he was reputed to have Nero's most ardent friendship. Without any delay the intrigue was followed by marriage.

Otho now began to praise his wife's beauty and accomplishments to the emperor, either from a lover's thoughtlessness or to inflame Nero's passion, in the hope of adding to his own influence by the further tie which would arise out of possession of the same woman. Often, as he rose from the emperor's table, was he heard repeatedly to say that he was going to her, to the high birth and beauty which had fallen to his lot, to that which all men pray for, the joy of the fortunate. These and like incitements allowed but of brief delay. Once having gained admission, Poppaea won her way by artful blandishments, pretending that she could not resist her passion and that she was captivated by Nero's person. Soon, as the emperor's love grew ardent, she would change and be supercilious, and, if she were detained more than one or two nights, would say again and again that she was a married woman and could not give up her husband attached as she was to Otho by a manner of life, which no one equalled. "His ideas and his style were grand; at his house everything worthy of the highest fortune was ever before her eyes. Nero, on the contrary, with his slave girl mistress, tied down by his attachment to Acte, had derived nothing from his slavish associations but what was low and degrading."

Otho was now cut off from Nero's usual familiar intercourse, and then even from interviews and from the royal suite, and at last was appointed governor of the province of Lusitania, that he might not be the emperor's rival at Rome. There he lived up to the time of the civil wars, not in the fashion of his disgraceful past, but uprightly and virtuously, a pleasure-loving man when idle, and self-restrained when in power.

Hitherto Nero had sought a veil for his abominations and wickedness. He was particularly suspicious of Cornelius Sulla, whose apathetic temper he interpreted as really the reverse, inferring that he was, in fact, an artful dissembler. Graptus, one of the emperor's freedmen, whose age and experience had made him thoroughly acquainted with the imperial household from the time of Tiberius, quickened these apprehensions by the following falsehood. The Mulvian bridge was then a famous haunt of nightly profligacy, and Nero used to go there that he might take his pleasures more freely outside the city. So Graptus, taking advantage of an idle panic into which the royal attendants had chanced to have been thrown on their return by one of those youthful frolics which were then everywhere practised, invented a story that a treacherous attack had been planned on the emperor, should he go back by the Flaminian road, and that through the favour of destiny he had escaped it, as he went home by a different way to Sallust's gardens. Sulla, he said, was the author of this plot. Not one, however, of Sulla's slaves or clients was recognised, and his character, despicable as it was and incapable of a daring act, was utterly at variance with the charge. Still, just as if he had been found guilty, he was ordered to leave his country, and confine himself within the walls of Massilia.

During the same consulship a hearing was given to two conflicting deputations from Puteoli, sent to the Senate by the town council and by the populace. The first spoke bitterly of the violence of the multitude; the second, of the rapacity of the magistrates and of all the chief citizens. That the disturbance, which had gone as far as stoning and threats of fire, might not lead on to bloodshed and armed fighting, Caius Cassius was appointed to apply some remedy. As they would not endure his rigour, the charge of the affair was at his own request transferred to the brothers Scribonii, to whom was given a praetorian cohort, the terror of which, coupled with the execution of a few persons, restored peace to the townspeople.

I should not mention a very trivial decree of the Senate which allowed the city of Syracuse to exceed the prescribed number in their gladiatorial shows, had not Paetus Thrasea spoken against it and furnished his traducers with a ground for censuring his motion. "Why," it was asked, "if he thought that the public welfare required freedom of speech in the Senate, did he pursue such trifling abuses? Why should he not speak for or against peace and war, or on the taxes and laws and other matters involving Roman interests? The senators, as often as they received the privilege of stating an opinion, were at liberty to say out what they pleased, and to claim that it should be put to the vote. Was it the only worthy object of reform to provide that the Syracusans should not give shows on a larger scale? Were all other matters in every department of the empire as admirable as if Thrasea and not Nero had the direction of them? But if the highest affairs were passed by and ignored, how much more ought there to be no meddling with things wholly insignificant."

Thrasea in reply, when his friends asked an explanation, said "that it was not in ignorance of Rome's actual condition that he sought to correct such decrees, but that he was giving what was due to the honour of the senators, in making it evident that those who attended even to the merest trifles, would not disguise their responsibility for important affairs."

That same year, repeated demands on the part of the people, who denounced the excessive greed of the revenue collectors, made Nero doubt whether he should not order the repeal of all indirect taxes, and so confer a most splendid boon on the human race. But this sudden impulse was checked by the senators, who, having first heartily praised the grandeur of his conception, pointed out "that the dissolution of the empire must ensue if the revenues which supported the State were to be diminished; for as soon as the customs were swept away, there would follow a demand for the abolition of the direct taxes. Many companies for the collection of the indirect taxes had been formed by consuls and tribunes, when the freedom of the Roman people was still in its vigour, and arrangements were subsequently made to insure an exact correspondence between the amount of income and the necessary disbursements. Certainly some restraint, they admitted, must be put on the cupidity of the revenue collectors, that they might not by new oppressions bring into odium what for so many years had been endured without a complaint."

Accordingly the emperor issued an edict that the regulations about every branch of the public revenue, which had hitherto been kept secret, should be published; that claims which had been dropped should not be revived after a year; that the praetor at Rome, the propraetor or proconsul in the provinces, should give judicial precedence to all cases against the collectors; that the soldiers should retain their immunities except when they traded for profit, with other very equitable arrangements, which for a short time were maintained and were subsequently disregarded. However, the repeal of the two per cent. and two-and-a-half per cent. taxes remains in force, as well as that of others bearing names invented by the collectors to cover their illegal exactions. In our transmarine provinces the conveyance of corn was rendered less costly, and it was decided that merchant ships should not be assessed with their owner's property, and that no tax should be paid on them.

Two men under prosecution from Africa, in which province they had held proconsular authority, Sulpicius Camerinus and Pomponius Silvanus, were acquitted by the emperor. Camerinus had against him a few private persons who charged him with cruelty rather than with extortion. Silvanus was beset by a host of accusers, who demanded time for summoning their witnesses, while the defendant insisted on being at once put on his defence. And he was successful, through his wealth, his childlessness, and his old age, which he prolonged beyond the life of those by whose corrupt influence he had escaped.

Up to this time everything had been quiet in Germany, from the temper of the generals, who, now that triumphal decorations had been vulgarised, hoped for greater glory by the maintenance of peace. Paulinus Pompeius and Lucius Vetus were then in command of the army. Still, to avoid keeping the soldiers in idleness, the first completed the embankment begun sixty-three years before by Drusus to confine the waters of the Rhine, while Vetus prepared to connect the Moselle and the Arar by a canal, so that troops crossing the sea and then conveyed on the Rhone and Arar might sail by this canal into the Moselle and the Rhine, and thence to the ocean. Thus the difficulties of the route being removed, there would be communication for ships between the shores of the west and of the north.

Aelius Gracilis, the governor of Belgica, discouraged the work by seeking to deter Vetus from bringing his legions into another man's province, and so drawing to himself the attachment of Gaul. This result he repeatedly said would excite the fears of the emperor, an assertion by which meritorious undertakings are often hindered.

Meantime, from the continued inaction of our armies, a rumour prevailed that the commanders had been deprived of the right of leading them against the enemy. Thereupon the Frisii moved up their youth to the forests and swamps, and their non-fighting population, over the lakes, to the river-bank, and established themselves in unoccupied lands, reserved for the use of our soldiers, under the leadership of Verritus and Malorix, the kings of the tribe, as far as Germans are under kings. Already they had settled themselves in houses, had sown the fields, and were cultivating the soil as if it had been their ancestors', when Dubius Avitus, who had succeeded Paulinus in the province, by threatening them with a Roman attack if they did not retire into their old country or obtain a new territory from the emperor, constrained Verritus and Malorix to become suppliants. They went to Rome, and while they waited for Nero, who was intent on other engagements, among the sights shown to the barbarians they were admitted into Pompey's theatre, where they might behold the vastness of the Roman people. There at their leisure (for in the entertainment, ignorant as they were, they found no amusement) they asked questions about the crowd on the benches, about the distinctions of classes, who were the knights, where was the Senate, till they observed some persons in a foreign dress on the seats of the senators. Having asked who they were, when they were told that this honour was granted to envoys from those nations which were distinguished for their bravery and their friendship to Rome, they exclaimed that no men on earth surpassed the Germans in arms or in loyalty. Then they went down and took their seat among the senators. The spectators hailed the act goodnaturedly, as due to the impulsiveness of a primitive people and to an honourable rivalry. Nero gave both of them the Roman franchise, and ordered the Frisii to withdraw from the territory in question. When they disdained obedience, some auxiliary cavalry by a sudden attack made it a necessity for them, capturing or slaughtering those who obstinately resisted.

Of this same territory, the Ampsivarii now possessed themselves, a tribe more powerful not only from their numbers, but from having the sympathy of the neighbouring peoples, as they had been expelled by the Chauci and had to beg, as homeless outcasts, a secure exile. Their cause was pleaded by a man, famous among those nations and loyal to Rome, Boiocalus by name, who reminded us that on the Cheruscan revolt he had been imprisoned by the order of Arminius, that afterwards he had served under the leadership of Tiberius and of Germanicus, and that to a fifty years' obedience he was adding the merit of subjecting his tribe to our dominion. "What an extent of plain," he would say, "lies open into which the flocks and herds of the Roman soldiers may some day be sent! Let them by all means keep retreats for their cattle, while men are starving; only let them not prefer a waste and a solitude to friendly nations. Once these fields belonged to the Chamavi; then to the Tubantes; after them to the Usipii. As heaven is for the gods, so the earth has been given to mankind, and lands uninhabited are common to all." Then looking up to the sun and invoking the other heavenly bodies, he asked them, as though standing in their presence, "whether they wished to behold an empty soil; rather let them submerge it beneath the sea against the plunderers of the land."

Avitus was impressed by this language and said that people must submit to the rule of their betters; that the gods to whom they appealed, had willed that the decision as to what should be given or taken from them, was to rest with the Romans, who would allow none but themselves to be judges. This was his public answer to the Ampsivarii; to Boiocalus his reply was that in remembrance of past friendship he would cede the lands in question. Boiocalus spurned the offer as the price of treason, adding, "We may lack a land to live in; we cannot lack one to die in." And so they parted with mutual exasperation. The Ampsivarii now called on the Bructeri, the Tencteri, and yet more distant tribes to be their allies in war. Avitus, having written to Curtilius Mancia, commander of the Upper army, asking him to cross the Rhine and display his troops in the enemy's rear, himself led his legions into the territory of the Tencteri, and threatened them with extermination unless they dissociated themselves from the cause. When upon this the Tencteri stood aloof, the Bructeri were cowed by a like terror. And so, as the rest too were for averting perils which did not concern them, the Ampsivarian tribe in its isolation retreated to the Usipii and Tubantes. Driven out of these countries, they sought refuge with the Chatti and then with the Cherusci, and after long wanderings, as destitute outcasts, received now as friends now as foes, their entire youth were slain in a strange land, and all who could not fight, were apportioned as booty.

The same summer a great battle was fought between the Hermunduri and the Chatti, both forcibly claiming a river which produced salt in plenty, and bounded their territories. They had not only a passion for settling every question by arms, but also a deep-rooted superstition that such localities are specially near to heaven, and that mortal prayers are nowhere more attentively heard by the gods. It is, they think, through the bounty of divine power, that in that river and in those forests salt is produced, not, as in other countries, by the drying up of an overflow of the sea, but by the combination of two opposite elements, fire and water, when the latter had been poured over a burning pile of wood. The war was a success for the Hermunduri, and the more disastrous to the Chatti because they had devoted, in the event of victory, the enemy's army to Mars and Mercury, a vow which consigns horses, men, everything indeed on the vanquished side to destruction. And so the hostile threat recoiled on themselves. Meanwhile, a state in alliance with us, that of the Ubii, suffered grievously from an unexpected calamity. Fires suddenly bursting from the earth seized everywhere on country houses, crops, and villages, and were rushing on to the very walls of the newly founded colony. Nor could they be extinguished by the fall of rain, or by river-water, or by any other moisture, till some countrymen, in despair of a remedy and in fury at the disaster, flung stones from a distance, and then, approaching nearer, as the flames began to sink, tried to scare them away, like so many wild beasts, with the blows of clubs and other weapons. At last they stript off their clothes and threw them on the fire, which they were the more likely to quench, the more they had been soiled by common use.

That same year, the fact that the tree in the Comitium, which 840 years before had sheltered the infancy of Romulus and Remus, was impaired by the decay of its boughs and by the withering of its stem, was accounted a portent, till it began to renew its life with fresh shoots.

BOOK XIV, A.D. 59-62

In the year of the consulship of Caius Vipstanus and Caius Fonteius, Nero deferred no more a long meditated crime. Length of power had matured his daring, and his passion for Poppaea daily grew more ardent. As the woman had no hope of marriage for herself or of Octavia's divorce while Agrippina lived, she would reproach the emperor with incessant vituperation and sometimes call him in jest a mere ward who was under the rule of others, and was so far from having empire that he had not even his liberty. "Why," she asked, "was her marriage put off? Was it, forsooth, her beauty and her ancestors, with their triumphal honours, that failed to please, or her being a mother, and her sincere heart? No; the fear was that as a wife at least she would divulge the wrongs of the Senate, and the wrath of the people at the arrogance and rapacity of his mother. If the only daughter-in-law Agrippina could bear was one who wished evil to her son, let her be restored to her union with Otho. She would go anywhere in the world, where she might hear of the insults heaped on the emperor, rather than witness them, and be also involved in his perils."

These and the like complaints, rendered impressive by tears and by the cunning of an adulteress, no one checked, as all longed to see the mother's power broken, while not a person believed that the son's hatred would steel his heart to her murder.

Cluvius relates that Agrippina in her eagerness to retain her influence went so far that more than once at midday, when Nero, even at that hour, was flushed with wine and feasting, she presented herself attractively attired to her half intoxicated son and offered him her person, and that when kinsfolk observed wanton kisses and caresses, portending infamy, it was Seneca who sought a female's aid against a woman's fascinations, and hurried in Acte, the freed-girl, who alarmed at her own peril and at Nero's disgrace, told him that the incest was notorious, as his mother boasted of it, and that the soldiers would never endure the rule of an impious sovereign. Fabius Rusticus tells us that it was not Agrippina, but Nero, who lusted for the crime, and that it was frustrated by the adroitness of that same freed-girl. Cluvius's account, however, is also that of all other authors, and popular belief inclines to it, whether it was that Agrippina really conceived such a monstrous wickedness in her heart, or perhaps because the thought of a strange passion seemed comparatively credible in a woman, who in her girlish years had allowed herself to be seduced by Lepidus in the hope of winning power, had stooped with a like ambition to the lust of Pallas, and had trained herself for every infamy by her marriage with her uncle.

Nero accordingly avoided secret interviews with her, and when she withdrew to her gardens or to her estates at Tusculum and Antium, he praised her for courting repose. At last, convinced that she would be too formidable, wherever she might dwell, he resolved to destroy her, merely deliberating whether it was to be accomplished by poison, or by the sword, or by any other violent means. Poison at first seemed best, but, were it to be administered at the imperial table, the result could not be referred to chance after the recent circumstances of the death of Britannicus. Again, to tamper with the servants of a woman who, from her familiarity with crime, was on her guard against treachery, appeared to be extremely difficult, and then, too, she had fortified her constitution by the use of antidotes. How again the dagger and its work were to be kept secret, no one could suggest, and it was feared too that whoever might be chosen to execute such a crime would spurn the order.

An ingenious suggestion was offered by Anicetus, a freedman, commander of the fleet at Misenum, who had been tutor to Nero in boyhood and had a hatred of Agrippina which she reciprocated. He explained that a vessel could be constructed, from which a part might by a contrivance be detached, when out at sea, so as to plunge her unawares into the water. "Nothing," he said, "allowed of accidents so much as the sea, and should she be overtaken by shipwreck, who would be so unfair as to impute to crime an offence committed by the winds and waves? The emperor would add the honour of a temple and of shrines to the deceased lady, with every other display of filial affection."

Nero liked the device, favoured as it also was by the particular time, for he was celebrating Minerva's five days' festival at Baiae. Thither he enticed his mother by repeated assurances that children ought to bear with the irritability of parents and to soothe their tempers, wishing thus to spread a rumour of reconciliation and to secure Agrippina's acceptance through the feminine credulity, which easily believes what joy. As she approached, he went to the shore to meet her (she was coming from Antium), welcomed her with outstretched hand and embrace, and conducted her to Bauli. This was the name of a country house, washed by a bay of the sea, between the promontory of Misenum and the lake of Baiae. Here was a vessel distinguished from others by its equipment, seemingly meant, among other things, to do honour to his mother; for she had been accustomed to sail in a trireme, with a crew of marines. And now she was invited to a banquet, that night might serve to conceal the crime. It was well known that somebody had been found to betray it, that Agrippina had heard of the plot, and in doubt whether she was to believe it, was conveyed to Baiae in her litter. There some soothing words allayed her fear; she was graciously received, and seated at table above the emperor. Nero prolonged the banquet with various conversation, passing from a youth's playful familiarity to an air of constraint, which seemed to indicate serious thought, and then, after protracted festivity, escorted her on her departure, clinging with kisses to her eyes and bosom, either to crown his hypocrisy or because the last sight of a mother on the even of destruction caused a lingering even in that brutal heart.

A night of brilliant starlight with the calm of a tranquil sea was granted by heaven, seemingly, to convict the crime. The vessel had not gone far, Agrippina having with her two of her intimate attendants, one of whom, Crepereius Gallus, stood near the helm, while Acerronia, reclining at Agrippina's feet as she reposed herself, spoke joyfully of her son's repentance and of the recovery of the mother's influence, when at a given signal the ceiling of the place, which was loaded with a quantity of lead, fell in, and Crepereius was crushed and instantly killed. Agrippina and Acerronia were protected by the projecting sides of the couch, which happened to be too strong to yield under the weight. But this was not followed by the breaking up of the vessel; for all were bewildered, and those too, who were in the plot, were hindered by the unconscious majority. The crew then thought it best to throw the vessel on one side and so sink it, but they could not themselves promptly unite to face the emergency, and others, by counteracting the attempt, gave an opportunity of a gentler fall into the sea. Acerronia, however, thoughtlessly exclaiming that she was Agrippina, and imploring help for the emperor's mother, was despatched with poles and oars, and such naval implements as chance offered. Agrippina was silent and was thus the less recognized; still, she received a wound in her shoulder. She swam, then met with some small boats which conveyed her to the Lucrine lake, and so entered her house.

There she reflected how for this very purpose she had been invited by a lying letter and treated with conspicuous honour, how also it was near the shore, not from being driven by winds or dashed on rocks, that the vessel had in its upper part collapsed, like a mechanism anything but nautical. She pondered too the death of Acerronia; she looked at her own wound, and saw that her only safeguard against treachery was to ignore it. Then she sent her freedman Agerinus to tell her son how by heaven's favour and his good fortune she had escaped a terrible disaster; that she begged him, alarmed, as he might be, by his mother's peril, to put off the duty of a visit, as for the present she needed repose. Meanwhile, pretending that she felt secure, she applied remedies to her wound, and fomentations to her person. She then ordered search to be made for the will of Acerronia, and her property to be sealed, in this alone throwing off disguise.

Nero, meantime, as he waited for tidings of the consummation of the deed, received information that she had escaped with the injury of a slight wound, after having so far encountered the peril that there could be no question as to its author. Then, paralysed with terror and protesting that she would show herself the next moment eager for vengeance, either arming the slaves or stirring up the soldiery, or hastening to the Senate and the people, to charge him with the wreck, with her wound, and with the destruction of her friends, he asked what resource he had against all this, unless something could be at once devised by Burrus and Seneca. He had instantly summoned both of them, and possibly they were already in the secret. There was a long silence on their part; they feared they might remonstrate in vain, or believed the crisis to be such that Nero must perish, unless Agrippina were at once crushed. Thereupon Seneca was so far the more prompt as to glance back on Burrus, as if to ask him whether the bloody deed must be required of the soldiers. Burrus replied "that the praetorians were attached to the whole family of the Caesars, and remembering Germanicus would not dare a savage deed on his offspring. It was for Anicetus to accomplish his promise."

Anicetus, without a pause, claimed for himself the consummation of the crime. At those words, Nero declared that that day gave him empire, and that a freedman was the author of this mighty boon. "Go," he said, "with all speed and take with you the men readiest to execute your orders." He himself, when he had heard of the arrival of Agrippina's messenger, Agerinus, contrived a theatrical mode of accusation, and, while the man was repeating his message, threw down a sword at his feet, then ordered him to be put in irons, as a detected criminal, so that he might invent a story how his mother had plotted the emperor's destruction and in the shame of discovered guilt had by her own choice sought death.

Meantime, Agrippina's peril being universally known and taken to be an accidental occurrence, everybody, the moment he heard of it, hurried down to the beach. Some climbed projecting piers; some the nearest vessels; others, as far as their stature allowed, went into the sea; some, again, stood with outstretched arms, while the whole shore rung with wailings, with prayers and cries, as different questions were asked and uncertain answers given. A vast multitude streamed to the spot with torches, and as soon as all knew that she was safe, they at once prepared to wish her joy, till the sight of an armed and threatening force scared them away. Anicetus then surrounded the house with a guard, and having burst open the gates, dragged off the slaves who met him, till he came to the door of her chamber, where a few still stood, after the rest had fled in terror at the attack. A small lamp was in the room, and one slave-girl with Agrippina, who grew more and more anxious, as no messenger came from her son, not even Agerinus, while the appearance of the shore was changed, a solitude one moment, then sudden bustle and tokens of the worst catastrophe. As the girl rose to depart, she exclaimed, "Do you too forsake me?" and looking round saw Anicetus, who had with him the captain of the trireme, Herculeius, and Obaritus, a centurion of marines. "If," said she, "you have come to see me, take back word that I have recovered, but if you are here to do a crime, I believe nothing about my son; he has not ordered his mother's murder."

The assassins closed in round her couch, and the captain of the trireme first struck her head violently with a club. Then, as the centurion bared his sword for the fatal deed, presenting her person, she exclaimed, "Smite my womb," and with many wounds she was slain.

So far our accounts agree. That Nero gazed on his mother after her death and praised her beauty, some have related, while others deny it. Her body was burnt that same night on a dining couch, with a mean funeral; nor, as long as Nero was in power, was the earth raised into a mound, or even decently closed. Subsequently, she received from the solicitude of her domestics, a humble sepulchre on the road to Misenum, near the country house of Caesar the Dictator, which from a great height commands a view of the bay beneath. As soon as the funeral pile was lighted, one of her freedmen, surnamed Mnester, ran himself through with a sword, either from love of his mistress or from the fear of destruction.

Many years before Agrippina had anticipated this end for herself and had spurned the thought. For when she consulted the astrologers about Nero, they replied that he would be emperor and kill his mother. "Let him kill her," she said, "provided he is emperor."

But the emperor, when the crime was at last accomplished, realised its portentous guilt. The rest of the night, now silent and stupified, now and still oftener starting up in terror, bereft of reason, he awaited the dawn as if it would bring with it his doom. He was first encouraged to hope by the flattery addressed to him, at the prompting of Burrus, by the centurions and tribunes, who again and again pressed his hand and congratulated him on his having escaped an unforeseen danger and his mother's daring crime. Then his friends went to the temples, and, an example having once been set, the neighbouring towns of Campania testified their joy with sacrifices and deputations. He himself, with an opposite phase of hypocrisy, seemed sad, and almost angry at his own deliverance, and shed tears over his mother's death. But as the aspects of places change not, as do the looks of men, and as he had ever before his eyes the dreadful sight of that sea with its shores (some too believed that the notes of a funereal trumpet were heard from the surrounding heights, and wailings from the mother's grave), he retired to Neapolis and sent a letter to the Senate, the drift of which was that Agerinus, one of Agrippina's confidential freedmen, had been detected with the dagger of an assassin, and that in the consciousness of having planned the crime she had paid its penalty.

He even revived the charges of a period long past, how she had aimed at a share of empire, and at inducing the praetorian cohorts to swear obedience to a woman, to the disgrace of the Senate and people; how, when she was disappointed, in her fury with the soldiers, the Senate, and the populace, she opposed the usual donative and largess, and organised perilous prosecutions against distinguished citizens. What efforts had it cost him to hinder her from bursting into the Senate-house and giving answers to foreign nations! He glanced too with indirect censure at the days of Claudius, and ascribed all the abominations of that reign to his mother, thus seeking to show that it was the State's good fortune which had destroyed her. For he actually told the story of the shipwreck; but who could be so stupid as to believe that it was accidental, or that a shipwrecked woman had sent one man with a weapon to break through an emperor's guards and fleets? So now it was not Nero, whose brutality was far beyond any remonstrance, but Seneca who was in ill repute, for having written a confession in such a style.

Still there was a marvellous rivalry among the nobles in decreeing thanksgivings at all the shrines, and the celebration with annual games of Minerva's festival, as the day on which the plot had been discovered; also, that a golden image of Minerva with a statue of the emperor by its side should be set up in the Senate-house, and that Agrippina's birthday should be classed among the inauspicious days. Thrasea Paetus, who had been used to pass over previous flatteries in silence or with brief assent, then walked out of the Senate, thereby imperilling himself, without communicating to the other senators any impulse towards freedom.

There occurred too a thick succession of portents, which meant nothing. A woman gave birth to a snake, and another was killed by a thunderbolt in her husband's embrace. Then the sun was suddenly darkened and the fourteen districts of the city were struck by lightning. All this happened quite without any providential design; so much so, that for many subsequent years Nero prolonged his reign and his crimes. Still, to deepen the popular hatred towards his mother, and prove that since her removal, his clemency had increased, he restored to their ancestral homes two distinguished ladies, Junia and Calpurnia, with two ex-praetors, Valerius Capito and Licinius Gabolus, whom Agrippina had formerly banished. He also allowed the ashes of Lollia Paulina to be brought back and a tomb to be built over them. Iturius and Calvisius, whom he had himself temporarily exiled, he now released from their penalty. Silana indeed had died a natural death at Tarentum, whither she had returned from her distant exile, when the power of Agrippina, to whose enmity she owed her fall, began to totter, or her wrath was at last appeased.

While Nero was lingering in the towns of Campania, doubting how he should enter Rome, whether he would find the Senate submissive and the populace enthusiastic, all the vilest courtiers, and of these never had a court a more abundant crop, argued against his hesitation by assuring him that Agrippina's name was hated and that her death had heightened his popularity. "He might go without a fear," they said, "and experience in his person men's veneration for him." They insisted at the same time on preceding him. They found greater enthusiasm than they had promised, the tribes coming forth to meet him, the Senate in holiday attire, troops of their children and wives arranged according to sex and age, tiers of seats raised for the spectacle, where he was to pass, as a triumph is witnessed. Thus elated and exulting over his people's slavery, he proceeded to the Capitol, performed the thanksgiving, and then plunged into all the excesses, which, though ill-restrained, some sort of respect for his mother had for a while delayed.

He had long had a fancy for driving a four-horse chariot, and a no less degrading taste for singing to the harp, in a theatrical fashion, when he was at dinner. This he would remind people was a royal custom, and had been the practice of ancient chiefs; it was celebrated too in the praises of poets and was meant to show honour to the gods. Songs indeed, he said, were sacred to Apollo, and it was in the dress of a singer that that great and prophetic deity was seen in Roman temples as well as in Greek cities. He could no longer be restrained, when Seneca and Burrus thought it best to concede one point that he might not persist in both. A space was enclosed in the Vatican valley where he might manage his horses, without the spectacle being public. Soon he actually invited all the people of Rome, who extolled him in their praises, like a mob which craves for amusements and rejoices when a prince draws them the same way. However, the public exposure of his shame acted on him as an incentive instead of sickening him, as men expected. Imagining that he mitigated the scandal by disgracing many others, he brought on the stage descendants of noble families, who sold themselves because they were paupers. As they have ended their days, I think it due to their ancestors not to hand down their names. And indeed the infamy is his who gave them wealth to reward their degradation rather than to deter them from degrading themselves. He prevailed too on some well-known Roman knights, by immense presents, to offer their services in the amphitheatre; only pay from one who is able to command, carries with it the force of compulsion.

Still, not yet wishing to disgrace himself on a public stage, he instituted some games under the title of "juvenile sports," for which people of every class gave in their names. Neither rank nor age nor previous high promotion hindered any one from practising the art of a Greek or Latin actor and even stooping to gestures and songs unfit for a man. Noble ladies too actually played disgusting parts, and in the grove, with which Augustus had surrounded the lake for the naval fight, there were erected places for meeting and refreshment, and every incentive to excess was offered for sale. Money too was distributed, which the respectable had to spend under sheer compulsion and which the profligate gloried in squandering. Hence a rank growth of abominations and of all infamy. Never did a more filthy rabble add a worse licentiousness to our long corrupted morals. Even, with virtuous training, purity is not easily upheld; far less amid rivalries in vice could modesty or propriety or any trace of good manners be preserved. Last of all, the emperor himself came on the stage, tuning his lute with elaborate care and trying his voice with his attendants. There were also present, to complete the show, a guard of soldiers with centurions and tribunes, and Burrus, who grieved and yet applauded. Then it was that Roman knights were first enrolled under the title of Augustani, men in their prime and remarkable for their strength, some, from a natural frivolity, others from the hope of promotion. Day and night they kept up a thunder of applause, and applied to the emperor's person and voice the epithets of deities. Thus they lived in fame and honour, as if on the strength of their merits.

Nero however, that he might not be known only for his accomplishments as an actor, also affected a taste for poetry, and drew round him persons who had some skill in such compositions, but not yet generally recognised. They used to sit with him, stringing together verses prepared at home, or extemporised on the spot, and fill up his own expressions, such as they were, just as he threw them off. This is plainly shown by the very character of the poems, which have no vigour or inspiration, or unity in their flow.

He would also bestow some leisure after his banquets on the teachers of philosophy, for he enjoyed the wrangles of opposing dogmatists. And some there were who liked to exhibit their gloomy faces and looks, as one of the amusements of the court.

About the same time a trifling beginning led to frightful bloodshed between the inhabitants of Nuceria and Pompeii, at a gladiatorial show exhibited by Livineius Regulus, who had been, as I have related, expelled from the Senate. With the unruly spirit of townsfolk, they began with abusive language of each other; then they took up stones and at last weapons, the advantage resting with the populace of Pompeii, where the show was being exhibited. And so there were brought to Rome a number of the people of Nuceria, with their bodies mutilated by wounds, and many lamented the deaths of children or of parents. The emperor entrusted the trial of the case to the Senate, and the Senate to the consuls, and then again the matter being referred back to the Senators, the inhabitants of Pompeii were forbidden to have any such public gathering for ten years, and all associations they had formed in defiance of the laws were dissolved. Livineius and the others who had excited the disturbance, were punished with exile.

Pedius Blaesus was also expelled from the Senate on the accusation of the people of Cyrene, that he had violated the treasury of Aesculapius and had tampered with a military levy by bribery and corruption. This same people prosecuted Acilius Strabo who had held the office of praetor, and had been sent by Claudius to adjudicate on some lands which were bequeathed by king Apion, their former possessor, together with his kingdom to the Roman people, and which had since been seized by the neighbouring proprietors, who trusted to a long continued licence in wrong, as if it constituted right and justice. Consequently, when the adjudication was against them, there arose a bitter feeling towards the judge, but the Senate replied that they knew nothing of the instructions given by Claudius, and that the emperor must be consulted. Nero, though he approved Strabo's decision, wrote word that nevertheless he was for relieving the allies, and that he waived all claim to what had been taken into possession.

Then followed the deaths of two illustrious men, Domitius Afer and Marcus Servilius, who had flourished through a career of the highest honours and great eloquence. The first was a pleader; Servilius, after long practice in the courts, distinguished himself by his history of Rome and by the refinement of his life, which the contrast of his character to that of Afer, whom he equalled in genius, rendered the more conspicuous.

In Nero's fourth consulship with Cornelius Cossus for his colleague, a theatrical entertainment to be repeated every five years was established at Rome in imitation of the Greek festival. Like all novelties, it was variously canvassed. There were some who declared that even Cnius Pompeius was censured by the older men of the day for having set up a fixed and permanent theatre. "Formerly," they said, "the games were usually exhibited with hastily erected tiers of benches and a temporary stage, and the people stood to witness them, that they might not, by having the chance of sitting down, spend a succession of entire days in idleness. Let the ancient character of these shows be retained, whenever the praetors exhibited them, and let no citizen be under the necessity of competing. As it was, the morality of their fathers, which had by degrees been forgotten, was utterly subverted by the introduction of a lax tone, so that all which could suffer or produce corruption was to be seen at Rome, and a degeneracy bred by foreign tastes was infecting the youth who devoted themselves to athletic sports, to idle loungings and low intrigues, with the encouragement of the emperor and Senate, who not only granted licence to vice, but even applied a compulsion to drive Roman nobles into disgracing themselves on the stage, under the pretence of being orators and poets. What remained for them but to strip themselves naked, put on the boxing-glove, and practise such battles instead of the arms of legitimate warfare? Would justice be promoted, or would they serve on the knights' commissions for the honourable office of a judge, because they had listened with critical sagacity to effeminate strains of music and sweet voices? Night too was given up to infamy, so that virtue had not a moment left to her, but all the vilest of that promiscuous throng dared to do in the darkness anything they had lusted for in the day."

Many people liked this very licence, but they screened it under respectable names. "Our ancestors," they said, "were not averse to the attractions of shows on a scale suited to the wealth of their day, and so they introduced actors from the Etruscans and horse-races from Thurii. When we had possessed ourselves of Achaia and Asia, games were exhibited with greater elaboration, and yet no one at Rome of good family had stooped to the theatrical profession during the 200 years following the triumph of Lucius Mummius, who first displayed this kind of show in the capital. Besides, even economy had been consulted, when a permanent edifice was erected for a theatre, in preference to a structure raised and fitted up yearly at vast expense. Nor would the magistrates, as hitherto, exhaust their substance, or would the populace have the same motive for demanding of them the Greek contests, when once the State undertakes the expenditure. The victories won by orators and poets would furnish a stimulus to genius, and it could not be a burden for any judge to bestow his attention on graceful pursuits or on legitimate recreations. It was to mirth rather than to profligacy that a few nights every five years were devoted, and in these amid such a blaze of illumination no lawless conduct could be concealed."

This entertainment, it is true, passed off without any notorious scandal. The enthusiasm too of the populace was not even slightly kindled, for the pantomimic actors, though permitted to return to the stage, were excluded from the sacred contests. No one gained the first prize for eloquence, but it was publicly announced that the emperor was victorious. Greek dresses, in which most people showed themselves during this festival, had then gone out of fashion.

A comet meantime blazed in the sky, which in popular opinion always portends revolution to kingdoms. So people began to ask, as if Nero was already dethroned, who was to be elected. In every one's mouth was the name of Rubellius Blandus, who inherited through his mother the high nobility of the Julian family. He was himself attached to the ideas of our ancestors; his manners were austere, his home was one of purity and seclusion, and the more he lived in retirement from fear, the more fame did he acquire. Popular talk was confirmed by an interpretation put with similar credulity on a flash of lightning. While Nero was reclining at dinner in his house named Sublaqueum on the Simbruine lake, the table with the banquet was struck and shattered, and as this happened close to Tibur, from which town Plautus derived his origin on his father's side, people believed him to be the man marked out by divine providence; and he was encouraged by that numerous class, whose eager and often mistaken ambition it is to attach themselves prematurely to some new and hazardous cause. This alarmed Nero, and he wrote a letter to Plautus, bidding "him consider the tranquillity of Rome and withdraw himself from mischievous gossip. He had ancestral possessions in Asia, where he might enjoy his youth safely and quietly." And so thither Plautus retired with his wife Antistia and a few intimate friends.

About the same time an excessive love of luxurious gratification involved Nero in disgrace and danger. He had plunged for a swim into the source of the stream which Quintus Marcius conveyed to Rome, and it was thought that, by thus immersing his person in it, he had polluted the sacred waters and the sanctity of the spot. A fit of illness which followed, convinced people of the divine displeasure.

Corbulo meanwhile having demolished Artaxata thought that he ought to avail himself of the recent panic by possessing himself of Tigranocerta, and either, by destroying it, increase the enemy's terror, or, by sparing it, win a name for mercy. Thither he marched his army, with no hostile demonstrations, lest might cut off all hope of quarter, but still without relaxing his vigilance, knowing, as he did, the fickle temper of the people, who are as treacherous, when they have an opportunity, as they are slow to meet danger. The barbarians, following their individual inclinations, either came to him with entreaties, or quitted their villages and dispersed into their deserts. Some there were who hid themselves in caverns with all that they held dearest. The Roman general accordingly dealt variously with them; he was merciful to suppliants, swift in pursuit of fugitives, pitiless towards those who had crept into hiding-places, burning them out after filling up the entrances and exits with brushwood and bushes. As he was on his march along the frontier of the Mardi, he was incessantly attacked by that tribe which is trained to guerilla warfare, and defended by mountains against an invader. Corbulo threw the Iberians on them, ravaged their country and punished the enemy's daring at the cost of the blood of the foreigner.

Both Corbulo and his army, though suffering no losses in battle, were becoming exhausted by short supplies and hardships, compelled as they were to stave off hunger solely by the flesh of cattle. Added to this was scarcity of water, a burning summer and long marches, all of which were alleviated only by the general's patient endurance. He bore indeed the same or even more burdens than the common soldier. Subsequently, they reached lands under cultivation, and reaped the crops, and of two fortresses in which the Armenians had fled for refuge, one was taken by storm; the other, which repulsed the first attack, was reduced by blockade. Thence the general crossed into the country of the Tauraunites, where he escaped an unforeseen peril. Near his tent, a barbarian of no mean rank was discovered with a dagger, who divulged under torture the whole method of the plot, its contrivance by himself, and his associates. The men who under a show of friendship planned the treachery, were convicted and punished.

Soon afterwards, Corbulo's envoys whom he had sent to Tigranocerta, reported that the city walls were open, and the inhabitants awaiting orders. They also handed him a gift denoting friendship, a golden crown, which he acknowledged in complimentary language. Nothing was done to humiliate the city, that remaining uninjured it might continue to yield a more cheerful obedience.

The citadel, however, which had been closed by an intrepid band of youths, was not stormed without a struggle. They even ventured on an engagement under the walls, but were driven back within their fortifications and succumbed at last only to our siege-works and to the swords of furious assailants. The success was the easier, as the Parthians were distracted by a war with the Hyrcanians, who had sent to the Roman emperor, imploring alliance, and pointing to the fact that they were detaining Vologeses as a pledge of amity. When these envoys were on their way home, Corbulo, to save them from being intercepted by the enemy's picquets after their passage of the Euphrates, gave them an escort, and conducted them to the shores of the Red Sea, whence, avoiding Parthian territory, they returned to their native possessions.

Corbulo too, as Tiridates was entering the Armenian frontier through Media, sent on Verulanus, his lieutenant-general with the auxiliaries, while he himself followed with the legions by forced marches, and compelled him to retreat to a distance and abandon the idea of war. Having harried with fire and sword all whom he had ascertained to be against us, he began to take possession of Armenia, when Tigranes arrived, whom Nero had selected to assume the sovereignty. Though a Cappadocian noble and grandson of king Archelaus, yet, from having long been a hostage at Rome, he had sunk into servile submissiveness. Nor was he unanimously welcomed, as some still cherished a liking for the Arsacids. Most, however, in their hatred of Parthian arrogance preferred a king given them by Rome. He was supported too with a force of a thousand legionaries, three allied cohorts and two squadrons of cavalry, that he might the more easily secure his new kingdom. Parts of Armenia, according to their respective proximities, were put under the subjection of Pharasmanes, Polemo, Aristobulus, and Antiochus. Corbulo retired into Syria, which province, as being vacant by the death of its governor Ummidius, was intrusted to him.

One of the famous cities of Asia, Laodicea, was that same year overthrown by an earthquake, and, without any relief from us, recovered itself by its own resources. In Italy meanwhile the old town of Puteoli obtained from Nero the privileges of a colony with an additional name. A further enrolment of veterans in Tarentum and Antium did but little for those thinly peopled places; for most scattered themselves in the provinces where they had completed their military service. Not being accustomed to tie themselves by marriage and rear children, they left behind them homes without families. For whole legions were no longer transplanted, as in former days, with tribunes and centurions and soldiers of every grade, so as to form a state by their unity and mutual attachment, but strangers to one another from different companies, without a head or any community of sentiment, were suddenly gathered together, as it might be out of any other class of human beings, and became a mere crowd rather than a colony.

As at the elections for praetors, now generally under the Senate's control there was the excitement of a particularly keen competition, the emperor quieted matters by promoting the three supernumerary candidates to legionary commands. He also raised the dignity of the Senate, by deciding that all who appealed from private judges to its house, were to incur the same pecuniary risk as those who referred their cause to the emperor. Hitherto such an appeal had been perfectly open, and free from penalty.

At the close of the year Vibius Secundus, a Roman knight, on the accusation of the Moors, was convicted of extortion, and banished from Italy, contriving through the influence of his brother Vibius Crispus to escape heavier punishment.

In the consulship of Caesonius Paetus and Petronius Turpilianus, a serious disaster was sustained in Britain, where Aulius Didius, the emperor's legate, had merely retained our existing possessions, and his successor Veranius, after having ravaged the Silures in some trifling raids, was prevented by death from extending the war. While he lived, he had a great name for manly independence, though, in his will's final words, he betrayed a flatterer's weakness; for, after heaping adulation on Nero, he added that he should have conquered the province for him, had he lived for the next two years. Now, however, Britain was in the hands of Suetonius Paulinus, who in military knowledge and in popular favour, which allows no one to be without a rival, vied with Corbulo, and aspired to equal the glory of the recovery of Armenia by the subjugation of Rome's enemies. He therefore prepared to attack the island of Mona which had a powerful population and was a refuge for fugitives. He built flat-bottomed vessels to cope with the shallows, and uncertain depths of the sea. Thus the infantry crossed, while the cavalry followed by fording, or, where the water was deep, swam by the side of their horses.

On the shore stood the opposing army with its dense array of armed warriors, while between the ranks dashed women, in black attire like the Furies, with hair dishevelled, waving brands. All around, the Druids, lifting up their hands to heaven, and pouring forth dreadful imprecations, scared our soldiers by the unfamiliar sight, so that, as if their limbs were paralysed, they stood motionless, and exposed to wounds. Then urged by their general's appeals and mutual encouragements not to quail before a troop of frenzied women, they bore the standards onwards, smote down all resistance, and wrapped the foe in the flames of his own brands. A force was next set over the conquered, and their groves, devoted to inhuman superstitions, were destroyed. They deemed it indeed a duty to cover their altars with the blood of captives and to consult their deities through human entrails.

Suetonius while thus occupied received tidings of the sudden revolt of the province. Prasutagus, king of the Iceni, famed for his long prosperity, had made the emperor his heir along with his two daughters, under the impression that this token of submission would put his kingdom and his house out of the reach of wrong. But the reverse was the result, so much so that his kingdom was plundered by centurions, his house by slaves, as if they were the spoils of war. First, his wife Boudicea was scourged, and his daughters outraged. All the chief men of the Iceni, as if Rome had received the whole country as a gift, were stript of their ancestral possessions, and the king's relatives were made slaves. Roused by these insults and the dread of worse, reduced as they now were into the condition of a province, they flew to arms and stirred to revolt the Trinobantes and others who, not yet cowed by slavery, had agreed in secret conspiracy to reclaim their freedom. It was against the veterans that their hatred was most intense. For these new settlers in the colony of Camulodunum drove people out of their houses, ejected them from their farms, called them captives and slaves, and the lawlessness of the veterans was encouraged by the soldiers, who lived a similar life and hoped for similar licence. A temple also erected to the Divine Claudius was ever before their eyes, a citadel, as it seemed, of perpetual tyranny. Men chosen as priests had to squander their whole fortunes under the pretence of a religious ceremonial. It appeared too no difficult matter to destroy the colony, undefended as it was by fortifications, a precaution neglected by our generals, while they thought more of what was agreeable than of what was expedient.

Meanwhile, without any evident cause, the statue of Victory at Camulodunum fell prostrate and turned its back to the enemy, as though it fled before them. Women excited to frenzy prophesied impending destruction; ravings in a strange tongue, it was said, were heard in their Senate-house; their theatre resounded with wailings, and in the estuary of the Tamesa had been seen the appearance of an overthrown town; even the ocean had worn the aspect of blood, and, when the tide ebbed, there had been left the likenesses of human forms, marvels interpreted by the Britons, as hopeful, by the veterans, as alarming. But as Suetonius was far away, they implored aid from the procurator, Catus Decianus. All he did was to send two hundred men, and no more, without regular arms, and there was in the place but a small military force. Trusting to the protection of the temple, hindered too by secret accomplices in the revolt, who embarrassed their plans, they had constructed neither fosse nor rampart; nor had they removed their old men and women, leaving their youth alone to face the foe. Surprised, as it were, in the midst of peace, they were surrounded by an immense host of the barbarians. All else was plundered or fired in the onslaught; the temple where the soldiers had assembled, was stormed after a two days' siege. The victorious enemy met Petilius Cerialis, commander of the ninth legion, as he was coming to the rescue, routed his troops, and destroyed all his infantry. Cerialis escaped with some cavalry into the camp, and was saved by its fortifications. Alarmed by this disaster and by the fury of the province which he had goaded into war by his rapacity, the procurator Catus crossed over into Gaul.

Suetonius, however, with wonderful resolution, marched amidst a hostile population to Londinium, which, though undistinguished by the name of a colony, was much frequented by a number of merchants and trading vessels. Uncertain whether he should choose it as a seat of war, as he looked round on his scanty force of soldiers, and remembered with what a serious warning the rashness of Petilius had been punished, he resolved to save the province at the cost of a single town. Nor did the tears and weeping of the people, as they implored his aid, deter him from giving the signal of departure and receiving into his army all who would go with him. Those who were chained to the spot by the weakness of their sex, or the infirmity of age, or the attractions of the place, were cut off by the enemy. Like ruin fell on the town of Verulamium, for the barbarians, who delighted in plunder and were indifferent to all else, passed by the fortresses with military garrisons, and attacked whatever offered most wealth to the spoiler, and was unsafe for defence. About seventy thousand citizens and allies, it appeared, fell in the places which I have mentioned. For it was not on making prisoners and selling them, or on any of the barter of war, that the enemy was bent, but on slaughter, on the gibbet, the fire and the cross, like men soon about to pay the penalty, and meanwhile snatching at instant vengeance.

Suetonius had the fourteenth legion with the veterans of the twentieth, and auxiliaries from the neighbourhood, to the number of about ten thousand armed men, when he prepared to break off delay and fight a battle. He chose a position approached by a narrow defile, closed in at the rear by a forest, having first ascertained that there was not a soldier of the enemy except in his front, where an open plain extended without any danger from ambuscades. His legions were in close array; round them, the light-armed troops, and the cavalry in dense array on the wings. On the other side, the army of the Britons, with its masses of infantry and cavalry, was confidently exulting, a vaster host than ever had assembled, and so fierce in spirit that they actually brought with them, to witness the victory, their wives riding in waggons, which they had placed on the extreme border of the plain.

Boudicea, with her daughters before her in a chariot, went up to tribe after tribe, protesting that it was indeed usual for Britons to fight under the leadership of women. "But now," she said, "it is not as a woman descended from noble ancestry, but as one of the people that I am avenging lost freedom, my scourged body, the outraged chastity of my daughters. Roman lust has gone so far that not our very persons, nor even age or virginity, are left unpolluted. But heaven is on the side of a righteous vengeance; a legion which dared to fight has perished; the rest are hiding themselves in their camp, or are thinking anxiously of flight. They will not sustain even the din and the shout of so many thousands, much less our charge and our blows. If you weigh well the strength of the armies, and the causes of the war, you will see that in this battle you must conquer or die. This is a woman's resolve; as for men, they may live and be slaves."

Nor was Suetonius silent at such a crisis. Though he confided in the valour of his men, he yet mingled encouragements and entreaties to disdain the clamours and empty threats of the barbarians. "There," he said, "you see more women than warriors. Unwarlike, unarmed, they will give way the moment they have recognised that sword and that courage of their conquerors, which have so often routed them. Even among many legions, it is a few who really decide the battle, and it will enhance their glory that a small force should earn the renown of an entire army. Only close up the ranks, and having discharged your javelins, then with shields and swords continue the work of bloodshed and destruction, without a thought of plunder. When once the victory has been won, everything will be in your power."

Such was the enthusiasm which followed the general's address, and so promptly did the veteran soldiery, with their long experience of battles, prepare for the hurling of the javelins, that it was with confidence in the result that Suetonius gave the signal of battle.

At first, the legion kept its position, clinging to the narrow defile as a defence; when they had exhausted their missiles, which they discharged with unerring aim on the closely approaching foe, they rushed out in a wedge-like column. Similar was the onset of the auxiliaries, while the cavalry with extended lances broke through all who offered a strong resistance. The rest turned their back in flight, and flight proved difficult, because the surrounding waggons had blocked retreat. Our soldiers spared not to slay even the women, while the very beasts of burden, transfixed by the missiles, swelled the piles of bodies. Great glory, equal to that of our old victories, was won on that day. Some indeed say that there fell little less than eighty thousand of the Britons, with a loss to our soldiers of about four hundred, and only as many wounded. Boudicea put an end to her life by poison. Poenius Postumus too, camp-prefect of the second legion, when he knew of the success of the men of the fourteenth and twentieth, feeling that he had cheated his legion out of like glory, and had contrary to all military usage disregarded the general's orders, threw himself on his sword.

The whole army was then brought together and kept under canvas to finish the remainder of the war. The emperor strengthened the forces by sending from Germany two thousand legionaries, eight cohorts of auxiliaries, and a thousand cavalry. On their arrival the men of the ninth had their number made up with legionary soldiers. The allied infantry and cavalry were placed in new winter quarters, and whatever tribes still wavered or were hostile were ravaged with fire and sword. Nothing however distressed the enemy so much as famine, for they had been careless about sowing corn, people of every age having gone to the war, while they reckoned on our supplies as their own. Nations, too, so high-spirited inclined the more slowly to peace, because Julius Classicanus, who had been sent as successor to Catus and was at variance with Suetonius, let private animosities interfere with the public interest, and had spread an idea that they ought to wait for a new governor who, having neither the anger of an enemy nor the pride of a conqueror, would deal mercifully with those who had surrendered. At the same time he stated in a despatch to Rome that no cessation of fighting must be expected, unless Suetonius were superseded, attributing that general's disasters to perverseness and his successes to good luck.

Accordingly one of the imperial freedmen, Polyclitus, was sent to survey the state of Britain, Nero having great hopes that his influence would be able not only to establish a good understanding between the governor and the pro-curator, but also to pacify the rebellious spirit of the barbarians. And Polyclitus, who with his enormous suite had been a burden to Italy and Gaul, failed not, as soon as he had crossed the ocean, to make his progresses a terror even to our soldiers. But to the enemy he was a laughing-stock, for they still retained some of the fire of liberty, knowing nothing yet of the power of freedmen, and so they marvelled to see a general and an army who had finished such a war cringing to slaves. Everything, however, was softened down for the emperor's ears, and Suetonius was retained in the government; but as he subsequently lost a few vessels on the shore with the crews, he was ordered, as though the war continued, to hand over his army to Petronius Turpilianus, who had just resigned his consulship. Petronius neither challenged the enemy nor was himself molested, and veiled this tame inaction under the honourable name of peace.

That same year two remarkable crimes were committed at Rome, one by a senator, the other by the daring of a slave. Domitius Balbus, an ex-praetor, from his prolonged old age, his childlessness and his wealth, was exposed to many a plot. His kinsman, Valerius Fabianus, who was marked out for a career of promotion, forged a will in his name with Vinicius Rufinus and Terentius Lentinus, Roman knights, for his accomplices. These men had associated with them Antonius Primus and Asinius Marcellus. Antonius was a man of ready audacity; Marcellus had the glory of being the great-grandson of Asinius Pollio, and bore a character far from contemptible, except that he thought poverty the greatest of all evils. So Fabianus, with the persons whom I have named and some others less distinguished, executed the will. The crime was proved against them before the Senate, and Fabianus and Antonius with Rufinus and Terentius were condemned under the Cornelian law. Marcellus was saved from punishment rather than from disgrace by the memory of his ancestors and the intercessions of the emperor.

That same day was fatal also to Pompeius Aelianus, a young ex-quaestor, suspected of complicity in the villanies of Fabianus. He was outlawed from Italy, and from Spain, where he was born. Valerius Pontius suffered the same degradation for having indicted the defendants before the praetor to save them from being prosecuted in the court of the city-prefect, purposing meanwhile to defeat justice on some legal pretext and subsequently by collusion. A clause was added to the Senate's decree, that whoever bought or sold such a service was to be just as liable to punishment as if he had been publicly convicted of false accusation.

Soon afterwards one of his own slaves murdered the city-prefect, Pedanius Secundus, either because he had been refused his freedom, for which he had made a bargain, or in the jealousy of a love in which he could not brook his master's rivalry. Ancient custom required that the whole slave-establishment which had dwelt under the same roof should be dragged to execution, when a sudden gathering of the populace, which was for saving so many innocent lives, brought matters to actual insurrection. Even in the Senate there was a strong feeling on the part of those who shrank from extreme rigour, though the majority were opposed to any innovation. Of these, Caius Cassius, in giving his vote, argued to the following effect:—

"Often have I been present, Senators, in this assembly when new decrees were demanded from us contrary to the customs and laws of our ancestors, and I have refrained from opposition, not because I doubted but that in all matters the arrangements of the past were better and fairer and that all changes were for the worse, but that I might not seem to be exalting my own profession out of an excessive partiality for ancient precedent. At the same time I thought that any influence I possess ought not to be destroyed by incessant protests, wishing that it might remain unimpaired, should the State ever need my counsels. To-day this has come to pass, since an ex-consul has been murdered in his house by the treachery of slaves, which not one hindered or divulged, though the Senate's decree, which threatens the entire slave-establishment with execution, has been till now unshaken. Vote impunity, in heaven's name, and then who will be protected by his rank, when the prefecture of the capital has been of no avail to its holder? Who will be kept safe by the number of his slaves when four hundred have not protected Pedanius Secundus? Which of us will be rescued by his domestics, who, even with the dread of punishment before them, regard not our dangers? Was the murderer, as some do not blush to pretend, avenging his wrongs because he had bargained about money from his father or because a family-slave was taken from him? Let us actually decide that the master was justly slain.

"Is it your pleasure to search for arguments in a matter already weighed in the deliberations of wiser men than ourselves? Even if we had now for the first time to come to a decision, do you believe that a slave took courage to murder his master without letting fall a threatening word or uttering a rash syllable? Granted that he concealed his purpose, that he procured his weapon without his fellows' knowledge. Could he pass the night-guard, could he open the doors of the chamber, carry in a light, and accomplish the murder, while all were in ignorance? There are many preliminaries to guilt; if these are divulged by slaves, we may live singly amid numbers, safe among a trembling throng; lastly, if we must perish, it will be with vengeance on the guilty. Our ancestors always suspected the temper of their slaves, even when they were born on the same estates, or in the same houses with themselves and thus inherited from their birth an affection for their masters. But now that we have in our households nations with different customs to our own, with a foreign worship or none at all, it is only by terror you can hold in such a motley rabble. But, it will be said, the innocent will perish. Well, even in a beaten army when every tenth man is felled by the club, the lot falls also on the brave. There is some injustice in every great precedent, which, though injurious to individuals, has its compensation in the public advantage."

No one indeed dared singly to oppose the opinion of Cassius, but clamorous voices rose in reply from all who pitied the number, age, or sex, as well as the undoubted innocence of the great majority. Still, the party which voted for their execution prevailed. But the sentence could not be obeyed in the face of a dense and threatening mob, with stones and firebrands. Then the emperor reprimanded the people by edict, and lined with a force of soldiers the entire route by which the condemned had to be dragged to execution. Cingonius Varro had proposed that even all the freedmen under the same roof should be transported from Italy. This the emperor forbade, as he did not wish an ancient custom, which mercy had not relaxed, to be strained with cruel rigour.

During the same consulship, Tarquitius Priscus was convicted of extortion on the prosecution of the Bithynians, to the great joy of the senators, who remembered that he had impeached Statilius, his own pro-consul. An assessment was made of Gaul by Quintus Volusius, Sextius Africanus, and Trebellius Maximus. There was a rivalry, on the score of rank, between Volusius and Africanus. While they both disdained Trebellius, they raised him above themselves.

In that year died Memmius Regulus, who from his solid worth and consistency was as distinguished as it is possible to be under the shadow of an emperor's grandeur, so much so, in fact, that Nero when he was ill, with flatterers round him, who said that if aught befell him in the course of destiny, there must be an end of the empire, replied that the State had a resource, and on their asking where it was specially to be found, he added, "in Memmius Regulus." Yet Regulus lived after this, protected by his retiring habits, and by the fact that he was a man of newly-risen family and of wealth which did not provoke envy. Nero, the same year, established a gymnasium, where oil was furnished to knights and senators after the lax fashion of the Greeks.

In the consulship of Publius Marius and Lucius Asinius, Antistius, the praetor, whose lawless behaviour as tribune of the people I have mentioned, composed some libellous verses on the emperor, which he openly recited at a large gathering, when he was dining at the house of Ostorius Scapula. He was upon this impeached of high treason by Cossutianus Capito, who had lately been restored to a senator's rank on the intercession of his father-in-law, Tigellinus. This was the first occasion on which the law of treason was revived, and men thought that it was not so much the ruin of Antistius which was aimed at, as the glory of the emperor, whose veto as tribune might save from death one whom the Senate had condemned. Though Ostorius had stated that he had heard nothing as evidence, the adverse witnesses were believed, and Junius Marullus, consul-elect, proposed that the accused should be deprived of his praetorship, and be put to death in the ancient manner. The rest assented, and then Paetus Thrasea, after much eulogy of Caesar, and most bitter censure of Antistius, argued that it was not what a guilty prisoner might deserve to suffer, which ought to be decreed against him, under so excellent a prince, and by a Senate bound by no compulsion. "The executioner and the halter," he said, "we have long ago abolished; still, there are punishments ordained by the laws, which prescribe penalties, without judicial cruelty and disgrace to our age. Rather send him to some island, after confiscating his property; there, the longer he drags on his guilty life, the more wretched will he be personally, and the more conspicuous as an example of public clemency."

Thrasea's freespokenness broke through the servility of the other senators. As soon as the consul allowed a division, they voted with him, with but few exceptions. Among these, the most enthusiastic in his flattery was Aulus Vitellius, who attacked all the best men with abuse, and was silent when they replied, the usual way of a cowardly temper. The consuls, however, did not dare to ratify the Senate's vote, and simply communicated their unanimous resolution to the emperor. Hesitating for a while between shame and rage, he at last wrote to them in reply "that Antistius, without having been provoked by any wrong, had uttered outrageous insults against the sovereign; that a demand for punishment had been submitted to the Senate, and that it was right that a penalty should be decreed proportioned to the offence; that for himself, inasmuch as he would have opposed severity in the sentence, he would not be an obstacle to leniency. They might determine as they pleased, and they had free liberty to acquit."

This and more to the same effect having been read out, clearly showing his displeasure, the consuls did not for that reason alter the terms of the motion, nor did Thrasea withdraw his proposal, or the Senate reject what it had once approved. Some were afraid of seeming to expose the emperor to odium; the majority felt safe in numbers, while Thrasea was supported by his usual firmness of spirit, and a determination not to let his fame perish.

A similar accusation caused the downfall of Fabricius Veiento. He had composed many libels on senators and pontiffs in a work to which he gave the title of "Codicils." Talius Geminus, the prosecutor, further stated that he had habitually trafficked in the emperor's favours and in the right of promotion. This was Nero's reason for himself undertaking the trial, and having convicted Veiento, he banished him from Italy, and ordered the burning of his books, which, while it was dangerous to procure them, were anxiously sought and much read. Soon full freedom for their possession caused their oblivion.

But while the miseries of the State were daily growing worse, its supports were becoming weaker. Burrus died, whether from illness or from poison was a question. It was supposed to be illness from the fact that from the gradual swelling of his throat inwardly and the closing up of the passage he ceased to breathe. Many positively asserted that by Nero's order his throat was smeared with some poisonous drug under the pretence of the application of a remedy, and that Burrus, who saw through the crime, when the emperor paid him a visit, recoiled with horror from his gaze, and merely replied to his question, "I indeed am well." Rome felt for him a deep and lasting regret, because of the remembrance of his worth, because too of the merely passive virtue of one of his successors and the very flagrant iniquities of the other. For the emperor had appointed two men to the command of the praetorian cohorts, Faenius Rufus, for a vulgar popularity, which he owed to his administration of the corn-supplies without profit to himself; and Sofonius Tigellinus, whose inveterate shamelessness and infamy were an attraction to him. As might have been expected from their known characters, Tigellinus had the greater influence with the prince, and was the associate of his most secret profligacy, while Rufus enjoyed the favour of the people and of the soldiers, and this, he found, prejudiced him with Nero.

The death of Burrus was a blow to Seneca's power, for virtue had not the same strength when one of its companions, so to say, was removed, and Nero too began to lean on worse advisers. They assailed Seneca with various charges, representing that he continued to increase a wealth which was already so vast as to be beyond the scale of a subject, and was drawing to himself the attachment of the citizens, while in the picturesqueness of his gardens and the magnificence of his country houses he almost surpassed the emperor. They further alleged against him that he claimed for himself alone the honours of eloquence, and composed poetry more assiduously, as soon as a passion for it had seized on Nero. "Openly inimical to the prince's amusements, he disparaged his ability in driving horses, and ridiculed his voice whenever he sang. When was there to be an end of nothing being publicly admired but what Seneca was thought to have originated? Surely Nero's boyhood was over, and he was all but in the prime of youthful manhood. He ought to shake off a tutor, furnished as he was with sufficiently noble instructors in his own ancestors."

Seneca, meanwhile, aware of these slanders, which were revealed to him by those who had some respect for merit, coupled with the fact that the emperor more and more shunned his intimacy, besought the opportunity of an interview. This was granted, and he spoke as follows:—

"It is fourteen years ago, Caesar, that I was first associated with your prospects, and eight years since you have been emperor. In the interval, you have heaped on me such honours and riches that nothing is wanting to my happiness but a right use of it. I will refer to great examples taken not from my own but from your position. Your great-grandfather Augustus granted to Marcus Agrippa the calm repose of Mitylene, to Caius Maecenas what was nearly equivalent to a foreign retreat in the capital itself. One of these men shared his wars; the other struggled with many laborious duties at Rome; both received awards which were indeed splendid, but only proportioned to their great merits. For myself, what other recompense had I for your munificence, than a culture nursed, so to speak, in the shade of retirement, and to which a glory attaches itself, because I thus seem to have helped on the early training of your youth, an ample reward for the service.

"You on the other hand have surrounded me with vast influence and boundless wealth, so that I often think within myself, Am I, who am but of an equestrian and provincial family, numbered among the chief men of Rome? Among nobles who can show a long succession of glories, has my new name become famous? Where is the mind once content with a humble lot? Is this the man who is building up his garden terraces, who paces grandly through these suburban parks, and revels in the affluence of such broad lands and such widely-spread investments? Only one apology occurs to me, that it would not have been right in me to have thwarted your bounty.

"And yet we have both filled up our respective measures, you in giving as much as a prince can bestow on a friend, and I in receiving as much as a friend can receive from a prince. All else only fosters envy, which, like all things human, sinks powerless beneath your greatness, though on me it weighs heavily. To me relief is a necessity. Just as I should implore support if exhausted by warfare or travel, so in this journey of life, old as I am and unequal even to the lightest cares, since I cannot any longer bear the burden of my wealth, I crave assistance. Order my property to be managed by your agents and to be included in your estate. Still I shall not sink myself into poverty, but having surrendered the splendours which dazzle me, I will henceforth again devote to my mind all the leisure and attention now reserved for my gardens and country houses. You have yet before you a vigorous prime, and that on which for so many years your eyes were fixed, supreme power. We, your older friends, can answer for our quiet behaviour. It will likewise redound to your honour that you have raised to the highest places men who could also bear moderate fortune."

Nero's reply was substantially this:—"My being able to meet your elaborate speech with an instant rejoinder is, I consider, primarily your gift, for you taught me how to express myself not only after reflection but at a moment's notice. My great-grandfather Augustus allowed Agrippa and Maecenas to enjoy rest after their labours, but he did it at an age carrying with it an authority sufficient to justify any boon, of any sort, he might have bestowed. But neither of them did he strip of the rewards he had given. It was by war and its perils they had earned them; for in these the youth of Augustus was spent. And if I had passed my years in arms, your sword and right hand would not have failed me. But, as my actual condition required, you watched over my boyhood, then over my youth, with wisdom, counsel, and advice. And indeed your gifts to me will, as long as life holds out, be lasting possessions; those which you owe to me, your parks, investments, your country houses, are liable to accidents. Though they seem much, many far inferior to you in merit have obtained more. I am ashamed to quote the names of freedmen who parade a greater wealth. Hence I actually blush to think that, standing as you do first in my affections, you do not as yet surpass all in fortune.

"Yours too is a still vigorous manhood, quite equal to the labours of business and to the fruit of those labours; and, as for myself, I am but treading the threshold of empire.

But perhaps you count yourself inferior to Vitellius, thrice a consul, and me to Claudius. Such wealth as long thrift has procured for Volusius, my bounty, you think, cannot fully make up to you. Why not rather, if the frailty of my youth goes in any respect astray, call me back and guide yet more zealously with your help the manhood which you have instructed? It will not be your moderation, if you restore me your wealth, not your love of quiet, if you forsake your emperor, but my avarice, the fear of my cruelty, which will be in all men's mouths. Even if your self-control were praised to the utmost, still it would not be seemly in a wise man to get glory for himself in the very act of bringing disgrace on his friend."

To these words the emperor added embraces and kisses; for he was formed by nature and trained by habit to veil his hatred under delusive flattery. Seneca thanked him, the usual end of an interview with a despot. But he entirely altered the practices of his former greatness; he kept the crowds of his visitors at a distance, avoided trains of followers, seldom appeared in Rome, as though weak health or philosophical studies detained him at home.

When Seneca had fallen, it was easy to shake the position of Faenius Rufus by making Agrippina's friendship a charge against him. Tigellinus, who was daily becoming more powerful and who thought that the wicked schemings which alone gave him strength, would be better liked if he could secure the emperor's complicity in guilt, dived into Nero's most secret apprehensions, and, as soon as he had ascertained that Plautus and Sulla were the men he most dreaded, Plautus having been lately sent away to Asia, Sulla to Gallia Narbonensis, he spoke much of their noble rank and of their respective proximity to the armies of the East and of Germany. "I have no eye," he said, "like Burrus, to two conflicting aims, but only to Nero's safety, which is at least secured against treachery in Rome by my presence. As for distant commotions, how can they be checked? Gaul is roused at the name of the great dictator, and I distrust no less the nations of Asia, because of the renown of such a grandfather as Drusus. Sulla is poor, and hence comes his surpassing audacity; he shams apathy, while he is seeking an opening for his reckless ambition. Plautus again, with his great wealth, does not so much as affect a love of repose, but he flaunts before us his imitations of the old Romans, and assumes the self-consciousness of the Stoics along with a philosophy, which makes men restless, and eager for a busy life."

There was not a moment's delay. Sulla, six days afterwards, was murdered by assassins brought over to Massilia, while he was reclining at the dinner-table, before he feared or heard of his danger. The head was taken to Rome, and Nero scoffed at its premature grey hairs as if they were a disfigurement.

It was less of a secret that there was a design to murder Plautus, as his life was dear to many. The distance too by land and sea, and the interval of time, had given rise to rumours, and the popular story was that he had tampered with Corbulo, who was then at the head of great armies, and would be a special mark for danger, if illustrious and innocent men were to be destroyed. Again Asia, it was said, from its partiality for the young man, had taken up arms, and the soldiers sent to do the crime, not being sufficient in number or decided in purpose, and, finding themselves unable to execute their orders, had gone over to the new cause. These absurdities, like all popular gossip, gathered strength from the idle leisure of a credulous society.

As it was, one of Plautus's freedmen, thanks to swift winds, arrived before the centurion and brought him a message from his father-in-law, Lucius Antistius. "He was to avoid the obvious refuge of a coward's death, and in the pity felt for a noble name he would soon find good men to help him, and daring spirits would rally round him. Meantime no resource was to be rejected. If he did but repel sixty soldiers (this was the number on the way), while tidings were being carried back to Nero, while another force was on its march, many events would follow which would ripen into war. Finally, by this plan he either secured safety, or he would suffer nothing worse by daring than by cowardice."

But all this had no effect on Plautus. Either he saw no resource before him, an unarmed exile as he was, or he was weary of an uncertain hope, or was swayed by his love of his wife and of his children, to whom he thought the emperor, if harassed by no anxiety, would be more merciful. Some say that another message came to him from his father-in-law, representing that no dreadful peril hung over him, and that two teachers of philosophy, Coeranus from Greece and Musonius from Etruria, advised him to await death with firmness rather than lead a precarious and anxious life. At all events, he was surprised at midday, when stripped for exercise. In that state the centurion slew him in the presence of Pelago, an eunuch, whom Nero had set over the centurion and his company, like a despot's minister over his satellites.

The head of the murdered man was brought to Rome. At its sight the emperor exclaimed (I give his very words), "Why would you have been a Nero?" Then casting off all fear he prepared to hurry on his marriage with Poppaea, hitherto deferred because of such alarms as I have described, and to divorce his wife Octavia, notwithstanding her virtuous life, because her father's name and the people's affection for her made her an offence to him. He wrote, however, a letter to the Senate, confessing nothing about the murders of Sulla and Plautus, but merely hinting that both had a restless temper, and that he gave the most anxious thought to the safety of the State. On this pretext a thanksgiving was decreed, and also the expulsion from the Senate of Sulla and Plautus, more grievous, however, as a farce than as an actual calamity.

Nero, on receiving this decree of the Senate and seeing that every piece of his wickedness was regarded as a conspicuous merit, drove Octavia from him, alleging that she was barren, and then married Poppaea. The woman who had long been Nero's mistress and ruled him first as a paramour, then as her husband, instigated one of Octavia's servants to accuse her an intrigue with a slave. The man fixed on as the guilty lover was one by name Eucaerus, an Alexandrine by birth, skilled in singing to the flute. As a consequence, her slave-girls were examined under torture, and though some were forced by the intensity of agony into admitting falsehoods, most of them persisted in upholding the virtue of their mistress. One of them said, in answer to the furious menaces of Tigellinus, that Octavia's person was purer than his mouth. Octavia, however, was dismissed under the form of an ordinary divorce, and received possession of the house of Burrus and of the estates of Plautus, an ill-starred gift. She was soon afterwards banished to Campania under military surveillance. This led to incessant and outspoken remonstrances among the common people, who have less discretion and are exposed to fewer dangers than others from the insignificance of their position. Upon this Nero, though he did not repent of his outrage, restored to Octavia her position as wife.

Then people in their joy went up to the Capitol and, at last, gave thanks to the gods. They threw down the statues of Poppaea; they bore on their shoulders the images of Octavia, covering them with flowers, and setting them up in the forum and in the temples. There was even a burst of applause for the emperor, men hailing the recalled Octavia. And now they were pouring into the Palace in crowds, with loud shoutings, when some companies of soldiers rushed out and dispersed the tumultuous throng with blows, and at the point of the sword. Whatever changes had been made in the riot, were reversed, and Poppaea's honours restored. Ever relentless in her hatred, she was now enraged by the fear that either the violence of the mob would burst on her with yet fiercer fury, or that Nero would be swayed by the popular bias, and so, flinging herself at his knees, she exclaimed that she was not in the position of a rival fighting for marriage, though that was dearer to her than life, but that her very life was brought into jeopardy by the dependants and slaves of Octavia, who had assumed the name of the people, and dared in peace what could hardly happen in war. "Those arms," she said, "have been taken up against the emperor; a leader only is wanting, and he will easily be found in a commotion. Only let her whose mere beck, though she is far away, stirs up tumult, quit Campania, and make her way in person to Rome. And, again, what is my sin? What offense have I caused any one? Is it that I am about to give to the house of the Caesars a lawful heir? Do the people of Rome prefer that the offspring of an Egyptian fluteplayer should be raised to the imperial throne? In a word, if it be expedient, Nero should of his own choice rather than on compulsion send for her who ruled him, or else secure his safety by a righteous vengeance. The beginning of a commotion has often been quieted by slight precautions; but if people once despair of Octavia being Nero's wife, they will soon find her a husband."

Her various arguments, tending both to frighten and to enrage, at once alarmed and incensed her listener. But the suspicion about the slave was of little weight, and the torture of the slave-girls exposed its absurdity. Consequently it was decided to procure a confession from some one on whom could also be fastened a charge of revolutionary designs. Fittest for this seemed the perpetrator of the mother's murder, Anicetus, commander, as I have already mentioned, of the fleet at Misenum, who got but scant gratitude after that atrocious deed, and subsequently all the more vehement hatred, inasmuch as men look on their instruments in crime as a sort of standing reproach to them.

The emperor accordingly sent for Anicetus, and reminded him of his former service. "He alone," he said, "had come to the rescue of the prince's life against a plotting mother. Close at hand was a chance of winning no less gratitude by ridding him of a malignant wife. No violence or weapons were needed; only let him confess to an intrigue with Octavia." Nero then promised him a secret but ample immediate recompense, and some delightful retreat, while he threatened him with death in case of refusal. Anicetus, with the moral insensibility of his nature and a promptness inspired by previous atrocities, invented even more than was required of him, and confessed before friends whom the prince had called in, as a sort of judicial council. He was then banished to Sardinia, where he endured exile without poverty, and died a natural death.

Nero meanwhile declared by edict that the prefect had been corrupted into a design of gaining over the fleet, and added, in forgetfulness of his late charge of barrenness against Octavia, that, conscious of her profligacies, she had procured abortion, a fact he had himself ascertained. Then he confined her in the island of Pandataria. No exile ever filled the eyes of beholders with tears of greater compassion. Some still remembered Agrippina, banished by Tiberius, and the yet fresher memory of Julia, whom Claudius exiled, was present to men's thoughts. But they had life's prime for their stay; they had seen some happiness, and the horror of the moment was alleviated by recollections of a better lot in the past. For Octavia, from the first, her marriage-day was a kind of funeral, brought, as she was, into a house where she had nothing but scenes of mourning, her father and, an instant afterwards, her brother, having been snatched from her by poison;

then, a slave-girl raised above the mistress; Poppaea married only to insure a wife's ruin, and, to end all, an accusation more horrible than any death.

And now the girl, in her twentieth year, with centurions and soldiers around her, already removed from among the living by the forecast of doom, still could not reconcile herself to death. After an interval of a few days, she received an order that she was to die, although she protested that she was now a widow and only a sister, and appealed to their common ancestors, the Germanici, and finally to the name of Agrippina, during whose life she had endured a marriage, which was miserable enough indeed, but not fatal. She was then tightly bound with cords, and the veins of every limb were opened; but as her blood was congealed by terror and flowed too slowly, she was killed outright by the steam of an intensely hot bath. To this was added the yet more appalling horror of Poppaea beholding the severed head which was conveyed to Rome.

And for all this offerings were voted to the temples. I record the fact with a special object. Whoever would study the calamities of that period in my pages or those of other authors, is to take it for granted that as often as the emperor directed banishments or executions, so often was there a thanksgiving to the gods, and what formerly commemorated some prosperous event, was then a token of public disaster. Still, if any decree of the Senate was marked by some new flattery, or by the lowest servility, I shall not pass it over in silence.

That same year Nero was believed to have destroyed by poison two of his most powerful freedmen, Doryphorus, on the pretext of his having opposed the marriage with Poppaea, Pallas for still keeping his boundless wealth by a prolonged old age. Romanus had accused Seneca in stealthy calumnies, of having been an accomplice of Caius Piso, but he was himself crushed more effectually by Seneca on the same charge. This alarmed Piso, and gave rise to a huge fabric of unsuccessful conspiracies against Nero.

BOOK XV, A.D. 62-65

Meanwhile, the Parthian king, Vologeses, when he heard of Corbulo's achievements and of a foreign prince, Tigranes, having been set over Armenia, though he longed at the same time to avenge the majesty of the Arsacids, which had been insulted by the expulsion of his brother Tiridates, was, on the other hand, drawn to different thoughts as he reflected on the greatness of Rome, and felt reverence for a hitherto unbroken treaty. Naturally irresolute, he was now hampered by a revolt of the Hyrcanians, a powerful tribe, and by several wars arising out of it. Suddenly, as he was wavering, fresh and further tidings of disgrace goaded him to action. Tigranes, quitting Armenia, had ravaged the Adiabeni, a people on its border, too extensively and continuously for mere plundering raids. The chief men of the tribes were indignant at having fallen into such contempt that they were victims to the inroads, not indeed of a Roman general, but of a daring hostage, who for so many years had been numbered among slaves. Their anger was inflamed by Monobazus, who ruled the Adiabeni, and repeatedly asked what protection he was to seek and from what quarter—"Already," he said, "Armenia has been given up, and its borders are being wrested from us, and unless the Parthians help us, we shall find that subjection to Rome is lighter for those who surrender than for the conquered." Tiridates too, exile as he was from his kingdom, by his silence or very moderate complaints made the deeper impression. "It is not," he urged, "by weak inaction that great empires are held together; there must be the struggle of brave men in arms; might is right with those who are at the summit of power. And though it is the glory of a private house to keep its own, it is the glory of a king to fight for the possessions of others."

Moved by these considerations Vologeses called a council, placed Tiridates by his side, and began to speak as follows:—

"This man before you, born from the same father as myself, having waived in my favour, on the ground of age, the highest title of all, was established by me in the possession of Armenia, which is accounted the third grade of power. As for Media, Pacorus was already in possession of it. And I thought to myself that I had duly arranged our family and home so as to guard against the old feuds and rivalries of brothers. The Romans thwart me, and though they have never with success to themselves disturbed the peace between us, they are now again breaking it to their own destruction. I will not attempt to deny one thing. It was by just dealing rather than by bloodshed, by having a good cause rather than by arms, that I had wished to retain what my ancestors had won. If I have sinned through irresolution, my valour shall make amends for it. Assuredly your strength and renown are at their height, and you have in addition the repute of obedience, which the greatest of mortals must not despise, and which the gods highly esteem."

As he spoke, he encircled Tiridates' brow with a diadem, and to Moneses, a noble, he entrusted a highly efficient body of cavalry, which was the king's customary escort, giving him also some auxiliaries from the Adiabeni, and orders that Tigranes was to be driven out of Armenia. He would himself abandon his feud with the Hyrcanians, and raise his own national force in all its warlike strength by way of menace to the Roman provinces.

When Corbulo had heard all this from messengers he could trust, he sent two legions under Verulanus Severus and Vettius Bolanus to the support of Tigranes, with secret instructions that they were to conduct all their operations with deliberation rather than despatch, as he would prefer to sustain rather than to make war. And indeed he had written to the emperor that a general was wanted specially for the defence of Armenia, and that Syria, threatened as it was by Vologeses, was in yet more imminent peril. Meanwhile he posted his remaining legions on the bank of the Euphrates, armed a hastily collected force of provincials, and occupied with troops the enemy's approaches. And as the country was deficient in water, he established forts to guard the wells, and concealed some of the streams with heaps of sand.

While Corbulo was thus preparing for the defence of Syria, Moneses rapidly pushed on his forces to anticipate the rumour of his advance, but he did not any the more find Tigranes unaware of or unprepared for his movement. He had, in fact, occupied Tigranocerta, a city strong from the multitude of its defenders and the vastness of its fortifications. In addition, the river Nicephorius, the breadth of which is far from contemptible, circled a portion of its walls, and a wide fosse was drawn where they distrusted the protection of the stream. There were some soldiers too, and supplies previously provided. In the conveyance of these a few men had hurried on too eagerly, and, having been surprised by a sudden attack from the enemy, had inspired their comrades with rage rather than fear. But the Parthian has not the daring in close combat needed for a successful siege. His thin showers of arrows do not alarm men within walls, and only disappoint himself. The Adiabeni, when they began to advance their scaling ladders and engines, were easily driven back, and then cut down by a sally of our men.

Corbulo, however, notwithstanding his successes thought he must use his good fortune with moderation, and sent Vologeses a message of remonstrance against the violence done to a Roman province, and the blockade of an allied and friendly king and of Roman cohorts. "He had better give up the siege, or he, Corbulo too would encamp in his territory, as on hostile ground." Casperius, a centurion selected for this mission, had an interview with the king at the town Nisibis, thirty-seven miles distant from Tigranocerta, and with fearless spirit announced his message. With Vologeses it was an old and deep conviction that he should shun the arms of Rome. Nor was the present going smoothly with him. The seige was a failure; Tigranes was safe with his troops and supplies; those who had undertaken the storming of the place had been routed; legions had been sent into Armenia, and other legions were ready to rush to the attack on behalf of Syria, while his own cavalry was crippled by want of food. A host of locusts, suddenly appearing, had devoured every blade of grass and every leaf. And so, hiding his fear and presenting a more conciliatory attitude, he replied that he would send envoys to the Roman emperor for the possession of Armenia and the conclusion of a lasting peace. He ordered Moneses to leave Tigranocerta, while he himself retired.

Many spoke highly of these results, as due to the king's alarm and the threats of Corbulo, and as splendid successes. Others explained them as a secret understanding that with the cessation of war on both sides and the departure of Vologeses, Tigranes also was to quit Armenia. "Why," it was asked, "had the Roman army been withdrawn from Tigranocerta? Why had they abandoned in peace what they had defended in war? Was it better for them to have wintered on the confines of Cappadocia in hastily constructed huts, than in the capital of a kingdom lately recovered? There had been, in short, a suspension of arms, in order that Vologeses might fight some other foe than Corbulo, and that Corbulo might not further risk the glory he had earned in so many years. For, as I have related, he had asked for a general exclusively for the defence of Armenia, and it was heard that Caesennius Paetus was on his way. And indeed he had now arrived, and the army was thus divided; the fourth and twelfth legions, with the fifth which had lately been raised in Moesia and the auxiliaries from Pontus, Galatia and Cappadocia, were under the command of Paetus, while the third, sixth, and tenth legions and the old soldiery of Syria remained with Corbulo. All else they were to share or divide between them according to circumstances. But as Corbulo could not endure a rival, so Paetus, who would have been sufficiently honoured by ranking second to him, disparaged the results of the war, and said repeatedly that there had been no bloodshed or spoil, that the sieges of cities were sieges only in name, and that he would soon impose on the conquered tribute and laws and Roman administration, instead of the empty shadow of a king.

About the same time the envoys of Vologeses, who had been sent, as I have related, to the emperor, returned without success, and the Parthians made open war. Nor did Paetus decline the challenge, but with two legions, the 4th and 12th, the first of which was then commanded by Funisulanus Vettonianus and the second by Calavius Sabinus, entered Armenia, with unlucky omen. In the passage of the Euphrates, which they crossed by a bridge, a horse which carried the consul's official emblems, took fright without any apparent cause and fled to the rear. A victim, too, standing by some of the winter-tents, which were being fortified, broke its way through them, when the work was but half finished, and got clear out of the entrenchments. Then again the soldiers' javelins gleamed with light, a prodigy the more significant because the Parthian foe fights with missiles.

Paetus, however, despising omens, before he had yet thoroughly fortified his winter-camp or provided for his corn supply, hurried his army across Mount Taurus, for the recovery, as he gave out, of Tigranocerta and the ravaging of the country which Corbulo had left untouched. Some forts too were taken, and some glory as well as plunder had been secured, if only he had enjoyed his glory modestly, and his plunder with vigilance. While he was overrunning in tedious expeditions districts which could not be held, the supplies which had been captured, were spoilt, and as winter was now at hand, he led back his army and wrote a letter to the emperor, as if the war was finished, in pompous language, but barren of facts.

Meanwhile Corbulo occupied the bank of the Euphrates, which he had never neglected, with troops at closer intervals. That he might have no hindrance in throwing a bridge over it from the enemy's cavalry, which was already scouring the adjoining plains with a formidable display, he launched on the river some vessels of remarkable size, linked together by beams, with towers rising from their decks, and with catapults and balistas he drove off the barbarians. The stones and spears penetrated their host at a range beyond the reach of the opposing volleys of arrows. The bridge was then completed, and the hills facing us were occupied by our auxiliary infantry, then, by the entrenchments of the legions, with such rapidity and such a display of force that the Parthians, giving up their preparations for the invasion of Syria, concentrated all their hopes on Armenia.

Paetus, ignorant of the impending danger, was keeping the 5th legion at a distance in Pontus; the rest he had weakened by indiscriminate furloughs, till it was heard that Vologeses was approaching with a powerful force bent on war. He summoned the 12th legion, and then was discovered the numerical feebleness of the source from which he had hoped for the repute of an augmented army. Yet even thus the camp might have been held, and the Parthian foe baffled, by protracting the war, had Paetus stood firm either by his own counsels or by those of others. But though military men had put him on his guard against imminent disasters, still, not wishing to seem to need the advice of others, he would fall back on some quite different and inferior plan. So now, leaving his winter quarters, and exclaiming that not the fosse or the rampart, but the men's bodies and weapons were given him for facing the foe, he led out his legions, as if he meant to fight a battle. Then, after losing a centurion and a few soldiers whom he had sent on in advance to reconnoitre the enemy's forces, he returned in alarm. And, as Vologeses had not pressed his advantage with much vigour, Paetus once again, with vain confidence, posted 3000 chosen infantry on the adjacent ridge of the Taurus, in order to bar the king's passage. He also stationed some Pannonian troopers, the flower of his cavalry, in a part of the plain. His wife and son he removed to a fortress named Arsamosata, with a cohort for their defence, thus dispersing the troops which, if kept together, could easily have checked the desultory skirmishing of the enemy. He could, it is said, scarcely be driven to confess to Corbulo how the enemy was pressing him. Corbulo made no haste, that, when the dangers thickened, the glory of the rescue might be enhanced. Yet he ordered 1000 men from each of his three legions with 800 cavalry, and an equal number of infantry to be in instant readiness.

Vologeses meanwhile, though he had heard that the roads were blocked by Paetus, here with infantry, there with cavalry, did not alter his plan, but drove off the latter by the menace of an attack, and crushed the legionaires, only one centurion of whom, Tarquitius Crescens, dared to defend a tower in which he was keeping guard. He had often sallied out, and cut to pieces such of the barbarians as came close up to the walls, till he was overwhelmed with volleys of firebrands. Every foot soldier still unwounded fled to remote wilds, and those who were disabled, returned to the camp, exaggerating in their terror the king's valour, and the warlike strength of his tribes, everything in short, to the simple credulity of those who trembled with like fear. Even the general did not struggle against his reverses. He had indeed wholly abandoned all the duties of a soldier, and had again sent an entreaty to Corbulo, that he would come with speed to save the standards and eagles, and the name yet left to the unfortunate army; they meantime, he said, would hold to their fidelity while life lasted.

Corbulo, perfectly fearless, left half his army in Syria to retain the forts built on the Euphrates, and taking the nearest route, which also was not deficient in supplies, marched through the country of Commagene, then through Cappadocia, and thence into Armenia. Beside the other usual accompaniments of war, his army was followed by a great number of camels laden with corn, to keep off famine as well as the enemy. The first he met of the defeated army was Paccius, a first-rank centurion, then many of the soldiers, whom, when they pleaded various excuses for flight, he advised to return to their standards and throw themselves on the mercy of Paetus. "For himself," he said, "he had no forgiveness but for the victorious."

As he spoke, he went up to his legions, cheering them and reminding them of their past career, and pointing the way to new glory. "It was not to villages or towns of Armenia, but to a Roman camp with two legions, a worthy recompense for their efforts, that they were bound. If each common soldier were to have bestowed on him by the emperor's hand the special honour of a crown for a rescued citizen, how wonderfully great the glory, when the numbers would be equal of those who had brought and of those had received deliverance." Roused by these and like words into a common enthusiasm, and some too were filled with an ardour peculiarly their own by the perils of brothers and kinsfolk, they hurried on by day and night their uninterrupted march.

All the more vigorously did Vologeses press the besieged, now attacking the legions' entrenchments, and now again the fortress, which guarded those whose years unfitted them for war. He advanced closer than is the Parthian practice, seeking to lure the enemy to an engagement by such rashness. They, however, could hardly be dragged out of their tents, and would merely defend their lives, some held back by the general's order, others by their own cowardice; they seemed to be awaiting Corbulo, and should they be overpowered by force, they had before them the examples of Candium and Numantia. "Neither the Samnites, Italian people as they were, nor the Carthaginians, the rivals of the Roman empire, were, it seemed, equally formidable, and even the men of old, with all their strength and glory, whenever fortune was adverse, had taken thought for safety."

The general, although he was overcome by the despair of his army, first wrote a letter to Vologeses, not a suppliant petition, but in a tone of remonstrance against the doing of hostile acts on behalf of the Armenians, who always had been under Roman dominion, or subject to a king chosen by the emperor. Peace, he reminded him, was equally for the interest of both, and it would be well for him not to look only at the present. He indeed had advanced with the whole strength of his kingdom against two legions, while the Romans had all the rest of the world with which to sustain the war.

To this Vologeses replied nothing to the purpose, but merely that he must wait for his brothers Pacorus and Tiridates, that the place and time of their meeting had been fixed on as the occasion when they would decide about Armenia, and that heaven had granted them a further honour, well worthy of the Arsacids, the having to determine the fate of Roman legions. Messengers were then despatched by Paetus and an interview requested with the king, who ordered Vasaces, the commander of the cavalry, to go. Thereupon Paetus dwelt on the memories of the Luculli and Pompeii, and of all that the Caesars had done in the way of holding or giving away Armenia, while Vasaces declared that we had the mere shadow of possession and of bestowing, but the Parthians, the reality of power. After much arguing on both sides, Monobazus of the Adiabeni was called the next day to be a witness to the stipulations into which they had entered. It was agreed that the legions should be released from the blockade, that all the troops should quit Armenian territory, and that the forts and supplies should be surrendered to the Parthians, and when all this had been completed, Vologeses was to have full permission to send envoys to Nero.

Meanwhile Paetus threw a bridge over the river Arsanias, which flowed by the camp, apparently with the view of facilitating his march. It was the Parthians, however, who had required this, as an evidence of their victory; for the bridge was of use to them, while our men went a different way. Rumour added that the legions had been passed under the yoke, with other miserable disgraces, of which the Armenians had borrowed imitations. For they not only entered our lines before the Roman army began to retire, but also stood about the camp streets, recognizing and dragging off slaves or beasts of burden which we had previously captured. They even seized clothes and detained weapons, for the soldiers were utterly cowed and gave up everything, so that no cause for fighting might arise. Vologeses having piled up the arms and bodies of the slain in order to attest our defeat, refrained from gazing on the fugitive legions. He sought a character for moderation after he had glutted his pride. Seated himself on an elephant, he crossed the river Arsanias, while those next to his person rushed through it at the utmost speed of their horses; for a rumour had gained ground that the bridge would give way, through the trickery of its builders. But those who ventured to go on it found it to be firm and trustworthy.

As for the besieged, it appeared that they had such an abundance of corn that they fired the granaries, and Corbulo declared that the Parthians on the other hand were in want of supplies, and would have abandoned the siege from their fodder being all but exhausted, and that he was himself only three days' march distant. He further stated that Paetus had guaranteed by an oath, before the standards, in the presence of those whom the king had sent to be witnesses, that no Roman was to enter Armenia until Nero's reply arrived as to whether he assented to the peace. Though this may have been invented to enhance our disgrace, yet about the rest of the story there is no obscurity, that, in a single day Paetus traversed forty miles, leaving his wounded behind him everywhere, and that the consternation of the fugitives was as frightful as if they had turned their backs in battle. Corbulo, as he met them with his forces on the bank of the Euphrates, did not make such a display of his standards and arms as to shame them by the contrast. His men, in their grief and pity for the lot of their comrades, could not even refrain from tears. There was scarce any mutual salutation for weeping. The spirit of a noble rivalry and the desire of glory, emotions which stir men in success, had died away; pity alone survived, the more strongly in the inferior ranks.

Then followed a short conversation between the generals. While Corbulo complained that his efforts had been fruitless and that the war might have been ended with the flight of the Parthians, Paetus replied that for neither of them was anything lost, and urged that they should reverse the eagles, and with their united forces invade Armenia, much weakened, as it was, by the departure of Vologeses. Corbulo said that he had no such instructions from the emperor; it was the peril of the legions which had stirred him to leave his province, and, as there was uncertainty about the designs of the Parthians, he should return to Syria, and, even as it was, he must pray for fortune under her most favourable aspect in order that the infantry, wearied out with long marches, might keep pace with the enemy's untiring cavalry, certain to outstrip him on the plains, which facilitated their movements. Paetus then went into winter quarters in Cappadocia. Vologeses, however, sent a message to Corbulo, requiring him to remove the fortresses on the further bank of the Euphrates, and to leave the river to be, as formerly, the boundary between them. Corbulo also demanded the evacuation of Armenia by the garrisons posted throughout it. At last the king yielded, all the positions fortified by Corbulo beyond the Euphrates were destroyed, and the Armenians too left without a master.

At Rome meanwhile trophies for the Parthian war, and arches were erected in the centre of the Capitoline hill; these had been decreed by the Senate, while the war was yet undecided, and even now they were not given up, appearances being consulted, in disregard of known facts. And to hide his anxious fears about foreign affairs, Nero threw the people's corn, which was so old as to be spoilt, into the Tiber, with the view of keeping up a sense of security about the supplies. There was no addition to the price, although about two hundred ships were destroyed in the very harbour by a violent storm, and one hundred more, which had sailed up the Tiber, by an accidental fire. Nero next appointed three ex-consuls, Lucius Piso, Ducennius Geminus, and Pompeius Paulinus, to the management of the public revenues, and inveighed at the same time against former emperors whose heavy expenditure had exceeded their legitimate income. He himself, he said, made the state an annual present of sixty million sesterces.

A very demoralizing custom had at this time become rife, of fictitious adoptions of children, on the eve of the elections or of the assignment of the provinces, by a number of childless persons, who, after obtaining along with real fathers praetorships and provinces, forthwith dismissed from paternal control the sons whom they had adopted. An appeal was made to the Senate under a keen sense of wrong. Parents pleaded natural rights and the anxieties of nurture against fraudulent evasions and the brief ceremony of adoption. "It was," they argued, "sufficient reward for the childless to have influence and distinction, everything, in short, easy and open to them, without a care and without a burden. For themselves, they found that the promises held out by the laws, for which they had long waited, were turned into mockery, when one who knew nothing of a parent's solicitude or of the sorrows of bereavement could rise in a moment to the level of a father's long deferred hopes."

On this, a decree of the Senate was passed that a fictitious adoption should be of no avail in any department of the public service, or even hold good for acquiring an inheritance.

Next came the prosecution of Claudius Timarchus of Crete, on such charges as often fall on very influential provincials, whom immense wealth has emboldened to the oppression of the weak. But one speech of his had gone to the extremity of a gross insult to the Senate; for he had repeatedly declared that it was in his power to decide whether the proconsuls who had governed Crete should receive the thanks of the province. Paetus Thrasea, turning the occasion to public advantage, after having stated his opinion that the accused ought to be expelled from Crete, further spoke as follows:—

"It is found by experience, Senators, that admirable laws and right precedents among the good have their origin in the misdeeds of others. Thus the license of advocates resulted in the Cincian bill; the corrupt practices of candidates, in the Julian laws; the rapacity of magistrates, in the Calpurnian enactments. For, in point of time, guilt comes before punishment, and correction follows after delinquency. And therefore, to meet the new insolence of provincials, let us adopt a measure worthy of Roman good faith and resolution, whereby our allies may lose nothing of our protection, while public opinion may cease to say of us, that the estimate of a man's character is to found anywhere rather than in the judgment of our citizens.

"Formerly, it was not only a praetor or a consul, but private persons also, who were sent to inspect the provinces, and to report what they thought about each man's loyalty. And nations were timidly sensitive to the opinion of individuals. But now we court foreigners and flatter them, and just as there is a vote of thanks at any one's pleasure, so even more eagerly is a prosecution decided on. Well; let it be decided on, and let the provincials retain the right of showing their power in this fashion, but as for false praise which has been extorted by entreaties, let it be as much checked as fraud or tyranny. More faults are often committed, while we are trying to oblige than while we are giving offence. Nay, some virtues are actually hated; inflexible strictness, for example, and a temper proof against partiality. Consequently, our magistrates' early career is generally better than its close, which deteriorates, when we are anxiously seeking votes, like candidates. If such practices are stopped, our provinces will be ruled more equitably and more steadily. For as the dread of a charge of extortion has been a check to rapacity, so, by prohibiting the vote of thanks, will the pursuit of popularity be restrained."

This opinion was hailed with great unanimity, but the Senate's resolution could not be finally passed, as the consuls decided that there had been no formal motion on the subject. Then, at the emperor's suggestion, they decreed that no one was to propose to any council of our allies that a vote of thanks ought to be given in the Senate to propraetors or proconsuls, and that no one was to discharge such a mission.

During the same consulship a gymnasium was wholly consumed by a stroke of lightning, and a statue of Nero within it was melted down to a shapeless mass of bronze. An earthquake too demolished a large part of Pompeii, a populous town in Campania. And one of the vestal virgins, Laelia, died, and in her place was chosen Cornelia, of the family of the Cossi.

During the consulship of Memmius Regulus and Verginius Rufus, Nero welcomed with something more than mortal joy the birth of a daughter by Poppaea, whom he called Augusta, the same title having also been given to Poppaea. The place of her confinement was the colony of Antium, where the emperor himself was born. Already had the Senate commended Poppaea's safety to the gods, and had made vows in the State's name, which were repeated again and again and duly discharged. To these was added a public thanksgiving, and a temple was decreed to the goddess of fecundity, as well as games and contests after the type of the ceremonies commemorative of Actium, and golden images of the two Fortunes were to be set up on the throne of Jupiter of the Capitol. Shows too of the circus were to be exhibited in honour of the Claudian and Domitian families at Antium, like those at Bovillae in commemoration of the Julii. Transient distinctions all of them, as within four months the infant died. Again there was an outburst of flattery, men voting the honours of deification, of a shrine, a temple, and a priest.

The emperor, too, was as excessive in his grief as he had been in his joy. It was observed that when all the Senate rushed out to Antium to honour the recent birth, Thrasea was forbidden to go, and received with fearless spirit an affront which foreboded his doom. Then followed, as rumour says, an expression from the emperor, in which he boasted to Seneca of his reconciliation with Thrasea, on which Seneca congratulated him. And now henceforth the glory and the peril of these illustrious men grew greater.

Meanwhile, in the beginning of spring, Parthian envoys brought a message from king Vologeses, with a letter to the same effect. "He did not," it was said, "repeat his former and frequent claims to the holding of Armenia, since the gods who ruled the destinies of the most powerful nations, had handed over its possession to the Parthians, not without disgrace to Rome. Only lately, he had besieged Tigranes; afterwards, he let Paetus and his legions depart in safety when he could have destroyed them. He had tried force with a satisfactory result; he had also given clemency a trial. Nor would Tiridates refuse a journey to Rome to receive the crown, were he not detained at home by the duties of a sacred office. He was ready to go to the emperor's image in the Roman headquarters, and there in the presence of the legions inaugurate his reign."

As Paetus's despatch contradicted this letter from Vologeses and implied that matters were unchanged, the centurion who had arrived with the envoys was questioned as to the state of Armenia. He replied that all the Romans had quitted it. Then was perceived the mockery of the barbarians in petitioning for what they had wrested from us, and Nero consulted with the chief men of the State whether they should accept a dangerous war or a disgraceful peace. There was no hesitation about war. Corbulo, who had known our soldiers and the enemy for so many years, was appointed to conduct it, that there might be no more blunders through any other officer's incapacity; for people were utterly disgusted with Paetus.

So the envoys were sent back without an answer, but with some presents, in order to inspire a hope that Tiridates would not make the same request in vain, if only he presented his petition in person. The administration of Syria was intrusted to Caius Itius, and the military forces to Corbulo, to which was added the fifteenth legion, under the leadership of Marius Celsus, from Pannonia. Written orders were sent to the tetrarchs, the tributaries, kings, prefects and procurators, and all the praetors who governed the neighbouring provinces, to obey Corbulo's commands, as his powers were enlarged on much the same scale as that which the Roman people had granted to Cneius Pompeius on the eve of his war against the Pirates. When Paetus returned and dreaded something worse, the emperor thought it enough to reproach him with a jest, to the effect that he pardoned him at once, lest one so ready to take fright might sink under prolonged suspense.

Corbulo meantime transferred to Syria the fourth and twelfth legions, which, from the loss of their bravest men and the panic of the remainder, seemed quite unfit for battle, and led thence into Armenia the third and sixth legions, troops in thorough efficiency, and trained by frequent and successful service. And he added to his army the fifth legion, which, having been quartered in Pontus, had known nothing of disaster, with men of the fifteenth, lately brought up, and picked veterans from Illyricum and Egypt, and all the allied cavalry and infantry, and the auxiliaries of the tributary princes, which had been concentrated at Melitene, where he was preparing to cross the Euphrates. Then, after the due lustration of his army, he called them together for an harangue, and began with grand allusions to the imperial auspices, and to his own achievements, while he attributed their disasters to the incapacity of Paetus. He spoke with much impressiveness, which in him, as a military man, was as good as eloquence.

He then pursued the route opened up in former days by Lucius Lucullus, clearing away the obstructions of long years. Envoys who came to him from Tiridates and Vologeses about peace, he did not repulse, but sent back with them some centurions with a message anything but harsh. "Matters," he said, "have not yet gone so far as to require the extremity of war. Many successes have fallen to the lot of Rome, some to that of Parthia, as a warning against pride. Therefore, it is to the advantage of Tiridates to accept as a gift a kingdom yet unhurt by the ravages of war, and Vologeses will better consult the welfare of the Parthian people by an alliance with Rome than by mutual injuries. I know how much there is of internal discord, and over what untamably fierce tribes he reigns. My emperor, on the other hand, has undisturbed peace all around him, and this is his only war."

In an instant Corbulo backed up his advice by a menacing attitude. He drove from their possessions the nobles of Armenia, who had been the first to revolt from us, destroyed their fortresses, and spread equal panic throughout the plain and the hill country, among the strong and among the weak.

Against the name of Corbulo no rage, nothing of the hatred of an enemy, was felt by the barbarians, and they therefore thought his advice trustworthy. Consequently Vologeses was not implacable to the uttermost, and he even asked a truce for some divisions of his kingdom. Tiridates demanded a place and a day for an interview. The time was to be soon, the place that in which Paetus and his legions had been lately besieged, for this was chosen by the barbarians in remembrance for their more prosperous fortune. Corbulo did not refuse, resolved that a widely different issue should enhance his renown. Nor did the disgrace of Paetus trouble him, as was clearly proved by the fact that he commanded Paetus' son, who was a tribune, to take some companies with him and cover up the relics of that ill-starred battle-field. On the day appointed, Tiberius Alexander, a distinguished Roman knight, sent to assist in the campaign, and Vinianus Annius, Corbulo's son-in-law, who, though not yet of a senator's age, had the command of the fifth legion as "legatus," entered the camp of Tiridates, by way of compliment to him, and to reassure him against treachery by so valuable a pledge. Each then took with him twenty horsemen. The king, seeing Corbulo, was the first to dismount, and Corbulo hesitated not a moment, but both on foot joined their right hands.

Then the Roman commended the young prince for abandoning rash courses, and adopting a safe and expedient policy. Tiridates first dwelt much on the nobility of his race, but went on to speak in a tone of moderation. He would go to Rome, and bring the emperor a new glory, a suppliant Arsacid, while Parthia was prosperous. It was then agreed that Tiridates should lay down his royal crown before Caesar's image, and resume it only from the hand of Nero. The interview then ended with a kiss. After an interval of a few days there was a grand display on both sides; on the one, cavalry ranged in squadrons with their national ensigns; on the other, stood the columns of our legions with glittering eagles and standards and images of deities, after the appearance of a temple. In the midst, on a tribunal, was a chair of state, and on the chair a statue of Nero. To this Tiridates advanced, and having slain the customary victims, he removed the crown from his head, and set it at the foot of the statue; whereupon all felt a deep thrill of emotion, rendered the more intense by the sight which yet lingered before their eyes, of the slaughter or siege of Roman armies. "But now," they thought, "the calamity is reversed; Tiridates is about to go, a spectacle to the world, little better than a prisoner."

To military glory Corbulo added courtesy and hospitality. When the king continually asked the reason of whatever he noticed which was new to him, the announcements, for example, by a centurion of the beginnings of each watch, the dismissal of the guests by the sound of a trumpet, and the lighting by a torch from beneath of an altar in front of the headquarters, Corbulo, by exaggerating everything, filled him with admiration of our ancient system. Next day Tiridates begged for time which, as he was about to enter on so long a journey, might suffice for a previous visit to his brothers and his mother. Meanwhile he gave up his daughter as a hostage, and prepared a suppliant letter to Nero.

He then departed, and found Pacorus in Media, and Vologeses at Ecbatana, who was by no means unconcerned for his brother. In fact, Vologeses had entreated Corbulo by special messengers, that Tiridates might not have to endure any badge of slavery, or have to deliver up his sword, or be debarred the honour of embracing the governors of the provinces, or have to present himself at their doors, and that he might be treated at Rome with as much respect as the consuls. Accustomed, forsooth, to foreign arrogance, he had no knowledge of us, who value the reality of empire and disregard its empty show.

That same year the emperor put into possession of the Latin franchise the tribes of the maritime Alps. To the Roman knights he assigned places in the circus in front of the seats of the people, for up to that time they used to enter in a promiscuous throng, as the Roscian law extended only to fourteen rows in the theatre. The same year witnessed shows of gladiators as magnificent as those of the past. Many ladies of distinction, however, and senators, disgraced themselves by appearing in the amphitheatre.

In the year of the consulship of Caius Laecanius and Marcus Licinius a yet keener impulse urged Nero to show himself frequently on the public stage. Hitherto he had sung in private houses or gardens, during the juvenile games, but these he now despised, as being but little frequented, and on too small a scale for so fine a voice. As, however, he did not venture to make a beginning at Rome, he chose Neapolis, because it was a Greek city. From this as his starting-point he might cross into Achaia, and there, winning the well-known and sacred garlands of antiquity, evoke, with increased fame, the enthusiasm of the citizens. Accordingly, a rabble of the townsfolk was brought together, with those whom the excitement of such an event had attracted from the neighbouring towns and colonies, and such as followed in the emperor's train to pay him honour or for various objects. All these, with some companies of soldiers, filled the theatre at Neapolis.

There an incident occurred, which many thought unlucky, though to the emperor it seemed due to the providence of auspicious deities. The people who had been present, had quitted the theatre, and the empty building then fell in without harm to anyone. Thereupon Nero in an elaborate ode thanked the gods, celebrating the good luck which attended the late downfall, and as he was on his way to cross the sea of Hadria, he rested awhile at Beneventum, where a crowded gladiatorial show was being exhibited by Vatinius. The man was one of the most conspicuously infamous sights in the imperial court, bred, as he had been, in a shoemaker's shop, of a deformed person and vulgar wit, originally introduced as a butt. After a time he grew so powerful by accusing all the best men, that in influence, wealth, and ability to injure, he was pre-eminent even in that bad company.

While Nero was frequently visiting the show, even amid his pleasures there was no cessation to his crimes. For during the very same period Torquatus Silanus was forced to die, because over and above his illustrious rank as one of the Junian family he claimed to be the great-grandson of Augustus. Accusers were ordered to charge him with prodigality in lavishing gifts, and with having no hope but in revolution. They said further that he had nobles about him for his letters, books, and accounts, titles all and rehearsals of supreme power. Then the most intimate of his freedmen were put in chains and torn from him, till, knowing the doom which impended, Torquatus divided the arteries in his arms. A speech from Nero followed, as usual, which stated that though he was guilty and with good reason distrusted his defence, he would yet have lived, had he awaited the clemency of the judge.

Soon afterwards, giving up Achaia for the present (his reasons were not certainly known), he returned to Rome, there dwelling in his secret imaginations on the provinces of the east, especially Egypt. Then having declared in a public proclamation that his absence would not be long and that all things in the State would remain unchanged and prosperous, he visited the temple of the Capitol for advice about his departure. There he adored the gods; then he entered also the temple of Vesta, and there feeling a sudden trembling throughout his limbs, either from terror inspired by the deity or because, from the remembrance of his crimes, he was never free from fear, he relinquished his purpose, repeatedly saying that all his plans were of less account than his love of his country. "He had seen the sad countenances of the citizens, he heard their secret complainings at the prospect of his entering on so long a journey, when they could not bear so much as his brief excursions, accustomed as they were to cheer themselves under mischances by the sight of the emperor. Hence, as in private relationships the closest ties were the strongest, so the people of Rome had the most powerful claims and must be obeyed in their wish to retain him."

These and the like sentiments suited the people, who craved amusement, and feared, always their chief anxiety, scarcity of corn, should he be absent. The Senate and leading citizens were in doubt whether to regard him as more terrible at a distance or among them. After a while, as is the way with great terrors, they thought what happened the worst alternative.

Nero, to win credit for himself of enjoying nothing so much as the capital, prepared banquets in the public places, and used the whole city, so to say, as his private house. Of these entertainments the most famous for their notorious profligacy were those furnished by Tigellinus, which I will describe as an illustration, that I may not have again and again to narrate similar extravagance. He had a raft constructed on Agrippa's lake, put the guests on board and set it in motion by other vessels towing it. These vessels glittered with gold and ivory; the crews were arranged according to age and experience in vice. Birds and beasts had been procured from remote countries, and sea monsters from the ocean. On the margin of the lake were set up brothels crowded with noble ladies, and on the opposite bank were seen naked prostitutes with obscene gestures and movements. As darkness approached, all the adjacent grove and surrounding buildings resounded with song, and shone brilliantly with lights. Nero, who polluted himself by every lawful or lawless indulgence, had not omitted a single abomination which could heighten his depravity, till a few days afterwards he stooped to marry himself to one of that filthy herd, by name Pythagoras, with all the forms of regular wedlock. The bridal veil was put over the emperor; people saw the witnesses of the ceremony, the wedding dower, the couch and the nuptial torches; everything in a word was plainly visible, which, even when a woman weds darkness hides.

A disaster followed, whether accidental or treacherously contrived by the emperor, is uncertain, as authors have given both accounts, worse, however, and more dreadful than any which have ever happened to this city by the violence of fire. It had its beginning in that part of the circus which adjoins the Palatine and Caelian hills, where, amid the shops containing inflammable wares, the conflagration both broke out and instantly became so fierce and so rapid from the wind that it seized in its grasp the entire length of the circus. For here there were no houses fenced in by solid masonry, or temples surrounded by walls, or any other obstacle to interpose delay. The blaze in its fury ran first through the level portions of the city, then rising to the hills, while it again devastated every place below them, it outstripped all preventive measures; so rapid was the mischief and so completely at its mercy the city, with those narrow winding passages and irregular streets, which characterised old Rome. Added to this were the wailings of terror-stricken women, the feebleness of age, the helpless inexperience of childhood, the crowds who sought to save themselves or others, dragging out the infirm or waiting for them, and by their hurry in the one case, by their delay in the other, aggravating the confusion. Often, while they looked behind them, they were intercepted by flames on their side or in their face. Or if they reached a refuge close at hand, when this too was seized by the fire, they found that, even places, which they had imagined to be remote, were involved in the same calamity. At last, doubting what they should avoid or whither betake themselves, they crowded the streets or flung themselves down in the fields, while some who had lost their all, even their very daily bread, and others out of love for their kinsfolk, whom they had been unable to rescue, perished, though escape was open to them. And no one dared to stop the mischief, because of incessant menaces from a number of persons who forbade the extinguishing of the flames, because again others openly hurled brands, and kept shouting that there was one who gave them authority, either seeking to plunder more freely, or obeying orders.

Nero at this time was at Antium, and did not return to Rome until the fire approached his house, which he had built to connect the palace with the gardens of Maecenas. It could not, however, be stopped from devouring the palace, the house, and everything around it. However, to relieve the people, driven out homeless as they were, he threw open to them the Campus Martius and the public buildings of Agrippa, and even his own gardens, and raised temporary structures to receive the destitute multitude. Supplies of food were brought up from Ostia and the neighbouring towns, and the price of corn was reduced to three sesterces a peck. These acts, though popular, produced no effect, since a rumour had gone forth everywhere that, at the very time when the city was in flames, the emperor appeared on a private stage and sang of the destruction of Troy, comparing present misfortunes with the calamities of antiquity.

At last, after five days, an end was put to the conflagration at the foot of the Esquiline hill, by the destruction of all buildings on a vast space, so that the violence of the fire was met by clear ground and an open sky. But before people had laid aside their fears, the flames returned, with no less fury this second time, and especially in the spacious districts of the city. Consequently, though there was less loss of life, the temples of the gods, and the porticoes which were devoted to enjoyment, fell in a yet more widespread ruin. And to this conflagration there attached the greater infamy because it broke out on the Aemilian property of Tigellinus, and it seemed that Nero was aiming at the glory of founding a new city and calling it by his name. Rome, indeed, is divided into fourteen districts, four of which remained uninjured, three were levelled to the ground, while in the other seven were left only a few shattered, half-burnt relics of houses.

It would not be easy to enter into a computation of the private mansions, the blocks of tenements, and of the temples, which were lost. Those with the oldest ceremonial, as that dedicated by Servius Tullius to Luna, the great altar and shrine raised by the Arcadian Evander to the visibly appearing Hercules, the temple of Jupiter the Stayer, which was vowed by Romulus, Numa's royal palace, and the sanctuary of Vesta, with the tutelary deities of the Roman people, were burnt. So too were the riches acquired by our many victories, various beauties of Greek art, then again the ancient and genuine historical monuments of men of genius, and, notwithstanding the striking splendour of the restored city, old men will remember many things which could not be replaced. Some persons observed that the beginning of this conflagration was on the 19th of July, the day on which the Senones captured and fired Rome. Others have pushed a curious inquiry so far as to reduce the interval between these two conflagrations into equal numbers of years, months, and days.

Nero meanwhile availed himself of his country's desolation, and erected a mansion in which the jewels and gold, long familiar objects, quite vulgarised by our extravagance, were not so marvellous as the fields and lakes, with woods on one side to resemble a wilderness, and, on the other, open spaces and extensive views. The directors and contrivers of the work were Severus and Celer, who had the genius and the audacity to attempt by art even what nature had refused, and to fool away an emperor's resources. They had actually undertaken to sink a navigable canal from the lake Avernus to the mouths of the Tiber along a barren shore or through the face of hills, where one meets with no moisture which could supply water, except the Pomptine marshes. The rest of the country is broken rock and perfectly dry. Even if it could be cut through, the labour would be intolerable, and there would be no adequate result. Nero, however, with his love of the impossible, endeavoured to dig through the nearest hills to Avernus, and there still remain the traces of his disappointed hope.

Of Rome meanwhile, so much as was left unoccupied by his mansion, was not built up, as it had been after its burning by the Gauls, without any regularity or in any fashion, but with rows of streets according to measurement, with broad thoroughfares, with a restriction on the height of houses, with open spaces, and the further addition of colonnades, as a protection to the frontage of the blocks of tenements. These colonnades Nero promised to erect at his own expense, and to hand over the open spaces, when cleared of the debris, to the ground landlords. He also offered rewards proportioned to each person's position and property, and prescribed a period within which they were to obtain them on the completion of so many houses or blocks of building. He fixed on the marshes of Ostia for the reception of the rubbish, and arranged that the ships which had brought up corn by the Tiber, should sail down the river with cargoes of this rubbish. The buildings themselves, to a certain height, were to be solidly constructed, without wooden beams, of stone from Gabii or Alba, that material being impervious to fire. And to provide that the water which individual license had illegally appropriated, might flow in greater abundance in several places for the public use, officers were appointed, and everyone was to have in the open court the means of stopping a fire. Every building, too, was to be enclosed by its own proper wall, not by one common to others. These changes which were liked for their utility, also added beauty to the new city. Some, however, thought that its old arrangement had been more conducive to health, inasmuch as the narrow streets with the elevation of the roofs were not equally penetrated by the sun's heat, while now the open space, unsheltered by any shade, was scorched by a fiercer glow.

Such indeed were the precautions of human wisdom. The next thing was to seek means of propitiating the gods, and recourse was had to the Sibylline books, by the direction of which prayers were offered to Vulcanus, Ceres, and Proserpina. Juno, too, was entreated by the matrons, first, in the Capitol, then on the nearest part of the coast, whence water was procured to sprinkle the fane and image of the goddess. And there were sacred banquets and nightly vigils celebrated by married women. But all human efforts, all the lavish gifts of the emperor, and the propitiations of the gods, did not banish the sinister belief that the conflagration was the result of an order. Consequently, to get rid of the report, Nero fastened the guilt and inflicted the most exquisite tortures on a class hated for their abominations, called Christians by the populace. Christus, from whom the name had its origin, suffered the extreme penalty during the reign of Tiberius at the hands of one of our procurators, Pontius Pilatus, and a most mischievous superstition, thus checked for the moment, again broke out not only in Judaea, the first source of the evil, but even in Rome, where all things hideous and shameful from every part of the world find their centre and become popular. Accordingly, an arrest was first made of all who pleaded guilty; then, upon their information, an immense multitude was convicted, not so much of the crime of firing the city, as of hatred against mankind. Mockery of every sort was added to their deaths. Covered with the skins of beasts, they were torn by dogs and perished, or were nailed to crosses, or were doomed to the flames and burnt, to serve as a nightly illumination, when daylight had expired.

Nero offered his gardens for the spectacle, and was exhibiting a show in the circus, while he mingled with the people in the dress of a charioteer or stood aloft on a car. Hence, even for criminals who deserved extreme and exemplary punishment, there arose a feeling of compassion; for it was not, as it seemed, for the public good, but to glut one man's cruelty, that they were being destroyed.

Meanwhile Italy was thoroughly exhausted by contributions of money, the provinces were ruined, as also the allied nations and the free states, as they were called. Even the gods fell victims to the plunder; for the temples in Rome were despoiled and the gold carried off, which, for a triumph or a vow, the Roman people in every age had consecrated in their prosperity or their alarm. Throughout Asia and Achaia not only votive gifts, but the images of deities were seized, Acratus and Secundus Carinas having been sent into those provinces. The first was a freedman ready for any wickedness; the latter, as far as speech went, was thoroughly trained in Greek learning, but he had not imbued his heart with sound principles. Seneca, it was said, to avert from himself the obloquy of sacrilege, begged for the seclusion of a remote rural retreat, and, when it was refused, feigning ill health, as though he had a nervous ailment, would not quit his chamber. According to some writers, poison was prepared for him at Nero's command by his own freedman, whose name was Cleonicus. This Seneca avoided through the freedman's disclosure, or his own apprehension, while he used to support life on the very simple diet of wild fruits, with water from a running stream when thirst prompted.

During the same time some gladiators in the town of Praeneste, who attempted to break loose, were put down by a military guard stationed on the spot to watch them, and the people, ever desirous and yet fearful of change, began at once to talk of Spartacus, and of bygone calamities. Soon afterwards, tidings of a naval disaster was received, but not from war, for never had there been so profound a peace. Nero, however, had ordered the fleet to return to Campania on a fixed day, without making any allowance for the dangers of the sea. Consequently the pilots, in spite of the fury of the waves, started from Formiae, and while they were struggling to double the promontory of Misenum, they were dashed by a violent south-west wind on the shores of Cumae, and lost, in all directions, a number of their triremes with some smaller vessels.

At the close of the year people talked much about prodigies, presaging impending evils. Never were lightning flashes more frequent, and a comet too appeared, for which Nero always made propitiation with noble blood. Human and other births with two heads were exposed to public view, or were discovered in those sacrifices in which it is usual to immolate victims in a pregnant condition. And in the district of Placentia, close to the road, a calf was born with its head attached to its leg. Then followed an explanation of the diviners, that another head was preparing for the world, which however would be neither mighty nor hidden, as its growth had been checked in the womb, and it had been born by the wayside.

Silius Nerva and Atticus Vestinus then entered on the consulship, and now a conspiracy was planned, and at once became formidable, for which senators, knights, soldiers, even women, had given their names with eager rivalry, out of hatred of Nero as well as a liking for Caius Piso. A descendant of the Calpurnian house, and embracing in his connections through his father's noble rank many illustrious families, Piso had a splendid reputation with the people from his virtue or semblance of virtue. His eloquence he exercised in the defence of fellow-citizens, his generosity towards friends, while even for strangers he had a courteous address and demeanour. He had, too, the fortuitous advantages of tall stature and a handsome face. But solidity of character and moderation in pleasure were wholly alien to him. He indulged in laxity, in display, and occasionally in excess. This suited the taste of that numerous class who, when the attractions of vice are so powerful, do not wish for strictness or special severity on the throne.

The origin of the conspiracy was not in Piso's personal ambition. But I could not easily narrate who first planned it, or whose prompting inspired a scheme into which so many entered. That the leading spirits were Subrius Flavus, tribune of a praetorian cohort, and Sulpicius Asper, a centurion, was proved by the fearlessness of their death. Lucanus Annaeus, too, and Plautius Lateranus, imported into it an intensely keen resentment. Lucanus had the stimulus of personal motives, for Nero tried to disparage the fame of his poems and, with the foolish vanity of a rival, had forbidden him to publish them. As for Lateranus, a consul-elect, it was no wrong, but love of the State which linked him with the others. Flavius Scaevinus and Afranius Quintianus, on the other hand, both of senatorial rank, contrary to what was expected of them, undertook the beginning of this daring crime. Scaevinus, indeed, had enfeebled his mind by excess, and his life, accordingly, was one of sleepy languor. Quintianus, infamous for his effeminate vice, had been satirised by Nero in a lampoon, and was bent on avenging the insult.

So, while they dropped hints among themselves or among their friends about the emperor's crimes, the approaching end of empire, and the importance of choosing some one to rescue the State in its distress, they associated with them Tullius Senecio, Cervarius Proculus, Vulcatius Araricus, Julius Augurinus, Munatius Gratus, Antonius Natalis, and Marcius Festus, all Roman knights. Of these Senecio, one of those who was specially intimate with Nero, still kept up a show of friendship, and had consequently to struggle with all the more dangers. Natalis shared with Piso all his secret plans. The rest built their hopes on revolution. Besides Subrius and Sulpicius, whom I have already mentioned, they invited the aid of military strength, of Gavius Silvanus and Statius Proximus, tribunes of praetorian cohorts, and of two centurions, Maximus Scaurus and Venetus Paulus. But their mainstay, it was thought, was Faenius Rufus, the commander of the guard, a man of esteemed life and character, to whom Tigellinus with his brutality and shamelessness was superior in the emperor's regard. He harassed him with calumnies, and had often put him in terror by hinting that he had been Agrippina's paramour, and from sorrow at her loss was intent on vengeance. And so, when the conspirators were assured by his own repeated language that the commander of the praetorian guard had come over to their side, they once more eagerly discussed the time and place of the fatal deed. It was said that Subrius Flavus had formed a sudden resolution to attack Nero when singing on the stage, or when his house was in flames and he was running hither and thither, unattended, in the darkness. In the one case was the opportunity of solitude; in the other, the very crowd which would witness so glorious a deed, had roused a singularly noble soul; it was only the desire of escape, that foe to all great enterprises, which held him back.

Meanwhile, as they hesitated in prolonged suspense between hope and fear, a certain Epicharis (how she informed herself is uncertain, as she had never before had a thought of anything noble) began to stir and upbraid the conspirators. Wearied at last of their long delay, she endeavoured, when staying in Campania, to shake the loyalty of the officers of the fleet at Misenum, and to entangle them in a guilty complicity. She began thus. There was a captain in the fleet, Volusius Proculus, who had been one of Nero's instruments in his mother's murder, and had not, as he thought, been promoted in proportion to the greatness of his crime. Either, as an old acquaintance of the woman, or on the strength of a recent intimacy, he divulged to her his services to Nero and their barren result to himself, adding complaints, and his determination to have vengeance, should the chance arise. He thus inspired the hope that he could be persuaded, and could secure many others. No small help was to be found in the fleet, and there would be numerous opportunities, as Nero delighted in frequent enjoyment of the sea off Puteoli and Misenum.

Epicharis accordingly said more, and began the history of all the emperor's crimes. "The Senate," she affirmed, "had no power left it; yet means had been provided whereby he might pay the penalty of having destroyed the State. Only let Proculus gird himself to do his part and bring over to their side his bravest soldiers, and then look for an adequate recompense." The conspirators' names, however, she withheld. Consequently the information of Proculus was useless, even though he reported what he had heard to Nero. For Epicharis being summoned and confronted with the informer easily silenced him, unsupported as he was by a single witness. But she was herself detained in custody, for Nero suspected that even what was not proved to be true, was not wholly false.

The conspirators, however, alarmed by the fear of disclosure, resolved to hurry on the assassination at Baiae, in Piso's villa, whither the emperor, charmed by its loveliness, often went, and where, unguarded and without the cumbrous grandeur of his rank, he would enjoy the bath and the banquet. But Piso refused, alleging the odium of an act which would stain with an emperor's blood, however bad he might be, the sanctity of the hospitable board and the deities who preside over it. "Better," he said, "in the capital, in that hateful mansion which was piled up with the plunder of the citizens, or in public, to accomplish what on the State's behalf they had undertaken."

So he said openly, with however a secret apprehension that Lucius Silanus might, on the strength of his distinguished rank and the teachings of Caius Cassius, under whom he had been trained, aspire to any greatness and seize an empire, which would be promptly offered him by all who had no part in the conspiracy, and who would pity Nero as the victim of a crime. Many thought that Piso shunned also the enterprising spirit of Vestinus, the consul, who might, he feared, rise up in the cause of freedom, or, by choosing another emperor, make the State his own gift. Vestinus, indeed, had no share in the conspiracy, though Nero on that charge gratified an old resentment against an innocent man.

At last they decided to carry out their design on that day of the circus games, which is celebrated in honour of Ceres, as the emperor, who seldom went out, and shut himself up in his house or gardens, used to go to the entertainments of the circus, and access to him was the easier from his keen enjoyment of the spectacle. They had so arranged the order of the plot, that Lateranus was to throw himself at the prince's knees in earnest entreaty, apparently craving relief for his private necessities, and, being a man of strong nerve and huge frame, hurl him to the ground and hold him down. When he was prostrate and powerless, the tribunes and centurions and all the others who had sufficient daring were to rush up and do the murder, the first blow being claimed by Scaevinus, who had taken a dagger from the Temple of Safety, or, according to another account, from that of Fortune, in the town of Ferentum, and used to wear the weapon as though dedicated to some noble deed. Piso, meanwhile, was wait in the sanctuary of Ceres, whence he was to be summoned by Faenius, the commander of the guard, and by the others, and then conveyed into the camp, accompanied by Antonia, the daughter of Claudius Caesar, with a view to evoke the people's enthusiasm. So it is related by Caius Pliny. Handed down from whatever source, I had no intention of suppressing it, however absurd it may seem, either that Antonia should have lent her name at her life's peril to a hopeless project, or that Piso, with his well-known affection for his wife, should have pledged himself to another marriage, but for the fact that the lust of dominion inflames the heart more than any other passion.

It was however wonderful how among people of different class, rank, age, sex, among rich and poor, everything was kept in secrecy till betrayal began from the house of Scaevinus. The day before the treacherous attempt, after a long conversation with Antonius Natalis, Scaevinus returned home, sealed his will, and, drawing from its sheath the dagger of which I have already spoken, and complaining that it was blunted from long disuse, he ordered it to be sharpened on a stone to a keen and bright point. This task he assigned to his freedman Milichus. At the same time sat down to a more than usually sumptuous banquet, and gave his favourite slaves their freedom, and money to others. He was himself depressed, and evidently in profound thought, though he affected gaiety in desultory conversation. Last of all, he directed ligatures for wounds and the means of stanching blood to be prepared by the same Milichus, who either knew of the conspiracy and was faithful up to this point, or was in complete ignorance and then first caught suspicions, as most authors have inferred from what followed. For when his servile imagination dwelt on the rewards of perfidy, and he saw before him at the same moment boundless wealth and power, conscience and care for his patron's life, together with the remembrance of the freedom he had received, fled from him. From his wife, too, he had adopted a womanly and yet baser suggestion; for she even held over him a dreadful thought, that many had been present, both freedmen and slaves, who had seen what he had; that one man's silence would be useless, whereas the rewards would be for him alone who was first with the information.

Accordingly at daybreak Milichus went to the Servilian gardens, and, finding the doors shut against him, said again and again that he was the bearer of important and alarming news. Upon this he was conducted by the gatekeepers to one of Nero's freedmen, Epaphroditus, and by him to Nero, whom he informed of the urgent danger, of the formidable conspiracy, and of all else which he had heard or inferred. He showed him too the weapon prepared for his destruction, and bade him summon the accused.

Scaevinus on being arrested by the soldiers began his defence with the reply that the dagger about which he was accused, had of old been regarded with a religious sentiment by his ancestors, that it had been kept in his chamber, and been stolen by a trick of his freedman. He had often, he said, signed his will without heeding the observance of particular days, and had previously given presents of money as well as freedom to some of his slaves, only on this occasion he gave more freely, because, as his means were now impoverished and his creditors were pressing him, he distrusted the validity of his will. Certainly his table had always been profusely furnished, and his life luxurious, such as rigid censors would hardly approve. As to the bandages for wounds, none had been prepared at his order, but as all the man's other charges were absurd, he added an accusation in which he might make himself alike informer and witness.

He backed up his words by an air of resolution. Turning on his accuser, he denounced him as an infamous and depraved wretch, with so fearless a voice and look that the information was beginning to collapse, when Milichus was reminded by his wife that Antonious Natalis had had a long secret conversation with Scaevinus, and that both were Piso's intimate friends.

Natalis was therefore summoned, and they were separately asked what the conversation was, and what was its subject. Then a suspicion arose because their answers did not agree, and they were both put in irons. They could not endure the sight and the threat of torture. Natalis however, taking the initiative, knowing as he did more of the whole conspiracy, and being also more practised in accusing, first confessed about Piso, next added the name of Annaeus Seneca, either as having been a messenger between him and Piso, or to win the favour of Nero, who hated Seneca and sought every means for his ruin. Then Scaevinus too, when he knew the disclosure of Natalis, with like pusillanimity, or under the impression that everything now divulged, and that there could be no advantage in silence, revealed the other conspirators. Of these, Lucanus, Quintianus, and Senecio long persisted in denial; after a time, when bribed by the promise of impunity, anxious to excuse their reluctance, Lucanus named his mother Atilla, Quintianus and Senecio, their chief friends, respectively, Glitius Gallus and Annius Pollio.

Nero, meanwhile, remembering that Epicharis was in custody on the information of Volusius Proculus, and assuming that a woman's frame must be unequal to the agony, ordered her to be torn on the rack. But neither the scourge nor fire, nor the fury of the men as they increased the torture that they might not be a woman's scorn, overcame her positive denial of the charge. Thus the first day's inquiry was futile. On the morrow, as she was being dragged back on a chair to the same torments (for with her limbs all dislocated she could not stand), she tied a band, which she had stript off her bosom, in a sort of noose to the arched back of the chair, put her neck in it, and then straining with the whole weight of her body, wrung out of her frame its little remaining breath. All the nobler was the example set by a freedwoman at such a crisis in screening strangers and those whom she hardly knew, when freeborn men, Roman knights, and senators, yet unscathed by torture, betrayed, every one, his dearest kinsfolk. For even Lucanus and Senecio and Quintianus failed not to reveal their accomplices indiscriminately, and Nero was more and more alarmed, though he had fenced his person with a largely augmented guard.

Even Rome itself he put, so to say, under custody, garrisoning its walls with companies of soldiers and occupying with troops the coast and the river-banks. Incessantly were there flying through the public places, through private houses, country fields, and the neighbouring villages, horse and foot soldiers, mixed with Germans, whom the emperor trusted as being foreigners. In long succession, troops of prisoners in chains were dragged along and stood at the gates of his gardens. When they entered to plead their cause, a smile of joy on any of the conspirators, a casual conversation, a sudden meeting, or the fact of having entered a banquet or a public show in company, was construed into a crime, while to the savage questionings of Nero and Tigellinus were added the violent menaces of Faenius Rufus, who had not yet been named by the informers, but who, to get the credit of complete ignorance, frowned fiercely on his accomplices. When Subius Flavus at his side asked him by a sign whether he should draw his sword in the middle of the trial and perpetrate the fatal deed, Rufus refused, and checked the man's impulse as he was putting his hand to his sword-hilt.

Some there were who, as soon as the conspiracy was betrayed, urged Piso, while Milichus' story was being heard, and Scaevinus was hesitating, to go to the camp or mount the Rostra and test the feelings of the soldiers and of the people. "If," said they, "your accomplices join your enterprise, those also who are yet undecided, will follow, and great will be the fame of the movement once started, and this in any new scheme is all-powerful. Against it Nero has taken no precaution. Even brave men are dismayed by sudden perils; far less will that stageplayer, with Tigellinus forsooth and his concubines in his train, raise arms against you. Many things are accomplished on trial which cowards think arduous. It is vain to expect secrecy and fidelity from the varying tempers and bodily constitutions of such a host of accomplices. Torture or reward can overcome everything. Men will soon come to put you also in chains and inflict on you an ignominious death. How much more gloriously will you die while you cling to the State and invoke aid for liberty. Rather let the soldiers fail, the people be traitors, provided that you, if prematurely robbed of life, justify your death to your ancestors and descendants."

Unmoved by these considerations, Piso showed himself a few moments in public, then sought the retirement of his house, and there fortified his spirit against the worst, till a troop of soldiers arrived, raw recruits, or men recently enlisted, whom Nero had selected, because he was afraid of the veterans, imbued, though they were, with a liking for him. Piso expired by having the veins in his arms severed. His will, full of loathsome flatteries of Nero, was a concession to his love of his wife, a base woman, with only a beautiful person to recommend her, whom he had taken away from her husband, one of his friends. Her name was Atria Galla; that of her former husband, Domitius Silus. The tame spirit of the man, the profligacy of the woman, blazoned Piso's infamy.

In quick succession Nero added the murder of Plautius Lateranus, consul-elect, so promptly that he did not allow him to embrace his children or to have the brief choice of his own death. He was dragged off to a place set apart for the execution of slaves, and butchered by the hand of the tribune Statius, maintaining a resolute silence, and not reproaching the tribune with complicity in the plot.

Then followed the destruction of Annaeus Seneca, a special joy to the emperor, not because he had convicted him of the conspiracy, but anxious to accomplish with the sword what poison had failed to do. It was, in fact, Natalis alone who divulged Seneca's name, to this extent, that he had been sent to Seneca when ailing, to see him and remonstrate with him for excluding Piso from his presence, when it would have been better to have kept up their friendship by familiar intercourse; that Seneca's reply was that mutual conversations and frequent interviews were to the advantage of neither, but still that his own life depended on Piso's safety. Gavius Silvanus, tribune of a praetorian cohort, was ordered to report this to Seneca and to ask him whether he acknowledged what Natalis said and his own answer. Either by chance or purposely Seneca had returned on that day from Campania, and had stopped at a country-house four miles from Rome. Thither the tribune came next evening, surrounded the house with troops of soldiers, and then made known the emperor's message to Seneca as he was at dinner with his wife, Pompeia Paulina, and two friends.

Seneca replied that Natalis had been sent to him and had complained to him in Piso's name because of his refusal to see Piso, upon which he excused himself on the ground of failing health and the desire of rest. "He had no reason," he said, for "preferring the interest of any private citizen to his own safety, and he had no natural aptitude for flattery. No one knew this better than Nero, who had oftener experienced Seneca's freespokenness than his servility." When the tribune reported this answer in the presence of Poppaea and Tigellinus, the emperor's most confidential advisers in his moments of rage, he asked whether Seneca was meditating suicide. Upon this the tribune asserted that he saw no signs of fear, and perceived no sadness in his words or in his looks. He was accordingly ordered to go back and to announce sentence of death. Fabius Rusticus tells us that he did not return the way he came, but went out of his course to Faenius, the commander of the guard, and having explained to him the emperor's orders, and asked whether he was to obey them, was by him admonished to carry them out, for a fatal spell of cowardice was on them all. For this very Silvanus was one of the conspirators, and he was now abetting the crimes which he had united with them to avenge. But he spared himself the anguish of a word or of a look, and merely sent in to Seneca one of his centurions, who was to announce to him his last doom.

Seneca, quite unmoved, asked for tablets on which to inscribe his will, and, on the centurion's refusal, turned to his friends, protesting that as he was forbidden to requite them, he bequeathed to them the only, but still the noblest possession yet remaining to him, the pattern of his life, which, if they remembered, they would win a name for moral worth and steadfast friendship. At the same time he called them back from their tears to manly resolution, now with friendly talk, and now with the sterner language of rebuke. "Where," he asked again and again, "are your maxims of philosophy, or the preparation of so many years' study against evils to come? Who knew not Nero's cruelty? After a mother's and a brother's murder, nothing remains but to add the destruction of a guardian and a tutor."

Having spoken these and like words, meant, so to say, for all, he embraced his wife; then softening awhile from the stern resolution of the hour, he begged and implored her to spare herself the burden of perpetual sorrow, and, in the contemplation of a life virtuously spent, to endure a husband's loss with honourable consolations. She declared, in answer, that she too had decided to die, and claimed for herself the blow of the executioner. There upon Seneca, not to thwart her noble ambition, from an affection too which would not leave behind him for insult one whom he dearly loved, replied: "I have shown you ways of smoothing life; you prefer the glory of dying. I will not grudge you such a noble example. Let the fortitude of so courageous an end be alike in both of us, but let there be more in your decease to win fame."

Then by one and the same stroke they sundered with a dagger the arteries of their arms. Seneca, as his aged frame, attenuated by frugal diet, allowed the blood to escape but slowly, severed also the veins of his legs and knees. Worn out by cruel anguish, afraid too that his sufferings might break his wife's spirit, and that, as he looked on her tortures, he might himself sink into irresolution, he persuaded her to retire into another chamber. Even at the last moment his eloquence failed him not; he summoned his secretaries, and dictated much to them which, as it has been published for all readers in his own words, I forbear to paraphrase.

Nero meanwhile, having no personal hatred against Paulina and not wishing to heighten the odium of his cruelty, forbade her death. At the soldiers' prompting, her slaves and freedmen bound up her arms, and stanched the bleeding, whether with her knowledge is doubtful. For as the vulgar are ever ready to think the worst, there were persons who believed that, as long as she dreaded Nero's relentlessness, she sought the glory of sharing her husband's death, but that after a time, when a more soothing prospect presented itself, she yielded to the charms of life. To this she added a few subsequent years, with a most praise worthy remembrance of her husband, and with a countenance and frame white to a degree of pallor which denoted a loss of much vital energy.

Seneca meantime, as the tedious process of death still lingered on, begged Statius Annaeus, whom he had long esteemed for his faithful friendship and medical skill, to produce a poison with which he had some time before provided himself, same drug which extinguished the life of those who were condemned by a public sentence of the people of Athens. It was brought to him and he drank it in vain, chilled as he was throughout his limbs, and his frame closed against the efficacy of the poison. At last he entered a pool of heated water, from which he sprinkled the nearest of his slaves, adding the exclamation, "I offer this liquid as a libation to Jupiter the Deliverer." He was then carried into a bath, with the steam of which he was suffocated, and he was burnt without any of the usual funeral rites. So he had directed in a codicil of his will, when even in the height of his wealth and power he was thinking of his life's close.

There was a rumour that Sabrius Flavus had held a secret consultation with the centurions, and had planned, not without Seneca's knowledge, that when Nero had been slain by Piso's instrumentality, Piso also was to be murdered, and the empire handed over to Seneca, as a man singled out for his splendid virtues by all persons of integrity. Even a saying of Flavus was popularly current, "that it mattered not as to the disgrace if a harp-player were removed and a tragic actor succeeded him." For as Nero used to sing to the harp, so did Piso in the dress of a tragedian.

The soldiers' part too in the conspiracy no longer escaped discovery, some in their rage becoming informers to betray Faenius Rufus, whom they could not endure to be both an accomplice and a judge. Accordingly Scaevinus, in answer to his browbeating and menaces, said with a smile that no one knew more than he did, and actually urged him to show gratitude to so good a prince. Faenius could not meet this with either speech or silence. Halting in his words and visibly terror-stricken, while the rest, especially Cervarius Proculus, a Roman knight, did their utmost to convict him, he was, at the emperor's bidding, seized and bound by Cassius, a soldier, who because of his well-known strength of limb was in attendance.

Shortly afterwards, the information of the same men proved fatal to Subrius Flavus. At first he grounded his defence on his moral contrast to the others, implying that an armed soldier, like himself, would never have shared such an attempt with unarmed and effeminate associates. Then, when he was pressed, he embraced the glory of a full confession. Questioned by Nero as to the motives which had led him on to forget his oath of allegiance, "I hated you," he replied; "yet not a soldier was more loyal to you while you deserved to be loved. I began to hate you when you became the murderer of your mother and your wife, a charioteer, an actor, and an incendiary." I have given the man's very words, because they were not, like those of Seneca, generally published, though the rough and vigorous sentiments of a soldier ought to be no less known.

Throughout the conspiracy nothing, it was certain, fell with more terror on the ears of Nero, who was as unused to be told of the crimes he perpetrated as he was eager in their perpetration. The punishment of Flavus was intrusted to Veianius Niger, a tribune. At his direction, a pit was dug in a neighbouring field. Flavus, on seeing it, censured it as too shallow and confined, saying to the soldiers around him, "Even this is not according to military rule." When bidden to offer his neck resolutely, "I wish," said he, "that your stroke may be as resolute." The tribune trembled greatly, and having only just severed his head at two blows, vaunted his brutality to Nero, saying that he had slain him with a blow and a half.

Sulpicius Asper, a centurion, exhibited the next example of fortitude. To Nero's question why he had conspired to murder him, he briefly replied that he could not have rendered a better service to his infamous career. He then underwent the prescribed penalty. Nor did the remaining centurions forget their courage in suffering their punishment. But Faenius Rufus had not equal spirit; he even put his laments into his will.

Nero waited in the hope that Vestinus also, the consul, whom he thought an impetuous and deeply disaffected man, would be involved in the charge. None however of the conspirators had shared their counsels with him, some from old feuds against him, most because they considered him a reckless and dangerous associate. Nero's hatred of him had had its origin in intimate companionship, Vestinus seeing through and despising the emperor's cowardice, while Nero feared the high spirit of his friend, who often bantered him with that rough humour which, when it draws largely on facts, leaves a bitter memory behind it. There was too a recent aggravation in the circumstance of Vestinus having married Statilia Messalina, without being ignorant that the emperor was one of her paramours.

As neither crime nor accuser appeared, Nero, being thus unable to assume the semblance of a judge, had recourse to the sheer might of despotism, and despatched Gerellanus, a tribune, with a cohort of soldiers, and with orders to forestall the designs of the consul, to seize what he might call his fortress, and crush his train of chosen youths. For Vestinus had a house towering over the Forum, and a host of handsome slaves of the same age. On that day he had performed all his duties as consul, and was entertaining some guests, fearless of danger, or perhaps by way of hiding his fears, when the soldiers entered and announced to him the tribune's summons. He rose without a moment's delay, and every preparation was at once made. He shut himself into his chamber; a physician was at his side; his veins were opened; with life still strong in him, he was carried into a bath, and plunged into warm water, without uttering a word of pity for himself. Meanwhile the guards surrounded those who had sat at his table, and it was only at a late hour of the night that they were dismissed, when Nero, having pictured to himself and laughed over their terror at the expectation of a fatal end to their banquet, said that they had suffered enough punishment for the consul's entertainment.

Next he ordered the destruction of Marcus Annaeus Lucanus. As the blood flowed freely from him, and he felt a chill creeping through his feet and hands, and the life gradually ebbing from his extremities, though the heart was still warm and he retained his mental power, Lucanus recalled some poetry he had composed in which he had told the story of a wounded soldier dying a similar kind of death, and he recited the very lines. These were his last words. After him, Senecio, Quintianus, and Scaevinus perished, not in the manner expected from the past effeminacy of their life, and then the remaining conspirators, without deed or word deserving record.

Rome all this time was thronged with funerals, the Capitol with sacrificial victims. One after another, on the destruction of a brother, a kinsman, or a friend, would return thanks to the gods, deck his house with laurels, prostrate himself at the knees of the emperor, and weary his hand with kisses. He, in the belief that this was rejoicing, rewarded with impunity the prompt informations of Antonius Natalis and Cervarius Proculus. Milichus was enriched with gifts and assumed in its Greek equivalent the name of Saviour. Of the tribunes, Gavius Silvanus, though acquitted, perished by his own hand; Statius Proximus threw away the benefit of the pardon he had accepted from the emperor by the folly of his end. Cornelius Martialis, Flavius Nepos, Statius Domitius were then deprived of the tribuneship, on the ground, not of actually hating the emperor, but of having the credit of it. Novius Priscus, as Seneca's friend, Glitius Gallus, and Annius Pollio, as men disgraced rather than convicted, escaped with sentences of banishment. Priscus and Gallus were accompanied respectively by their wives, Artoria Flaccilla and Egnatia Maximilla. The latter possessed at first a great fortune, still unimpaired, and was subsequently deprived of it, both which circumstances enhanced her fame.

Rufius Crispinus too was banished, on the opportune pretext of the conspiracy, but he was in fact hated by Nero, because he had once been Poppaea's husband. It was the splendour of their name which drove Verginius Flavus and Musonius Rufus into exile. Verginius encouraged the studies of our youth by his eloquence; Rufus by the teachings of philosophy. Cluvidienus Quietus, Julius Agrippa, Blitius Catulinus, Petronius Priscus, Julius Altinus, mere rank and file, so to say, had islands in the Aegean Sea assigned to them. Caedicia, the wife of Scaevinus, and Caesonius Maximus were forbidden to live in Italy, their penalty being the only proof they had of having been accused. Atilla, the mother of Annaeus Lucanus, without either acquittal or punishment, was simply ignored.

All this having been completed, Nero assembled the troops and distributed two thousand sesterces to every common soldier, with an addition of as much corn without payment, as they had previously the use of at the market price. Then, as if he was going to describe successes in war, he summoned the Senate, and awarded triumphal honours to Petronius Turpilianus, an ex-consul, to Cocceius Nerva, praetor-elect, and to Tigellinus, commander of the praetorians. Tigellinus and Nerva he so distinguished as to place busts of them in the palace in addition to triumphal statues in the Forum. He granted a consul's decorations to Nymphidius, on whose origin, as he now appears for the first time, I will briefly touch. For he too will be a part of Rome's calamities.

The son of a freedwoman, who had prostituted a handsome person among the slaves and freedmen of the emperors, he gave out that he was the offspring of Caius Caesar, for he happened to be of tall stature and to have a fierce look, or possibly Caius Caesar, who liked even harlots, had also amused himself with the man's mother.

Nero meanwhile summoned the Senate, addressed them in a speech, and further added a proclamation to the people, with the evidence which had been entered on records, and the confessions of the condemned. He was indeed perpetually under the lash of popular talk, which said that he had destroyed men perfectly innocent out of jealousy or fear. However, that a conspiracy was begun, matured, and conclusively proved was not doubted at the time by those who took pains to ascertain the truth, and is admitted by those who after Nero's death returned to the capital. When every one in the Senate, those especially who had most cause to mourn, abased himself in flattery, Salienus Clemens denounced Junius Gallio, who was terror-stricken at his brother Seneca's death was pleading for his life. He called him an enemy and traitor to the State, till the unanimous voice of the senators deterred him from perverting public miseries into an occasion for a personal resentment, and thus importing fresh bitterness into what by the prince's clemency had been hushed up or forgotten.

Then offerings and thanksgivings to the gods were decreed, with special honours to the Sun, who has an ancient temple in the circus where the crime was planned, as having revealed by his power the secrets of the conspiracy. The games too of Ceres in the circus were to be celebrated with more horse-races, and the month of April was to be called after the name of Nero. A temple also was to be erected to Safety, on the spot whence Scaevinus had taken his dagger. The emperor himself dedicated the weapon in the temple of the capital, and inscribed on it, "To Jupiter the Avenger." This passed without notice at the moment, but after the war of Julius Vindex it was construed as an omen and presage of impending vengeance. I find in the registers of the Senate that Cerialis Anicius, consul-elect, proposed a motion that a temple should as soon as possible be built at the public expense to the Divine Nero. He implied indeed by this proposal that the prince had transcended all mortal grandeur and deserved the adoration of mankind. Some however interpreted it as an omen of his death, seeing that divine honours are not paid to an emperor till he has ceased to live among men.

BOOK XVI, A.D. 65, 66

Fortune soon afterwards made a dupe of Nero through his own credulity and the promises of Caesellius Bassus, a Carthaginian by birth and a man of a crazed imagination, who wrested a vision seen in the slumber of night into a confident expectation. He sailed to Rome, and having purchased admission to the emperor, he explained how he had discovered on his land a cave of immense depth, which contained a vast quantity of gold, not in the form of coin, but in the shapeless and ponderous masses of ancient days. In fact, he said, ingots of great weight lay there, with bars standing near them in another part of the cave, a treasure hidden for so many ages to increase the wealth of the present. Phoenician Dido, as he sought to show by inference, after fleeing from Tyre and founding Carthage, had concealed these riches in the fear that a new people might be demoralised by a superabundance of money, or that the Numidian kings, already for other reasons hostile, might by lust of gold be provoked to war.

Nero upon this, without sufficiently examining the credibility of the author of the story, or of the matter itself, or sending persons through whom he might ascertain whether the intelligence was true, himself actually encouraged the report and despatched men to bring the spoil, as if it were already acquired. They had triremes assigned them and crews specially selected to promote speed. Nothing else at the time was the subject of the credulous gossip of the people, and of the very different conversation of thinking persons. It happened, too, that the quinquennial games were being celebrated for the second time, and the orators took from this same incident their chief materials for eulogies on the emperor. "Not only," they said, "were there the usual harvests, and the gold of the mine with its alloy, but the earth now teemed with a new abundance, and wealth was thrust on them by the bounty of the gods." These and other servile flatteries they invented, with consummate eloquence and equal sycophancy, confidently counting on the facility of his belief.

Extravagance meanwhile increased, on the strength of a chimerical hope, and ancient wealth was wasted, as apparently the emperor had lighted on treasures he might squander for many a year. He even gave away profusely from this source, and the expectation of riches was one of the causes of the poverty of the State. Bassus indeed dug up his land and extensive plains in the neighbourhood, while he persisted that this or that was the place of the promised cave, and was followed not only by our soldiers but by the rustic population who were engaged to execute the work, till at last he threw off his infatuation, and expressing wonder that his dreams had never before been false, and that now for the first time he had been deluded, he escaped disgrace and danger by a voluntary death. Some have said that he was imprisoned and soon released, his property having been taken from him as a substitute for the royal treasure.

Meanwhile the Senate, as they were now on the eve of the quinquennial contest, wishing to avert scandal, offered the emperor the "victory in song," and added the "crown of eloquence," that thus a veil might be thrown over a shameful exposure on the stage. Nero, however, repeatedly declared that he wanted neither favour nor the Senate's influence, as he was a match for his rivals, and was certain, in the conscientious opinion of the judges, to win the honour by merit. First, he recited a poem on the stage; then, at the importunate request of the rabble that he would make public property of all his accomplishments (these were their words), he entered the theatre, and conformed to all the laws of harp-playing, not sitting down when tired, nor wiping off the perspiration with anything but the garment he wore, or letting himself be seen to spit or clear his nostrils. Last of all, on bended knee he saluted the assembly with a motion of the hand, and awaited the verdict of the judges with pretended anxiety. And then the city-populace, who were wont to encourage every gesture even of actors, made the place ring with measured strains of elaborate applause. One would have thought they were rejoicing, and perhaps they did rejoice, in their indifference to the public disgrace.

All, however, who were present from remote towns, and still retained the Italy of strict morals and primitive ways; all too who had come on embassies or on private business from distant provinces, where they had been unused to such wantonness, were unable to endure the spectacle or sustain the degrading fatigue, which wearied their unpractised hands, while they disturbed those who knew their part, and were often struck by soldiers, stationed in the seats, to see that not a moment of time passed with less vigorous applause or in the silence of indifference. It was a known fact that several knights, in struggling through the narrow approaches and the pressure of the crowd, were trampled to death, and that others while keeping their seats day and night were seized with some fatal malady. For it was a still worse danger to be absent from the show, as many openly and many more secretly made it their business to scrutinize names and faces, and to note the delight or the disgust of the company. Hence came cruel severities, immediately exercised on the humble, and resentments, concealed for the moment, but subsequently paid off, towards men of distinction. There was a story that Vespasian was insulted by Phoebus, a freedman, for closing his eyes in a doze, and that having with difficulty been screened by the intercessions of the well disposed, he escaped imminent destruction through his grander destiny.

After the conclusion of the games Poppaea died from a casual outburst of rage in her husband, who felled her with a kick when she was pregnant. That there was poison I cannot believe, though some writers so relate, from hatred rather than from belief, for the emperor was desirous of children, and wholly swayed by love of his wife. Her body was not consumed by fire according to Roman usage, but after the custom of foreign princes was filled with fragrant spices and embalmed, and then consigned to the sepulchre of the Julii. She had, however, a public funeral, and Nero himself from the rostra eulogized her beauty, her lot in having been the mother of a deified child, and fortune's other gifts, as though they were virtues.

To the death of Poppaea, which, though a public grief, was a delight to those who recalling the past thought of her shamelessness and cruelty, Nero added fresh and greater odium by forbidding Caius Cassius to attend the funeral. This was the first token of mischief. Nor was it long delayed. Silanus was coupled with Cassius, no crime being alleged, but that Cassius was eminent for his ancestral wealth and dignity of character, Silanus for the nobility of his birth and the quiet demeanour of his youth. The emperor accordingly sent the Senate a speech in which he argued that both ought to be removed from the State, and made it a reproach against Cassius that among his ancestors' busts he had specially revered that of Caius Cassius, which bore the inscription "to the Party-Leader." In fact, he had thereby sought to sow the seeds of civil war and revolt from the House of the Caesars. And that he might not merely avail himself of the memory of a hated name to stir up strife, he had associated with him Lucius Silanus, a youth of noble birth and reckless spirit, to whom he might point as an instrument of revolution.

Nero next denounced Silanus himself in the same terms as he had his uncle Torquatus, implying that he was already arranging the details of imperial business, and setting freedmen to manage his accounts, papers, and correspondence, imputations utterly groundless and false. Silanus, in truth, was intensely apprehensive, and had been frightened into caution by his uncle's destruction. Nero then procured persons, under the name of informers, to invent against Lepida, the wife of Cassius and aunt of Silanus, a charge of incest with her brother's son, and of some ghastly religious ceremonial. Volcatius Tullinus, and Marcellus Cornelius, senators, and Fabatus, a Roman knight, were drawn in as accomplices. By an appeal to the emperor these men eluded an impending doom and subsequently, as being too insignificant, escaped from Nero, who was busy with crimes on a far greater scale.

The Senate was then consulted and sentences of exile were passed on Cassius and Silanus. As to Lepida, the emperor was to decide. Cassius was transported to the island of Sardinia, and he was quietly left to old age. Silanus was removed to Ostia, whence, it was pretended, he was to be conveyed to Naxos. He was afterwards confined in a town of Apulia named Barium. There, as he was wisely enduring a most undeserved calamity, he was suddenly seized by a centurion sent to slay him. When the man advised him to sever his veins, he replied that, though he had resolved in his heart to die, he would not let a cutthroat have the glory of the service. The centurion seeing that, unarmed as he was, he was very powerful, and more an enraged than a frightened man, ordered his soldiers to overpower him. And Silanus failed not to resist and to strike blows, as well as he could with his bare hands, till he was cut down by the centurion, as though in battle, with wounds in his breast.

With equal courage Lucius Vetus, his mother-in-law Sextia, and his daughter Pollutia submitted to death. They were hated by the emperor because they seemed a living reproach to him for the murder of Rubellius Plautus, son-in-law of Lucius Vetus. But the first opportunity of unmasking his savage wrath was furnished by Fortunatus, a freedman, who having embezzled his patron's property, deserted him to become his accuser. He had as his accomplice Claudius Demianus, whom Vetus, when proconsul of Asia, had imprisoned for his gross misdeeds, and whom Nero now released as a recompense for the accusation.

When the accused knew this and saw that he and his freedman were pitted against each other on an equal footing, he retired to his estate at Formiae. There he was put under the secret surveillance of soldiers. With him was his daughter, who, to say nothing of the now imminent peril, had all the fury of a long grief ever since she had seen the murderers of her husband Plautus. She had clasped his bleeding neck, and still kept by her the blood-stained apparel, clinging in her widowhood to perpetual sorrow, and using only such nourishment as might suffice to avert starvation. Then at her father's bidding she went to Neapolis. And as she was forbidden to approach Nero, she would haunt his doors; and implore him to hear an innocent man, and not surrender to a freedman one who had once been his colleague in the consulship, now pleading with the cries of a woman, now again forgetting her sex and lifting up her voice in a tone of menace, till the emperor showed himself unmoved alike by entreaty and reproach.

She therefore told her father by message that she cast hope aside and yielded to necessity. He was at the same time informed that judicial proceedings in the Senate and a dreadful sentence were hanging over him. Some there were who advised him to name the emperor as his chief heir, and so secure the remainder for his grandchildren. But he spurned the notion, and unwilling to disgrace a life which had clung to freedom by a final act of servility, he bestowed on his slaves all his ready money, and ordered each to convey away for himself whatever he could carry, leaving only three couches for the last scene. Then in the same chamber, with the same weapon, they sundered their veins, and speedily hurried into a bath, covered each, as delicacy required, with a single garment, the father gazing intently on his daughter, the grandmother on her grandchild, she again on both, while with rival earnestness they prayed that the ebbing life might have a quick departure, each wishing to leave a relative still surviving, but just on the verge of death. Fortune preserved the due order; the oldest died first, then the others according to priority of age. They were prosecuted after their burial, and the sentence was that "they should be punished in ancient fashion." Nero interposed his veto, allowing them to die without his interference. Such were the mockeries added to murders already perpetrated.

Publius Gallus, a Roman knight, was outlawed for having been intimate with Faenius Rufus and somewhat acquainted with Vetus. To the freedman who was the accuser, was given, as a reward for his service, a seat in the theatre among the tribune's officers. The month too following April, or Neroneus, was changed from Maius into the name of Claudius, and Junius into that of Germanicus, Cornelius Orfitus, the proposer of the motion, publicly declaring that the month Junius had been passed over because the execution of the two Torquati for their crimes had now rendered its name inauspicious.

A year of shame and of so many evil deeds heaven also marked by storms and pestilence. Campania was devastated by a hurricane, which destroyed everywhere country-houses, plantations and crops, and carried its fury to the neighbourhood of Rome, where a terrible plague was sweeping away all classes of human beings without any such derangement of the atmosphere as to be visibly apparent. Yet the houses were filled with lifeless forms and the streets with funerals. Neither age nor sex was exempt from peril. Slaves and the free-born populace alike were suddenly cut off, amid the wailings of wives and children, who were often consumed on the very funeral pile of their friends by whom they had been sitting and shedding tears. Knights and senators perished indiscriminately, and yet their deaths were less deplored because they seemed to forestal the emperor's cruelty by an ordinary death. That same year levies of troops were held in Narbon Gaul, Africa and Asia, to fill up the legions of Illyricum, all soldiers in which, worn out by age or ill-health, were receiving their discharge. Lugdunum was consoled by the prince for a ruinous disaster by a gift of four million sesterces, so that what was lost to the city might be replaced. Its people had previously offered this same amount for the distresses of Rome.

In the consulship of Caius Suetonius and Lucius Telesinus, Antistius Sosianus, who, as I have stated, had been punished with exile for repeated satires on Nero, having heard that there was such honour for informers and that the emperor was so partial to bloodshed, being himself too of a restless temper and quick to seize opportunities, made a friend of a man in like condition with himself, one Pammenes, an exile in the same place, noted for his skill as an astrologer, and consequently bound to many in close intimacy. He thought there must be a meaning in the frequent messages and the consultations, and he learnt at the same time that an annual payment was furnished him by Publius Anteius. He knew too that Anteius was hated by Nero for his love of Agrippina, and that his wealth was sufficiently conspicuous to provoke cupidity, and that this was the cause of the destruction of many. Accordingly he intercepted a letter from Anteius, and having also stolen some notes about the day of his nativity and his future career, which were hidden away among Pammenes' secret papers, and having further discovered some remarks on the birth and life of Ostorius Scapula, he wrote to the emperor that he would communicate important news which would contribute to his safety, if he could but obtain a brief reprieve of his exile. Anteius and Ostorius were, he hinted, grasping at empire and prying into the destinies of themselves and of the prince. Some swift galleys were then despatched and Sosianus speedily arrived. On the disclosure of his information, Anteius and Ostorius were classed with condemned criminals rather than with men on their trial, so completely, indeed, that no one would attest the will of Anteius, till Tigellinus interposed to sanction it. Anteius had been previously advised by him not to delay this final document. Then he drank poison, but disgusted at its slowness, he hastened death by severing his veins.

Ostorius was living at the time on a remote estate on the Ligurian frontier. Thither a centurion was despatched to hurry on his destruction. There was a motive for promptitude arising out of the fact that Ostorius, with his great military fame and the civic crown he had won in Britain, possessed, too, as he was of huge bodily strength and skill in arms, had made Nero, who was always timid and now more frightened than ever by the lately discovered conspiracy, fearful of a sudden attack. So the centurion, having barred every exit from the house, disclosed the emperor's orders to Ostorius. That fortitude which he had often shown in fighting the enemy Ostorius now turned against himself. And as his veins, though severed, allowed but a scanty flow of blood, he used the help of a slave, simply to hold up a dagger firmly, and then pressing the man's hand towards him, he met the point with his throat.

Even if I had to relate foreign wars and deaths encountered in the service of the State with such a monotony of disaster, I should myself have been overcome by disgust, while I should look for weariness in my readers, sickened as they would be by the melancholy and continuous destruction of our citizens, however glorious to themselves. But now a servile submissiveness and so much wanton bloodshed at home fatigue the mind and paralyze it with grief. The only indulgence I would ask from those who will acquaint themselves with these horrors is that I be not thought to hate men who perished so tamely. Such was the wrath of heaven against the Roman State that one may not pass over it with a single mention, as one might the defeat of armies and the capture of cities. Let us grant this privilege to the posterity of illustrious men, that just as in their funeral obsequies such men are not confounded in a common burial, so in the record of their end they may receive and retain a special memorial.

Within a few days, in quick succession, Annaeus Mela, Cerialis Anicius, Rufius Crispinus, and Petronius fell, Mela and Crispinus being Roman knights with senatorial rank. The latter had once commanded the praetorians and had been rewarded with the decorations of the consulate. He had lately been banished to Sardinia on a charge of conspiracy, and on receiving a message that he was doomed to die had destroyed himself. Mela, son of the same parents as Gallio and Seneca, had refrained from seeking promotion out of a perverse vanity which wished to raise a Roman knight to an equality with ex-consuls. He also thought that there was a shorter road to the acquisition of wealth through offices connected with the administration of the emperor's private business. He had too in his son Annaeus Lucanus a powerful aid in rising to distinction. After the death of Lucanus, he rigorously called in the debts due to his estate, and thereby provoked an accuser in the person of Fabius Romanus, one of the intimate friends of Lucanus. A story was invented that the father and son shared between them a knowledge of the conspiracy, and a letter was forged in Lucanus's name. This Nero examined, and ordered it to be conveyed to Mela, whose wealth he ravenously desired. Mela meanwhile, adopting the easiest mode of death then in fashion, opened his veins, after adding a codicil to his will bequeathing an immense amount to Tigellinus and his son-in-law, Cossutianus Capito, in order to save the remainder. In this codicil he is also said to have written, by way of remonstrance against the injustice of his death, that he died without any cause for punishment, while Rufius Crispinus and Anicius Cerialis still enjoyed life, though bitter foes to the prince. It was thought that he had invented this about Crispinus, because the man had been already murdered; about Cerialis, with the object of procuring his murder. Soon afterwards Cerialis laid violent hands on himself, and received less pity than the others, because men remembered that he had betrayed a conspiracy to Caius Caesar.

With regard to Caius Petronius, I ought to dwell a little on his antecedents. His days he passed in sleep, his nights in the business and pleasures of life. Indolence had raised him to fame, as energy raises others, and he was reckoned not a debauchee and spendthrift, like most of those who squander their substance, but a man of refined luxury. And indeed his talk and his doings, the freer they were and the more show of carelessness they exhibited, were the better liked, for their look of natural simplicity. Yet as proconsul of Bithynia and soon afterwards as consul, he showed himself a man of vigour and equal to business. Then falling back into vice or affecting vice, he was chosen by Nero to be one of his few intimate associates, as a critic in matters of taste, while the emperor thought nothing charming or elegant in luxury unless Petronius had expressed to him his approval of it. Hence jealousy on the part of Tigellinus, who looked on him as a rival and even his superior in the science of pleasure. And so he worked on the prince's cruelty, which dominated every other passion, charging Petronius with having been the friend of Scaevinus, bribing a slave to become informer, robbing him of the means of defence, and hurrying into prison the greater part of his domestics.

It happened at the time that the emperor was on his way Campania and that Petronius, after going as far as Cumae, was there detained. He bore no longer the suspense of fear or of hope. Yet he did not fling away life with precipitate haste, but having made an incision in his veins and then, according to his humour, bound them up, he again opened them, while he conversed with his friends, not in a serious strain or on topics that might win for him the glory of courage. And he listened to them as they repeated, not thoughts on the immortality of the soul or on the theories of philosophers, but light poetry and playful verses. To some of his slaves he gave liberal presents, a flogging to others. He dined, indulged himself in sleep, that death, though forced on him, might have a natural appearance. Even in his will he did not, as did many in their last moments, flatter Nero or Tigellinus or any other of the men in power. On the contrary, he described fully the prince's shameful excesses, with the names of his male and female companions and their novelties in debauchery, and sent the account under seal to Nero. Then he broke his signet-ring, that it might not be subsequently available for imperilling others.

When Nero was in doubt how the ingenious varieties of his nightly revels became notorious, Silia came into his mind, who, as a senator's wife, was a conspicuous person, and who had been his chosen associate in all his profligacy and was very intimate with Petronius. She was banished for not having, as was suspected, kept secret what she had seen and endured, a sacrifice to his personal resentment. Minucius Thermus, an ex-praetor, he surrendered to the hate of Tigellinus, because a freedman of Thermus had brought criminal charges against Tigellinus, such that the man had to atone for them himself by the torture of the rack, his patron by an undeserved death.

Nero after having butchered so many illustrious men, at last aspired to extirpate virtue itself by murdering Thrasea Paetus and Barea Soranus. Both men he had hated of old, Thrasea on additional grounds, because he had walked out of the Senate when Agrippina's case was under discussion, as I have already related, and had not given the Juvenile games any conspicuous encouragement. Nero's displeasure at this was the deeper, since this same Thrasea had sung in a tragedian's dress at Patavium, his birth-place, in some games instituted by the Trojan Antenor. On the day, too, on which the praetor Antistius was being sentenced to death for libels on Nero, Thrasea proposed and carried a more merciful decision. Again, when divine honours were decreed to Poppaea, he was purposely absent and did not attend her funeral. All this Capito Cossutianus would not allow to be forgotten. He had a heart eager for the worst wickedness, and he also bore ill-will to Thrasea, the weight of whose influence had crushed him, while envoys from Cilicia, supported by Thrasea's advocacy, were accusing him of extortion.

He alleged, too, against him the following charges:—"Thrasea," he said, "at the beginning of the year always avoided the usual oath of allegiance; he was not present at the recital of the public prayers, though he had been promoted to the priesthood of the Fifteen; he had never offered a sacrifice for the safety of the prince or for his heavenly voice. Though formerly he had been assiduous and unwearied in showing himself a supporter or an opponent even of the most ordinary motions of senators, he had not entered the Senate-house for three years, and very lately, when all were rushing thither with rival eagerness to put down Silanus and Vetus, he had attended by preference to the private business of his clients. This was political schism, and, should many dare to do the like, it was actual war."

Capito further added, "The country in its eagerness for discord is now talking of you, Nero, and of Thrasea, as it talked once of Caius Caesar and Marcus Cato. Thrasea has his followers or rather his satellites, who copy, not indeed as yet the audacious tone of his sentiments, but only his manners and his looks, a sour and gloomy set, bent on making your mirthfulness a reproach to you. He is the only man who cares not for your safety, honours not your accomplishments. The prince's prosperity he despises. Can it be that he is not satisfied with your sorrows and griefs? It shows the same spirit not to believe in Poppaea's divinity as to refuse to swear obedience to the acts of the Divine Augustus and the Divine Julius. He contemns religious rites; he annuls laws. The daily records of the Roman people are read attentively in the provinces and the armies that they may know what Thrasea has not done.

"Either let us go over to his system, if it is better than ours, or let those who desire change have their leader and adviser taken from them. That sect of his gave birth to the Tuberones and Favonii, names hateful even to the old republic. They make a show of freedom, to overturn the empire; should they destroy it, they will attack freedom itself. In vain have you banished Cassius, if you are going to allow rivals of the Bruti to multiply and flourish. Finally, write nothing yourself about Thrasea; leave the Senate to decide for us." Nero further stimulated the eager wrath of Cossutianus, and associated with him the pungent eloquence of Marcellus Eprius.

As for the impeachment of Barea Soranus, Ostorius Sabinus, a Roman knight, had already claimed it for himself. It arose out of his proconsulate of Asia, where he increased the prince's animosity by his uprightness and diligence, as well as by having bestowed pains on opening the port of Ephesus and passed over without punishment the violence of the citizens of Pergamos in their efforts to hinder Acratus, one of the emperor's freedmen, from carrying off statues and pictures. But the crime imputed to him was friendship with Plautus and intrigues to lure the province into thoughts of revolt. The time chosen for the fatal sentence was that at which Tiridates was on his way to receive the sovereignty of Armenia, so that crime at home might be partially veiled amid rumours on foreign affairs, or that Nero might display his imperial grandeur by the murder of illustrious men, as though it were a kingly exploit.

Accordingly when all Rome rushed out to welcome the emperor and see the king, Thrasea, though forbidden to appear, did not let his spirit be cast down, but wrote a note to Nero, in which he demanded to know the charges against him, and asserted that he would clear himself, if he were informed of the crimes alleged and had an opportunity of refuting them. This note Nero received with eagerness, in the hope that Thrasea in dismay had written something to enhance the emperor's glory and to tarnish his own honour. When it turned out otherwise, and he himself, on the contrary, dreaded the glance and the defiant independence of the guiltless man, he ordered the Senate to be summoned.

Thrasea then consulted his most intimate friends whether he should attempt or spurn defence. Conflicting advice was offered. Those who thought it best for him to enter the Senate house said that they counted confidently on his courage, and were sure that he would say nothing but what would heighten his renown. "It was for the feeble and timid to invest their last moments with secrecy. Let the people behold a man who could meet death. Let the Senate hear words, almost of divine inspiration, more than human. It was possible that the very miracle might impress even a Nero. But should he persist in his cruelty, posterity would at least distinguish between the memory of an honourable death and the cowardice of those who perished in silence."

Those, on the other hand, who thought that he ought to wait at home, though their opinion of him was the same, hinted that mockeries and insults were in store for him. "Spare your ears" they said, "taunts and revilings. Not only are Cossutianus and Eprius eagerly bent on crime; there are numbers more, daring enough, perchance, to raise the hand of violence in their brutality. Even good men through fear do the like. Better save the Senate which you have adorned to the last the infamy of such an outrage, and leave it a matter of doubt what the senators would have decided, had they seen Thrasea on his trial. It is with a vain hope we are aiming to touch Nero with shame for his abominations, and we have far more cause to fear that he will vent his fury on your wife, your household, on all others dear to you. And therefore, while you are yet stainless and undisgraced, seek to close life with the glory of those in whose track and pursuits you have passed it."

Present at this deliberation was Rusticus Arulenus, an enthusiastic youth, who, in his ardour for renown, offered, as he was tribune of the people, to protest against the sentence of the Senate. Thrasea checked his impetuous temper, not wishing him to attempt what would be as futile, and useless to the accused, as it would be fatal to the protester. "My days," he said, "are ended, and I must not now abandon a scheme of life in which for so many years I have persevered. You are at the beginning of a career of office, and your future is yet clear. Weigh thoroughly with yourself beforehand, at such a crisis as this, the path of political life on which you enter." He then reserved for his own consideration the question whether it became him to enter the Senate.

Next day, however, two praetorian cohorts under arms occupied the temple of Venus Genetrix. A group of ordinary citizens with swords which they did not conceal, had blocked the approach to the Senate. Through the squares and colonnades were scattered bodies of soldiers, amid whose looks of menace the senators entered their house. A speech from the emperor was read by his quaestor. Without addressing any one by name, he censured the senators for neglecting their public duties, and drawing by their example the Roman knights into idleness. "For what wonder is it," he asked, "that men do not come from remote provinces when many, after obtaining the consulate or some sacred office, give all their thoughts by choice to the beauty of their gardens?" Here was, so to say, a weapon for the accusers, on which they fastened.

Cossutianus made a beginning, and then Marcellus in more violent tones exclaimed that the whole commonwealth was at stake. "It is," he said, "the stubbornness of inferiors which lessens the clemency of our ruler. We senators have hitherto been too lenient in allowing him to be mocked with impunity by Thrasea throwing off allegiance, by his son-in-law Helvidius Priscus indulging similar frenzies, by Paconius Agrippinus, the inheritor of his father's hatred towards emperors, and by Curtius Montanus, the habitual composer of abominable verses. I miss the presence of an ex-consul in the Senate, of a priest when we offer our vows, of a citizen when we swear obedience, unless indeed, in defiance of the manners and rites of our ancestors, Thrasea has openly assumed the part of a traitor and an enemy. In a word, let the man, wont to act the senator and to screen those who disparage the prince, come among us; let him propose any reform or change he may desire. We shall more readily endure his censure of details than we can now bear the silence by which he condemns everything. Is it the peace throughout the world or victories won without loss to our armies which vex him? A man who grieves at the country's prosperity, who treats our public places, theatres and temples as if they were a desert, and who is ever threatening us with exile, let us not enable such an one to gratify his perverse vanity. To him the decrees of this house, the offices of State, the city of Rome seem as nothing. Let him sever his life from a country all love for which he has long lost and the very sight of which he has now put from him."

While Marcellus, with the savage and menacing look he usually wore, spoke these and like words with rising fury in his voice, countenance, and eye, that familiar grief to which a thick succession of perils had habituated the Senate gave way to a new and profounder panic, as they saw the soldiers' hands on their weapons. At the same moment the venerable form of Thrasea rose before their imagination, and some there were who pitied Helvidius too, doomed as he was to suffer for an innocent alliance. "What again," they asked, "was the charge against Agrippinus except his father's sad fate, since he too, though guiltless as his son, fell beneath the cruelty of Tiberius? As for Montanus, a youth without a blemish, author of no libellous poem, he was positively driven out an exile because he had exhibited genius."

And meanwhile Ostorius Sabinus, the accuser of Soranus, entered, and began by speaking of his friendship with Rubellius Plautus and of his proconsulate in Asia which he had, he said, adapted to his own glory rather than to the public welfare, by fostering seditious movements in the various states. These were bygones, but there was a fresh charge involving the daughter in the peril of the father, to the effect that she had lavished money on astrologers. This indeed had really occurred through the filial affection of Servilia (that was the girl's name), who, out of love for her father and the thoughtlessness of youth, had consulted them, only however about the safety of her family, whether Nero could be appeased, and the trial before the Senate have no dreadful result.

She was accordingly summoned before the Senate, and there they stood facing one another before the consuls' tribunal, the aged parent, and opposite to him the daughter, in the twentieth year of her age, widowed and forlorn, her husband Annius Pollio having lately been driven into banishment, without so much as a glance at her father, whose peril she seemed to have aggravated.

Then on the accuser asking her whether she had sold her bridal presents or stript her neck of its ornaments to raise money for the performance of magical rites, she at first flung herself on the ground and wept long in silence. After awhile, clasping the altar steps and altar, she exclaimed, "I have invoked no impious deities, no enchantments, nor aught else in my unhappy prayers, but only that thou, Caesar, and you, senators, might preserve unharmed this best of fathers. My jewels, my apparel, and the signs of my rank I gave up, as I would have given up my life-blood had they demanded it. They must have seen this, those men before unknown to me, both as to the name they bear and the arts they practise. No mention was made by me of the emperor, except as one of the divinities. But my most unhappy father knows nothing, and, if it is a crime, I alone am guilty."

While she was yet speaking, Soranus caught up her words, and exclaimed that she had not gone with him into the province; that, from her youth, she could not have been known to Plautus, and that she was not involved in the charges against her husband. "Treat separately," he said, "the case of one who is guilty only of an exaggerated filial piety, and as for myself, let me undergo any fate." He was rushing, as he spoke, into the embraces of his daughter who hurried towards him, but the lictors interposed and stopped them both. Place was then given to the witnesses, and the appearance among them of Publius Egnatius provoked as much indignation as the cruelty of the prosecution had excited pity. A client of Soranus, and now hired to ruin his friend, he professed the dignified character of a Stoic, and had trained himself in demeanour and language to exhibit an ideal of virtue. In his heart, however, treacherous and cunning, he concealed greed and sensuality. As soon as money had brought these vices to light, he became an example, warning us to beware just as much of those who under the guise of virtuous tastes are false and deceitful in friendship, as of men wholly entangled in falsehoods and stained with every infamy.

That same day brought with it a noble pattern in Cassius Asclepiodotus, whose vast wealth made him a foremost man in Bithynia. He had honoured Soranus in his prosperity with a respect which he did not cast off in his fall, and he was now stript of all his property and driven into exile; so impartially indifferent is heaven to examples of virtue and vice. Thrasea, Soranus, and Servilia were allowed the choice of death. Helvidius and Paconius were banished from Italy. Montanus was spared to his father's intercessions on the understanding that he was not to be admitted to political life. The prosecutors, Eprius and Cossutianus, received each five million sesterces, Ostorius twelve hundred thousand, with the decorations of the quaestorship.

Then, as evening approached, the consul's quaestor was sent to Thrasea, who was passing his time in his garden. He had had a crowded gathering of distinguished men and women, giving special attention to Demetrius, a professor of the Cynic philosophy. With him, as might be inferred from his earnest expression of face and from words heard when they raised their voices, he was speculating on the nature of the soul and on the separation of the spirit from the body, till Domitius Caecilianus, one of his intimate friends, came to him and told him in detail what the Senate had decided. When all who were present, wept and bitterly complained, Thrasea urged them to hasten their departure and not mingle their own perils with the fate of a doomed man. Arria, too, who aspired to follow her husband's end and the example of Arria, her mother, he counselled to preserve her life, and not rob the daughter of their love of her only stay.

Then he went out into a colonnade, where he was found by the quaestor, joyful rather than otherwise, as he had learnt that Helvidius, his son-in-law, was merely excluded from Italy. When he heard the Senate's decision, he led Helvidius and Demetrius into a chamber, and having laid bare the arteries of each arm, he let the blood flow freely, and, as he sprinkled it on the ground, he called the quaestor to his side and said, "We pour out a libation to Jupiter the Deliverer. Behold, young man, and may the gods avert the omen, but you have been born into times in which it is well to fortify the spirit with examples of courage." Then as the slowness of his end brought with it grievous anguish, turning his eyes on Demetrius. . . .

[At this point the Annals are broken off. Much remained to be told about the last two years of Nero's reign.]

THE END

Printed in the United States
48547LVS00004B/18

9 781420 926682